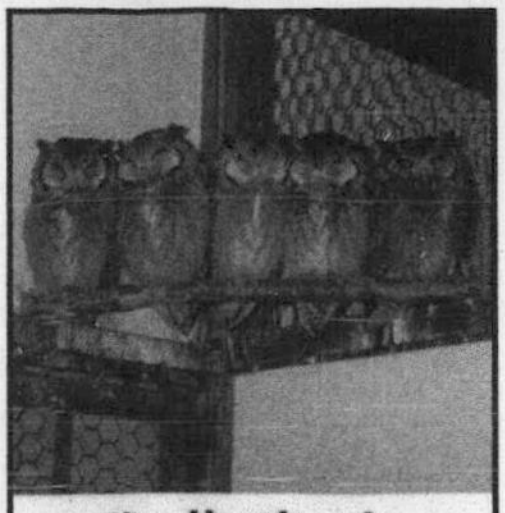

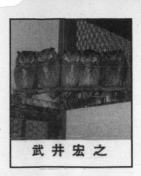

武井宏之

Owls are really cute.
—Hiroyuki Takei

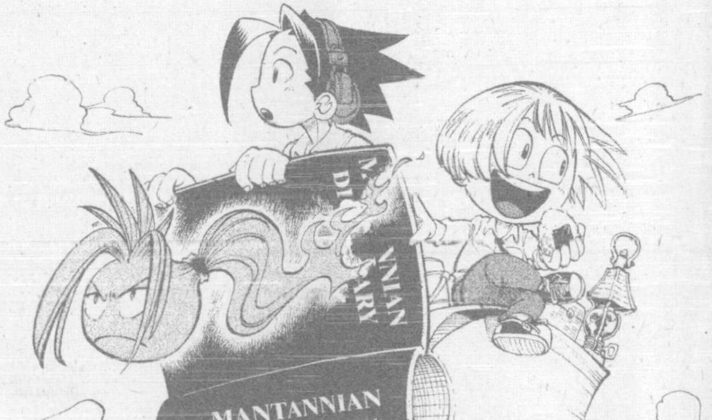
MANTANNIAN

Unconventional author/artist Hiroyuki Takei began his career by winning the coveted Hop Step Award (for new manga artists) and the Osamu Tezuka Award (named after the famous artist of the same name). After working as an assistant to famed artist Nobuhiro Watsuki, Takei debuted in **Weekly Shonen Jump** in 1997 with **Butsu Zone**, an action series based on Buddhist mythology. His multicultural adventure manga **Shaman King**, which debuted in 1998, became a hit and was adapted into an anime TV series. Takei lists Osamu Tezuka, American comics and robot anime among his many influences.

SHAMAN KING VOL. 14
SHONEN JUMP Manga Edition

STORY AND ART BY
HIROYUKI TAKEI

English Adaptation/Lance Caselman
Translation/Lillian Olsen
Touch-up Art & Lettering/John Hunt
Additional Lettering/Josh Simpson
Cover Design/Sean Lee
Interior Design/Nozomi Akashi
Editors/Joel Enos & Carol Fox

VP, Production/Alvin Lu
VP, Sales & Product Marketing/Gonzalo Ferreyra
VP, Creative/Linda Espinosa
Publisher/Hyoe Narita

Published by VIZ Media, LLC
P.O. Box 77010
San Francisco, CA 94107

10 9 8 7 6 5 4 3 2
First printing, January 2008
Second printing, July 2009

T 252528

www.viz.com

THE WORLD'S
MOST POPULAR MANGA
SHONEN JUMP
www.shonenjump.com

SHONEN JUMP MANGA

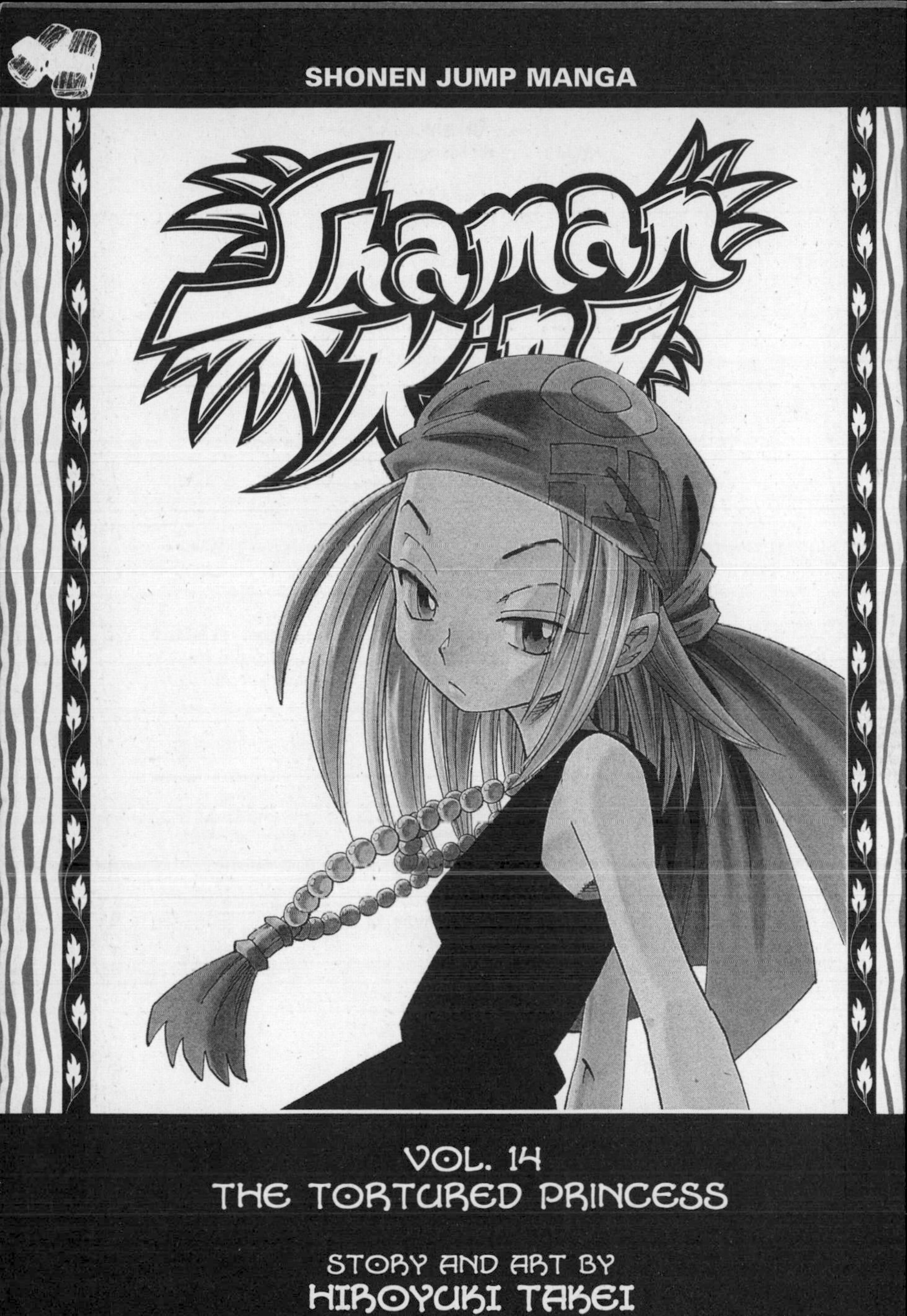
Shaman King

VOL. 14
THE TORTURED PRINCESS

STORY AND ART BY
HIROYUKI TAKEI

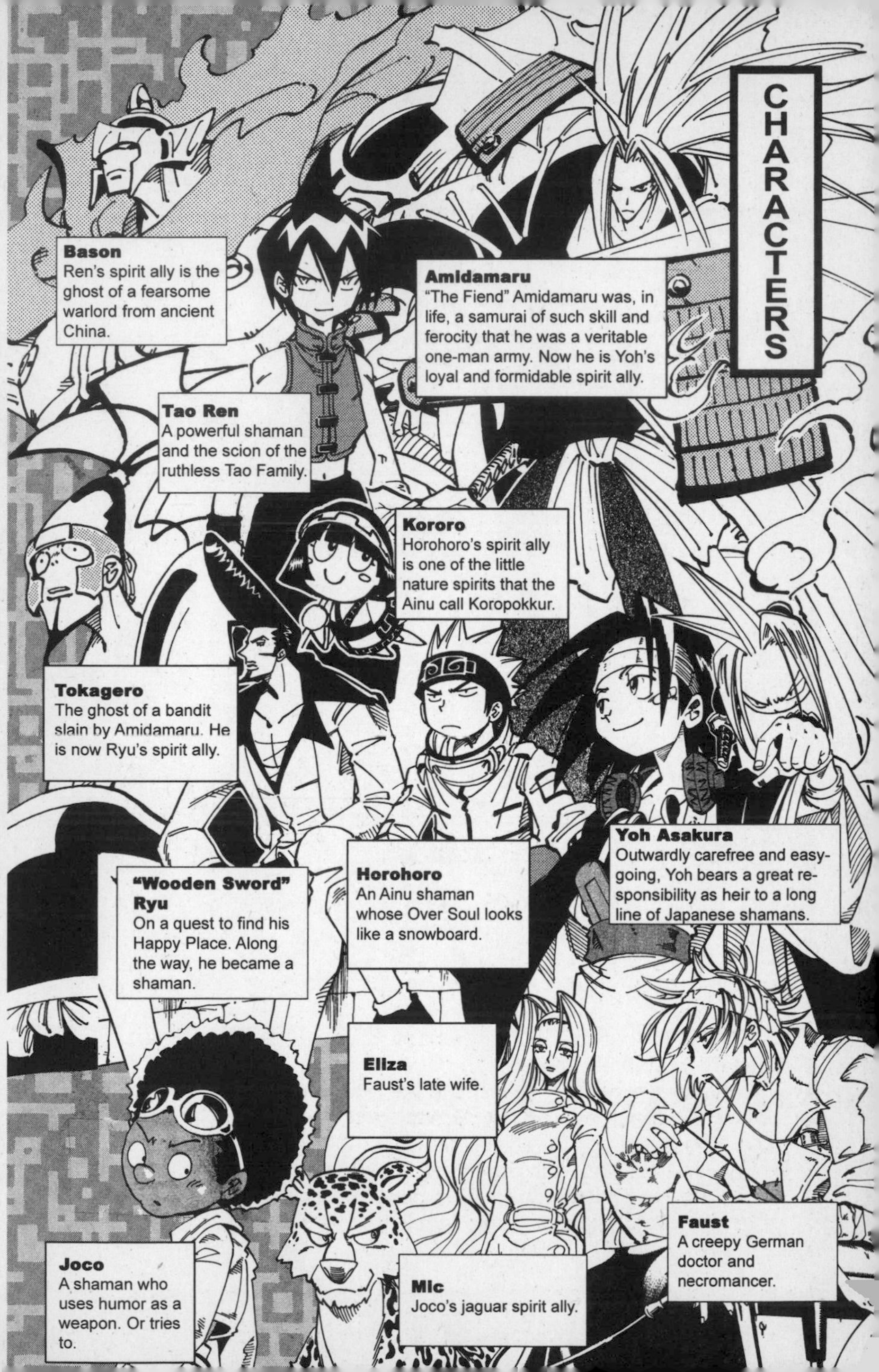
CHARACTERS
Amidamaru
"The Fiend" Amidamaru was, in life, a samurai of such skill and ferocity that he was a veritable one-man army. Now he is Yoh's loyal and formidable spirit ally.
Bason
Ren's spirit ally is the ghost of a fearsome warlord from ancient China.
Tao Ren
A powerful shaman and the scion of the ruthless Tao Family.
Kororo
Horohoro's spirit ally is one of the little nature spirits that the Ainu call Koropokkur.
Tokagero
The ghost of a bandit slain by Amidamaru. He is now Ryu's spirit ally.
Yoh Asakura
Outwardly carefree and easy-going, Yoh bears a great responsibility as heir to a long line of Japanese shamans.
Horohoro
An Ainu shaman whose Over Soul looks like a snowboard.
"Wooden Sword" Ryu
On a quest to find his Happy Place. Along the way, he became a shaman.
Eliza
Faust's late wife.
Faust
A creepy German doctor and necromancer.
Mic
Joco's jaguar spirit ally.
Joco
A shaman who uses humor as a weapon. Or tries to.

Morphea
Lyserg's flower fairy spirit ally.

Marco
The leader of the X-LAWS.

Manta Oyamada
A high-strung boy with a huge dictionary. He has enough sixth sense to see ghosts, but not enough to control them.

Lyserg
A young shaman with a vendetta against Hao.

Hao
An enigmatic figure who calls himself the "Future King."

Anna Kyoyama
Yoh's butt-kicking fiancée. Anna is an itako, a traditional Japanese village shaman.

THE STORY THUS FAR

Yoh Asakura not only sees dead people, he talks and fights with them, too. That's because Yoh is a shaman, a traditional holy man able to interact with the spirit world. Yoh is now a competitor in the "Shaman Fight," a tournament held every 500 years to decide who will become the Shaman King and shape humanity's future.

Yoh and crew finally reach the Patch Village and are awe-struck by the power of the Great Spirit. Now they must separate into teams of three for the first round of the tournament. Yoh goes with Ryu and Faust, while Ren and Horohoro team up with their new friend Joco. But does either team have what it takes to defeat the terrible Tecolote and his skeletal minions?

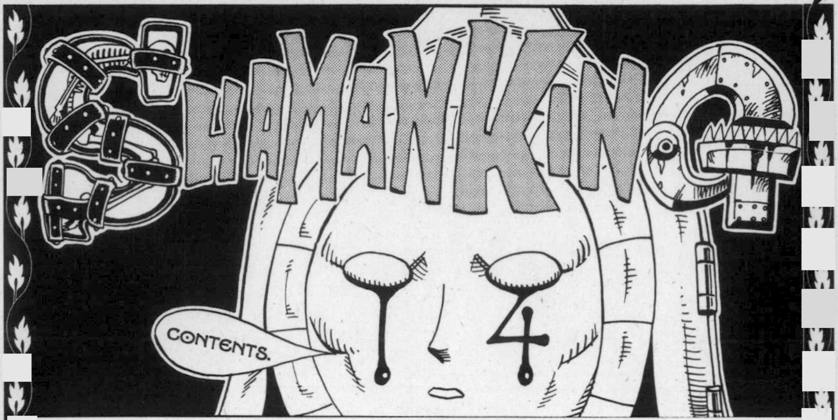
SHAMAN KING
CONTENTS.

VOL. 14
THE TORTURED PRINCESS

CONTENTS

Reincarnation 117: His Name was Olona

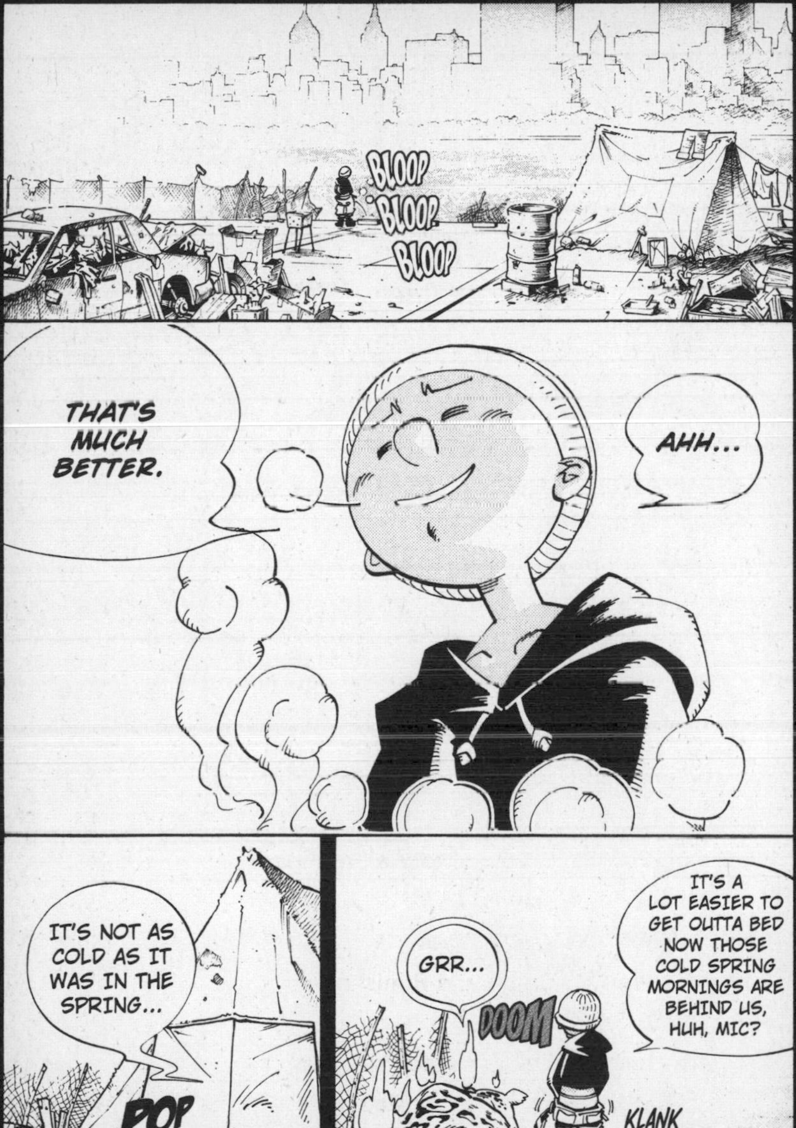
BLOOP
BLOOP
BLOOP
AHH...
THAT'S MUCH BETTER.
IT'S A LOT EASIER TO GET OUTTA BED NOW THOSE COLD SPRING MORNINGS ARE BEHIND US, HUH, MIC?
GRR...
DOOM
KLANK KLANK
IT'S NOT AS COLD AS IT WAS IN THE SPRING...
POP

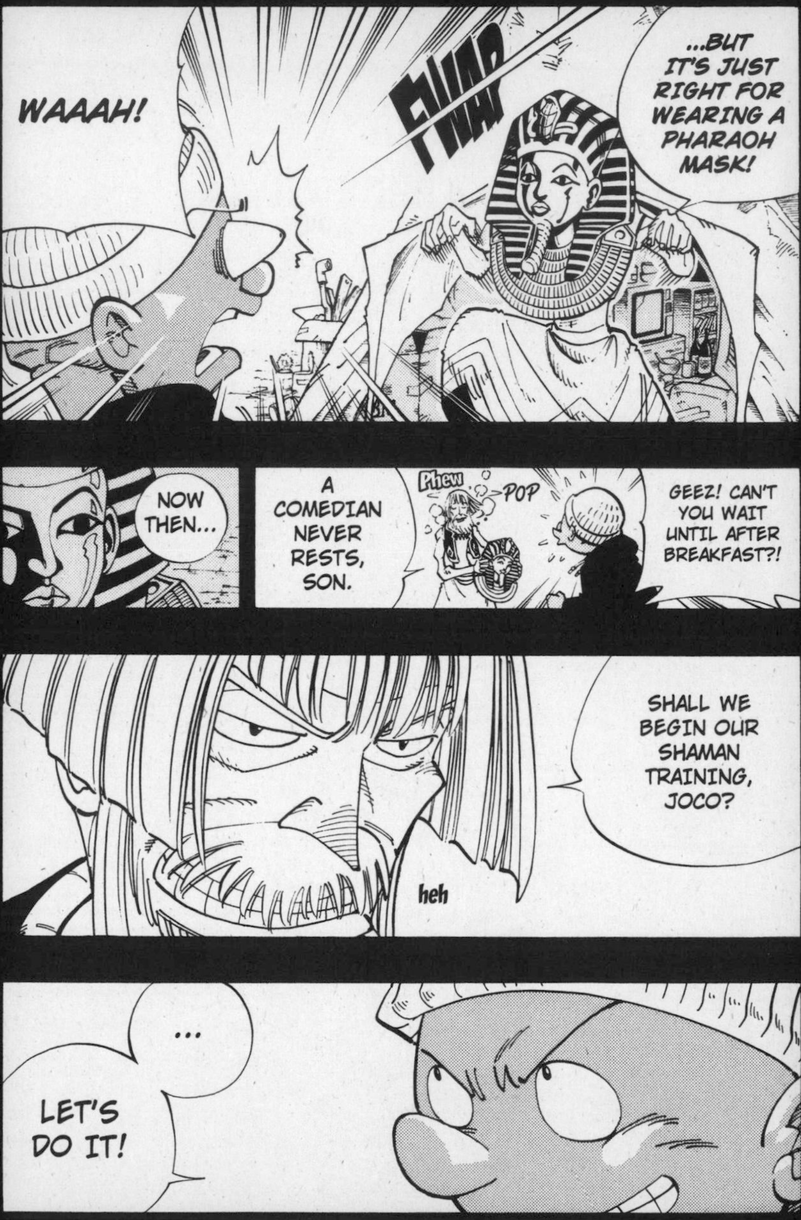
...BUT IT'S JUST RIGHT FOR WEARING A PHARAOH MASK!
FWAP
WAAAH!
GEEZ! CAN'T YOU WAIT UNTIL AFTER BREAKFAST?!
POP
Phew
A COMEDIAN NEVER RESTS, SON.
NOW THEN...
SHALL WE BEGIN OUR SHAMAN TRAINING, JOCO?
heh
...
LET'S DO IT!

Reincarnation 117:

His Name was Olona

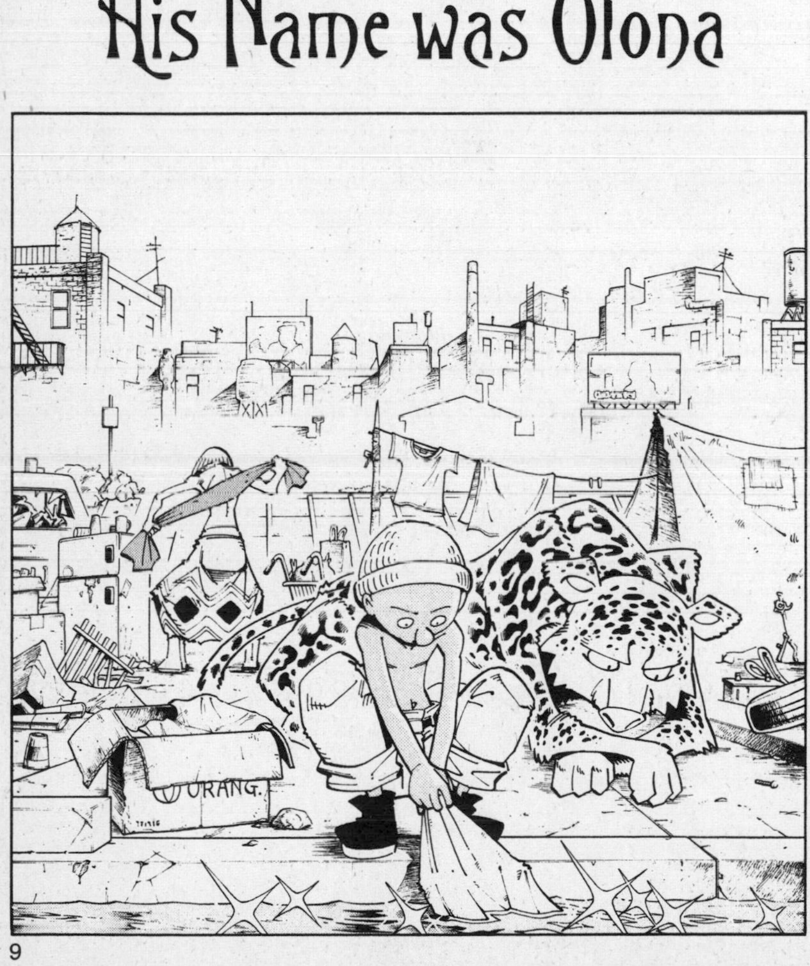
ORANG.

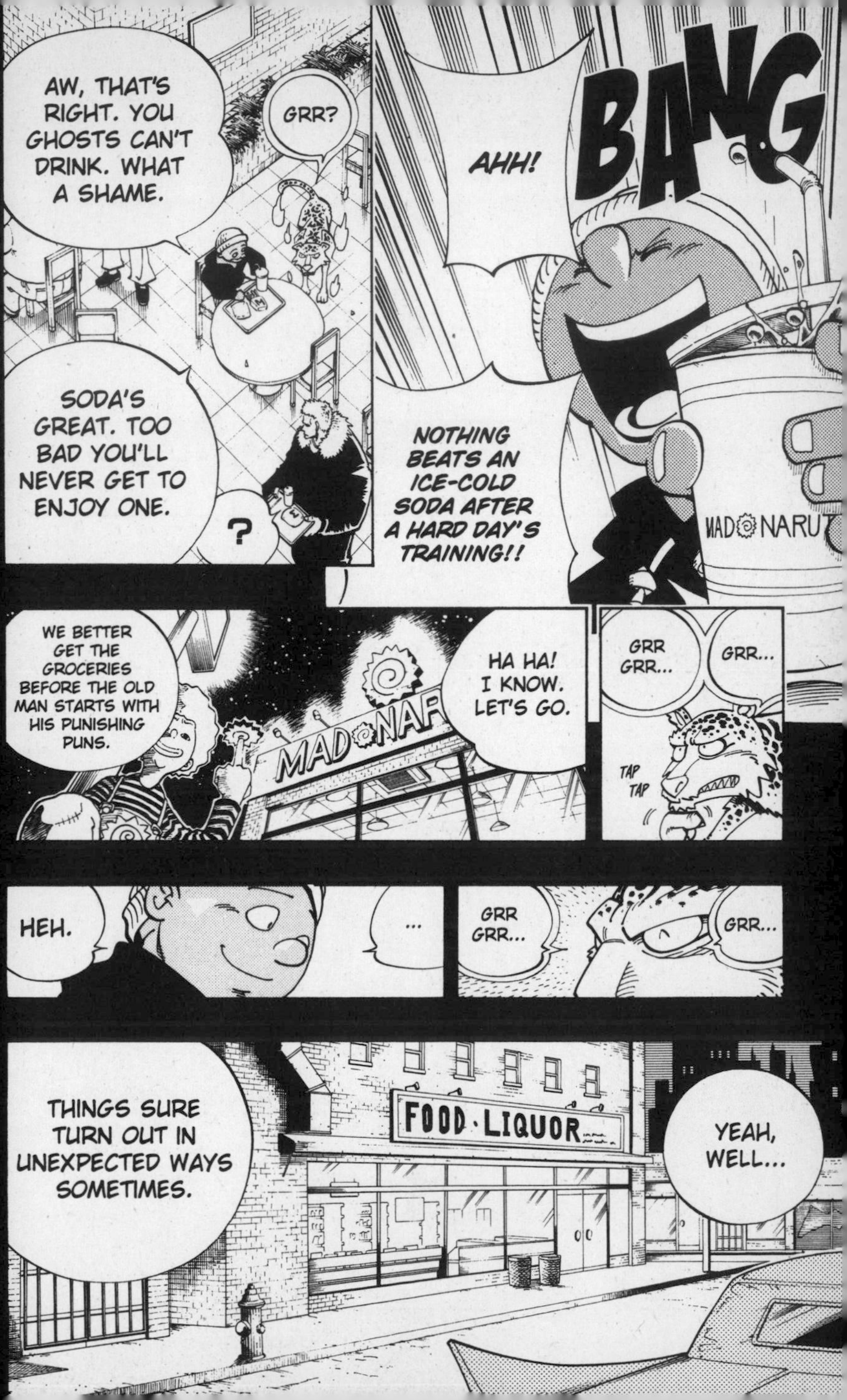
BANG
AHH!
NOTHING BEATS AN ICE-COLD SODA AFTER A HARD DAY'S TRAINING!!
MAD NARU
AW, THAT'S RIGHT. YOU GHOSTS CAN'T DRINK. WHAT A SHAME.
GRR?
SODA'S GREAT. TOO BAD YOU'LL NEVER GET TO ENJOY ONE.
?
GRR GRR...
GRR...
TAP TAP
WE BETTER GET THE GROCERIES BEFORE THE OLD MAN STARTS WITH HIS PUNISHING PUNS.
MAD NAR
HA HA! I KNOW. LET'S GO.
GRR GRR...
GRR...
...
HEH.
FOOD · LIQUOR
THINGS SURE TURN OUT IN UNEXPECTED WAYS SOMETIMES.
YEAH, WELL...

READ THIS WAY

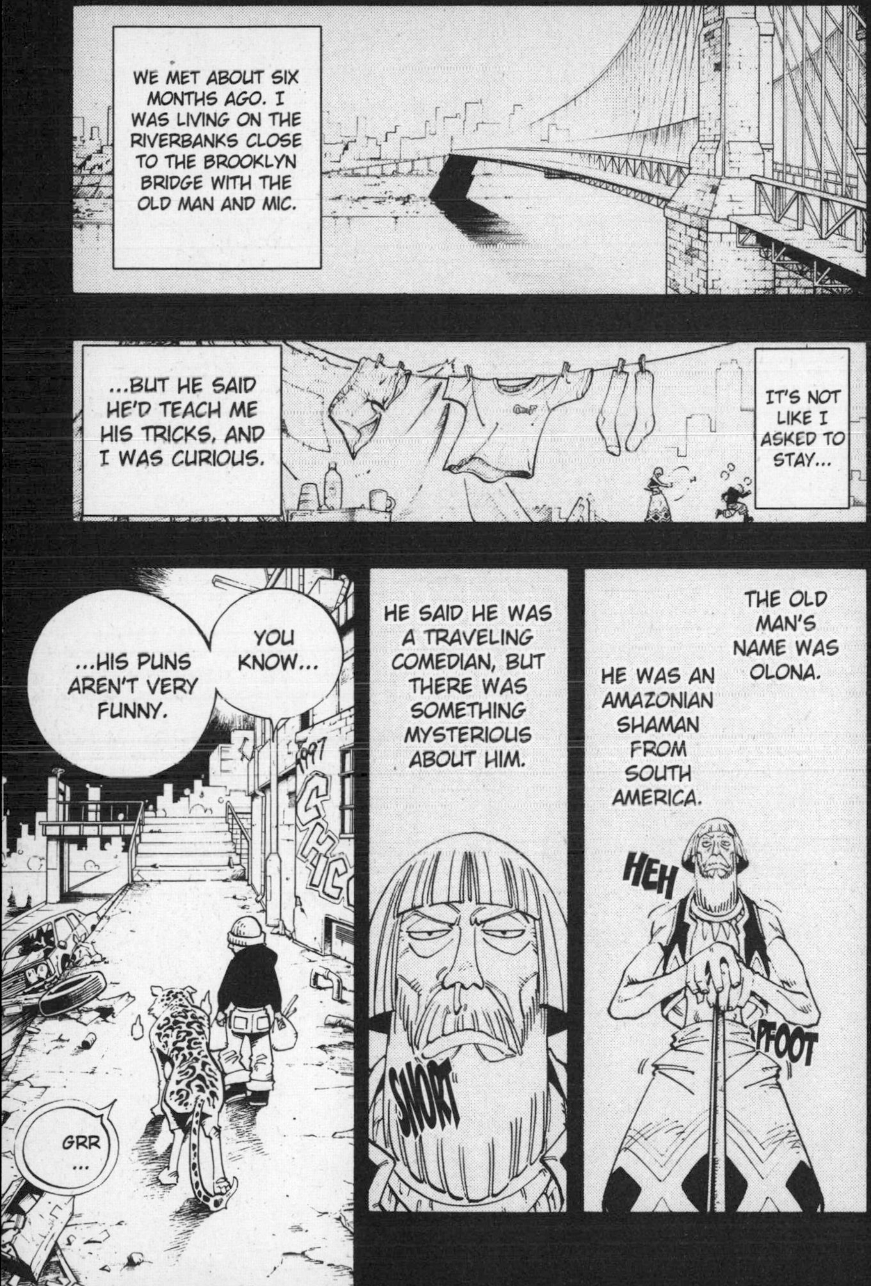

WE MET ABOUT SIX MONTHS AGO. I WAS LIVING ON THE RIVERBANKS CLOSE TO THE BROOKLYN BRIDGE WITH THE OLD MAN AND MIC.
IT'S NOT LIKE I ASKED TO STAY...
...BUT HE SAID HE'D TEACH ME HIS TRICKS, AND I WAS CURIOUS.
THE OLD MAN'S NAME WAS OLONA.
HE WAS AN AMAZONIAN SHAMAN FROM SOUTH AMERICA.
HEH
PFOOT
HE SAID HE WAS A TRAVELING COMEDIAN, BUT THERE WAS SOMETHING MYSTERIOUS ABOUT HIM.
SNORT
YOU KNOW...
...HIS PUNS AREN'T VERY FUNNY.
GRR ...

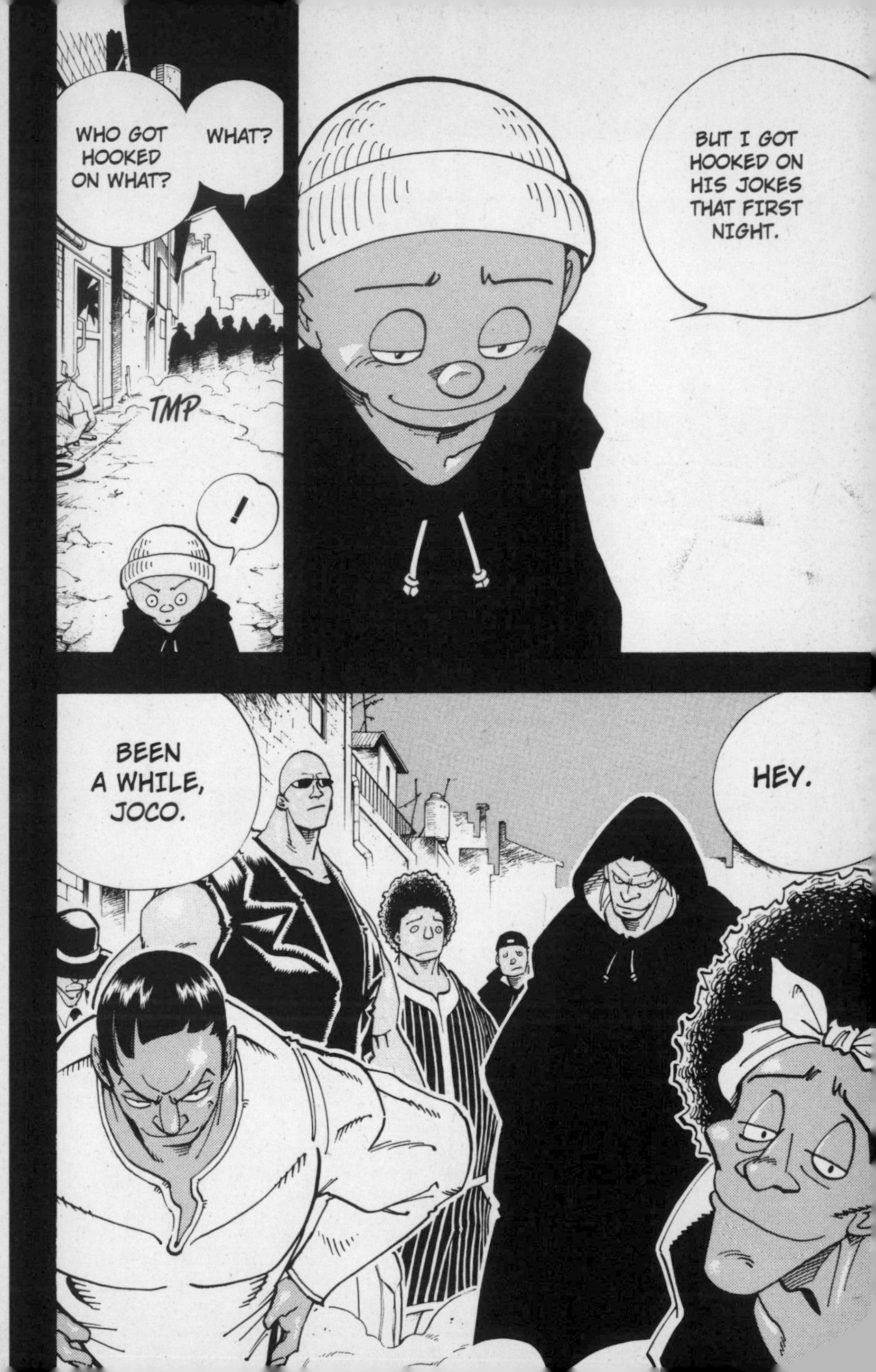
BUT I GOT HOOKED ON HIS JOKES THAT FIRST NIGHT.
WHAT?
WHO GOT HOOKED ON WHAT?
TMP
!
HEY.
BEEN A WHILE, JOCO.

READ THIS WAY

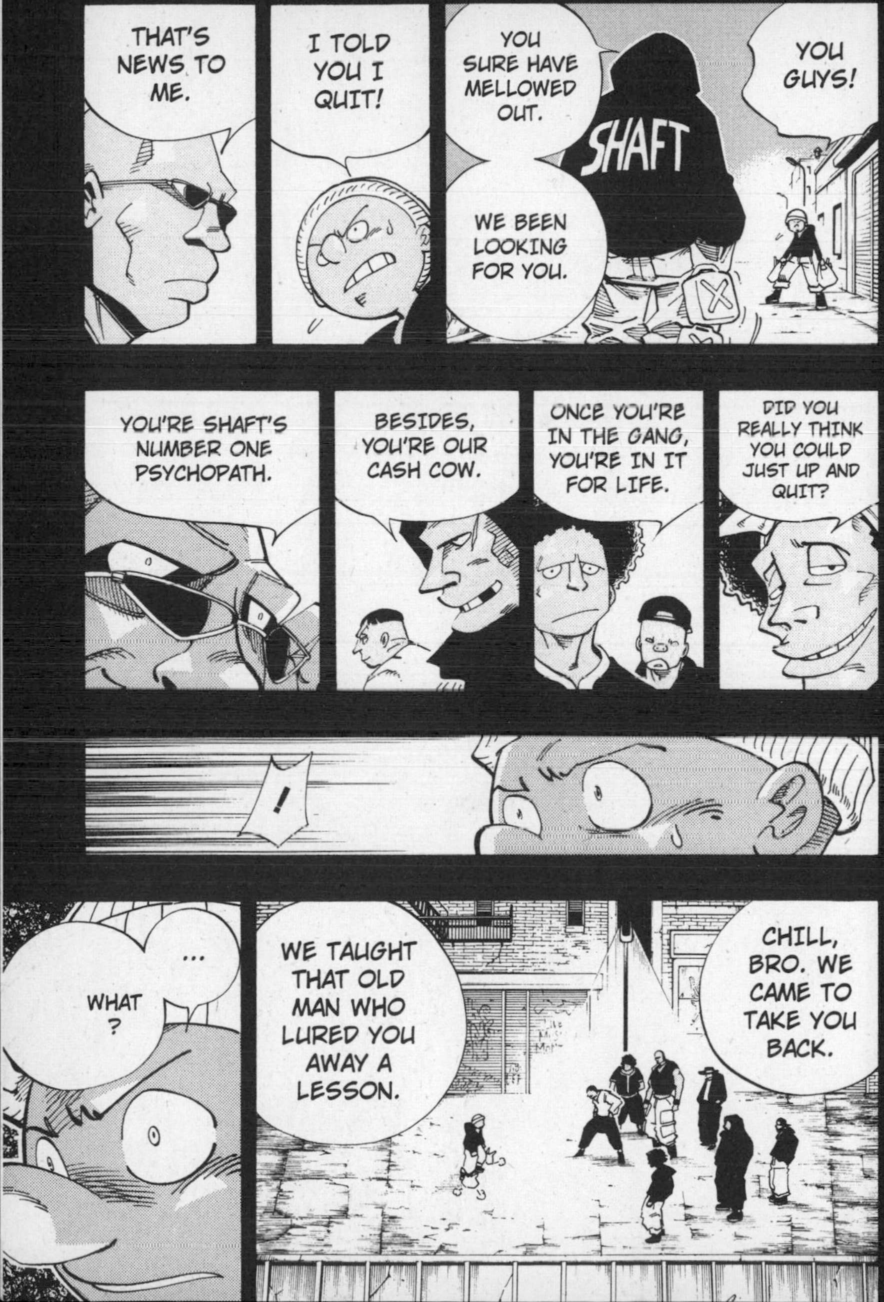

YOU GUYS!
YOU SURE HAVE MELLOWED OUT.
SHAFT
WE BEEN LOOKING FOR YOU.
I TOLD YOU I QUIT!
THAT'S NEWS TO ME.
DID YOU REALLY THINK YOU COULD JUST UP AND QUIT?
ONCE YOU'RE IN THE GANG, YOU'RE IN IT FOR LIFE.
BESIDES, YOU'RE OUR CASH COW.
YOU'RE SHAFT'S NUMBER ONE PSYCHOPATH.
!
CHILL, BRO. WE CAME TO TAKE YOU BACK.
WE TAUGHT THAT OLD MAN WHO LURED YOU AWAY A LESSON.
...
WHAT ?

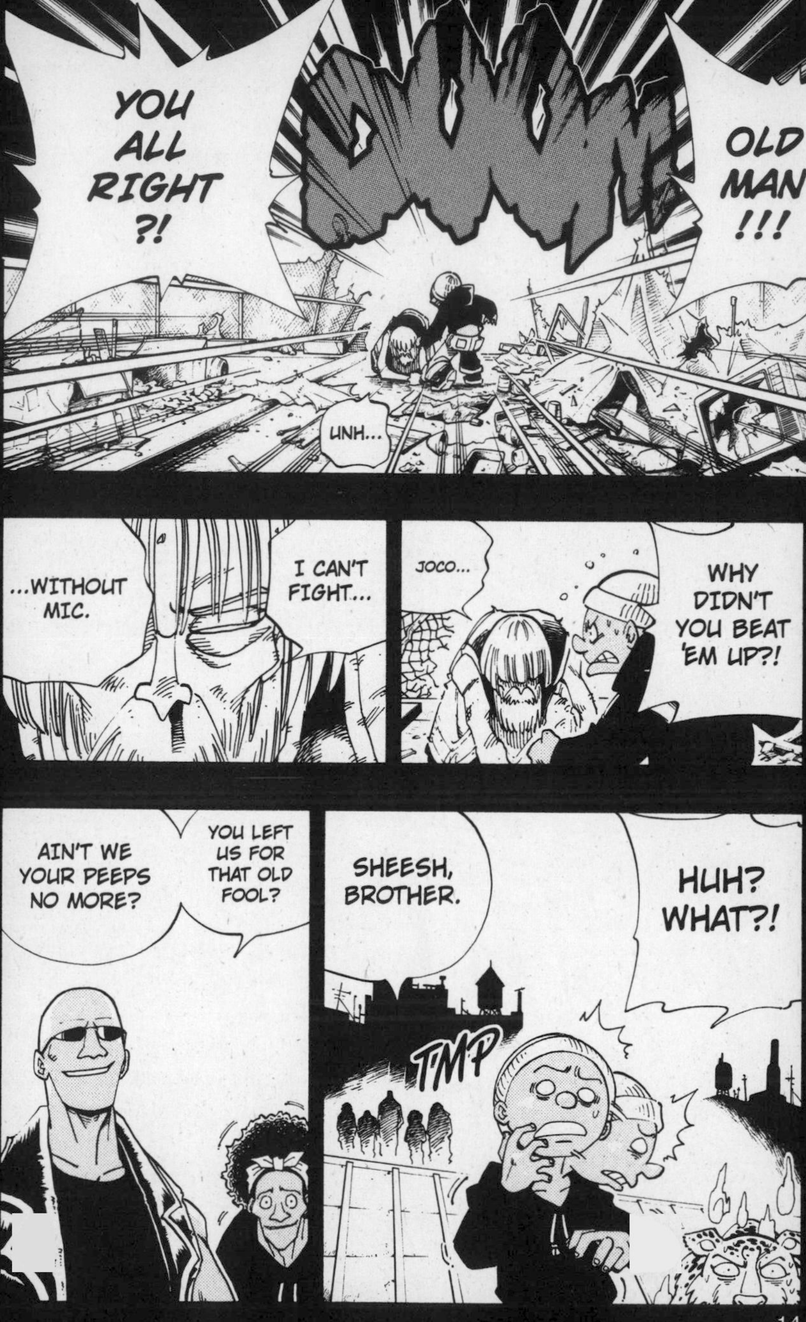
OLD MAN!!!
YOU ALL RIGHT?!
UNH...
WHY DIDN'T YOU BEAT 'EM UP?!
JOCO...
I CAN'T FIGHT...
...WITHOUT MIC.
HUH? WHAT?!
SHEESH, BROTHER.
TMP
YOU LEFT US FOR THAT OLD FOOL?
AIN'T WE YOUR PEEPS NO MORE?

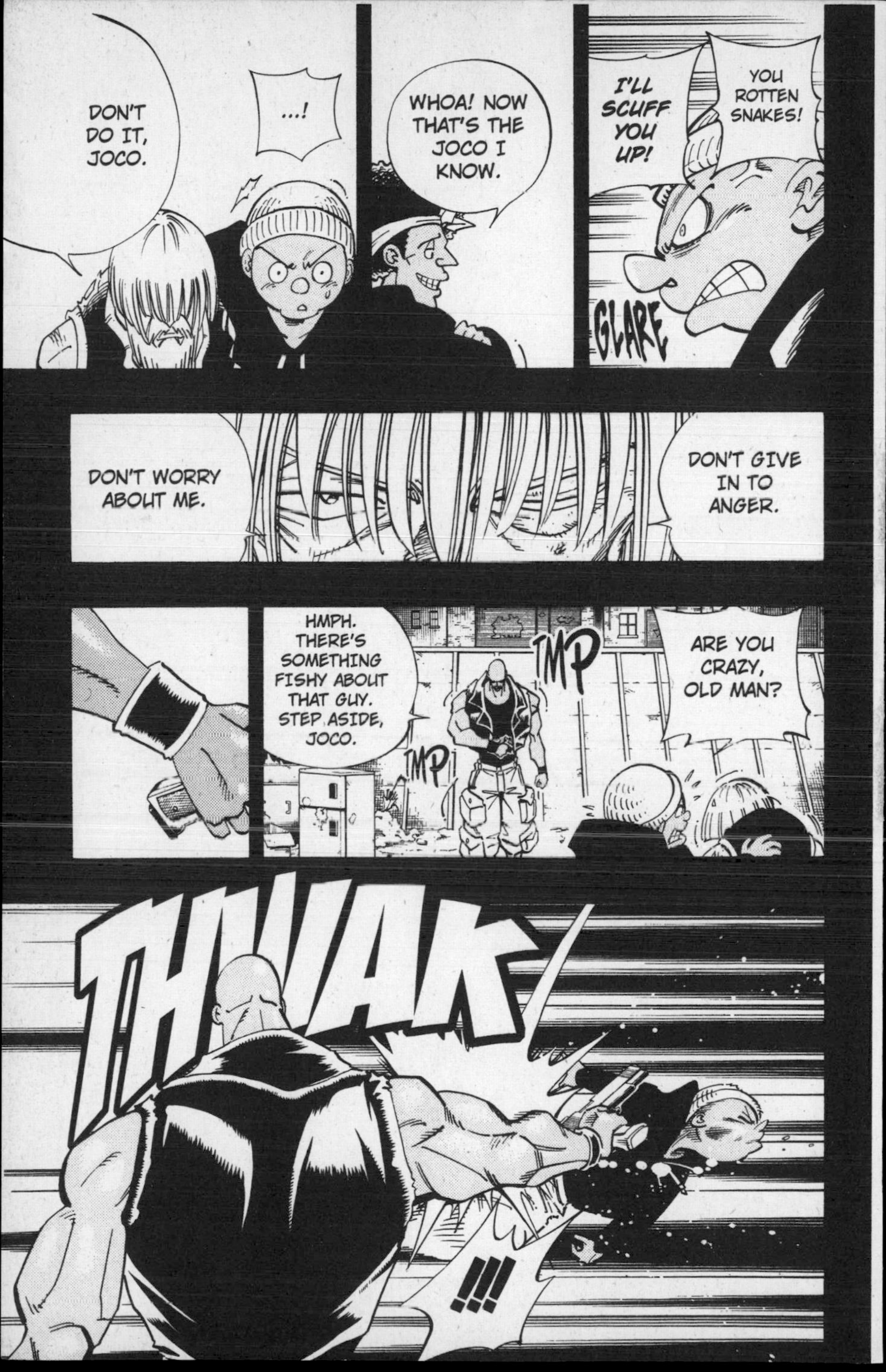
YOU ROTTEN SNAKES!
I'LL SCUFF YOU UP!
GLARE
WHOA! NOW THAT'S THE JOCO I KNOW.
...!
DON'T DO IT, JOCO.
DON'T GIVE IN TO ANGER.
DON'T WORRY ABOUT ME.
ARE YOU CRAZY, OLD MAN?
TMP
HMPH. THERE'S SOMETHING FISHY ABOUT THAT GUY. STEP ASIDE, JOCO.
TMP
THWAK
!!!

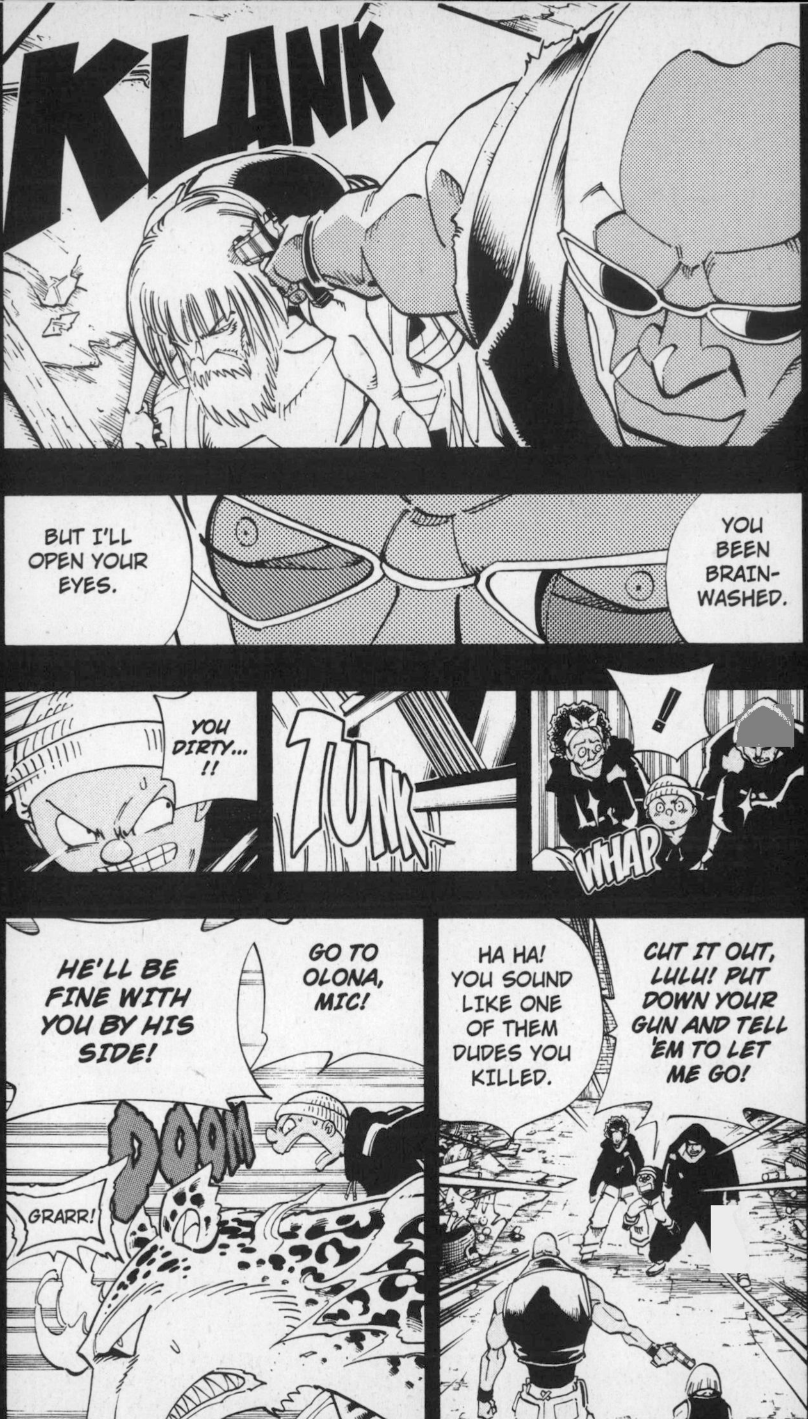
KLANK
YOU BEEN BRAIN-WASHED.
BUT I'LL OPEN YOUR EYES.
!
WHAP
TUNK
YOU DIRTY... !!
CUT IT OUT, LULU! PUT DOWN YOUR GUN AND TELL 'EM TO LET ME GO!
HA HA! YOU SOUND LIKE ONE OF THEM DUDES YOU KILLED.
GO TO OLONA, MIC!
HE'LL BE FINE WITH YOU BY HIS SIDE!
DOOM
GRARR!

READ THIS WAY

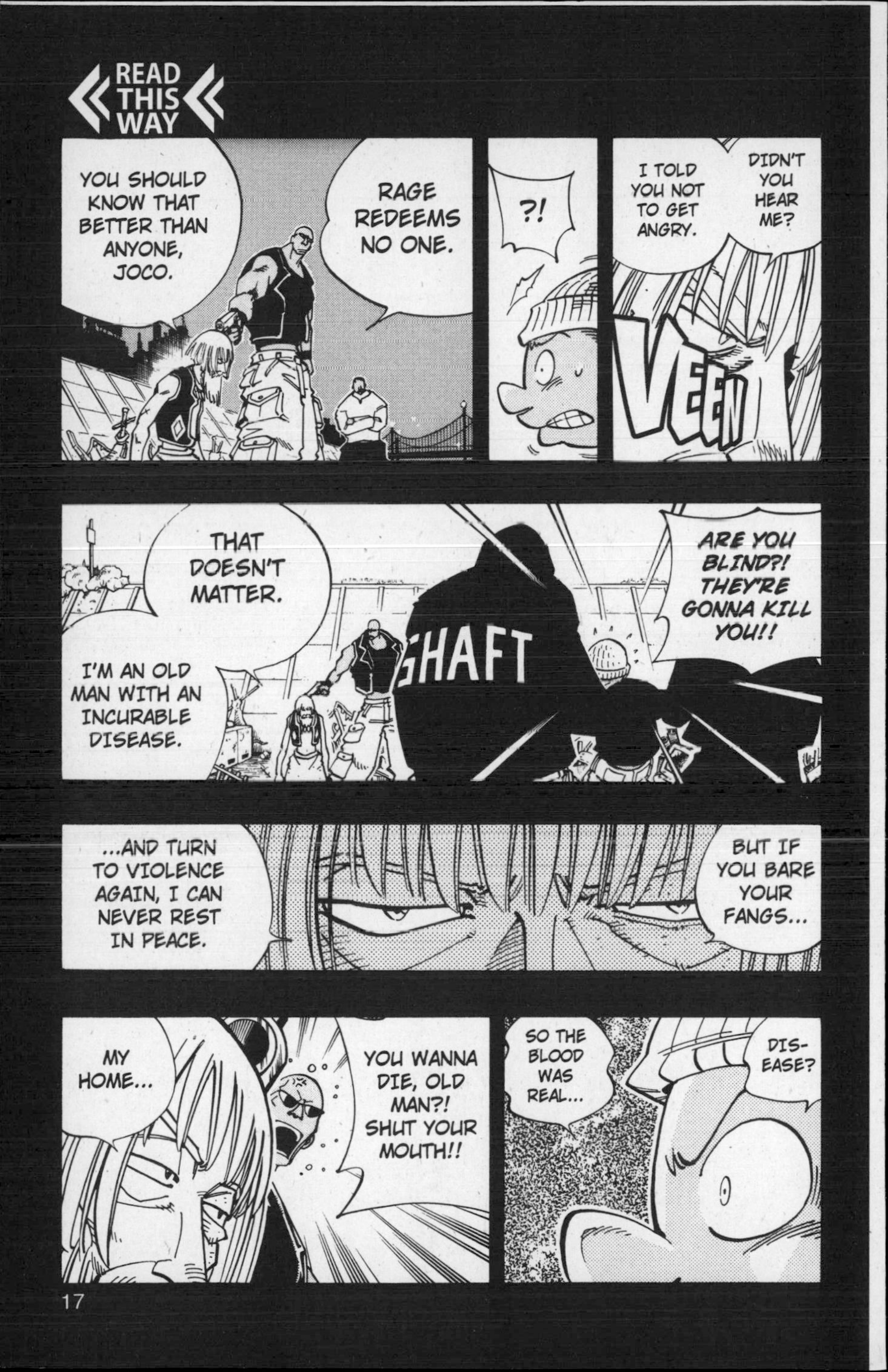

DIDN'T YOU HEAR ME?
I TOLD YOU NOT TO GET ANGRY.
VEEN
?!
RAGE REDEEMS NO ONE.
YOU SHOULD KNOW THAT BETTER THAN ANYONE, JOCO.
ARE YOU BLIND?! THEY'RE GONNA KILL YOU!!
SHAFT
THAT DOESN'T MATTER.
I'M AN OLD MAN WITH AN INCURABLE DISEASE.
BUT IF YOU BARE YOUR FANGS...
...AND TURN TO VIOLENCE AGAIN, I CAN NEVER REST IN PEACE.
DIS-EASE?
SO THE BLOOD WAS REAL...
YOU WANNA DIE, OLD MAN?! SHUT YOUR MOUTH!!
MY HOME...

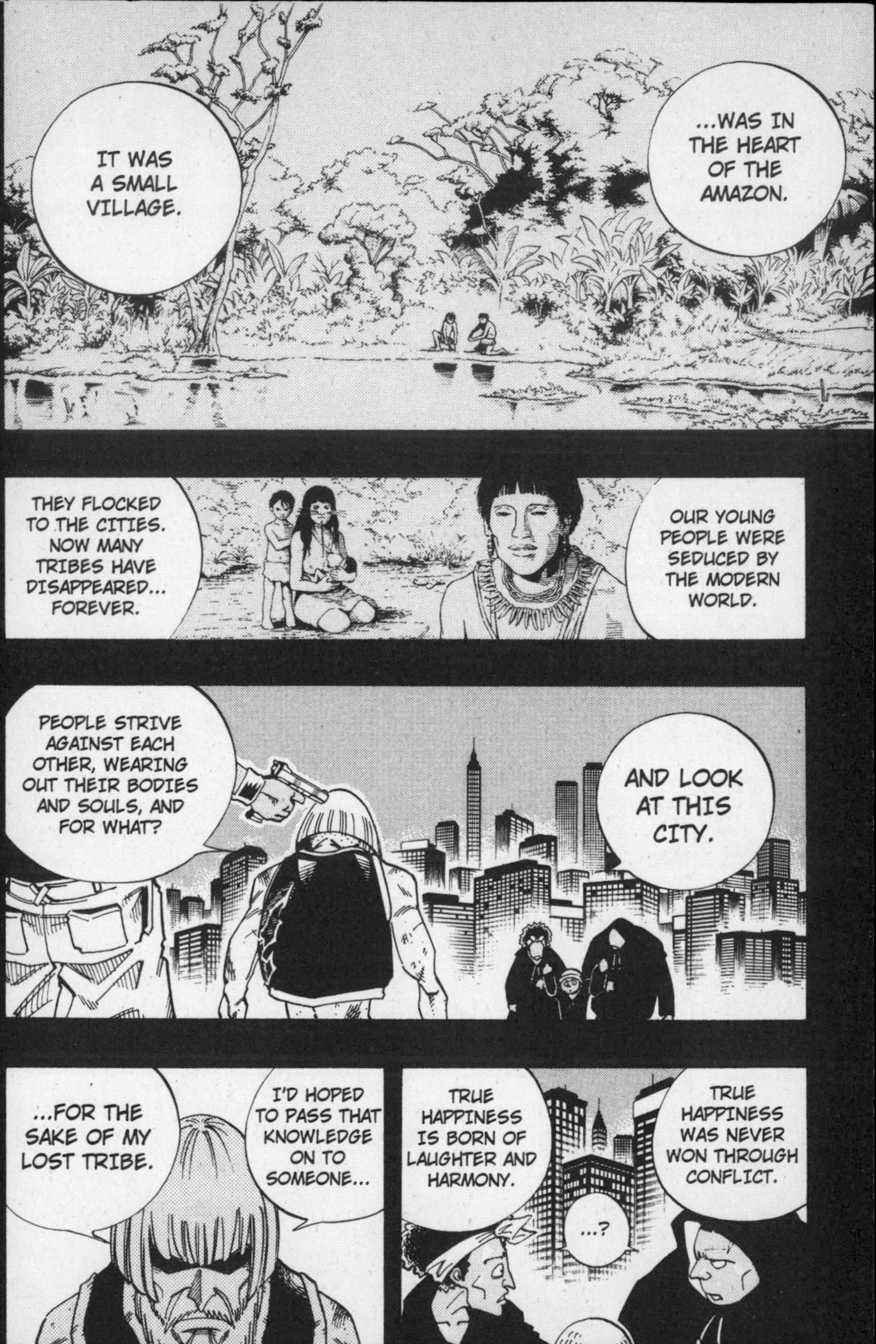
...WAS IN THE HEART OF THE AMAZON.
IT WAS A SMALL VILLAGE.
OUR YOUNG PEOPLE WERE SEDUCED BY THE MODERN WORLD.
THEY FLOCKED TO THE CITIES. NOW MANY TRIBES HAVE DISAPPEARED... FOREVER.
AND LOOK AT THIS CITY.
PEOPLE STRIVE AGAINST EACH OTHER, WEARING OUT THEIR BODIES AND SOULS, AND FOR WHAT?
TRUE HAPPINESS WAS NEVER WON THROUGH CONFLICT.
TRUE HAPPINESS IS BORN OF LAUGHTER AND HARMONY.
...?
I'D HOPED TO PASS THAT KNOWLEDGE ON TO SOMEONE...
...FOR THE SAKE OF MY LOST TRIBE.

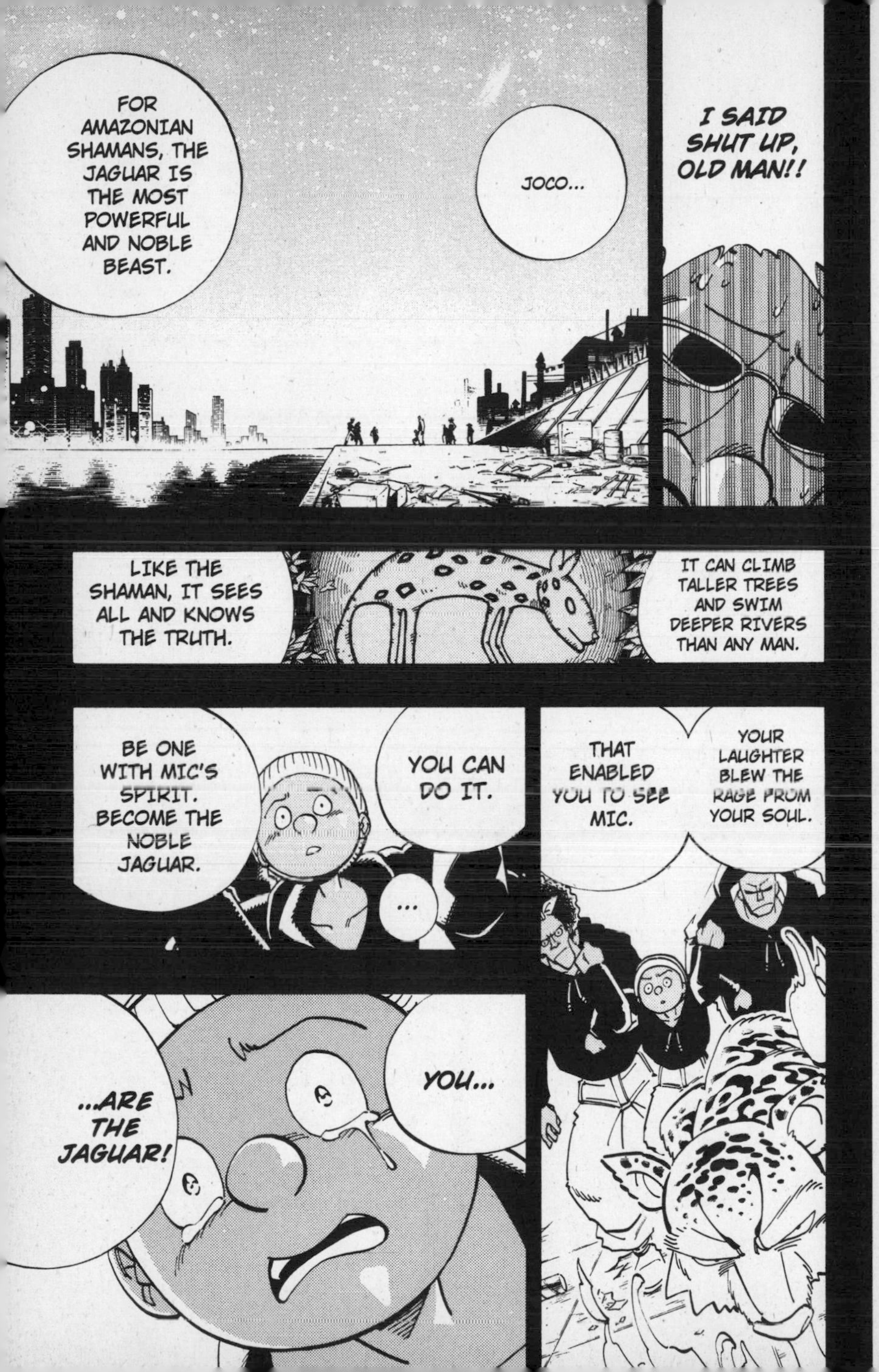
I SAID SHUT UP, OLD MAN!!
JOCO...
FOR AMAZONIAN SHAMANS, THE JAGUAR IS THE MOST POWERFUL AND NOBLE BEAST.
IT CAN CLIMB TALLER TREES AND SWIM DEEPER RIVERS THAN ANY MAN.
LIKE THE SHAMAN, IT SEES ALL AND KNOWS THE TRUTH.
YOUR LAUGHTER BLEW THE RAGE FROM YOUR SOUL.
THAT ENABLED YOU TO SEE MIC.
YOU CAN DO IT.
BE ONE WITH MIC'S SPIRIT. BECOME THE NOBLE JAGUAR.
...
YOU...
...ARE THE JAGUAR!

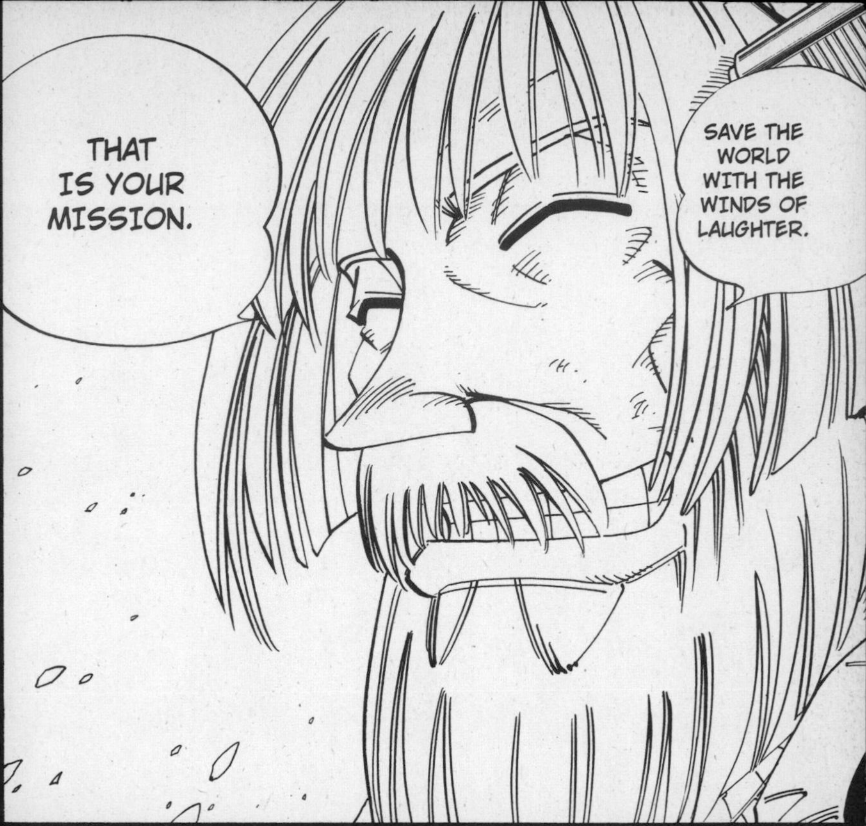
SAVE THE WORLD WITH THE WINDS OF LAUGHTER.
THAT IS YOUR MISSION.

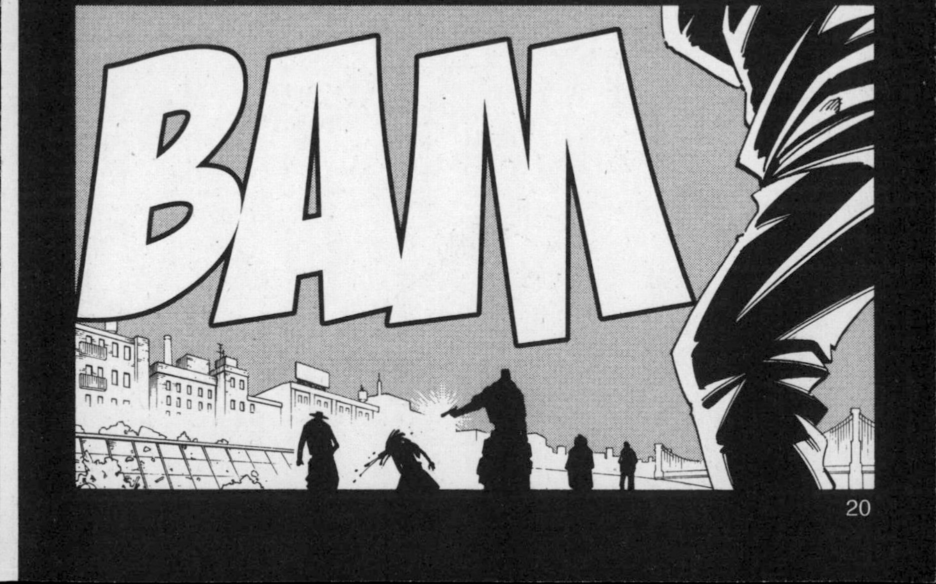
BAM

READ THIS WAY

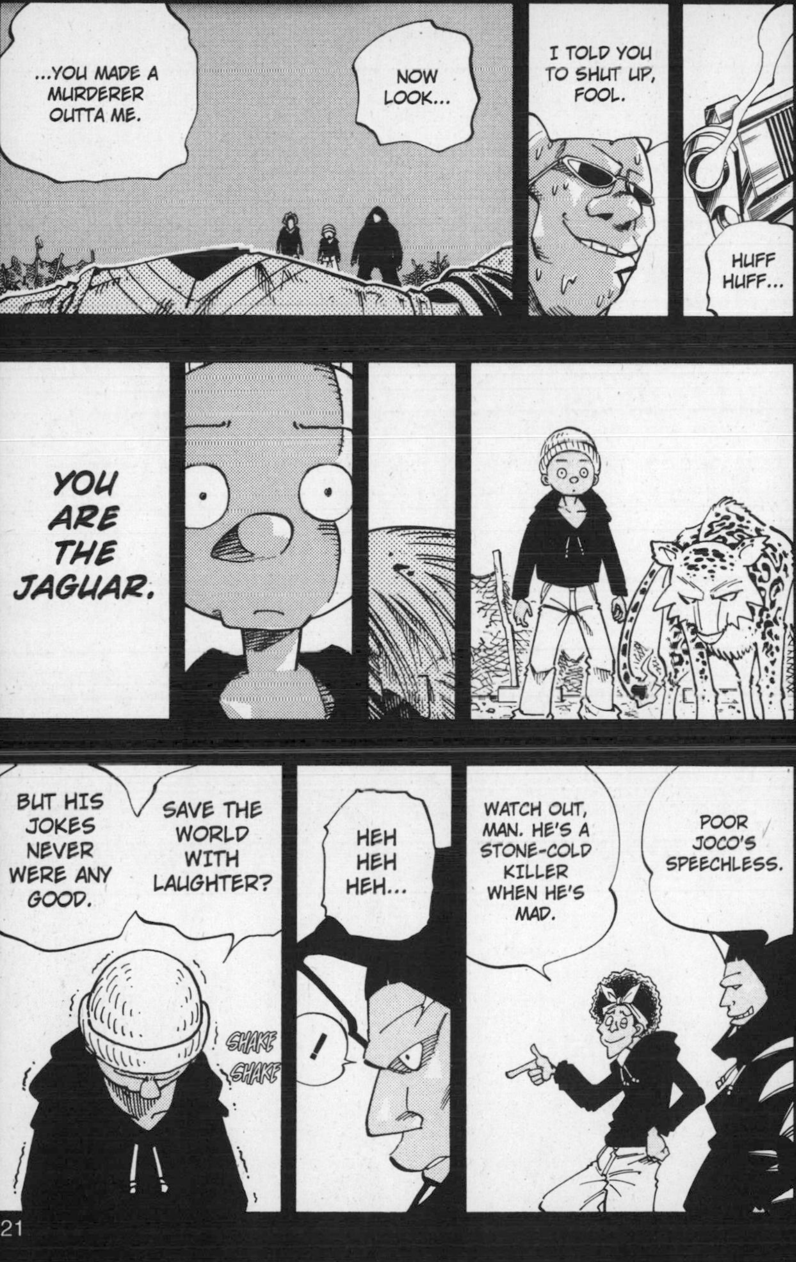
HUFF HUFF...
I TOLD YOU TO SHUT UP, FOOL.
NOW LOOK...
...YOU MADE A MURDERER OUTTA ME.
YOU ARE THE JAGUAR.
POOR JOCO'S SPEECHLESS.
WATCH OUT, MAN. HE'S A STONE-COLD KILLER WHEN HE'S MAD.
HEH HEH HEH...
!
SAVE THE WORLD WITH LAUGHTER?
BUT HIS JOKES NEVER WERE ANY GOOD.
SHAKE
SHAKE

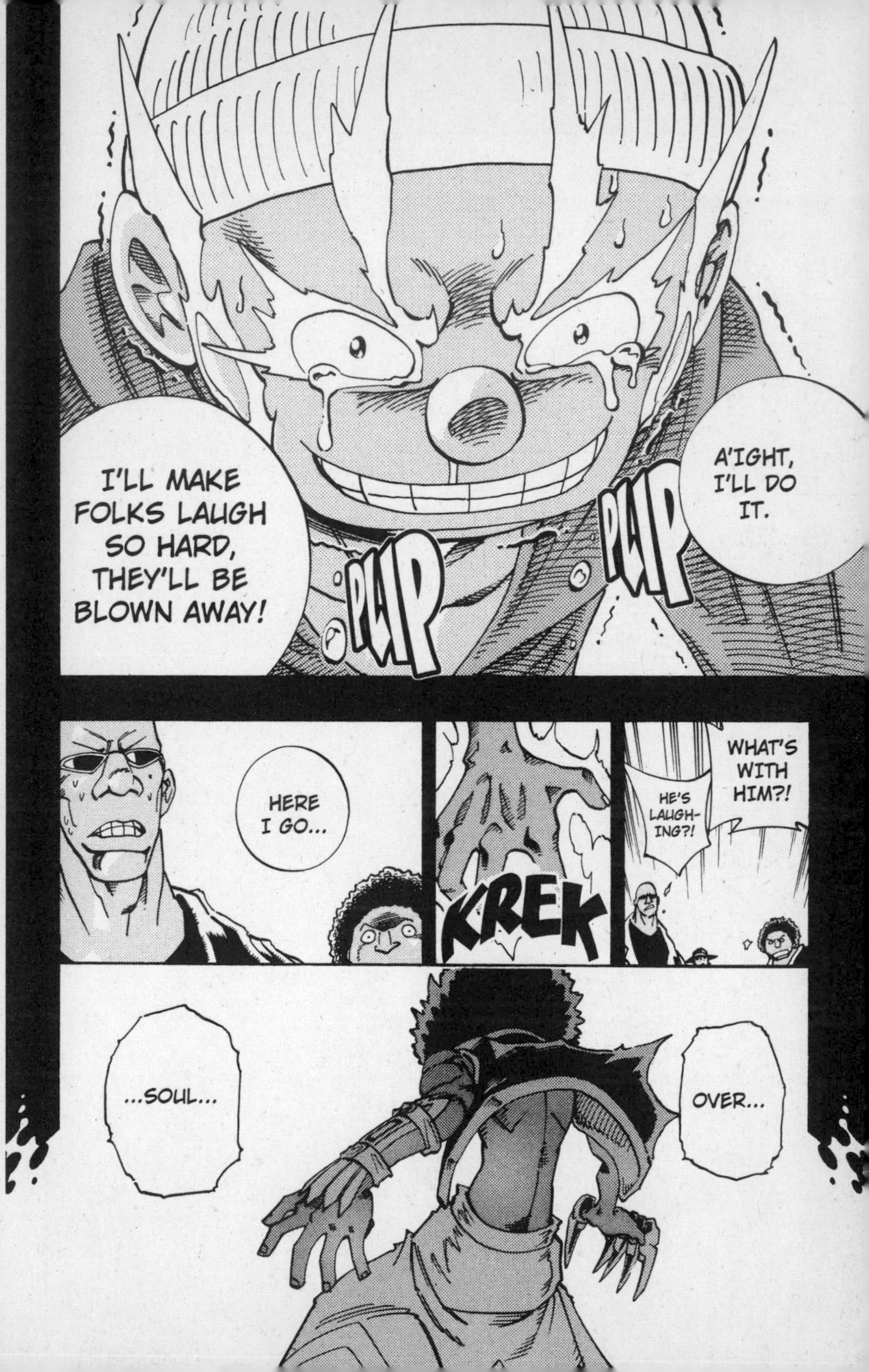
A'IGHT, I'LL DO IT.
PLIP
PLIP
I'LL MAKE FOLKS LAUGH SO HARD, THEY'LL BE BLOWN AWAY!
WHAT'S WITH HIM?!
HE'S LAUGH-ING?!
KREK
HERE I GO...
OVER...
...SOUL...

READ THIS WAY

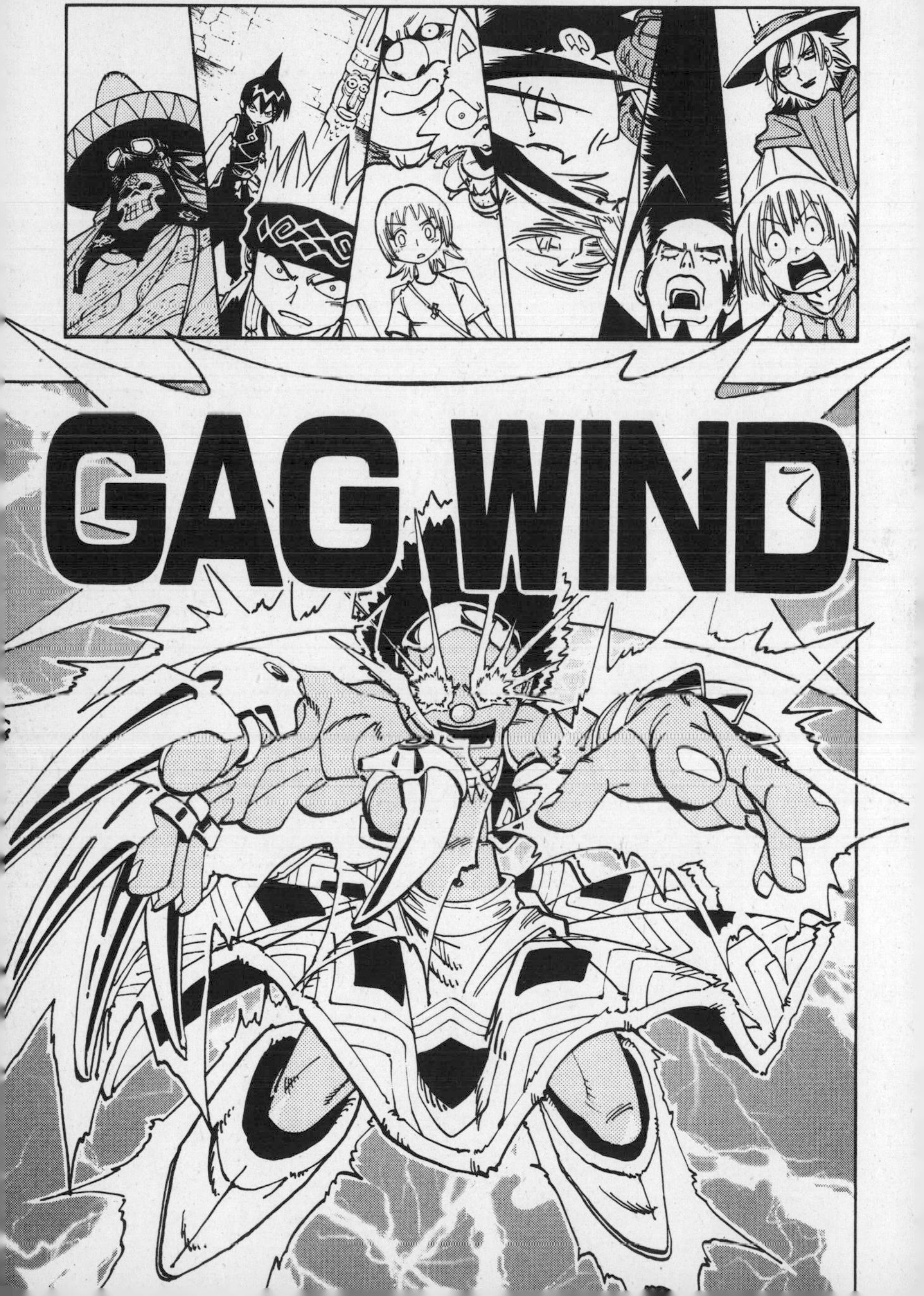

GAG WIND

SHAMAN KING CHARACTER FILE No.64

アナテル
ANATEL

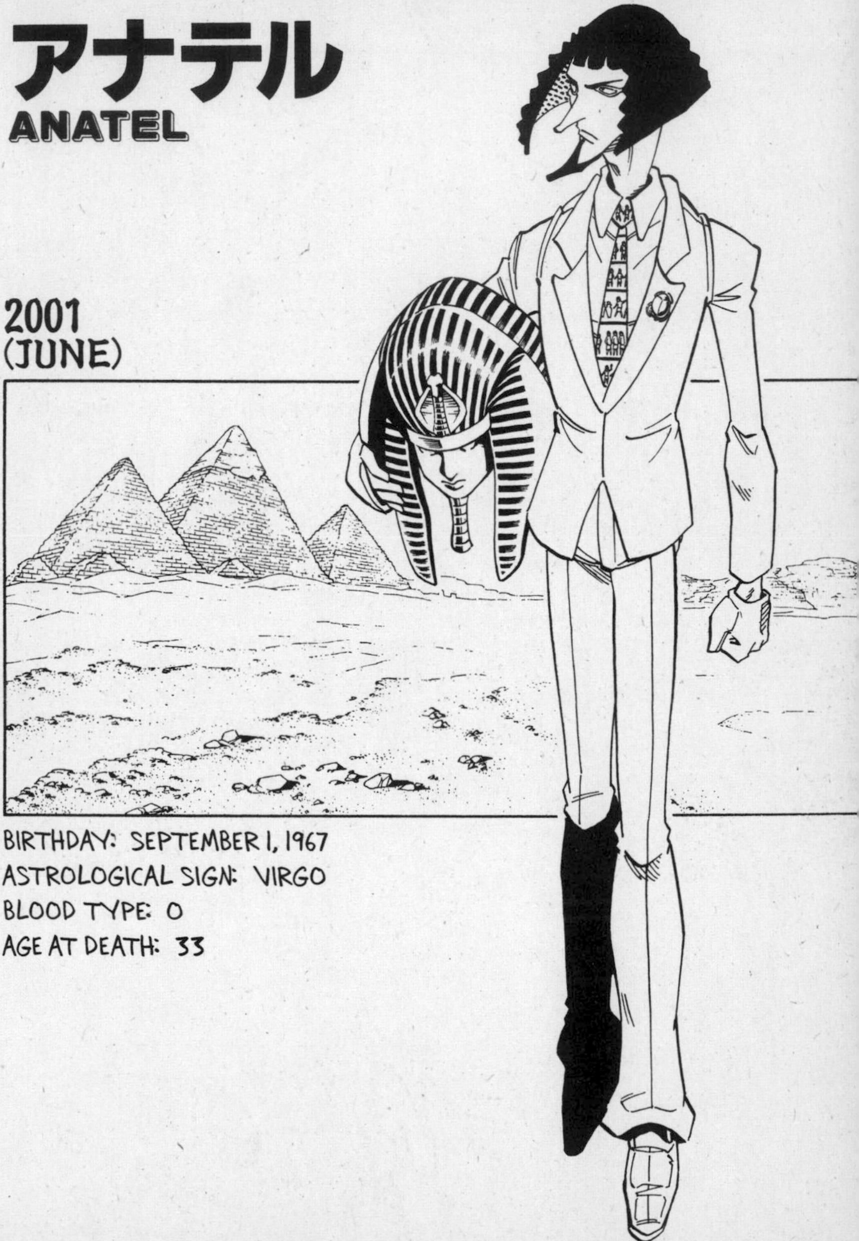

2001
(JUNE)

BIRTHDAY: SEPTEMBER 1, 1967
ASTROLOGICAL SIGN: VIRGO
BLOOD TYPE: O
AGE AT DEATH: 33

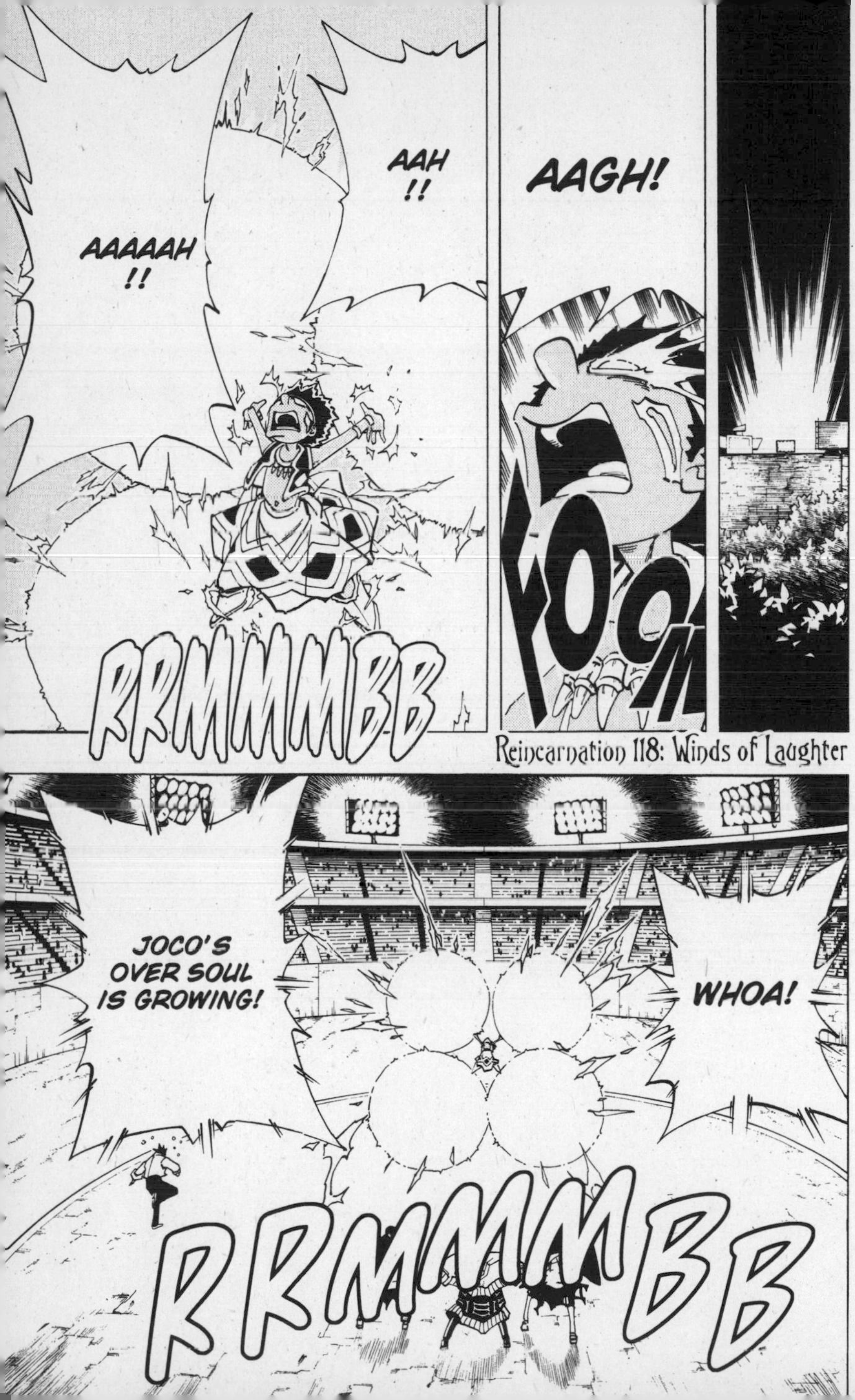
AAGH!
VOOM
AAH !!
AAAAAH !!
RRMMMMBB
Reincarnation 118: Winds of Laughter
WHOA!
JOCO'S OVER SOUL IS GROWING!
RRMMMBB

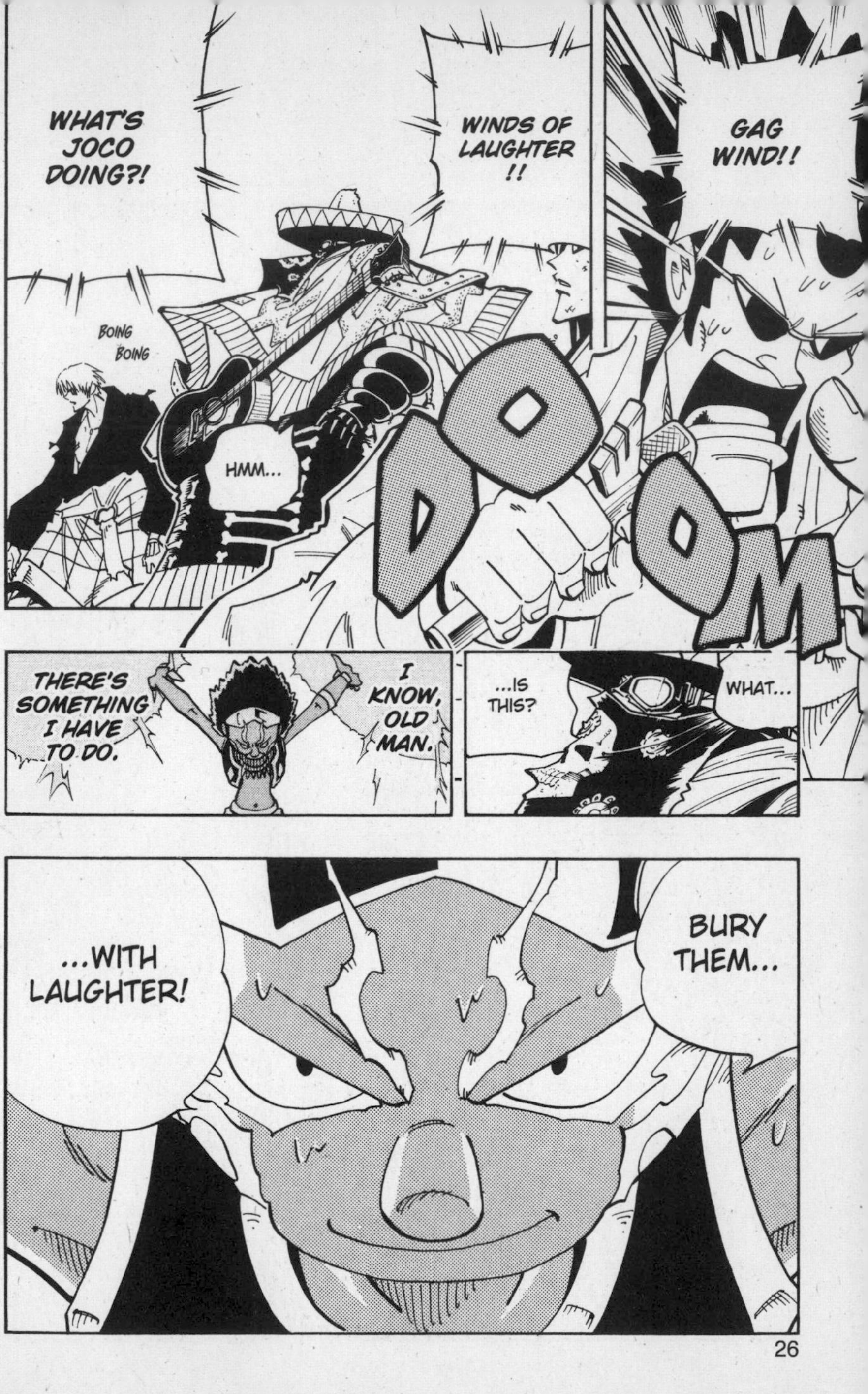
GAG WIND!!
WINDS OF LAUGHTER !!
DOOM
WHAT'S JOCO DOING?!
BOING BOING
HMM...
WHAT...
...IS THIS?
I KNOW, OLD MAN.
THERE'S SOMETHING I HAVE TO DO.
BURY THEM...
...WITH LAUGHTER!

Reincarnation 118:
Winds of Laughter

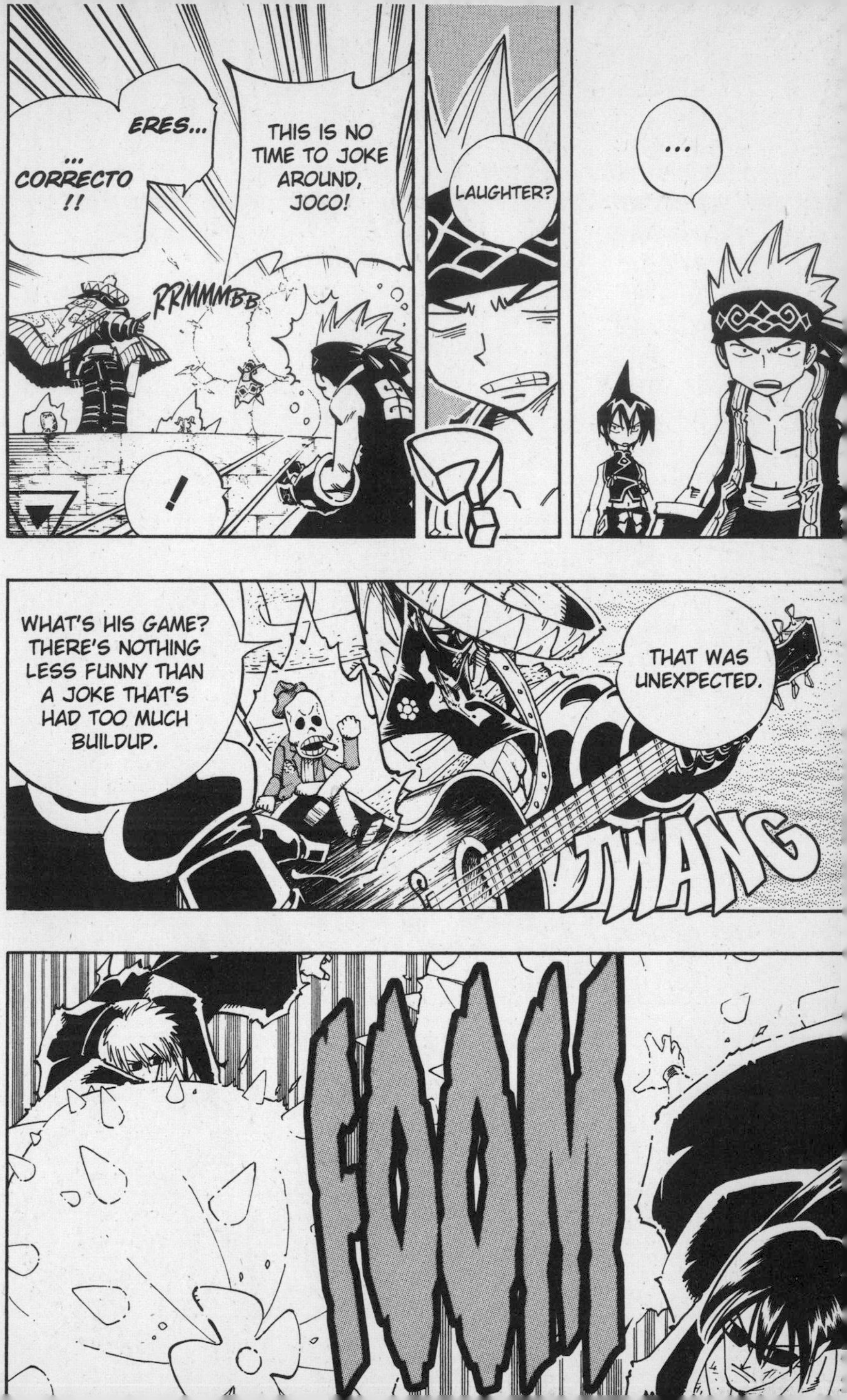
...
LAUGHTER?
THIS IS NO TIME TO JOKE AROUND, JOCO!
ERES...
... CORRECTO !!
RRMMMBB
!
THAT WAS UNEXPECTED.
WHAT'S HIS GAME? THERE'S NOTHING LESS FUNNY THAN A JOKE THAT'S HAD TOO MUCH BUILDUP.
TWANG
FOOM

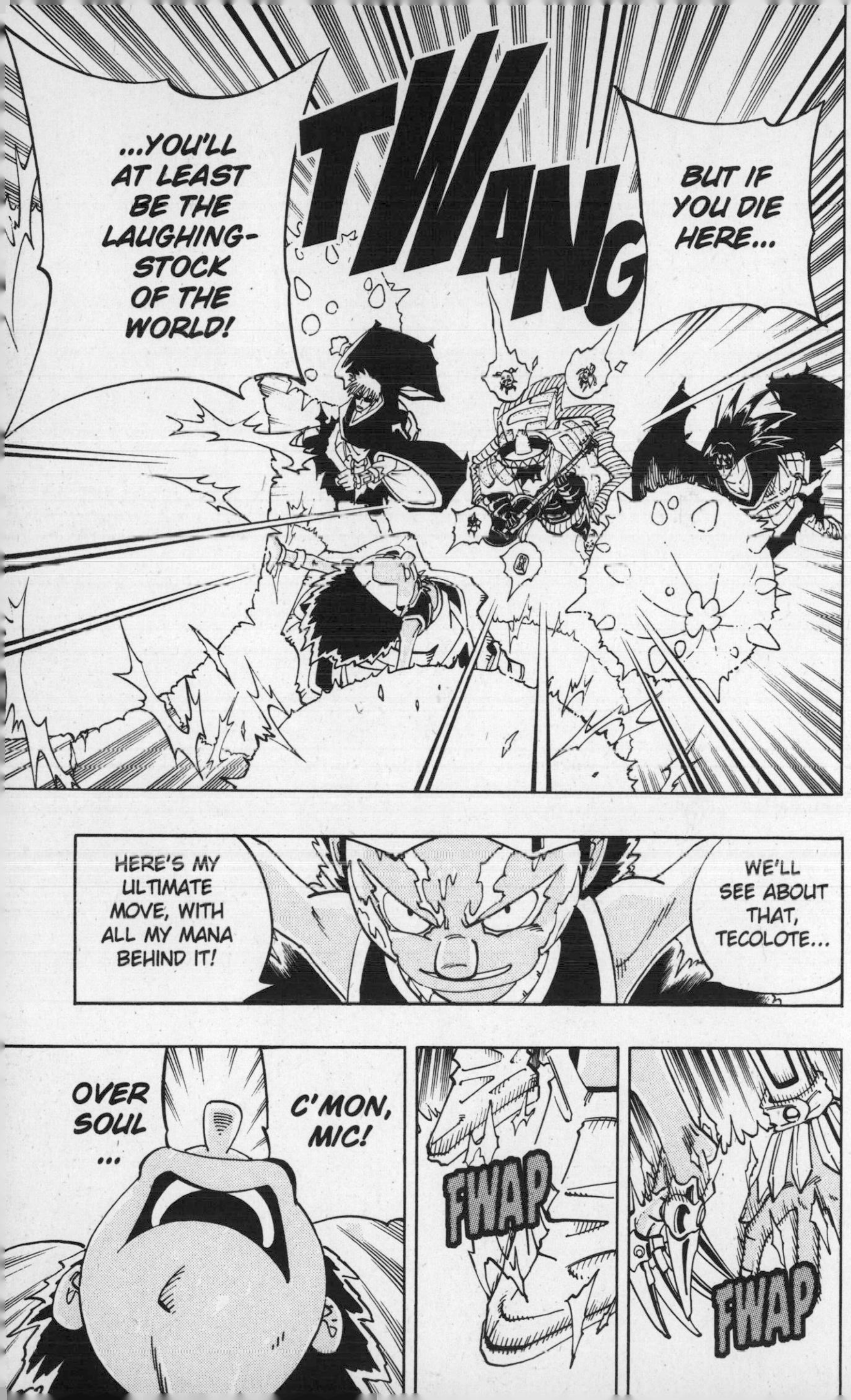
BUT IF YOU DIE HERE...
TWANG
...YOU'LL AT LEAST BE THE LAUGHING-STOCK OF THE WORLD!
WE'LL SEE ABOUT THAT, TECOLOTE...
HERE'S MY ULTIMATE MOVE, WITH ALL MY MANA BEHIND IT!
FWAP
FWAP
C'MON, MIC!
OVER SOUL ...

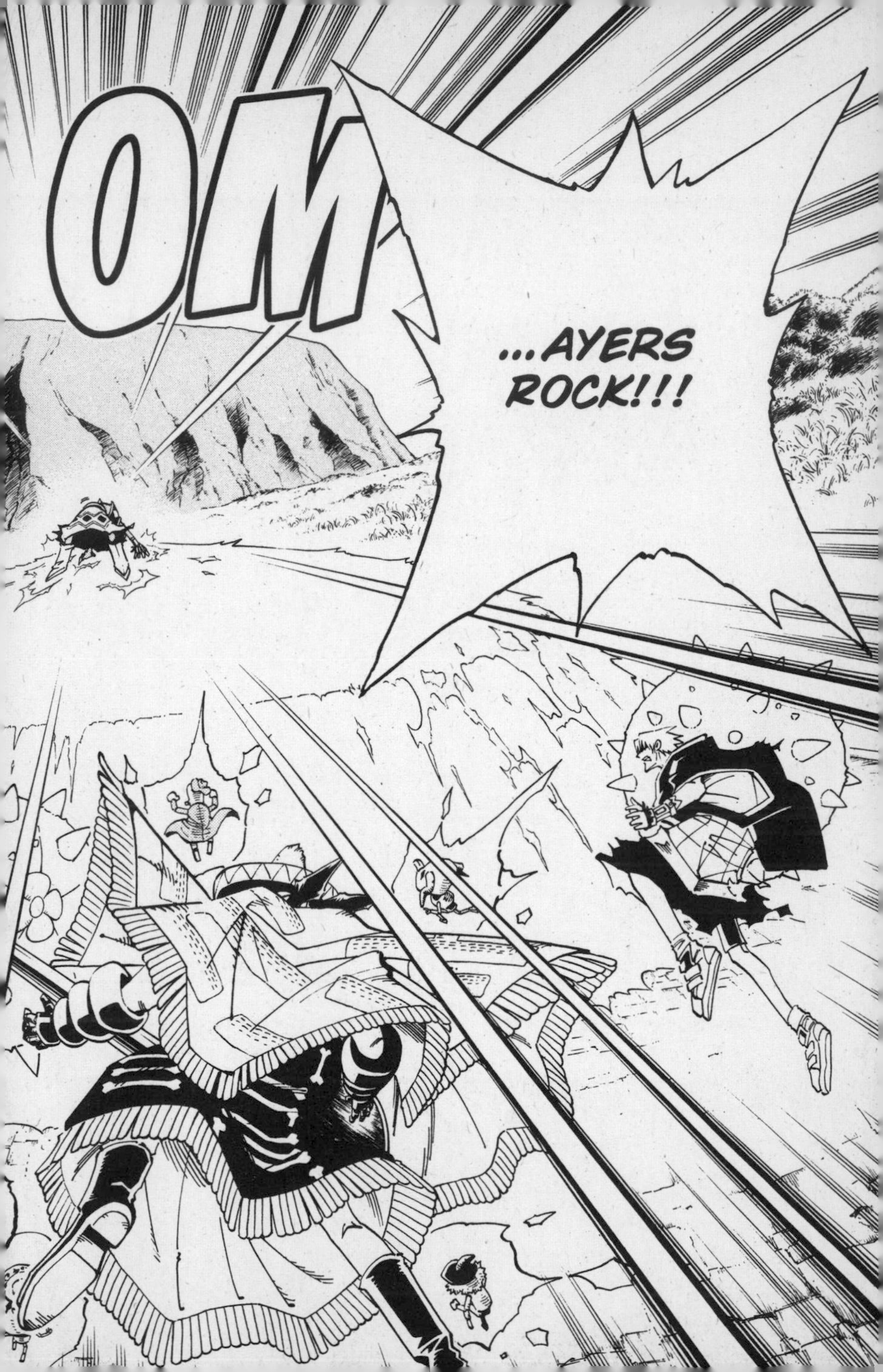
OM
...AYERS
ROCK!!!

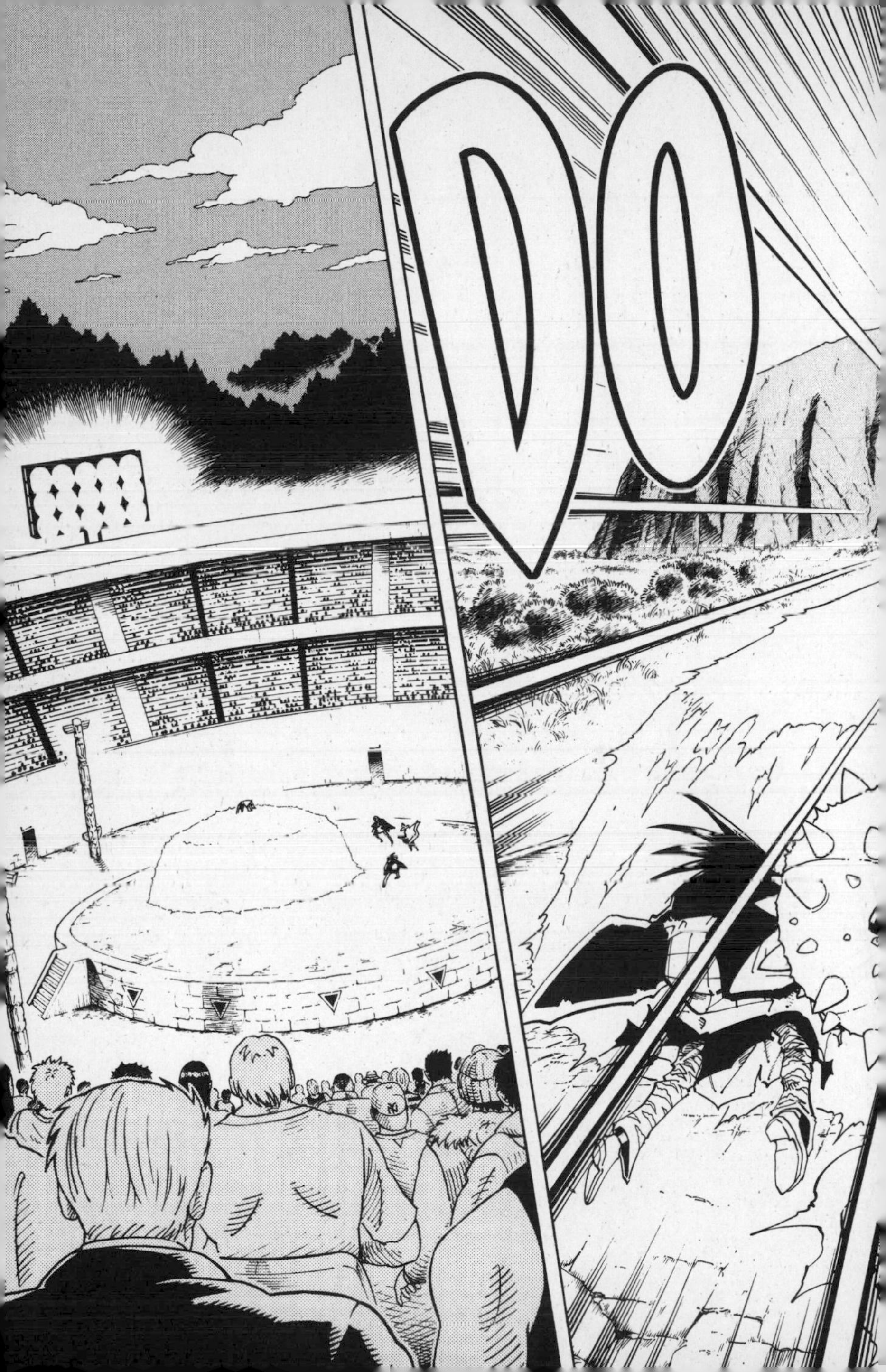
DO

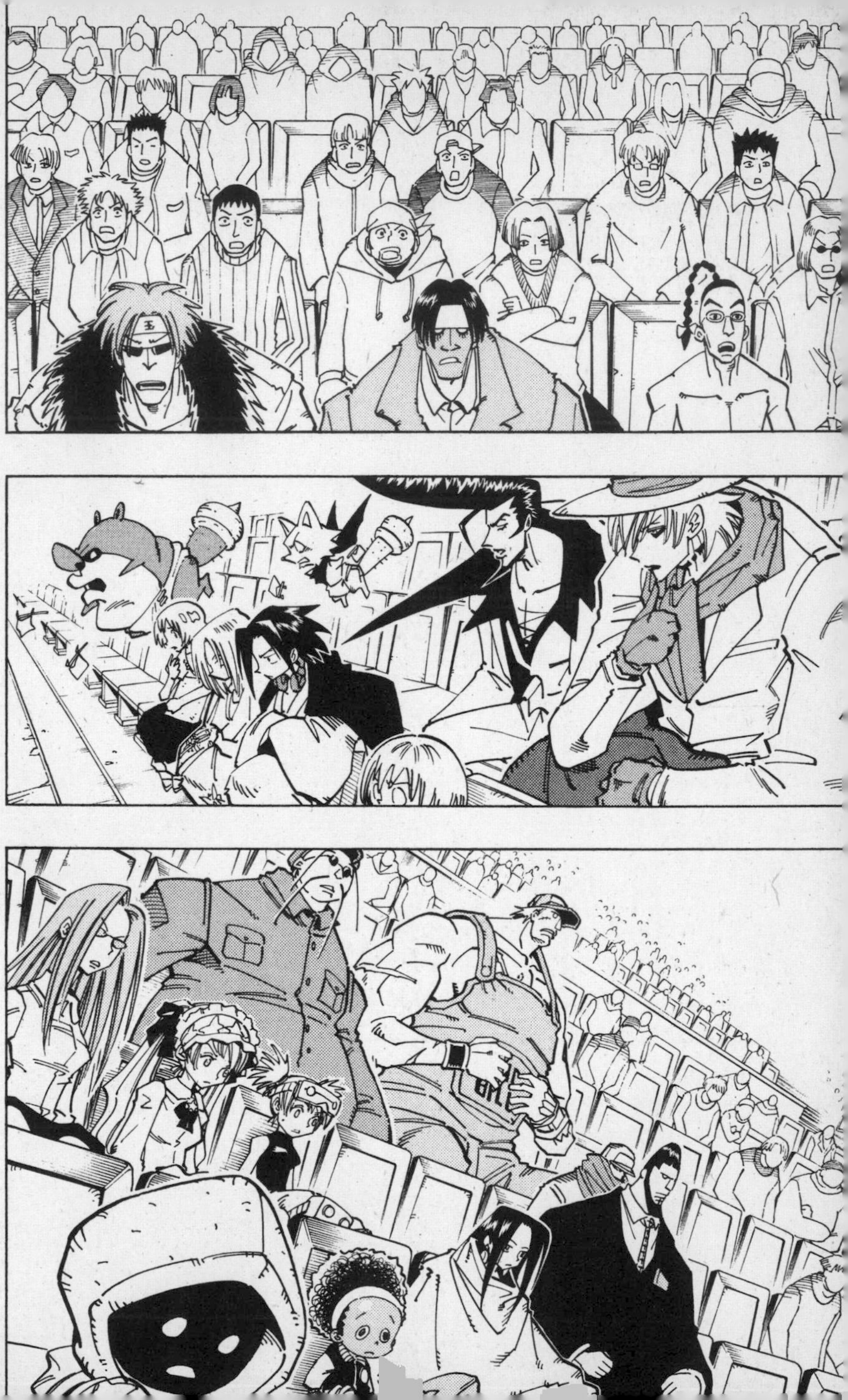

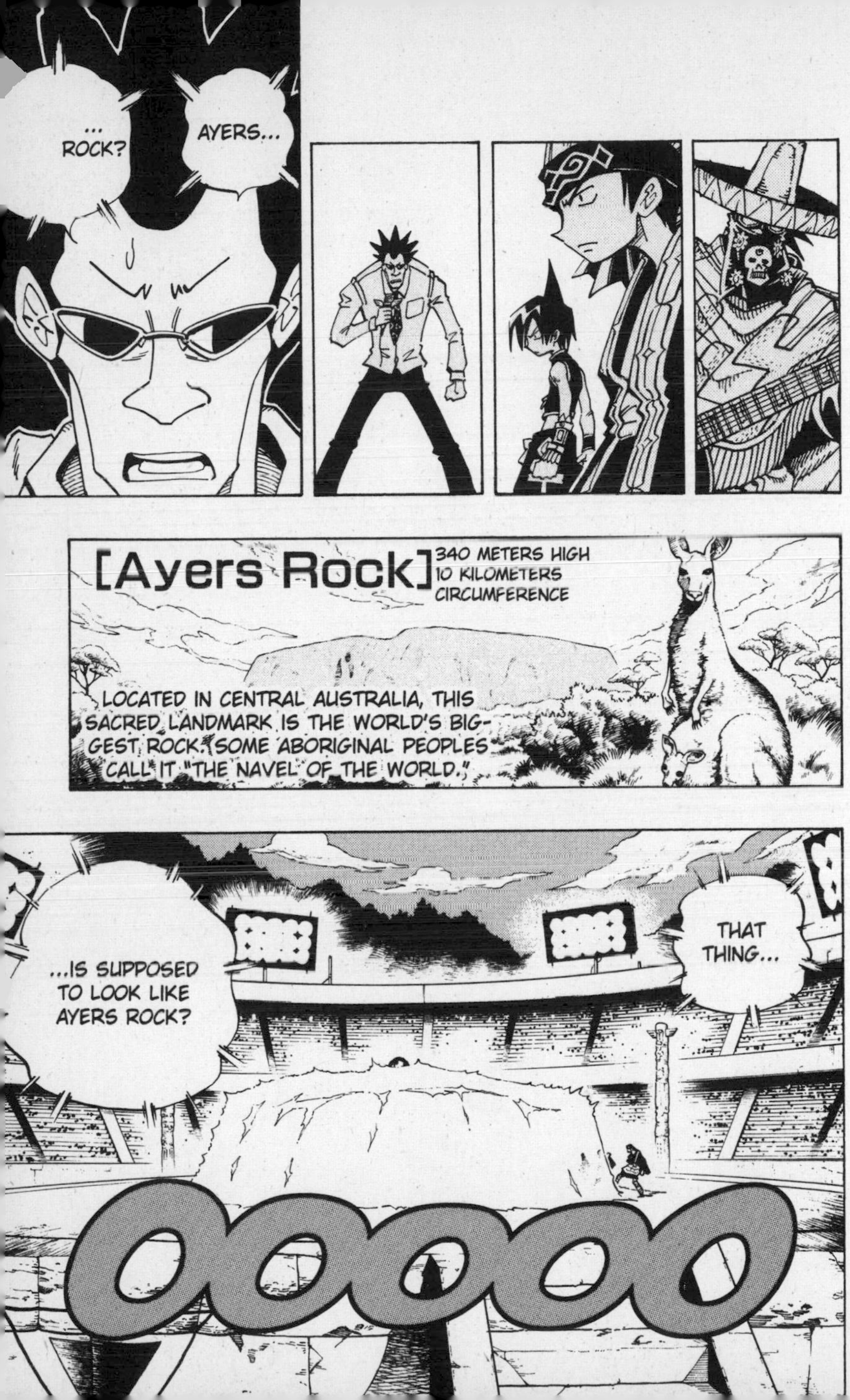
AYERS...
...ROCK?
[Ayers Rock]
340 METERS HIGH
10 KILOMETERS CIRCUMFERENCE
LOCATED IN CENTRAL AUSTRALIA, THIS SACRED LANDMARK IS THE WORLD'S BIGGEST ROCK. SOME ABORIGINAL PEOPLES CALL IT "THE NAVEL OF THE WORLD."
THAT THING...
...IS SUPPOSED TO LOOK LIKE AYERS ROCK?

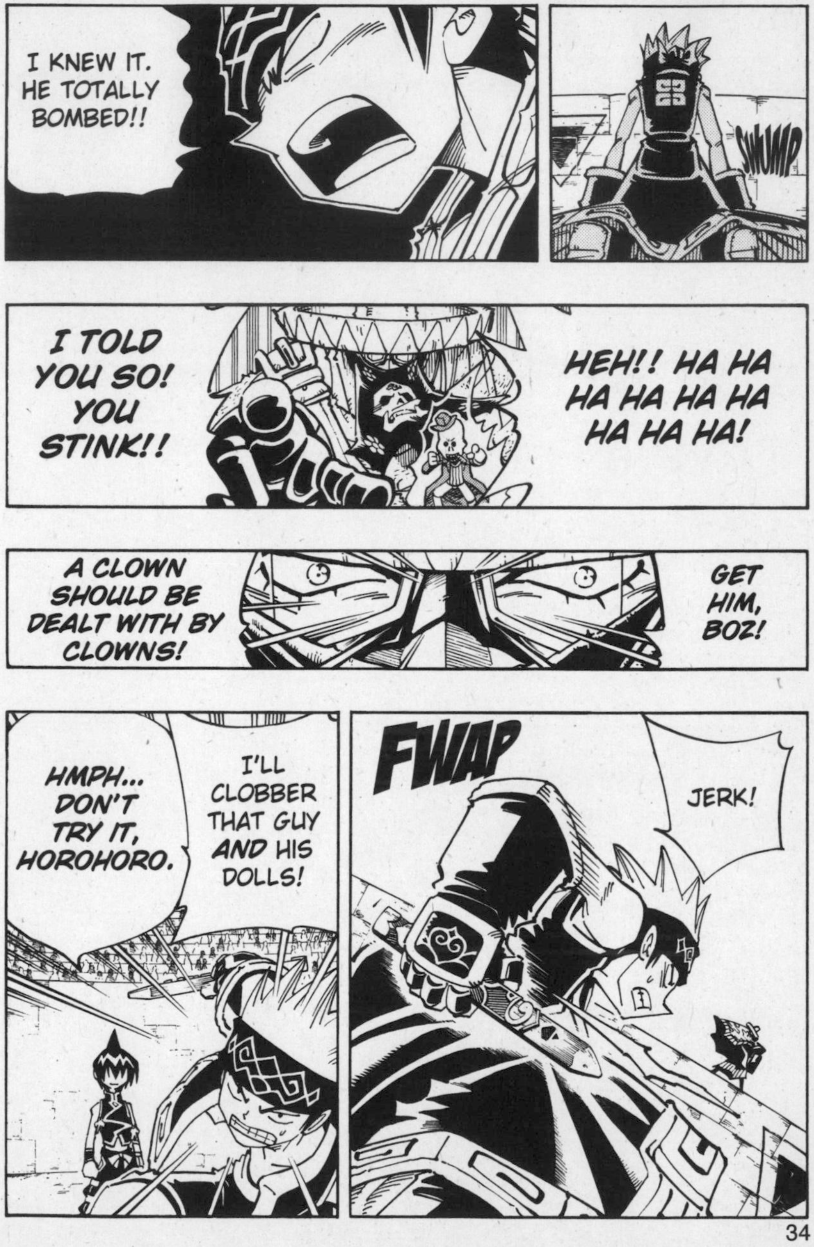
SHUMP
I KNEW IT. HE TOTALLY BOMBED!!
HEH!! HA HA HA HA HA HA HA HA HA!
I TOLD YOU SO! YOU STINK!!
GET HIM, BOZ!
A CLOWN SHOULD BE DEALT WITH BY CLOWNS!
JERK!
FWAP
I'LL CLOBBER THAT GUY AND HIS DOLLS!
HMPH... DON'T TRY IT, HOROHORO.

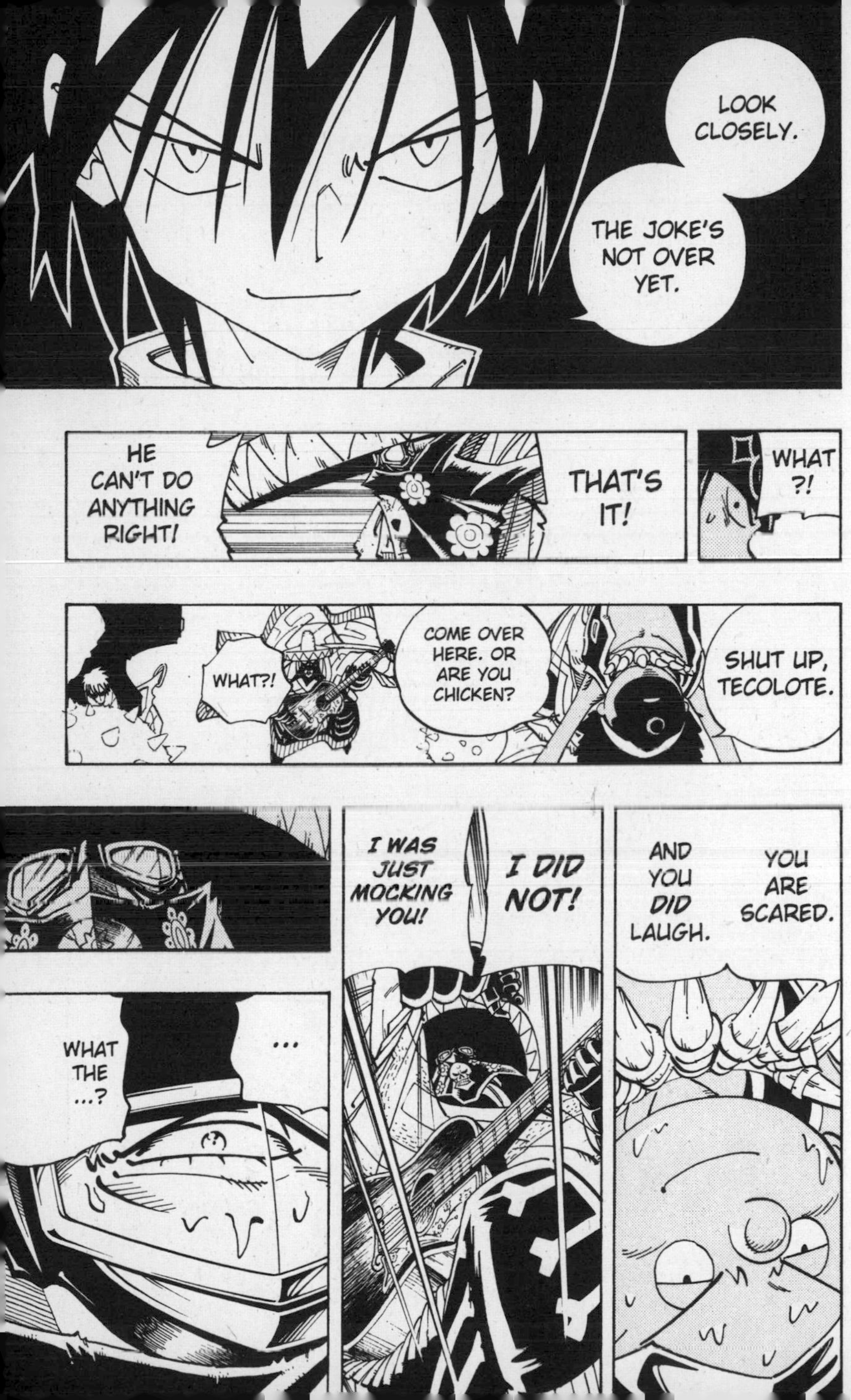
LOOK CLOSELY.
THE JOKE'S NOT OVER YET.
WHAT ?!
THAT'S IT!
HE CAN'T DO ANYTHING RIGHT!
SHUT UP, TECOLOTE.
COME OVER HERE. OR ARE YOU CHICKEN?
WHAT?!
YOU ARE SCARED.
AND YOU DID LAUGH.
I DID NOT!
I WAS JUST MOCKING YOU!
...
WHAT THE ...?

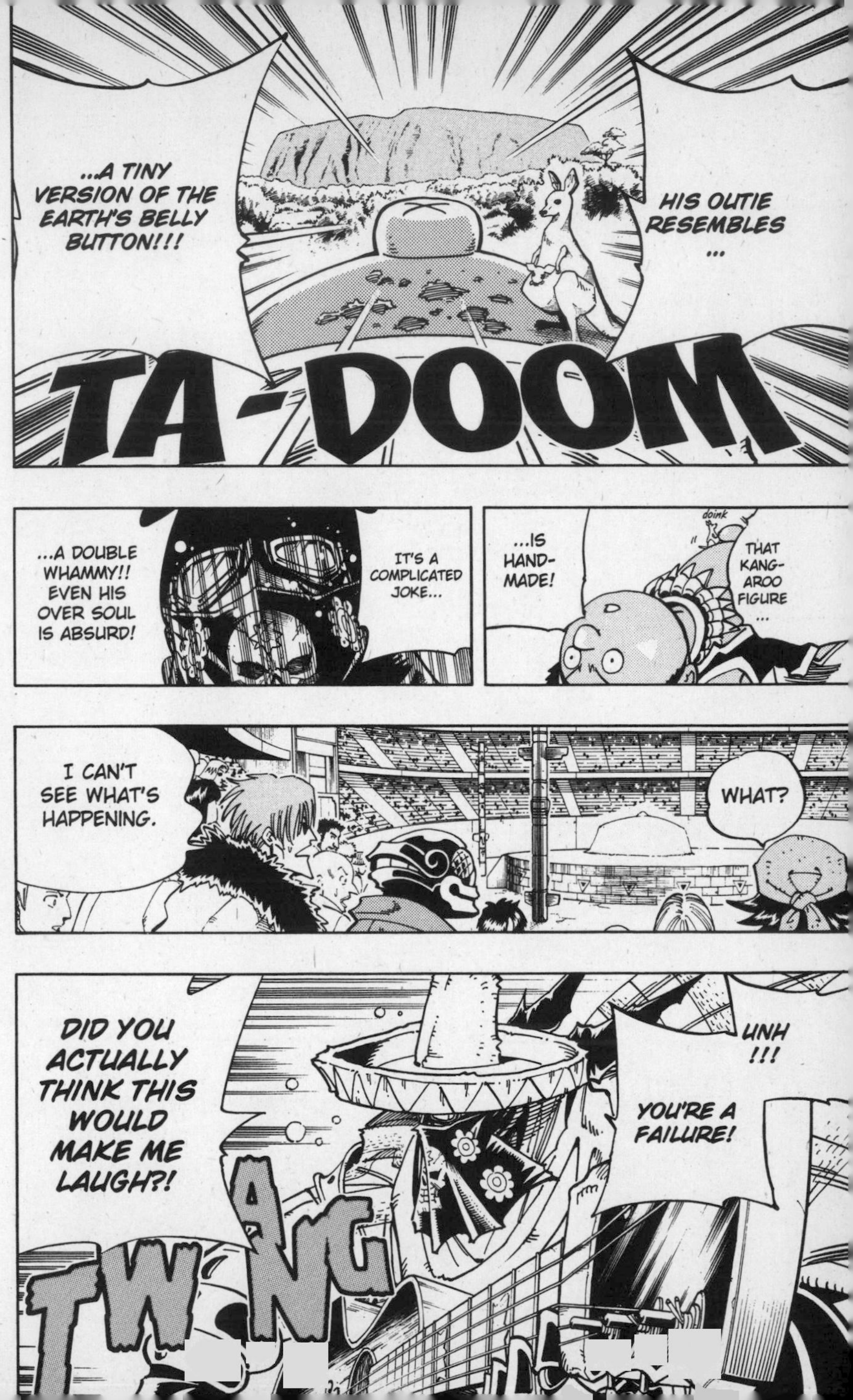
HIS OUTIE RESEMBLES ...
...A TINY VERSION OF THE EARTH'S BELLY BUTTON!!!
TA-DOOM
doink
THAT KANG-AROO FIGURE ...
...IS HAND-MADE!
IT'S A COMPLICATED JOKE...
...A DOUBLE WHAMMY!! EVEN HIS OVER SOUL IS ABSURD!
WHAT?
I CAN'T SEE WHAT'S HAPPENING.
UNH !!!
YOU'RE A FAILURE!
DID YOU ACTUALLY THINK THIS WOULD MAKE ME LAUGH?!
TWANG

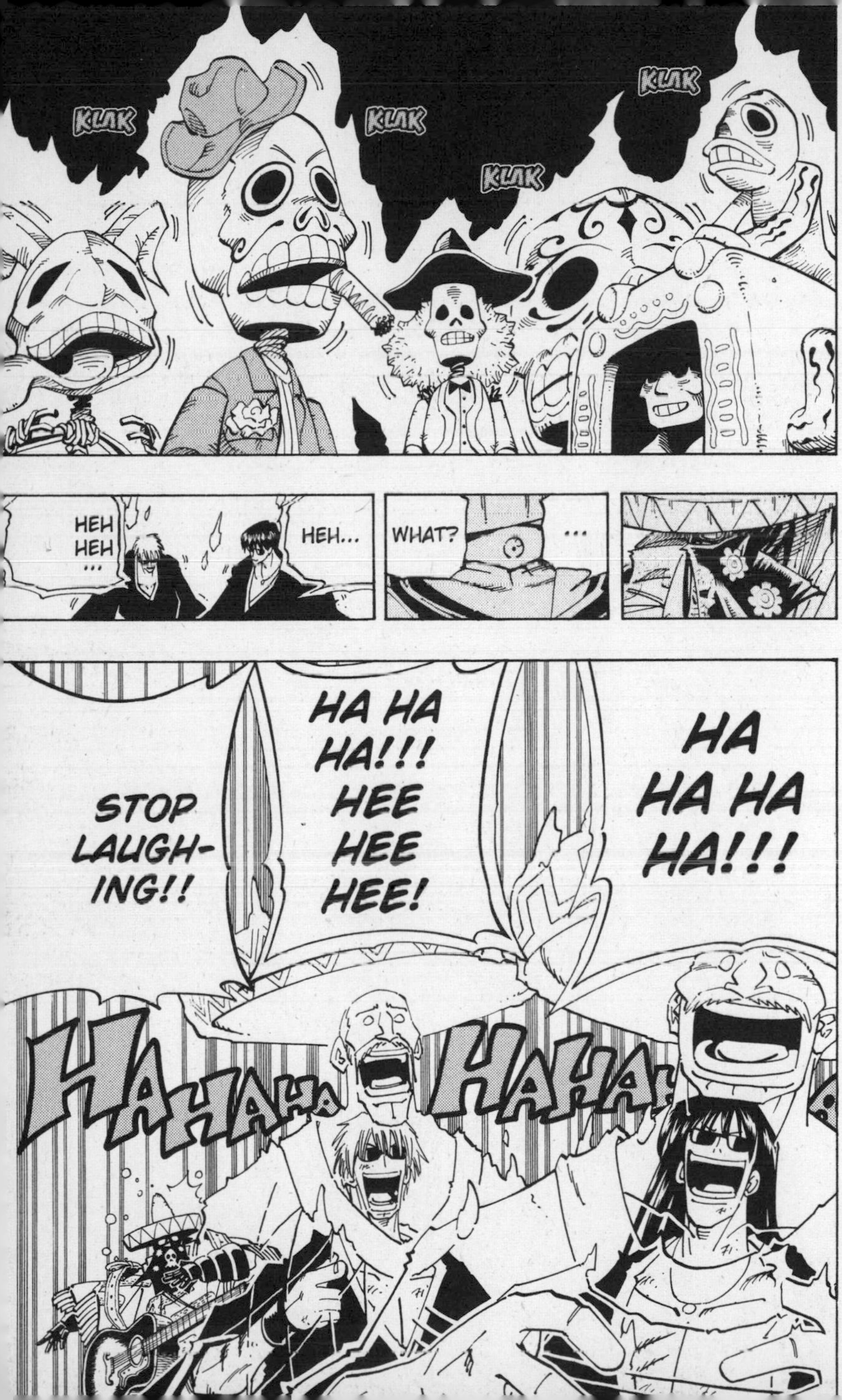
KLAK
KLAK
KLAK
KLAK
WHAT?
...
HEH...
HEH HEH ...
HA HA HA HA!!!
HA HA HA!!! HEE HEE HEE!
STOP LAUGH-ING!!
HAHAHA
HAHAHA

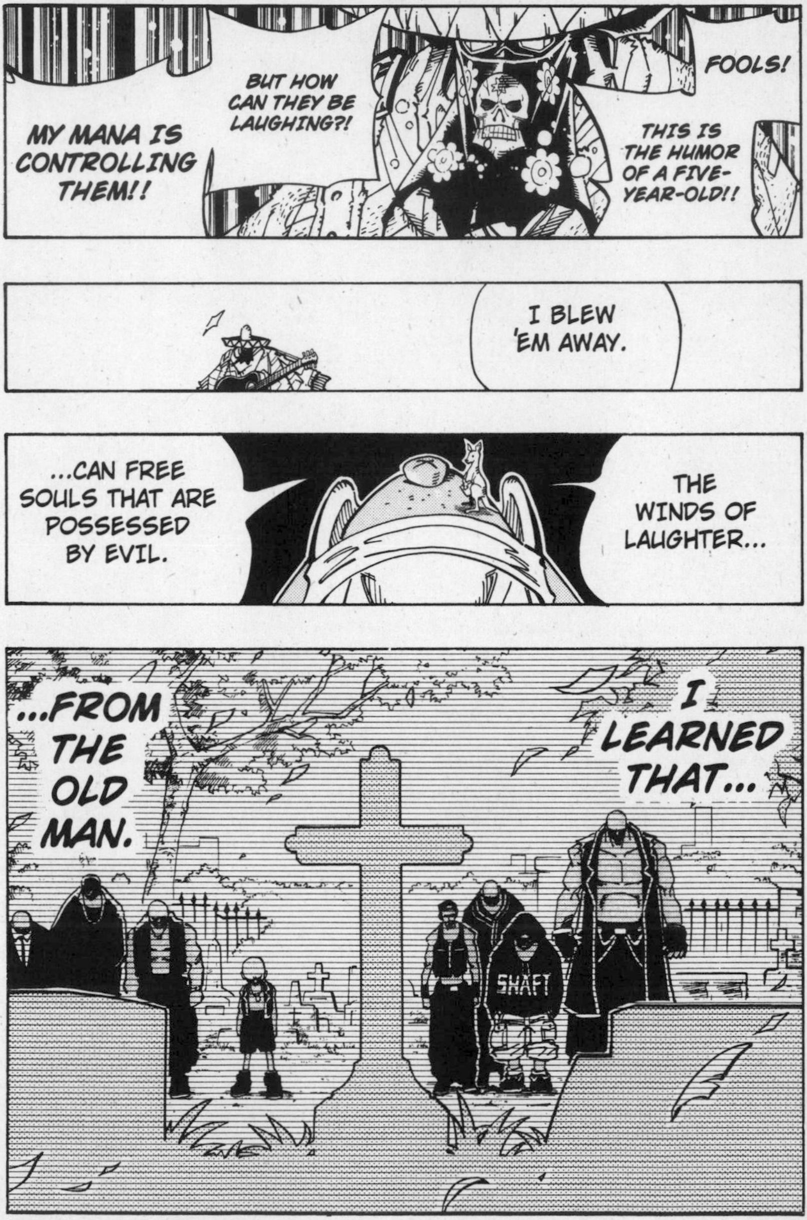
FOOLS!
THIS IS THE HUMOR OF A FIVE-YEAR-OLD!!
BUT HOW CAN THEY BE LAUGHING?!
MY MANA IS CONTROLLING THEM!!
I BLEW 'EM AWAY.
THE WINDS OF LAUGHTER...
...CAN FREE SOULS THAT ARE POSSESSED BY EVIL.
I LEARNED THAT...
...FROM THE OLD MAN.
SHAFT

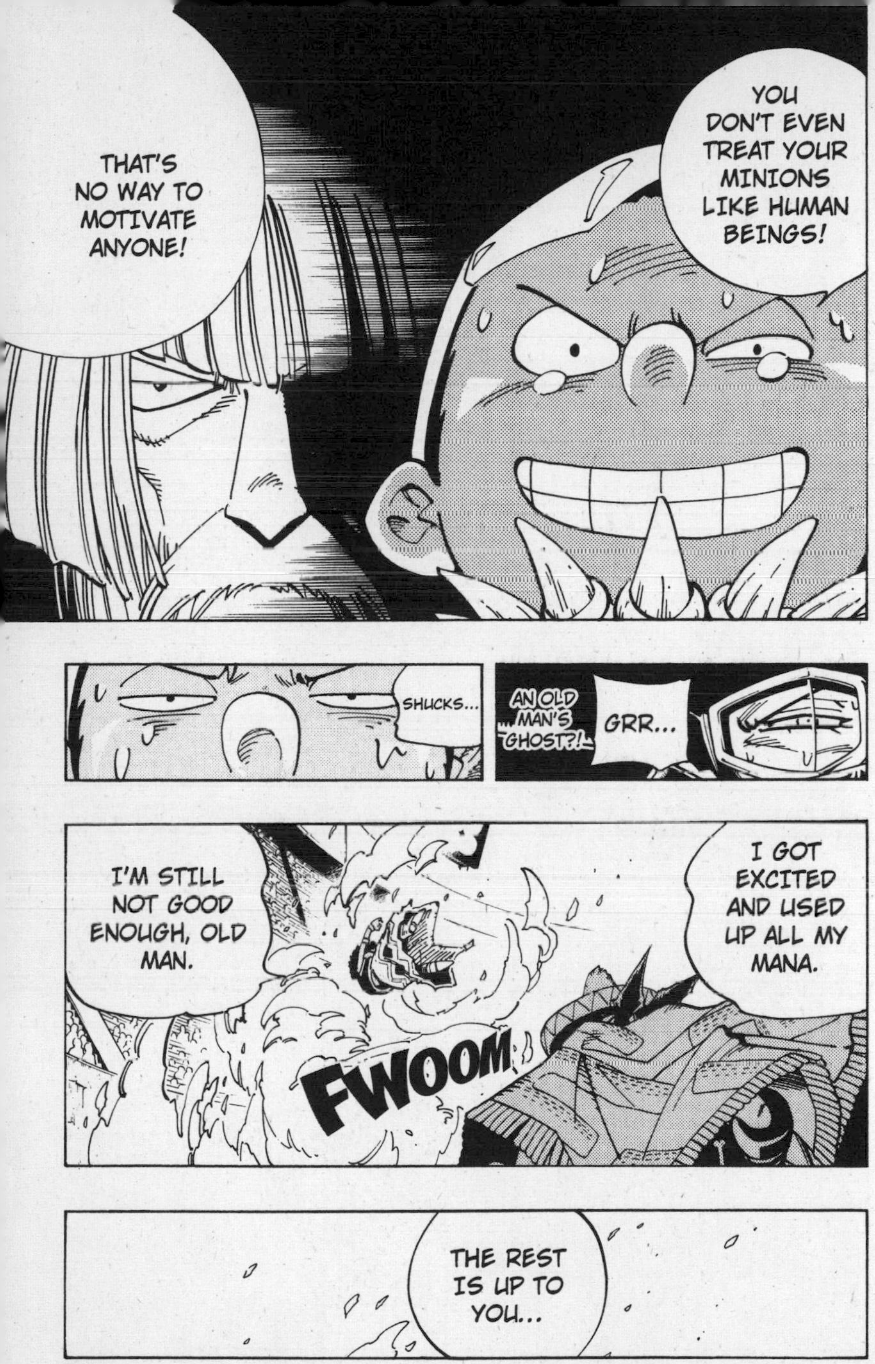

YOU DON'T EVEN TREAT YOUR MINIONS LIKE HUMAN BEINGS!
THAT'S NO WAY TO MOTIVATE ANYONE!
GRR...
AN OLD MAN'S GHOST?!
SHUCKS...
I GOT EXCITED AND USED UP ALL MY MANA.
I'M STILL NOT GOOD ENOUGH, OLD MAN.
FWOOM
THE REST IS UP TO YOU...

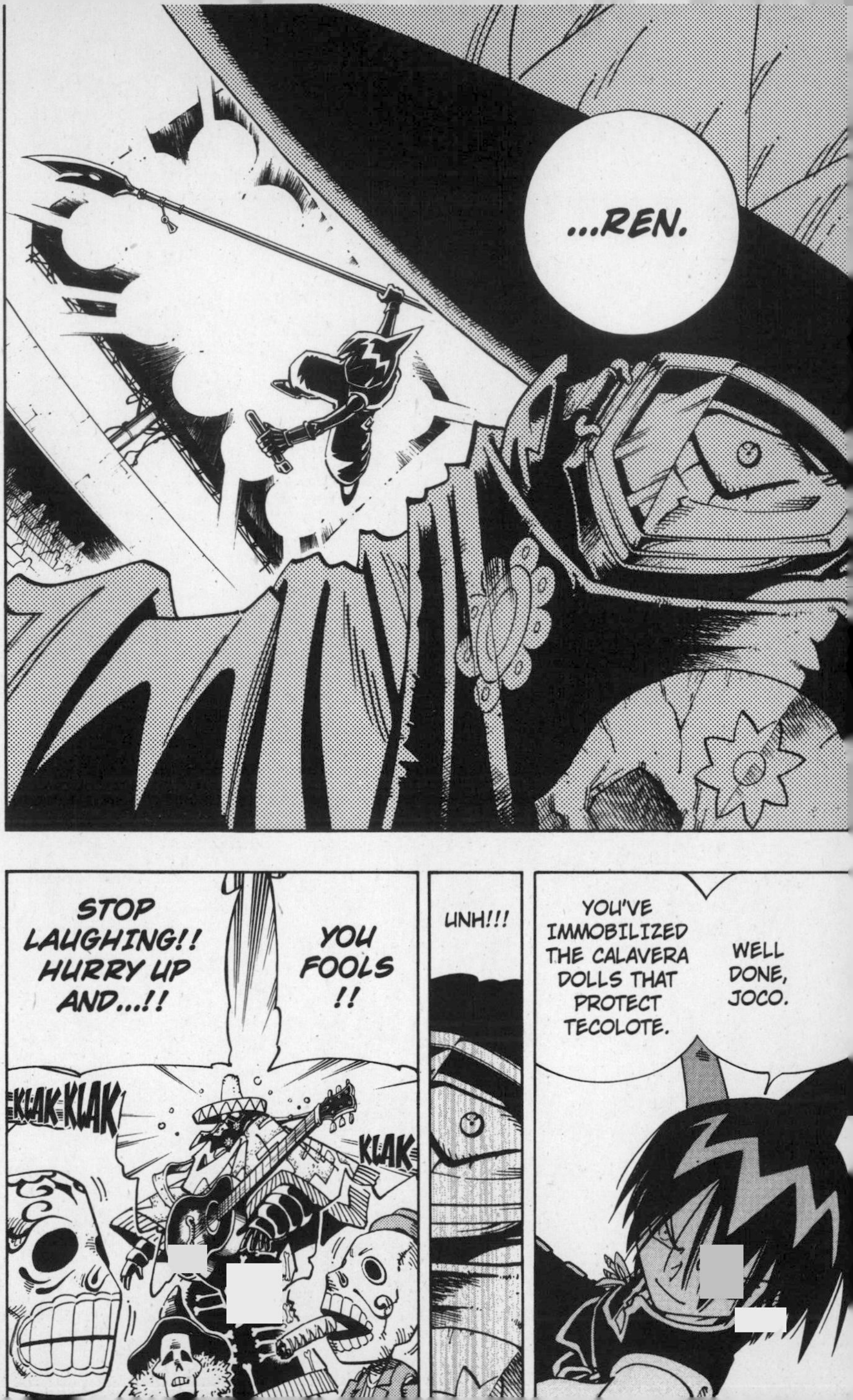
...REN.
WELL DONE, JOCO.
YOU'VE IMMOBILIZED THE CALAVERA DOLLS THAT PROTECT TECOLOTE.
UNH!!!
YOU FOOLS!!
STOP LAUGHING!! HURRY UP AND...!!
KLAK KLAK
KLAK

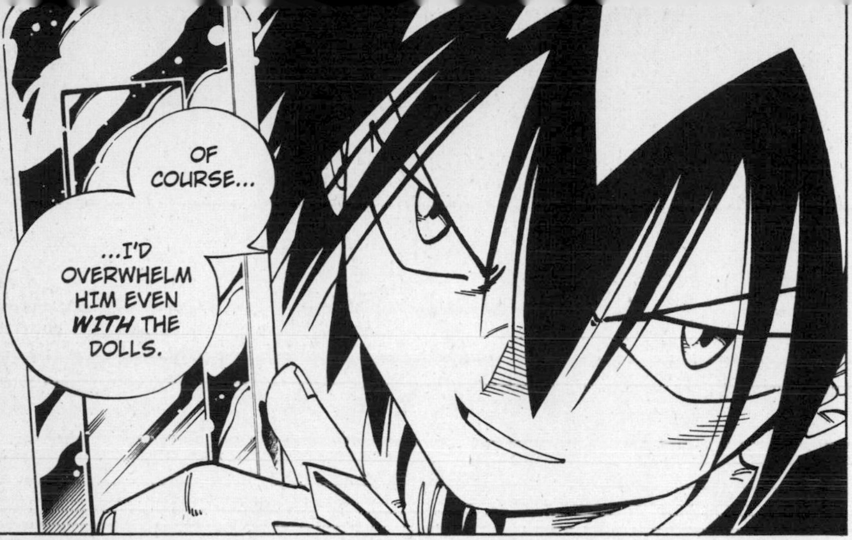
OF COURSE...
...I'D OVERWHELM HIM EVEN WITH THE DOLLS.

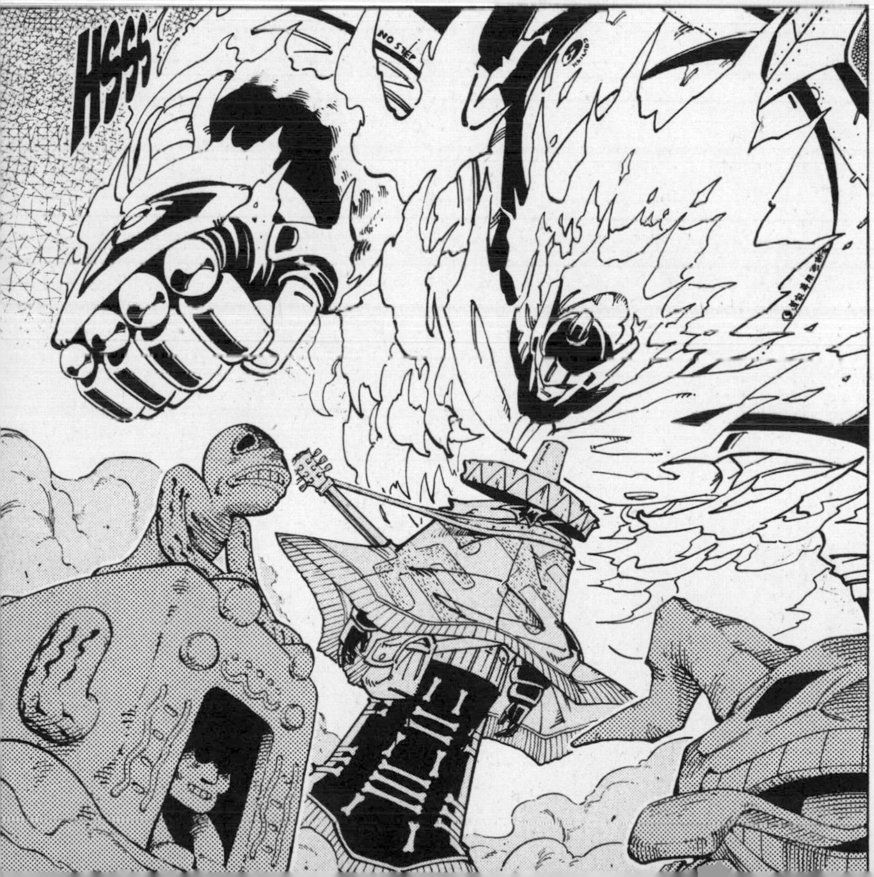
HSSS
NO STEP

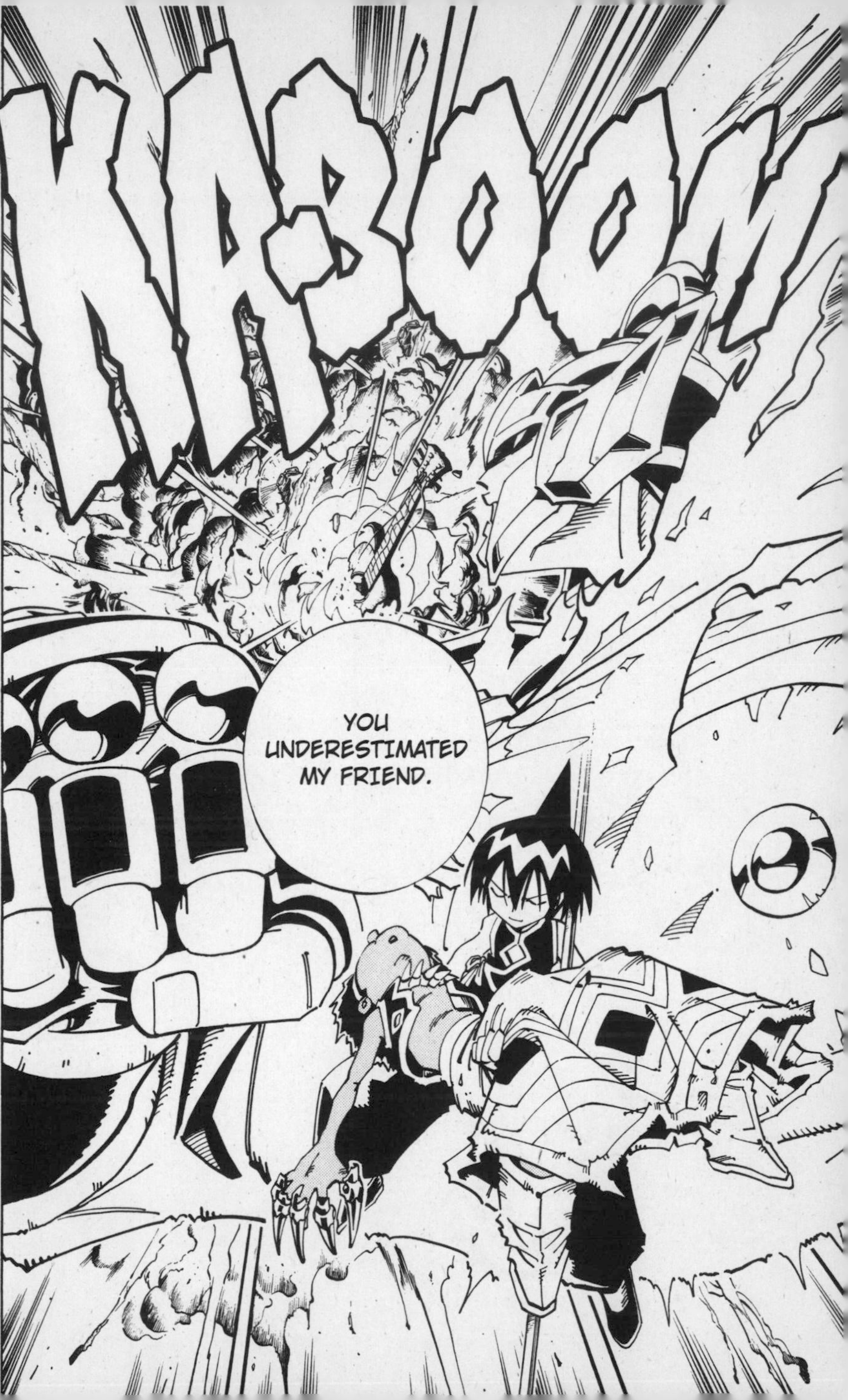
KABOOM
YOU UNDERESTIMATED MY FRIEND.

Shaman King™

SHAMAN KING CHARACTER FILE No.65

ナクト
NAKHT

2001
(JUNE)

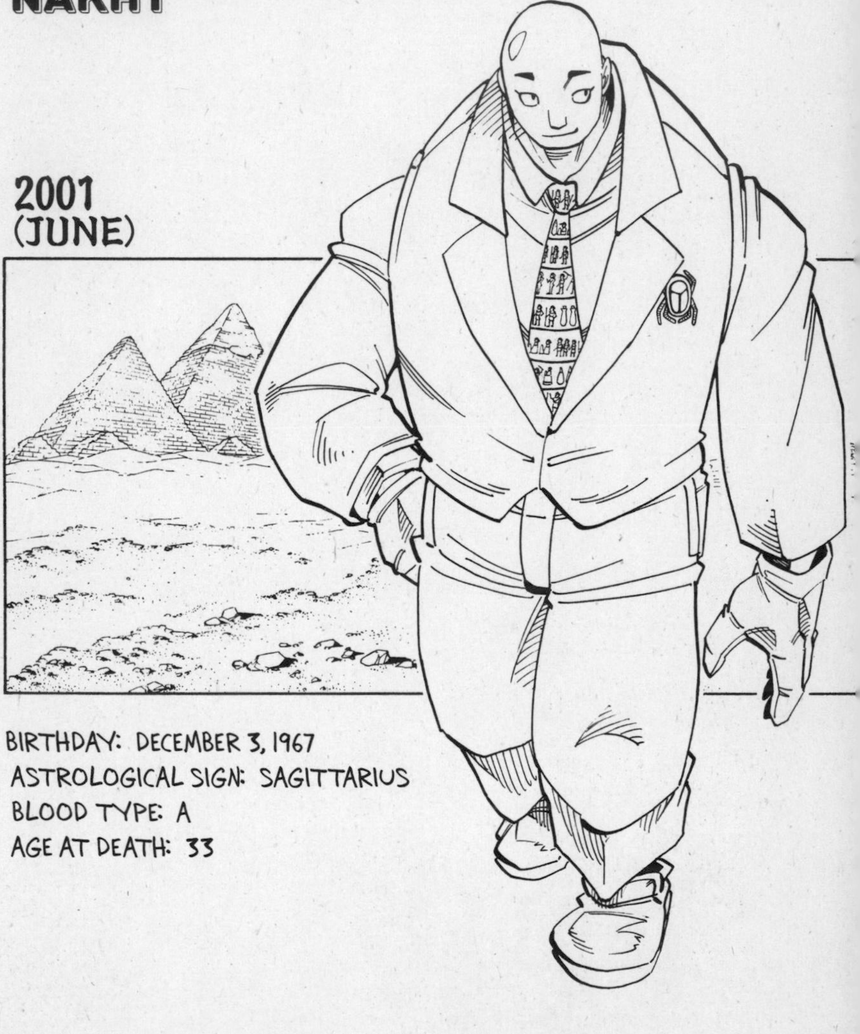

BIRTHDAY: DECEMBER 3, 1967
ASTROLOGICAL SIGN: SAGITTARIUS
BLOOD TYPE: A
AGE AT DEATH: 33

Reincarnation 119:

Motto #2

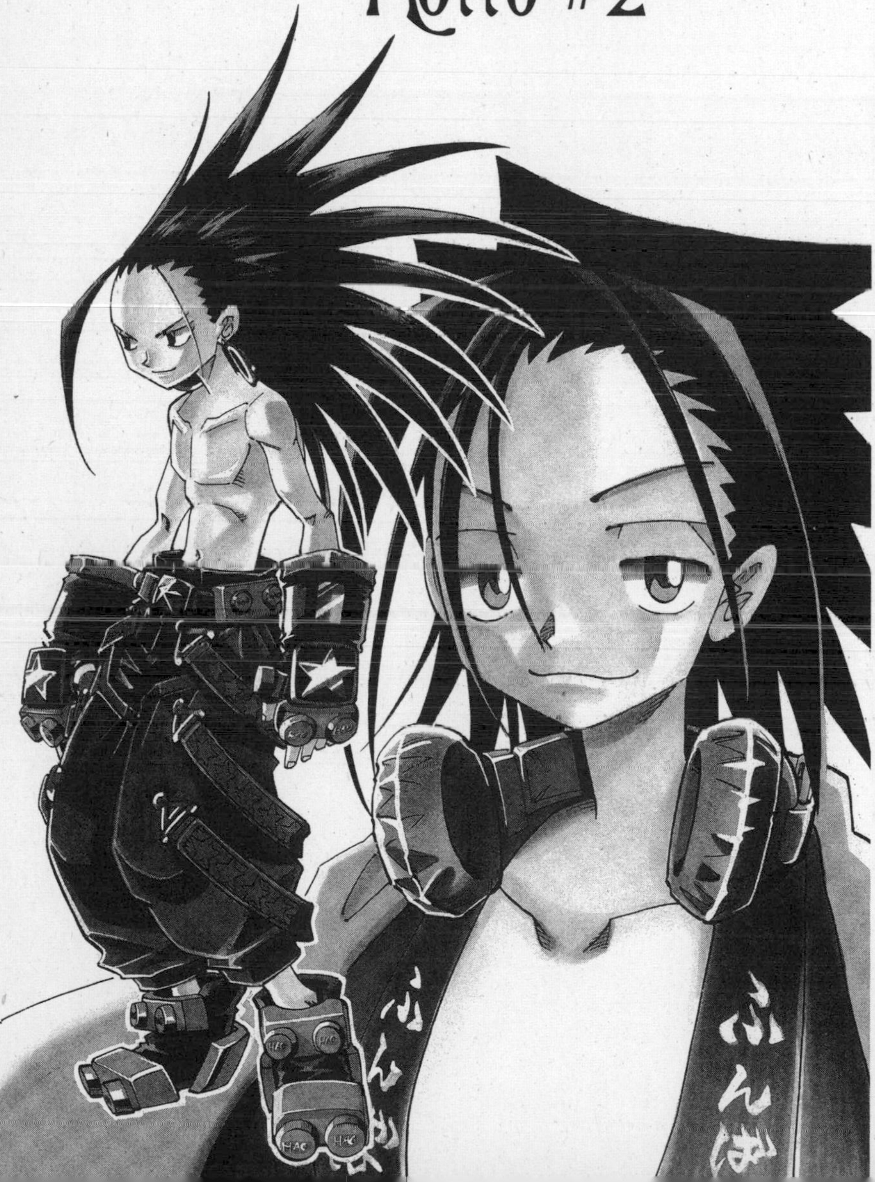

READ THIS WAY

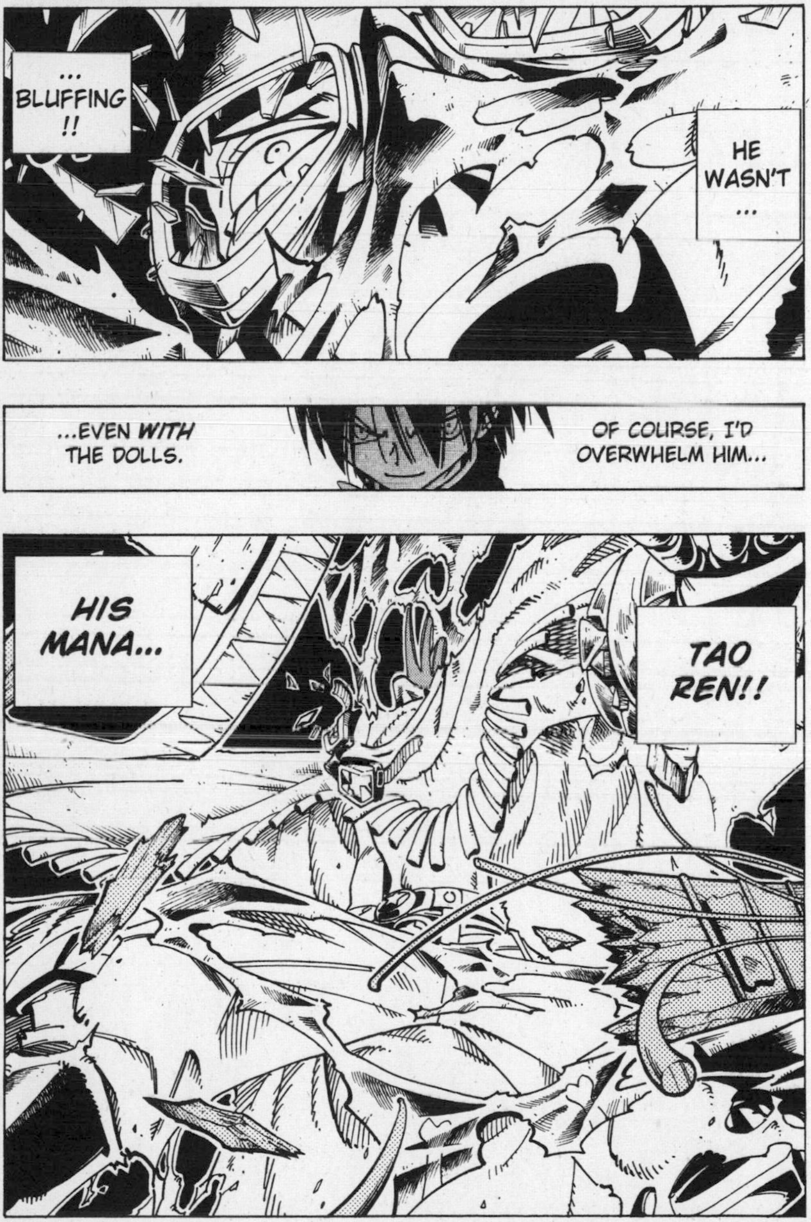
HE WASN'T ...
... BLUFFING !!
OF COURSE, I'D OVERWHELM HIM...
...EVEN WITH THE DOLLS.
TAO REN!!
HIS MANA...

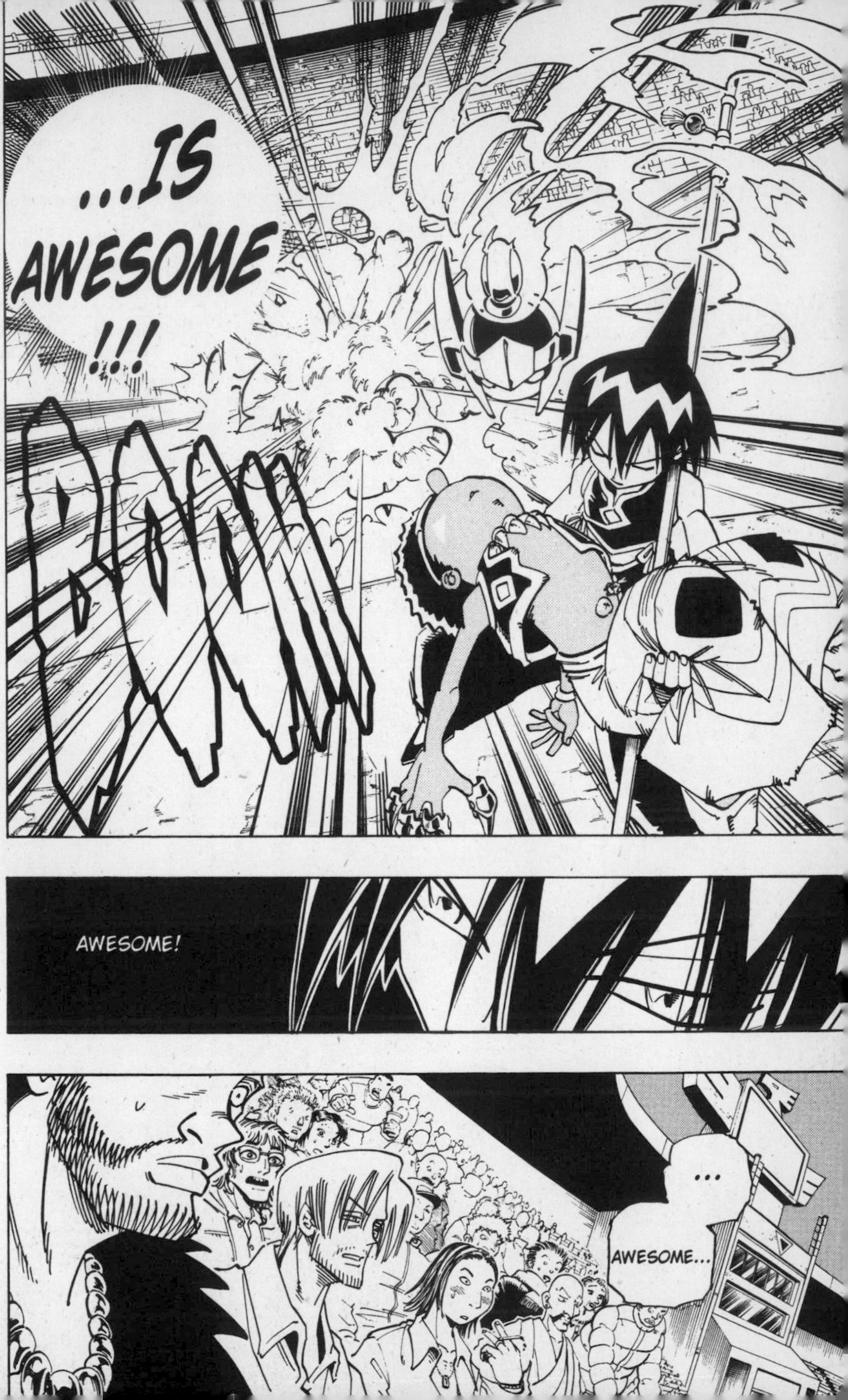
...IS AWESOME !!!
BOOM
AWESOME!
...
AWESOME...

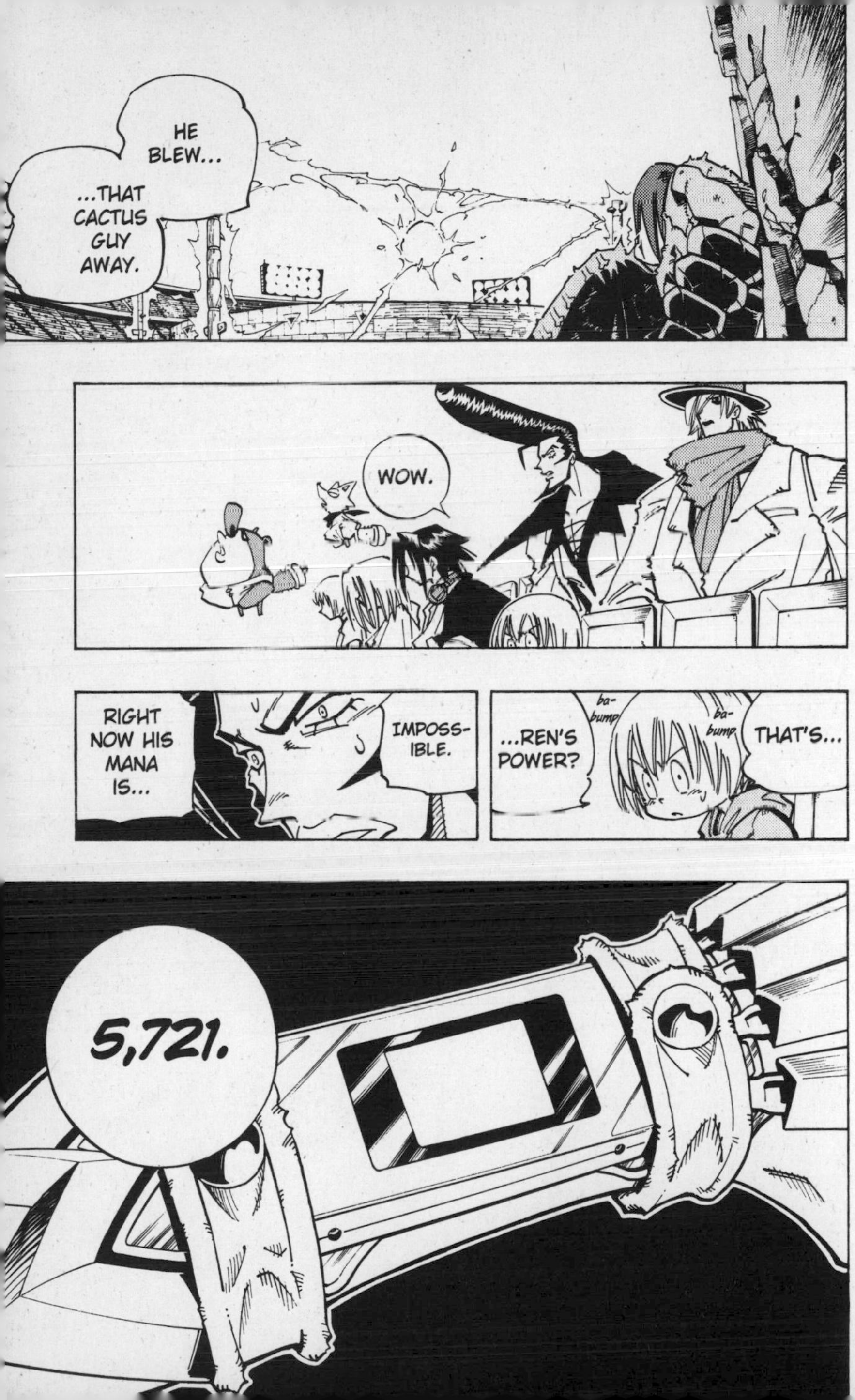
HE BLEW...
...THAT CACTUS GUY AWAY.
WOW.
ba-bump
ba-bump
THAT'S...
...REN'S POWER?
IMPOSS-IBLE.
RIGHT NOW HIS MANA IS...
5,721.

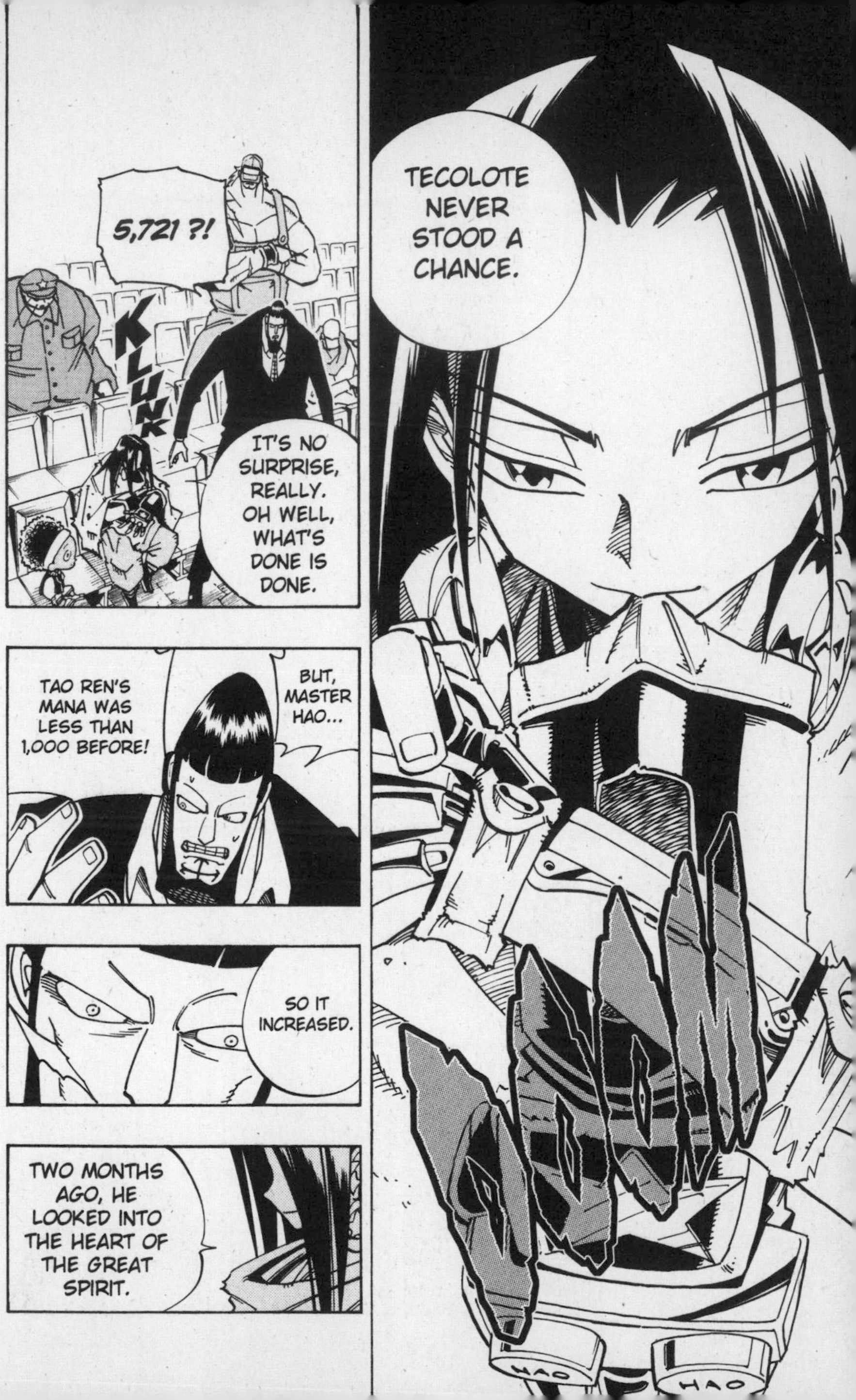

TECOLOTE NEVER STOOD A CHANCE.
5,721 ?!
KLUNK
IT'S NO SURPRISE, REALLY. OH WELL, WHAT'S DONE IS DONE.
BUT, MASTER HAO...
TAO REN'S MANA WAS LESS THAN 1,000 BEFORE!
SO IT INCREASED.
TWO MONTHS AGO, HE LOOKED INTO THE HEART OF THE GREAT SPIRIT.
HAO
HAO

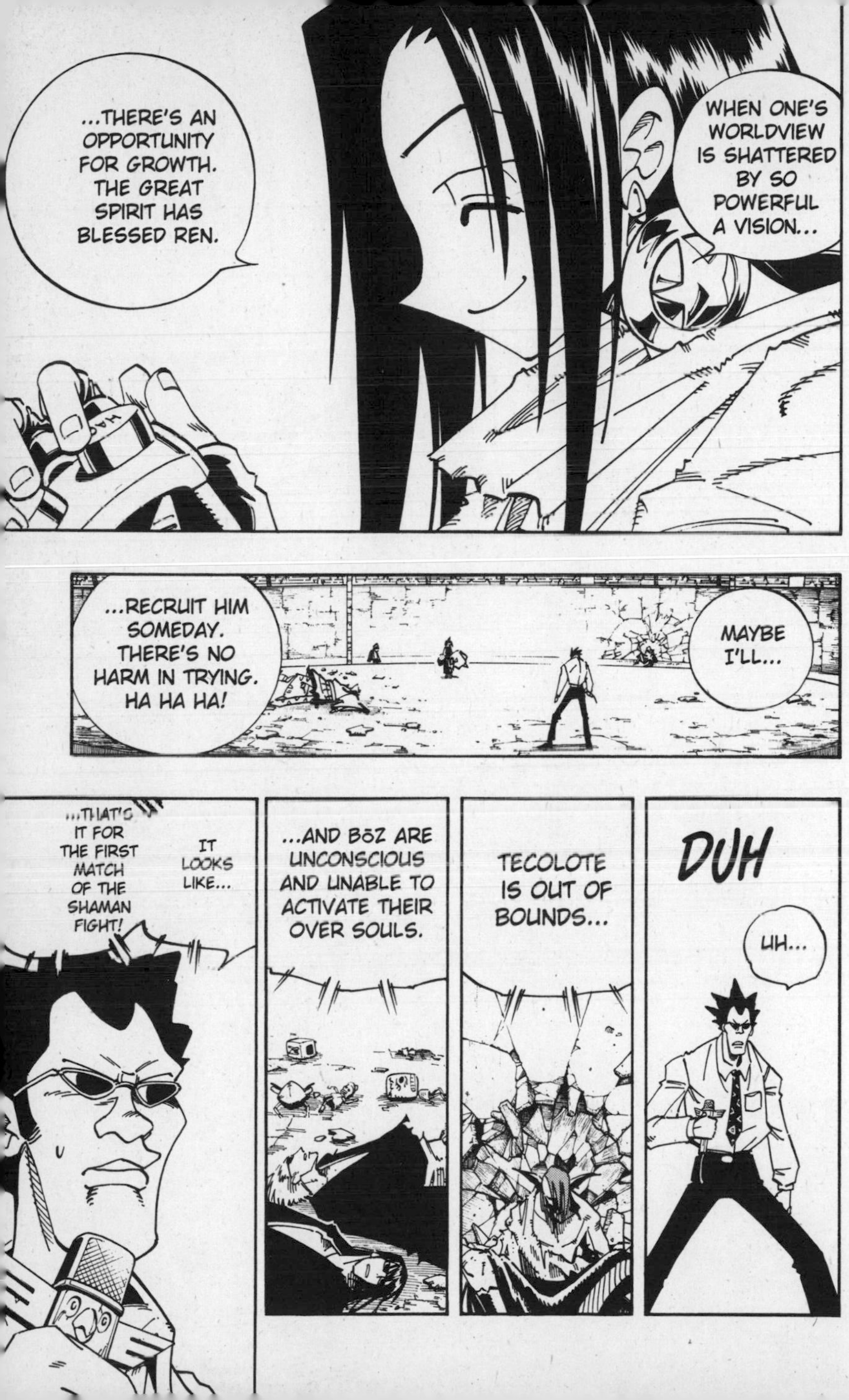
WHEN ONE'S WORLDVIEW IS SHATTERED BY SO POWERFUL A VISION...
...THERE'S AN OPPORTUNITY FOR GROWTH. THE GREAT SPIRIT HAS BLESSED REN.
MAYBE I'LL...
...RECRUIT HIM SOMEDAY. THERE'S NO HARM IN TRYING. HA HA HA!
DUH
UH...
TECOLOTE IS OUT OF BOUNDS...
...AND BŌZ ARE UNCONSCIOUS AND UNABLE TO ACTIVATE THEIR OVER SOULS.
IT LOOKS LIKE...
...THAT'S IT FOR THE FIRST MATCH OF THE SHAMAN FIGHT!

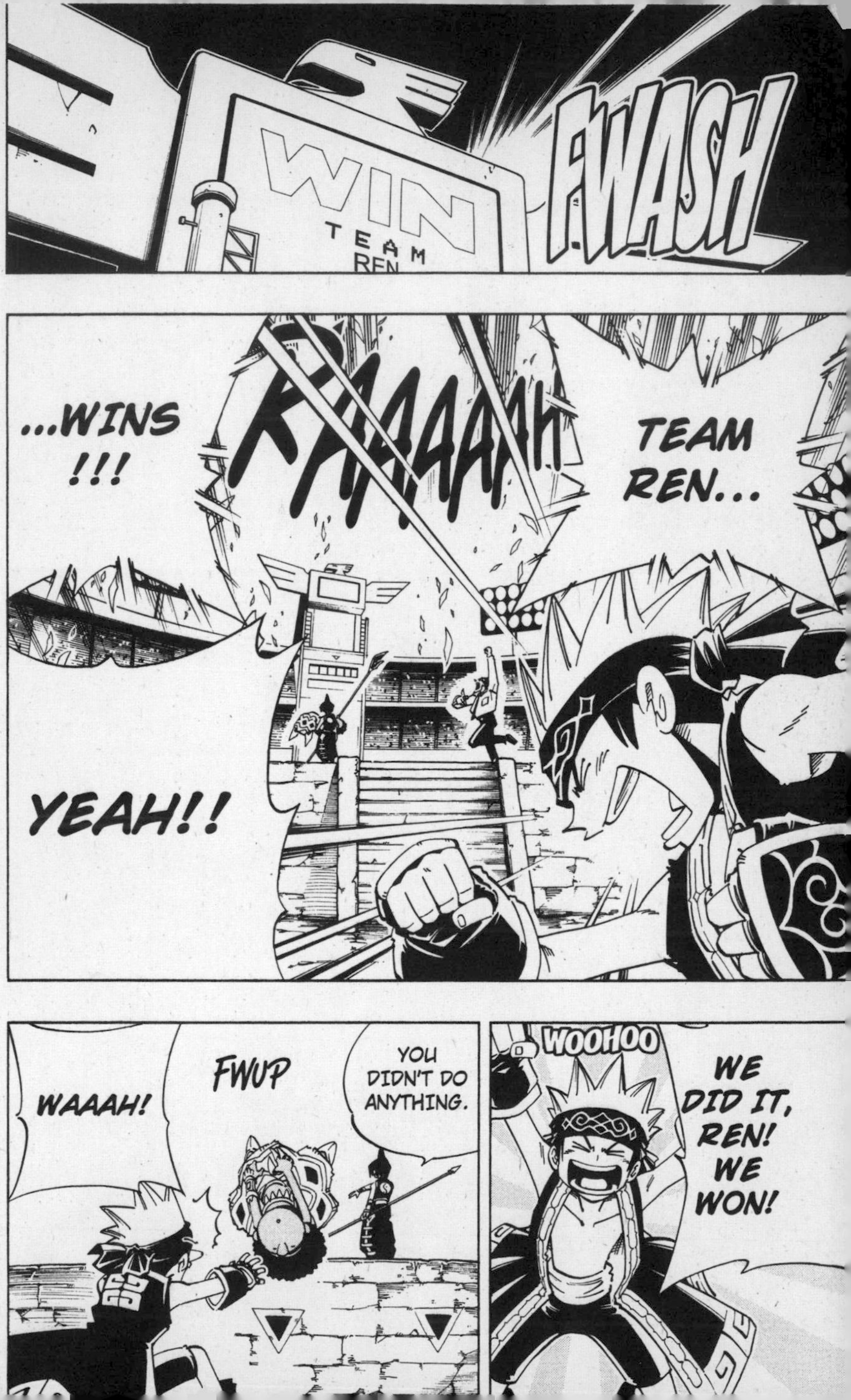
FWASH
WIN
TEAM
REN
TEAM REN...
RAAAAAH
...WINS !!!
YEAH!!
WOOHOO
WE DID IT, REN! WE WON!
YOU DIDN'T DO ANYTHING.
FWUP
WAAAH!

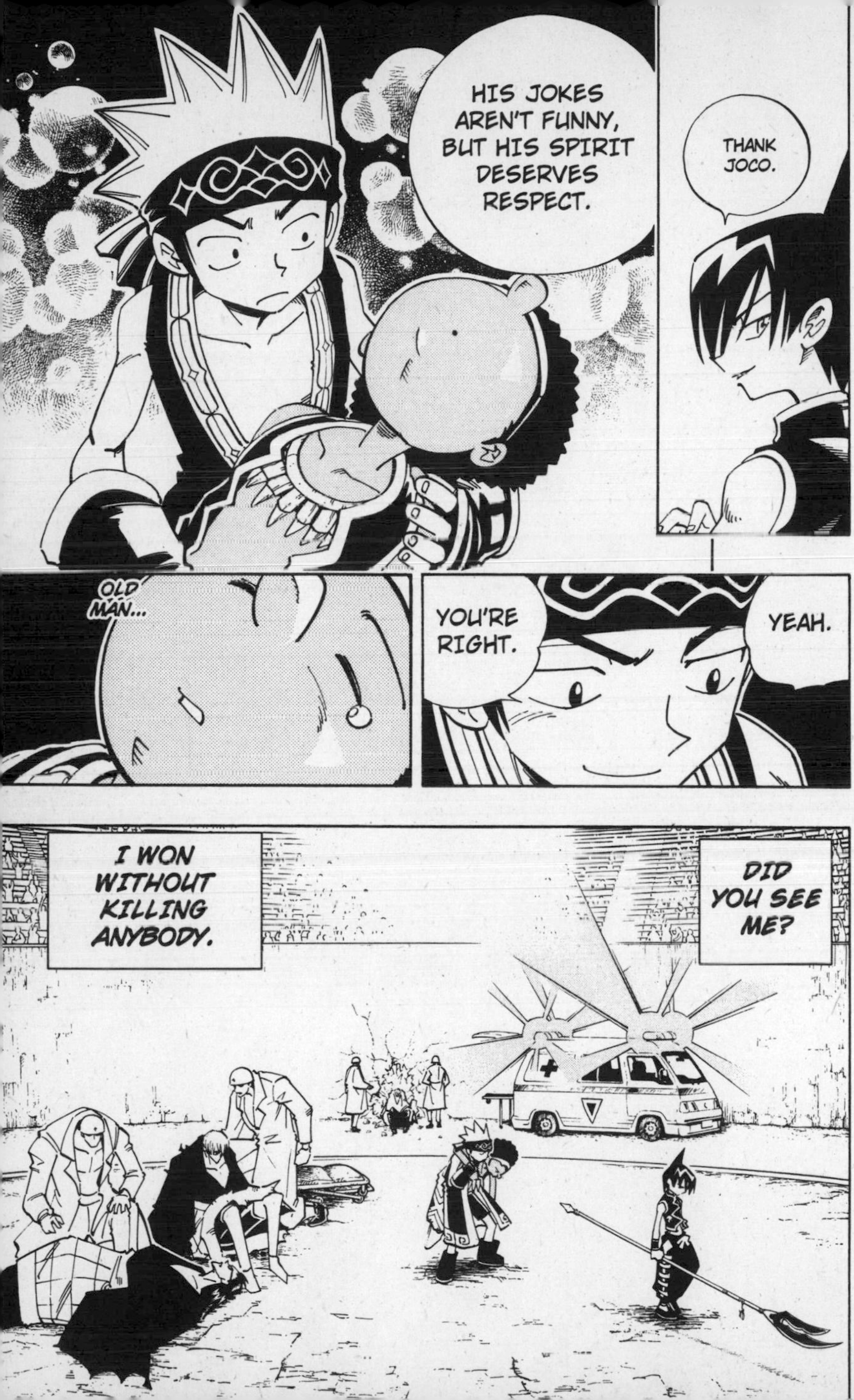
THANK JOCO.
HIS JOKES AREN'T FUNNY, BUT HIS SPIRIT DESERVES RESPECT.
YEAH.
YOU'RE RIGHT.
OLD MAN...
DID YOU SEE ME?
I WON WITHOUT KILLING ANYBODY.

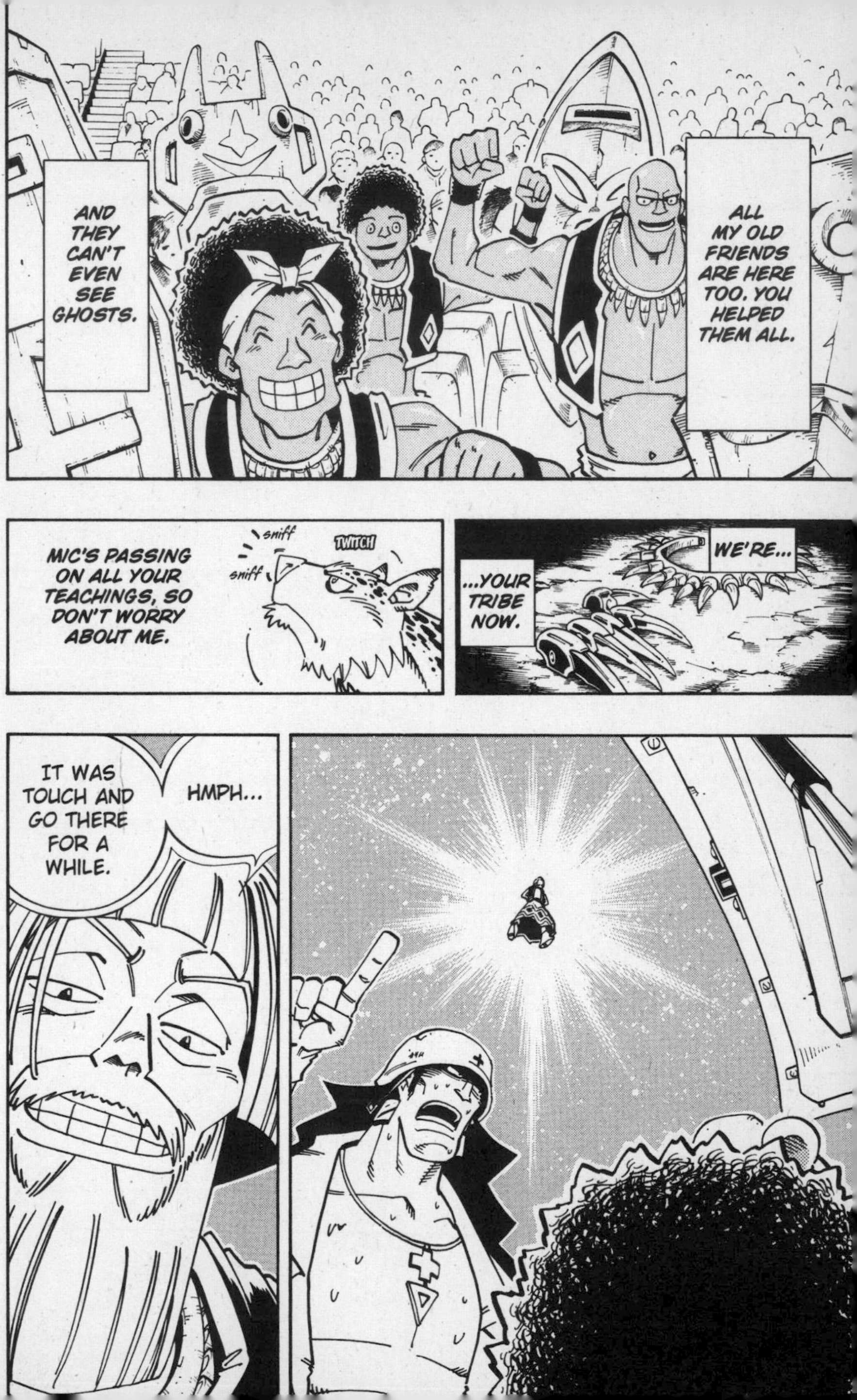
ALL MY OLD FRIENDS ARE HERE TOO. YOU HELPED THEM ALL.
AND THEY CAN'T EVEN SEE GHOSTS.
WE'RE...
...YOUR TRIBE NOW.
TWITCH
sniff
sniff
MIC'S PASSING ON ALL YOUR TEACHINGS, SO DON'T WORRY ABOUT ME.
HMPH...
IT WAS TOUCH AND GO THERE FOR A WHILE.

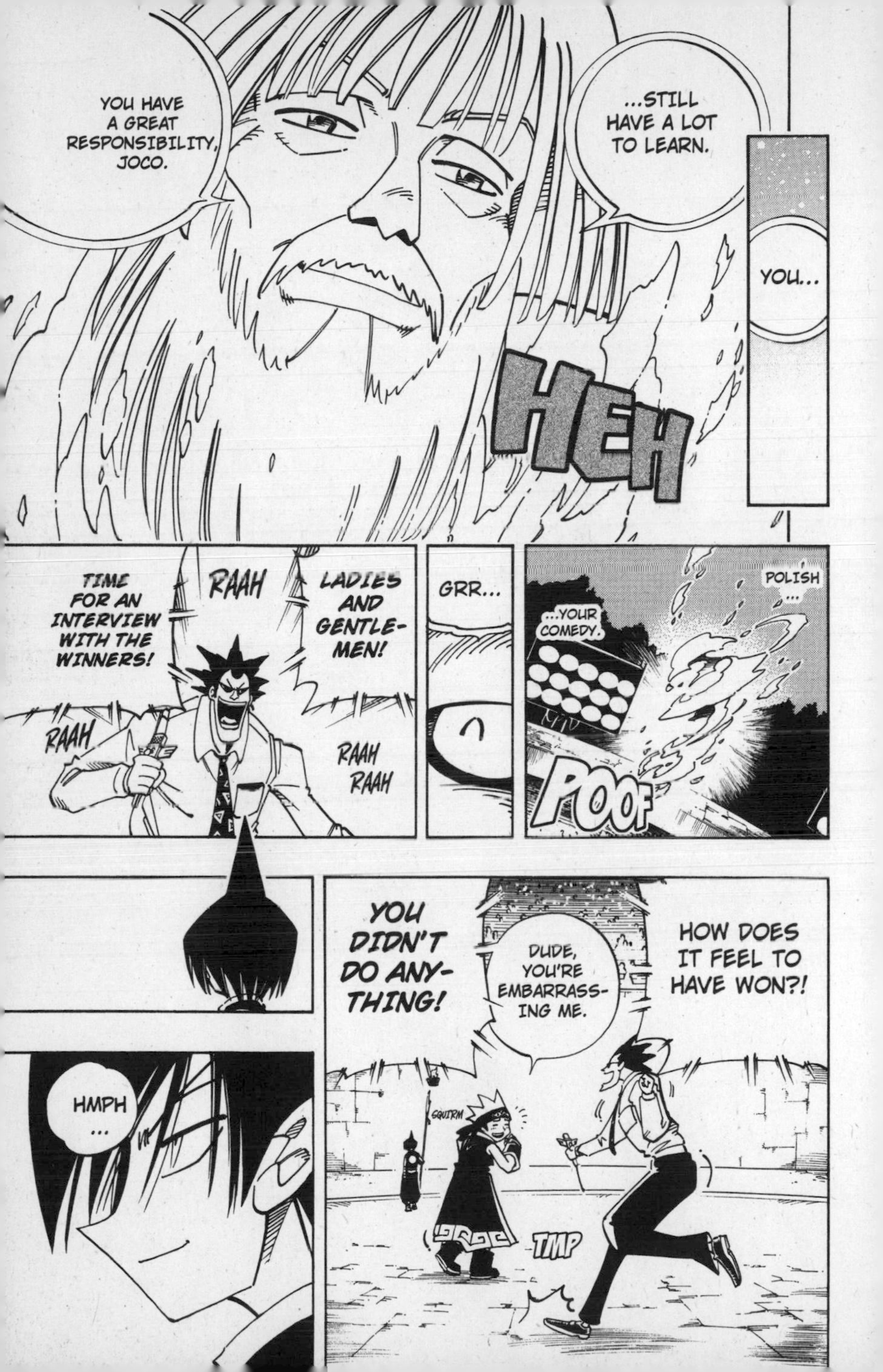
YOU...
...STILL HAVE A LOT TO LEARN.
YOU HAVE A GREAT RESPONSIBILITY, JOCO.
HEH
POLISH ...
...YOUR COMEDY.
POOF
GRR...
LADIES AND GENTLE-MEN!
RAAH
TIME FOR AN INTERVIEW WITH THE WINNERS!
RAAH
RAAH RAAH
HOW DOES IT FEEL TO HAVE WON?!
DUDE, YOU'RE EMBARRASS-ING ME.
YOU DIDN'T DO ANY-THING!
SQUIRM
TMP
HMPH ...

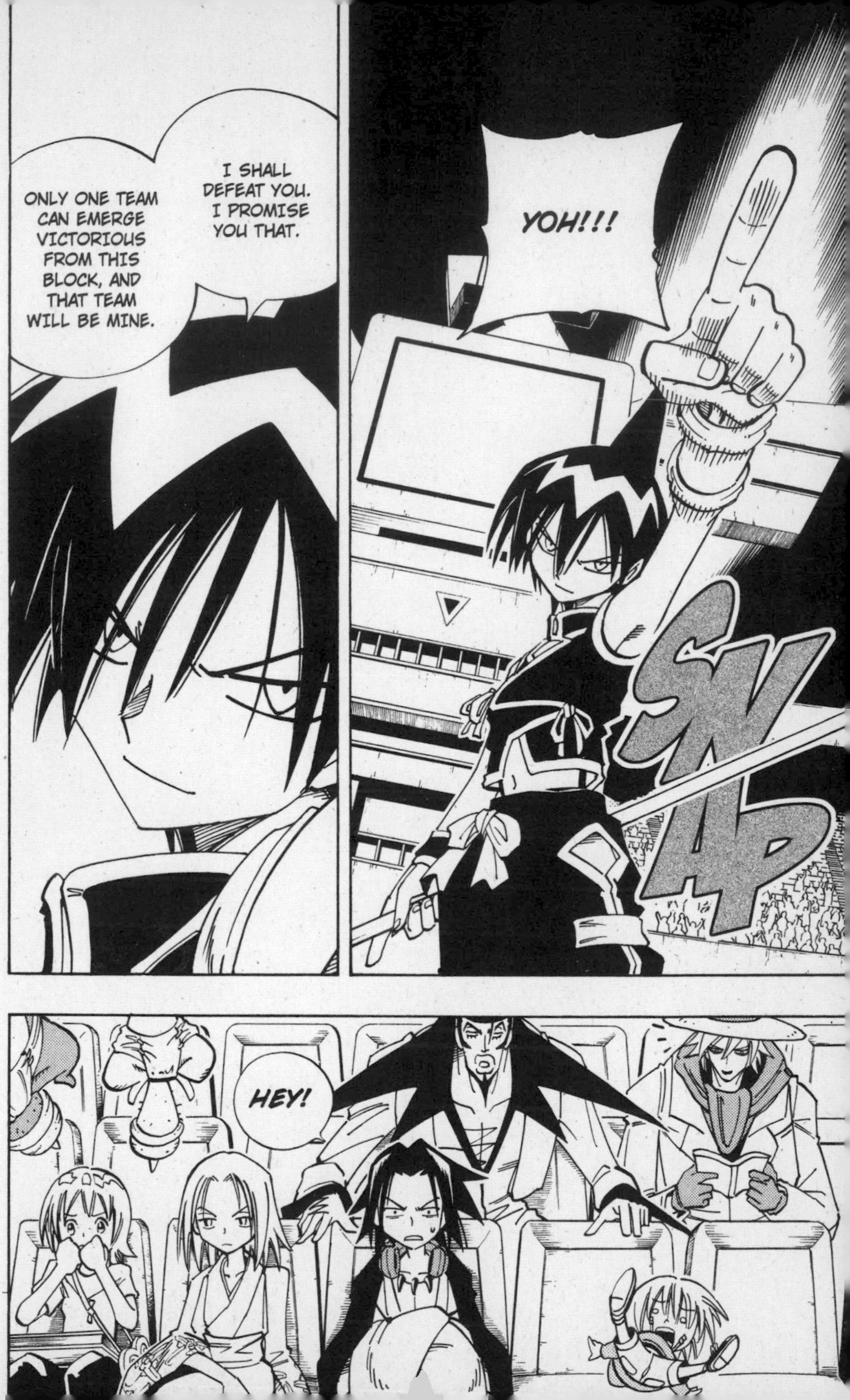

YOH!!!
SNAP
I SHALL DEFEAT YOU. I PROMISE YOU THAT.
ONLY ONE TEAM CAN EMERGE VICTORIOUS FROM THIS BLOCK, AND THAT TEAM WILL BE MINE.
HEY!

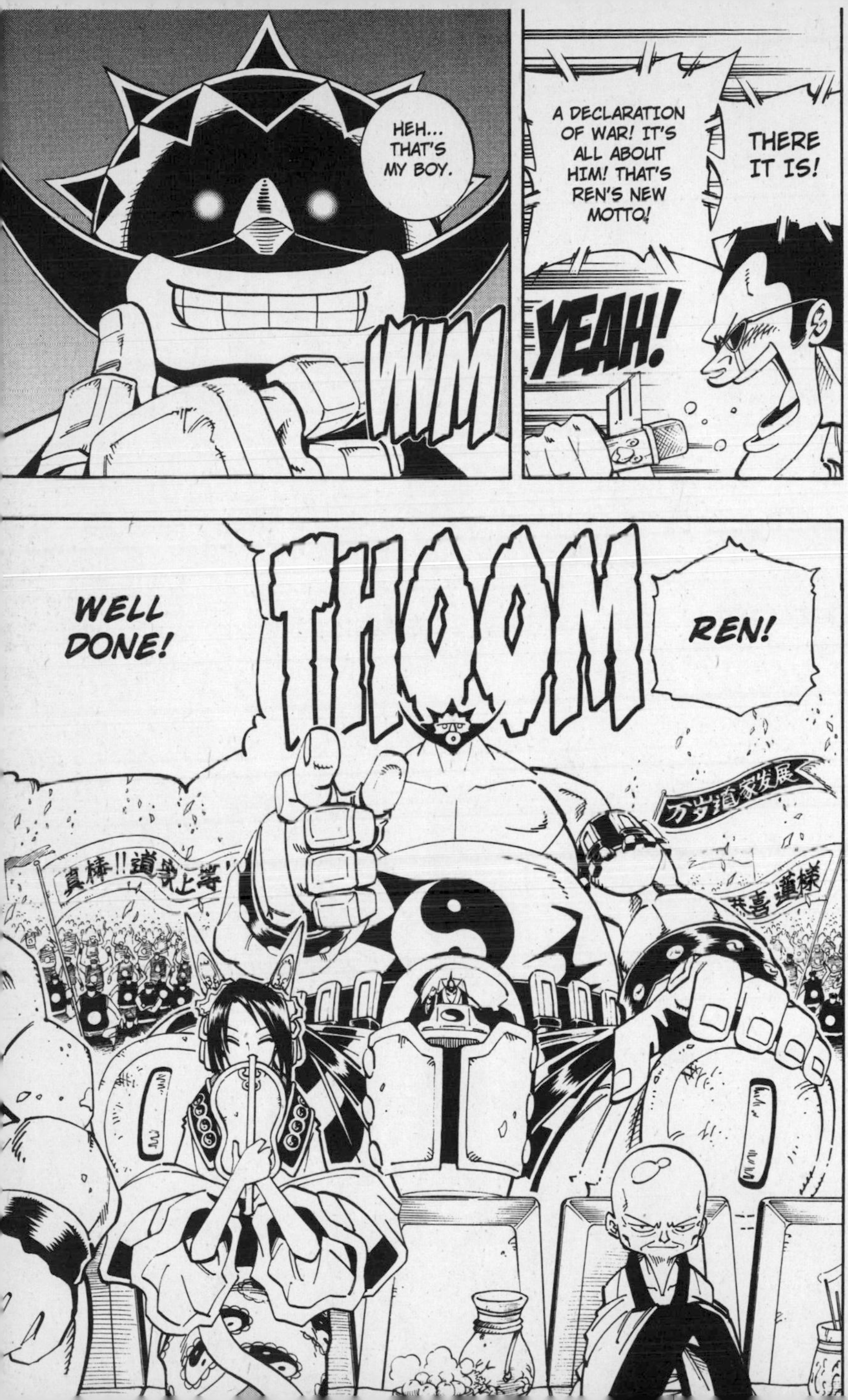
THERE IT IS!
A DECLARATION OF WAR! IT'S ALL ABOUT HIM! THAT'S REN'S NEW MOTTO!
YEAH!
HEH... THAT'S MY BOY.
WWM
REN!
THOOM
WELL DONE!
万岁道家发展

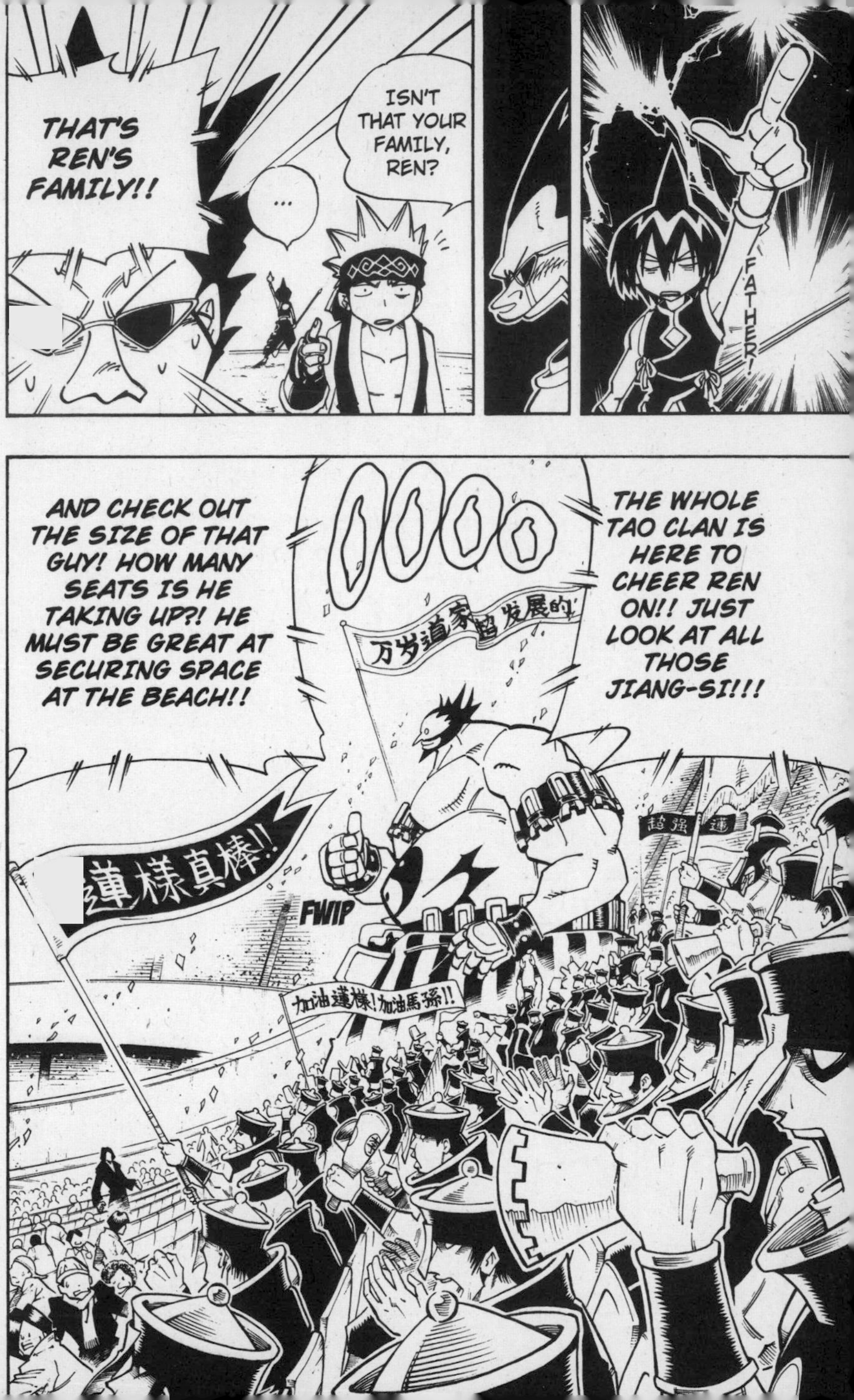

FATHER!
ISN'T THAT YOUR FAMILY, REN?
...
THAT'S REN'S FAMILY!!
THE WHOLE TAO CLAN IS HERE TO CHEER REN ON!! JUST LOOK AT ALL THOSE JIANG-SI!!!
OOOO
万岁道家超发展的
AND CHECK OUT THE SIZE OF THAT GUY! HOW MANY SEATS IS HE TAKING UP?! HE MUST BE GREAT AT SECURING SPACE AT THE BEACH!!
蓮様真棒!!
FWIP
加油蓮様!加油馬孫!!

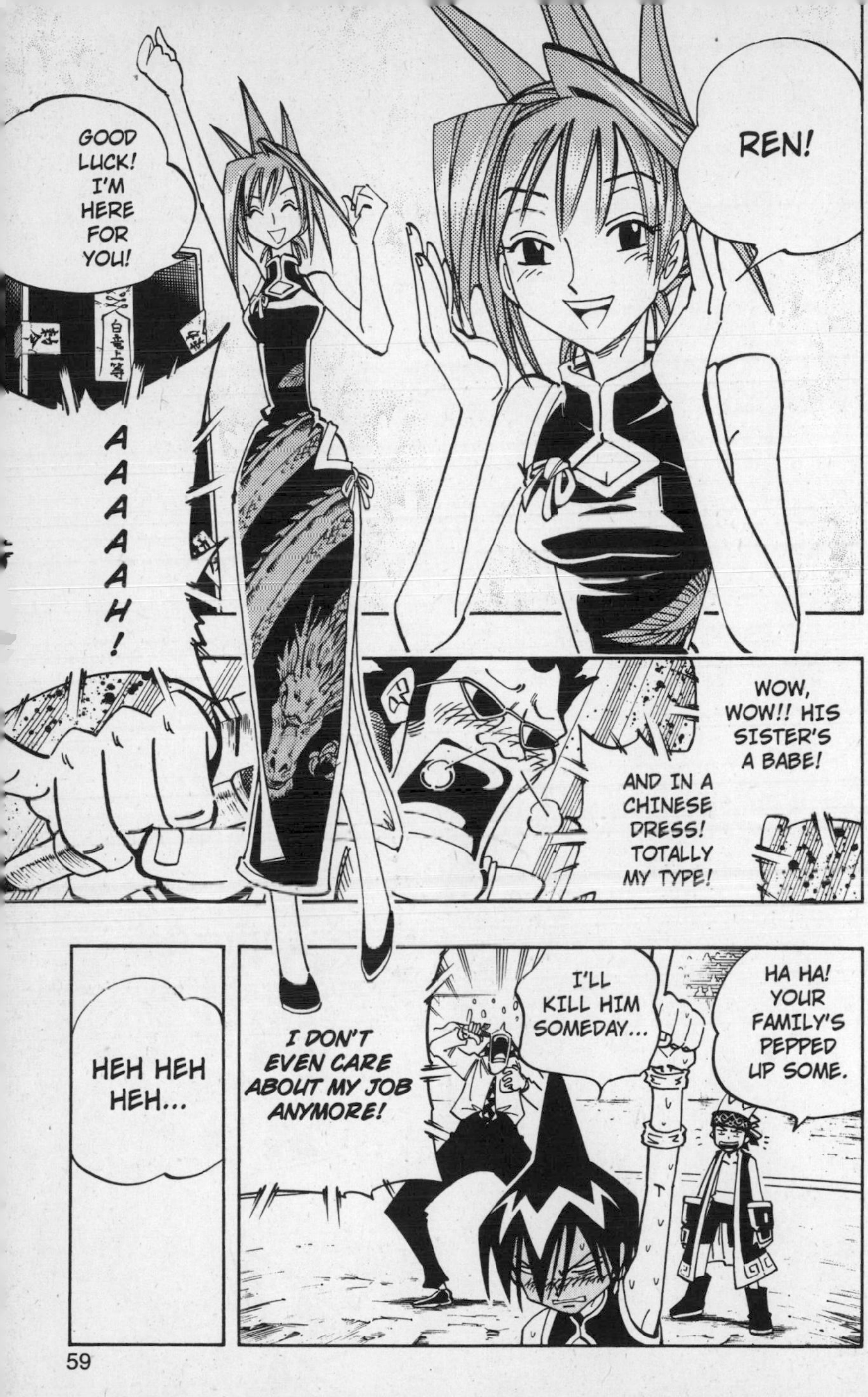
REN!
GOOD LUCK! I'M HERE FOR YOU!
白竜上等
AAAAAAH!
WOW, WOW!! HIS SISTER'S A BABE!
AND IN A CHINESE DRESS! TOTALLY MY TYPE!
HA HA! YOUR FAMILY'S PEPPED UP SOME.
I'LL KILL HIM SOMEDAY...
I DON'T EVEN CARE ABOUT MY JOB ANYMORE!
HEH HEH HEH...

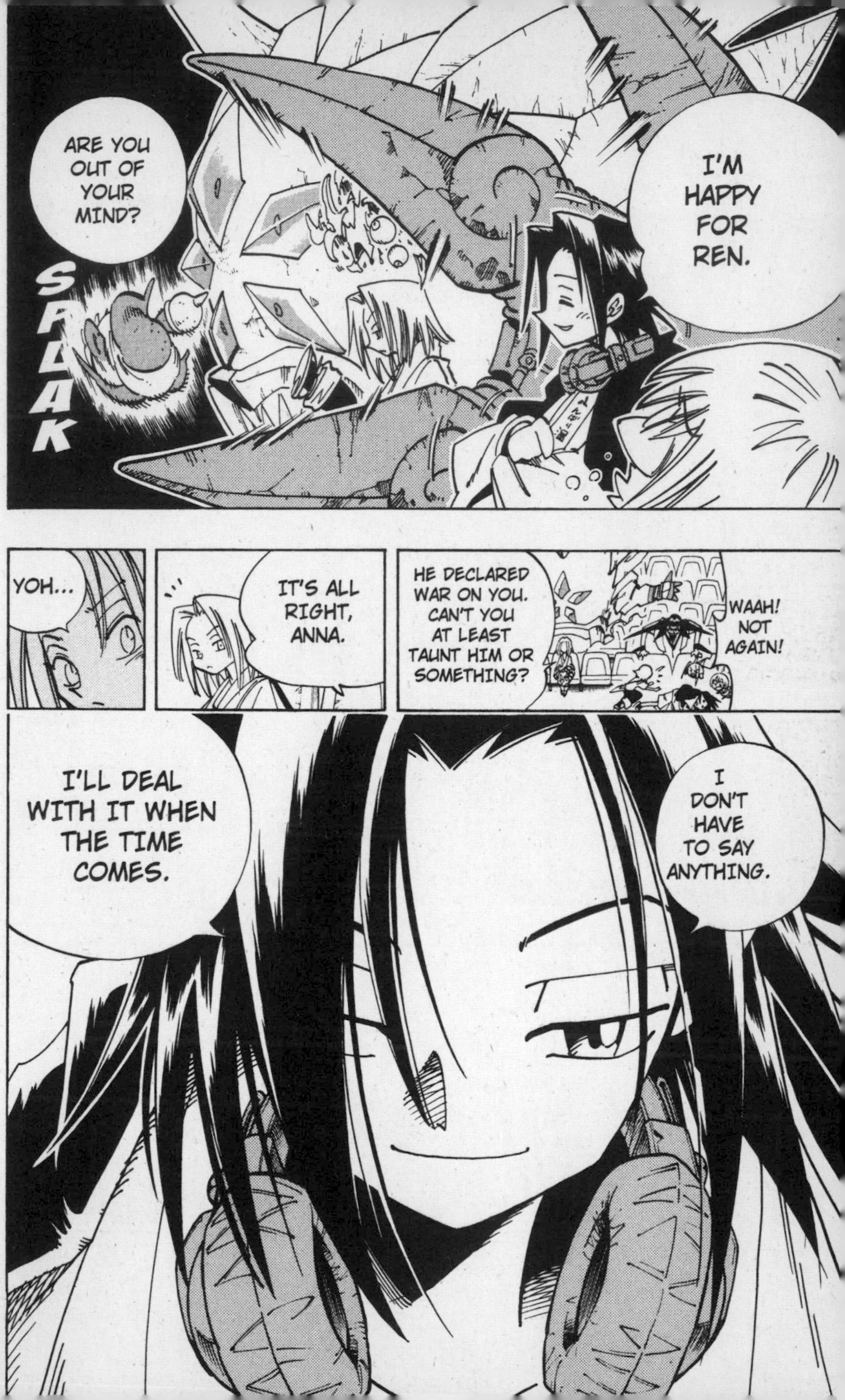
I'M HAPPY FOR REN.
ARE YOU OUT OF YOUR MIND?
SPLAAK
WAAH! NOT AGAIN!
HE DECLARED WAR ON YOU. CAN'T YOU AT LEAST TAUNT HIM OR SOMETHING?
IT'S ALL RIGHT, ANNA.
YOH...
I DON'T HAVE TO SAY ANYTHING.
I'LL DEAL WITH IT WHEN THE TIME COMES.

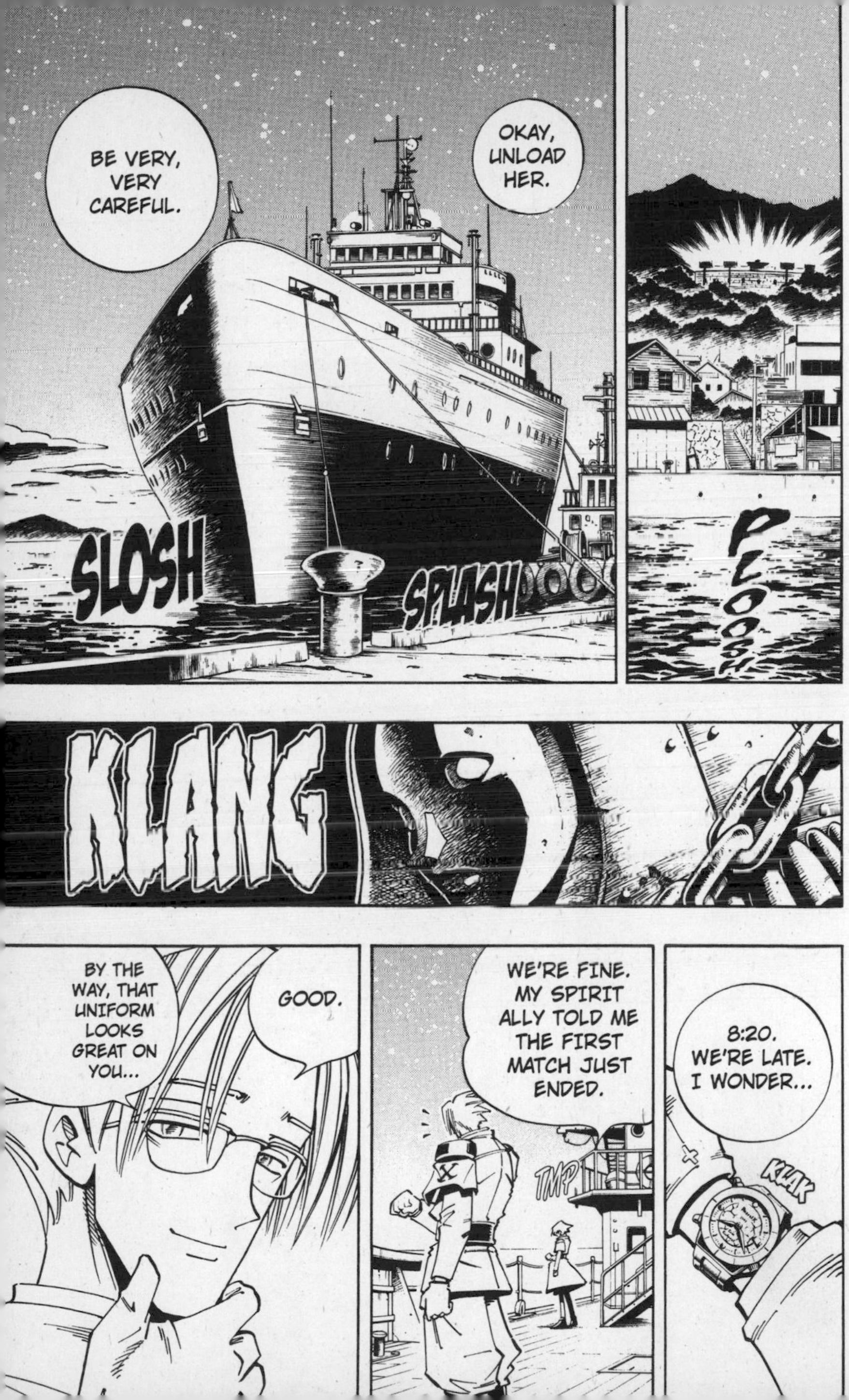
PLOOOSH
OKAY, UNLOAD HER.
BE VERY, VERY CAREFUL.
SPLASH
SLOSH
KLANG
8:20. WE'RE LATE. I WONDER...
KLAK
WE'RE FINE. MY SPIRIT ALLY TOLD ME THE FIRST MATCH JUST ENDED.
TMP
GOOD.
BY THE WAY, THAT UNIFORM LOOKS GREAT ON YOU...

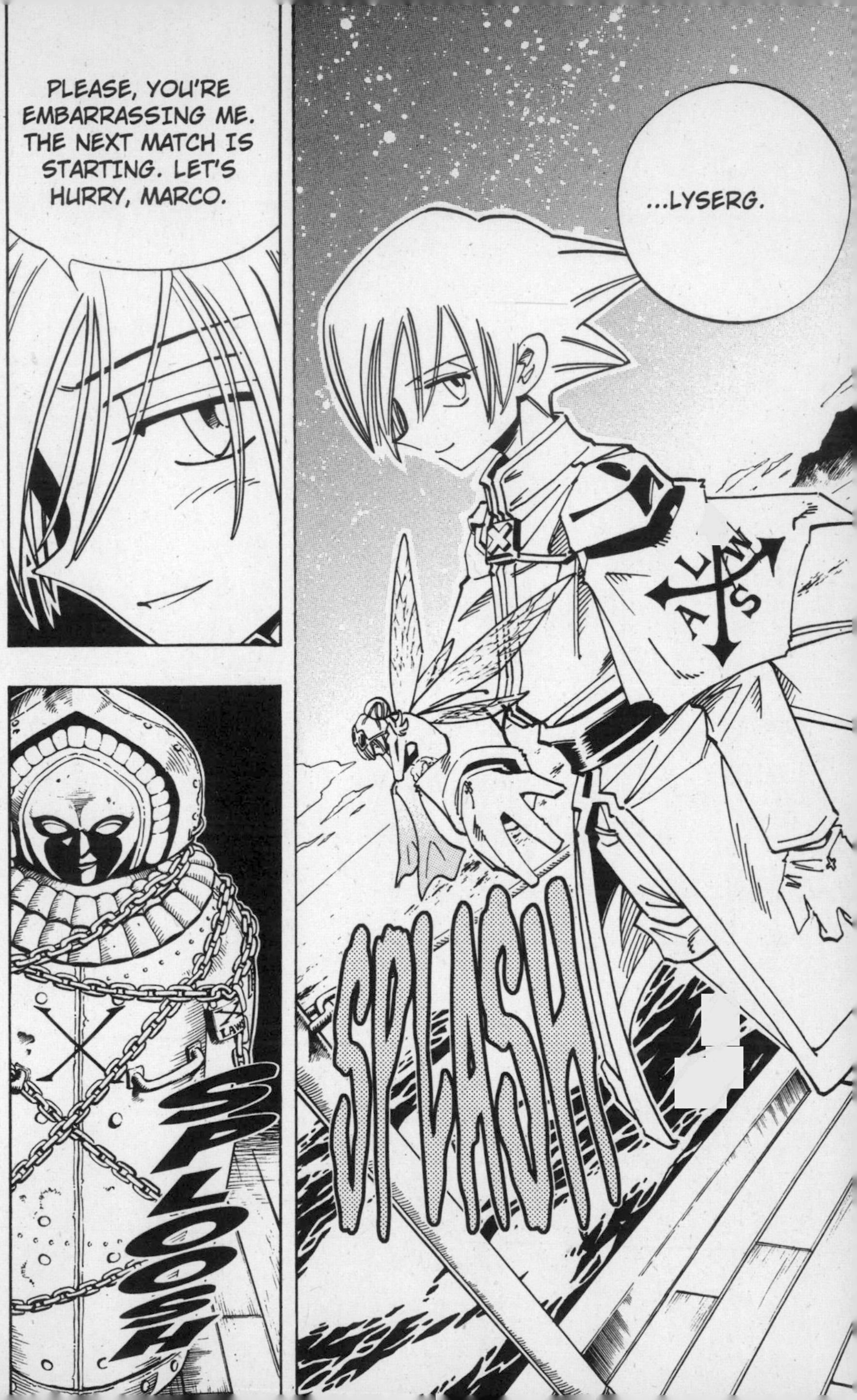
...LYSERG.
SPLASH
PLEASE, YOU'RE EMBARRASSING ME. THE NEXT MATCH IS STARTING. LET'S HURRY, MARCO.
SPLOOSH

Shaman King™

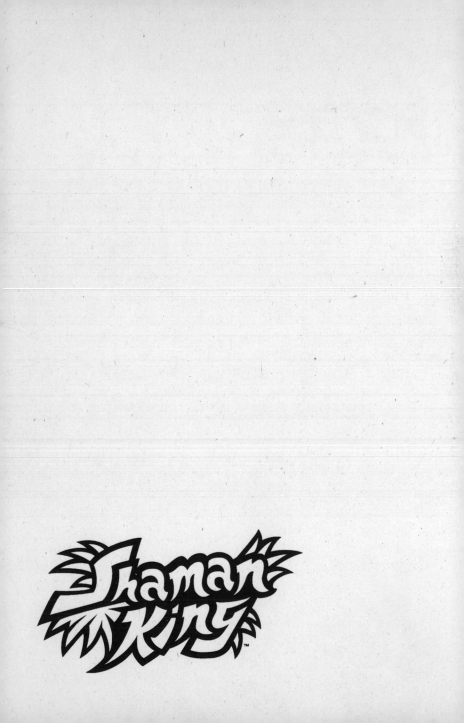

SHAMAN KING CHARACTER FILE No.66

カフラー
KHAFRE

2001
(JUNE)

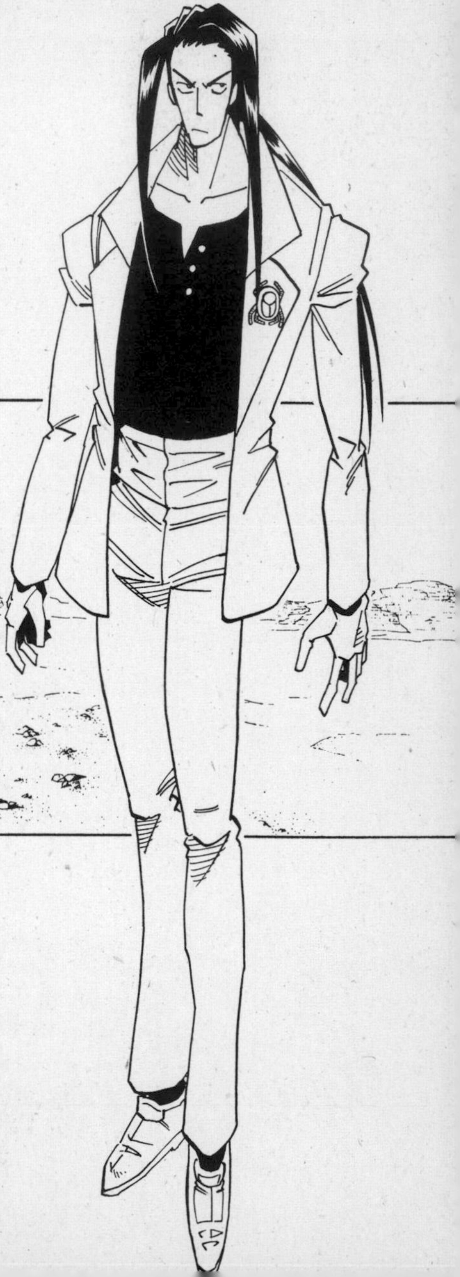

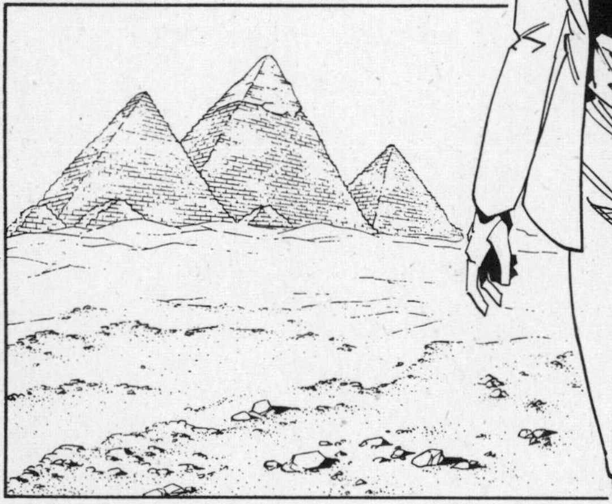

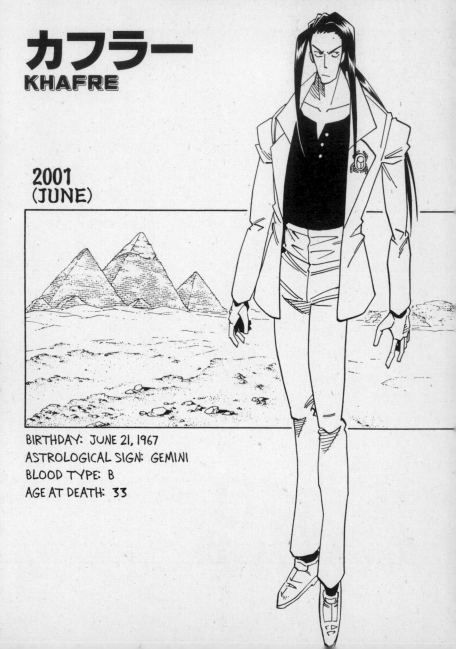

BIRTHDAY: JUNE 21, 1967
ASTROLOGICAL SIGN: GEMINI
BLOOD TYPE: B
AGE AT DEATH: 33

Reincarnation 120: From Inn to Waiting Room

パッチメディカルセンター
Patch Medical Center
Patch Studio Medico
补丁诊疗所

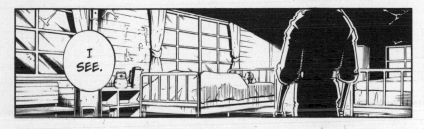

I SEE.

SO MASTER HAO...

...LAUGHED OFF MY DEFEAT.

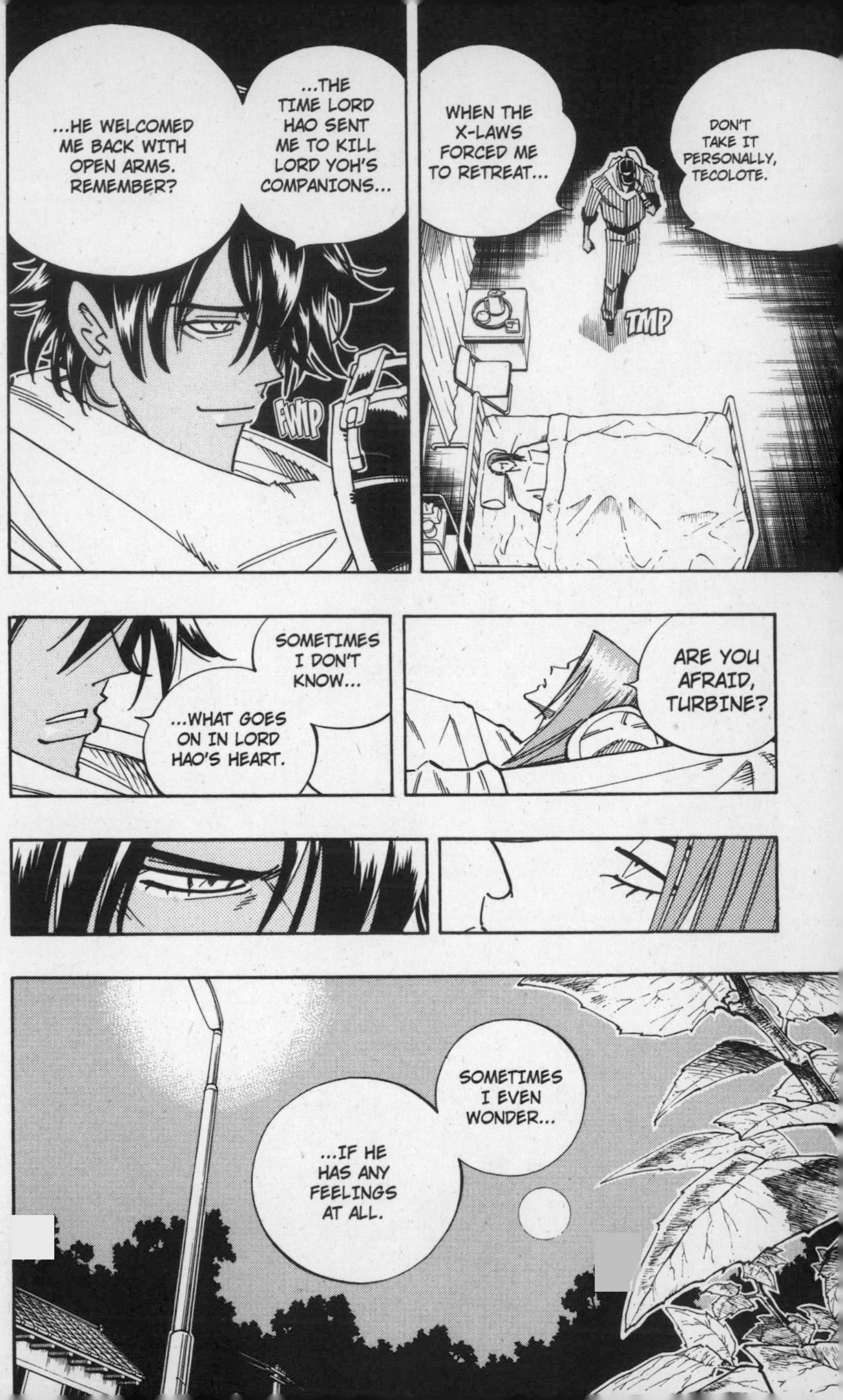
DON'T TAKE IT PERSONALLY, TECOLOTE.
WHEN THE X-LAWS FORCED ME TO RETREAT...
TMP
...THE TIME LORD HAO SENT ME TO KILL LORD YOH'S COMPANIONS...
...HE WELCOMED ME BACK WITH OPEN ARMS. REMEMBER?
FWIP
ARE YOU AFRAID, TURBINE?
SOMETIMES I DON'T KNOW...
...WHAT GOES ON IN LORD HAO'S HEART.
SOMETIMES I EVEN WONDER...
...IF HE HAS ANY FEELINGS AT ALL.

Reincarnation 120:

From Inn to Waiting Room

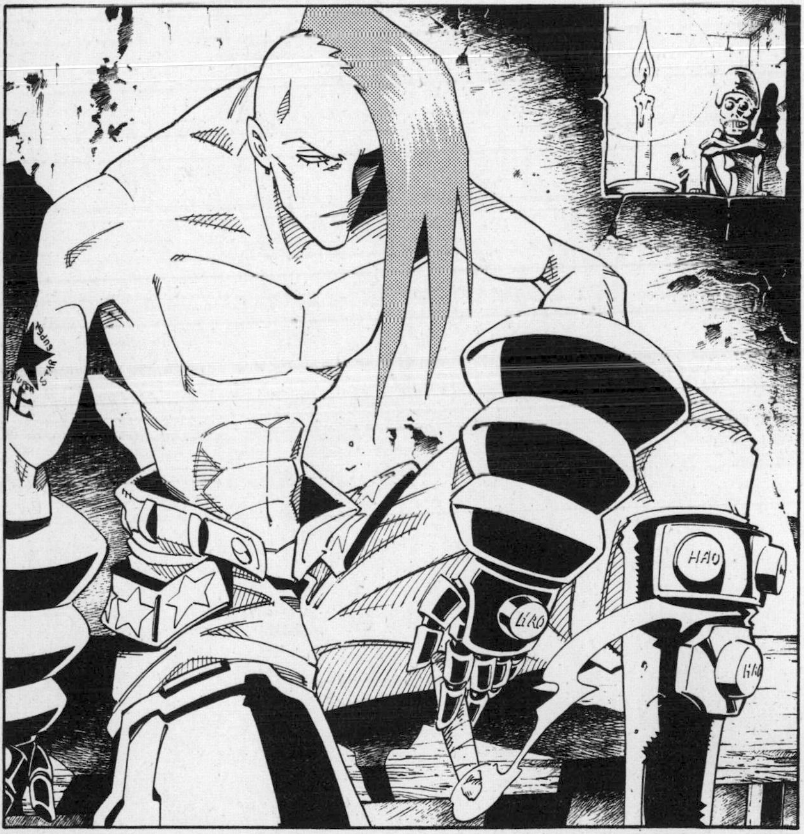
SUPER STAR
SUPER S-TAR
HAO
HAO
HAO

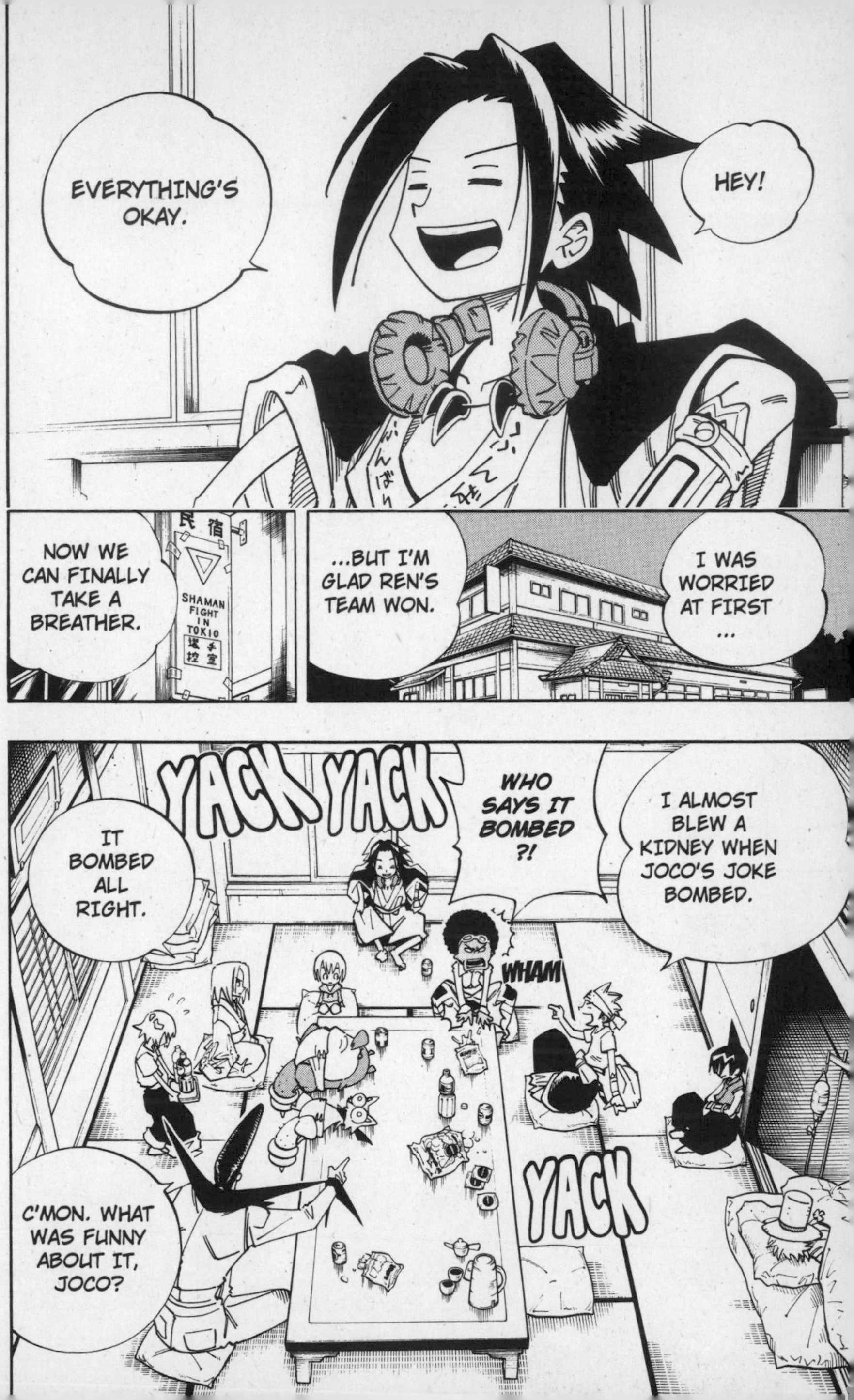
HEY!
EVERYTHING'S OKAY.
I WAS WORRIED AT FIRST ...
...BUT I'M GLAD REN'S TEAM WON.
民宿
SHAMAN FIGHT IN TOKIO
選手控室
NOW WE CAN FINALLY TAKE A BREATHER.
I ALMOST BLEW A KIDNEY WHEN JOCO'S JOKE BOMBED.
WHO SAYS IT BOMBED?!
YACK YACK
IT BOMBED ALL RIGHT.
WHAM
YACK
C'MON. WHAT WAS FUNNY ABOUT IT, JOCO?

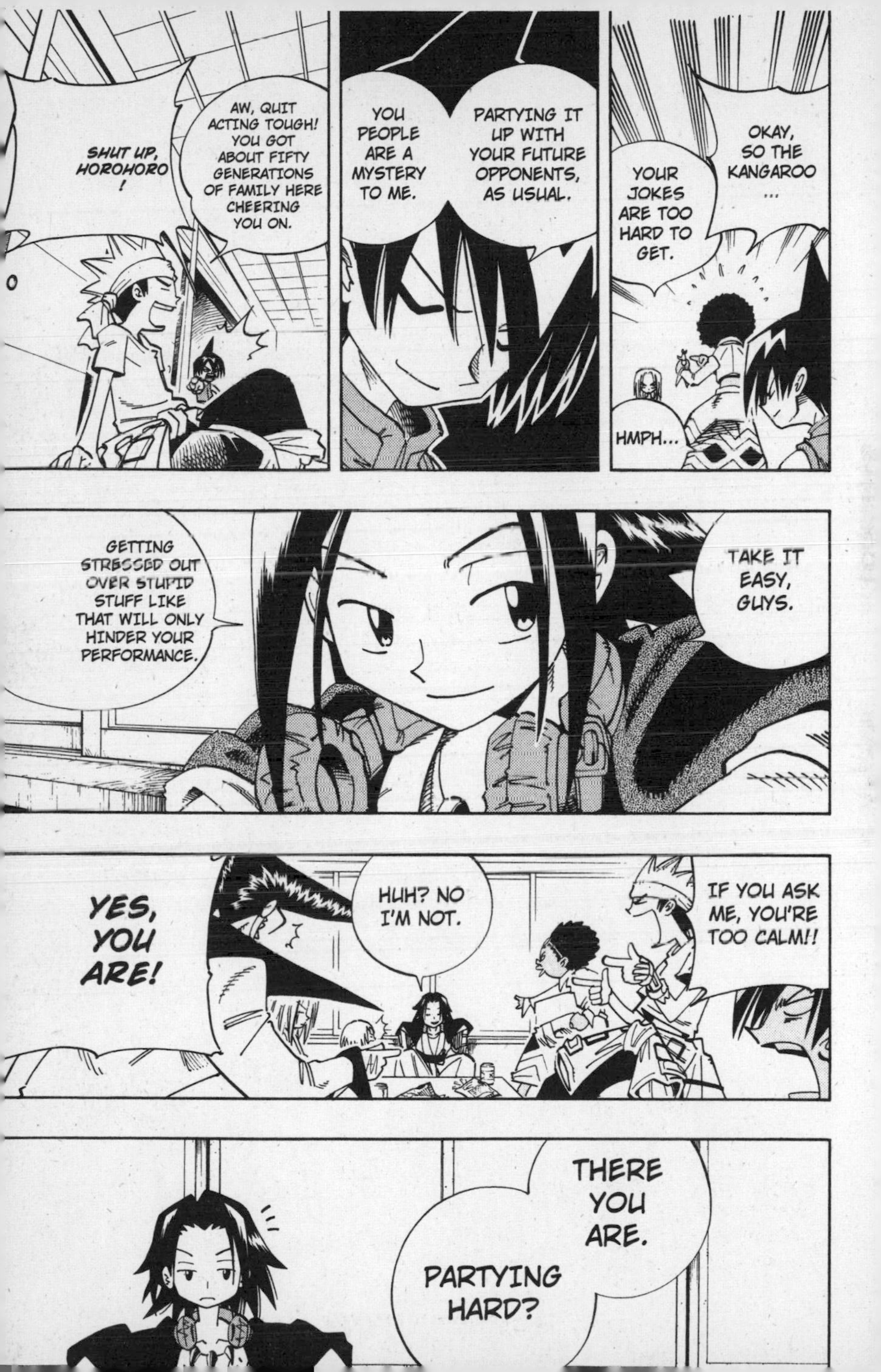
OKAY, SO THE KANGAROO...
YOUR JOKES ARE TOO HARD TO GET.
HMPH...
PARTYING IT UP WITH YOUR FUTURE OPPONENTS, AS USUAL.
YOU PEOPLE ARE A MYSTERY TO ME.
AW, QUIT ACTING TOUGH! YOU GOT ABOUT FIFTY GENERATIONS OF FAMILY HERE CHEERING YOU ON.
SHUT UP, HOROHORO!
TAKE IT EASY, GUYS.
GETTING STRESSED OUT OVER STUPID STUFF LIKE THAT WILL ONLY HINDER YOUR PERFORMANCE.
IF YOU ASK ME, YOU'RE TOO CALM!!
HUH? NO I'M NOT.
YES, YOU ARE!
THERE YOU ARE.
PARTYING HARD?

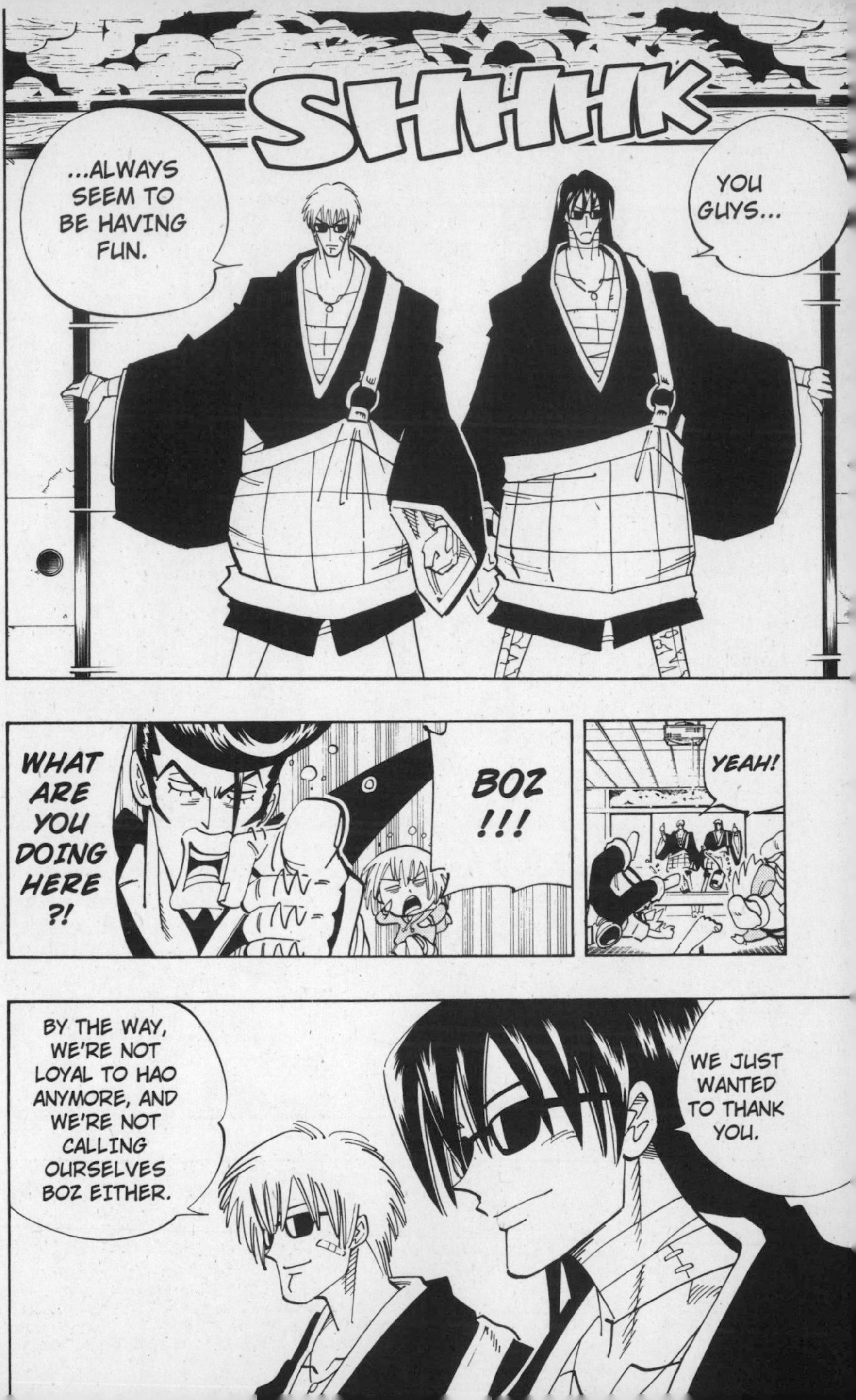
SHHHK
YOU GUYS...
...ALWAYS SEEM TO BE HAVING FUN.
YEAH!
BOZ!!!
WHAT ARE YOU DOING HERE?!
WE JUST WANTED TO THANK YOU.
BY THE WAY, WE'RE NOT LOYAL TO HAO ANYMORE, AND WE'RE NOT CALLING OURSELVES BOZ EITHER.

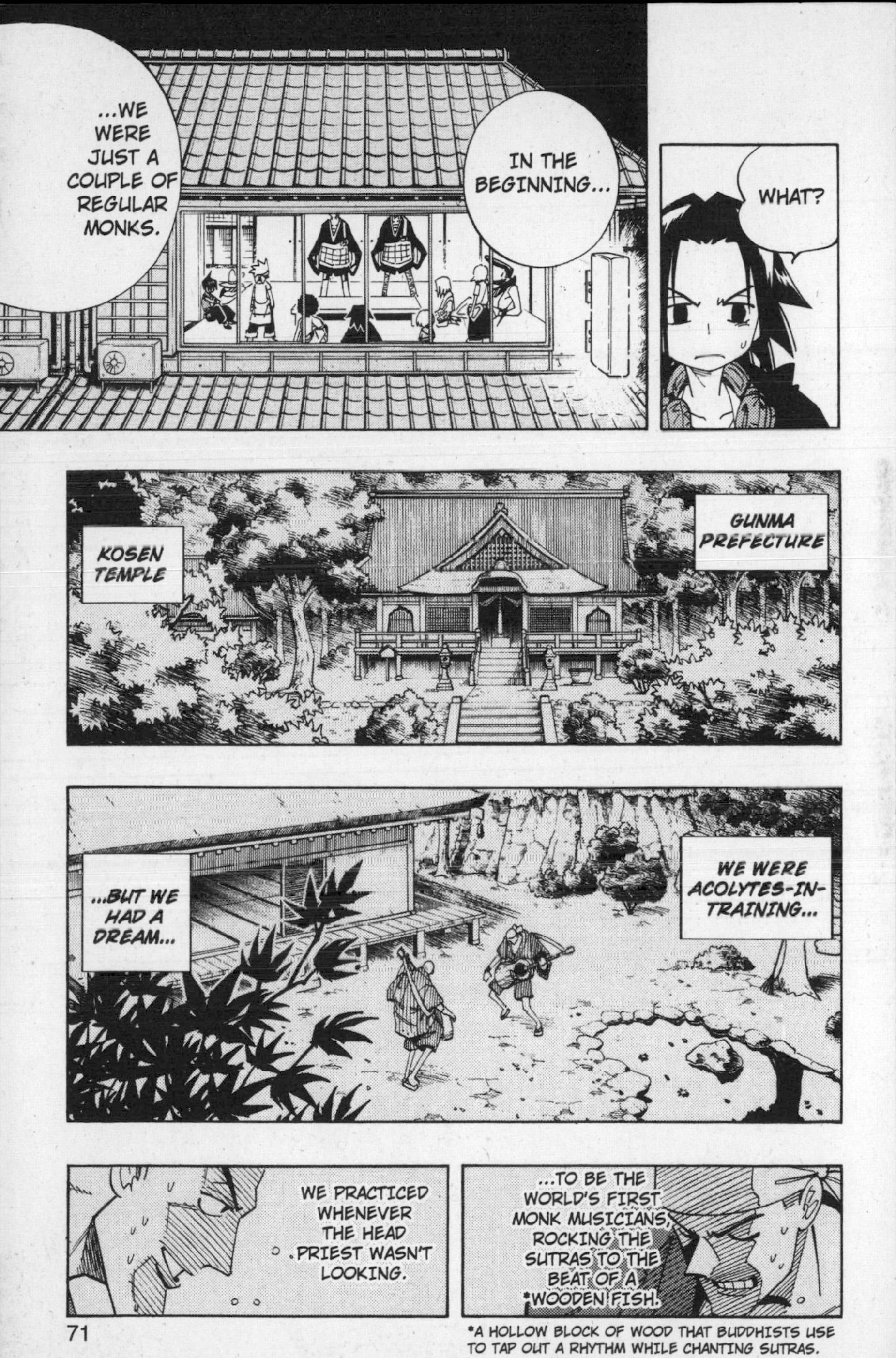
WHAT?
IN THE BEGINNING...
...WE WERE JUST A COUPLE OF REGULAR MONKS.
GUNMA PREFECTURE
KOSEN TEMPLE
WE WERE ACOLYTES-IN-TRAINING...
...BUT WE HAD A DREAM...
...TO BE THE WORLD'S FIRST MONK MUSICIANS, ROCKING THE SUTRAS TO THE BEAT OF A *WOODEN FISH.
WE PRACTICED WHENEVER THE HEAD PRIEST WASN'T LOOKING.

*A HOLLOW BLOCK OF WOOD THAT BUDDHISTS USE TO TAP OUT A RHYTHM WHILE CHANTING SUTRAS.

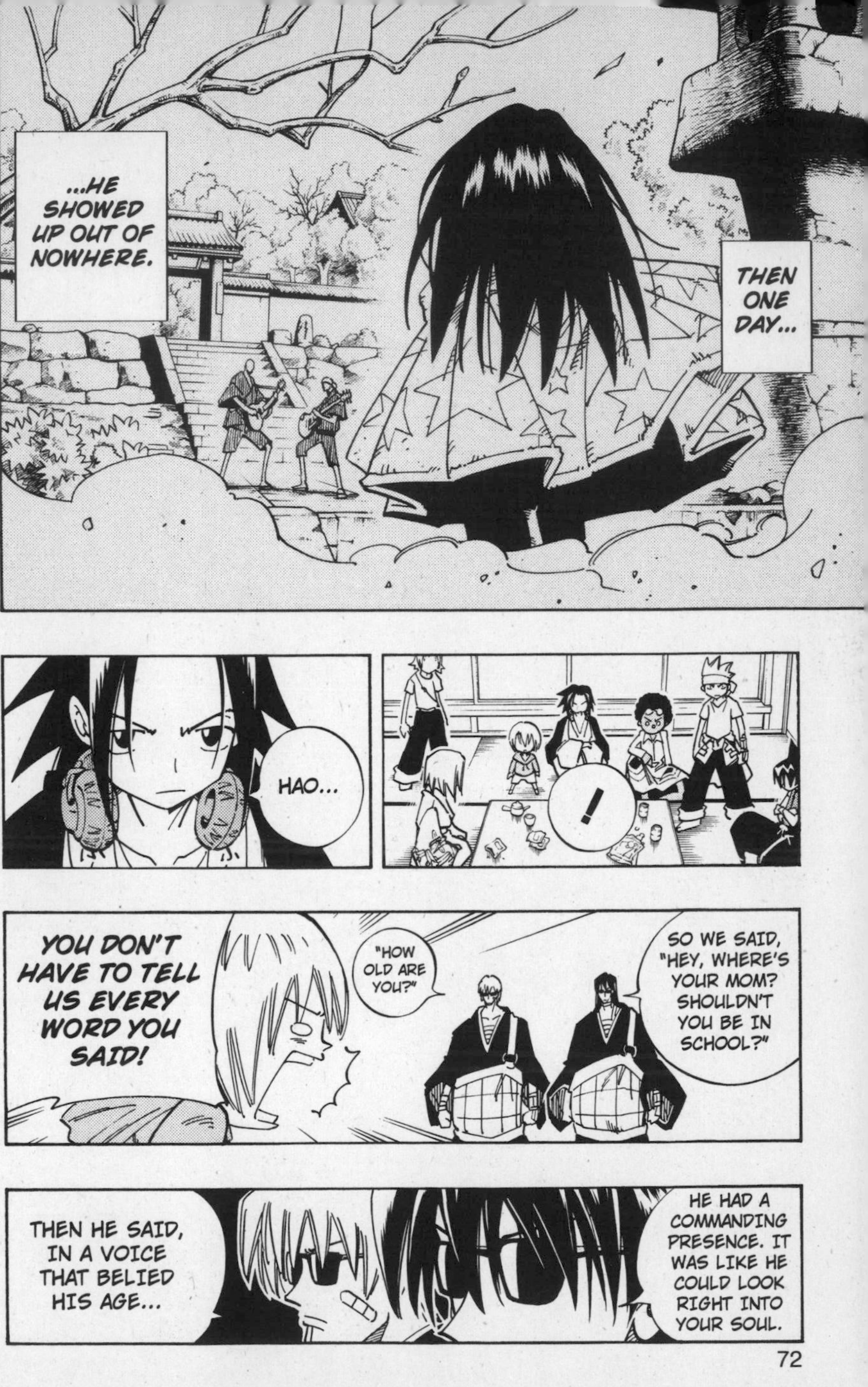
THEN ONE DAY...
...HE SHOWED UP OUT OF NOWHERE.
!
HAO...
SO WE SAID, "HEY, WHERE'S YOUR MOM? SHOULDN'T YOU BE IN SCHOOL?"
"HOW OLD ARE YOU?"
YOU DON'T HAVE TO TELL US EVERY WORD YOU SAID!
HE HAD A COMMANDING PRESENCE. IT WAS LIKE HE COULD LOOK RIGHT INTO YOUR SOUL.
THEN HE SAID, IN A VOICE THAT BELIED HIS AGE...

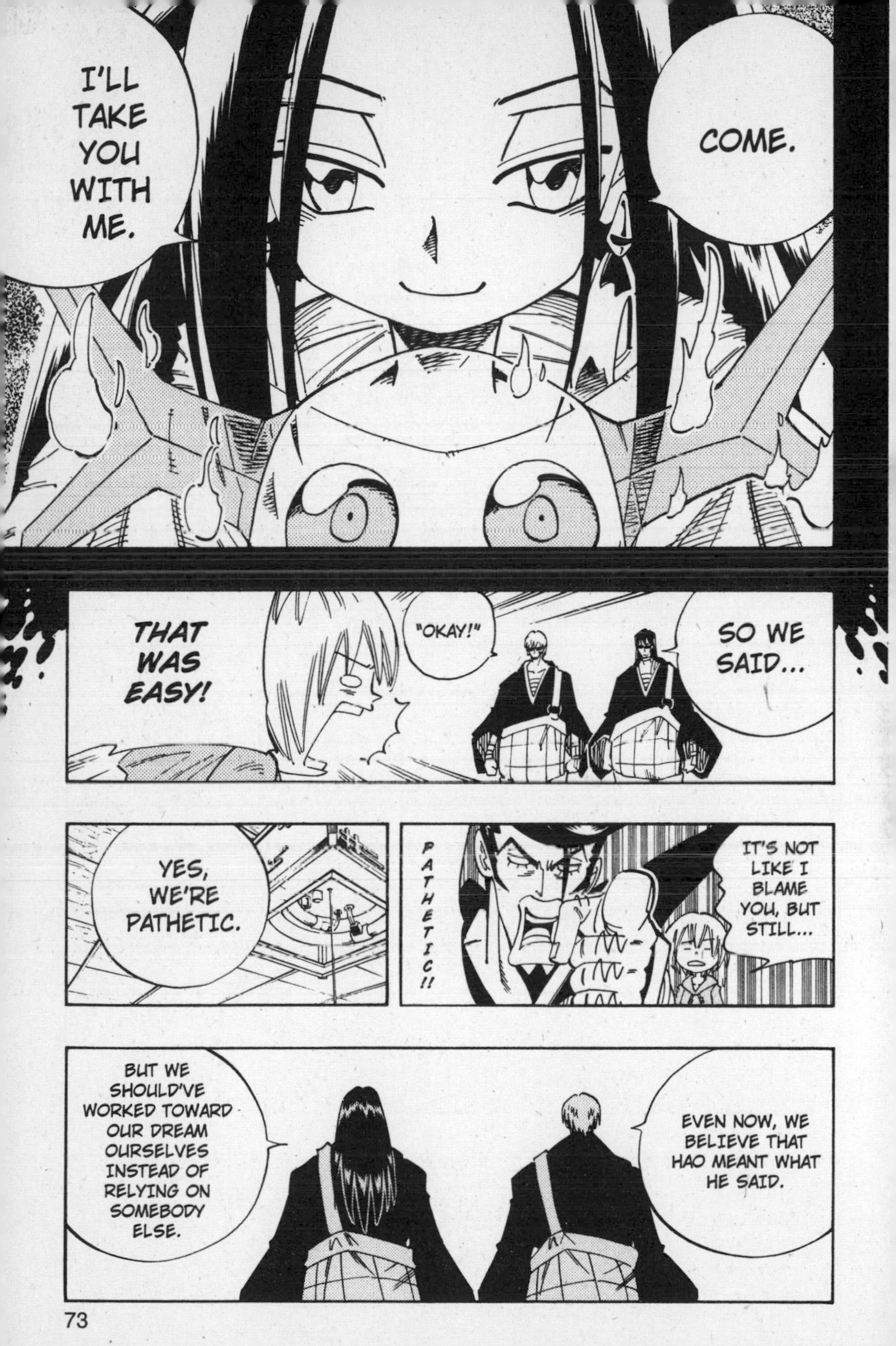
COME.
I'LL TAKE YOU WITH ME.
SO WE SAID...
"OKAY!"
THAT WAS EASY!
IT'S NOT LIKE I BLAME YOU, BUT STILL...
PATHETIC!!
YES, WE'RE PATHETIC.
EVEN NOW, WE BELIEVE THAT HAO MEANT WHAT HE SAID.
BUT WE SHOULD'VE WORKED TOWARD OUR DREAM OURSELVES INSTEAD OF RELYING ON SOMEBODY ELSE.

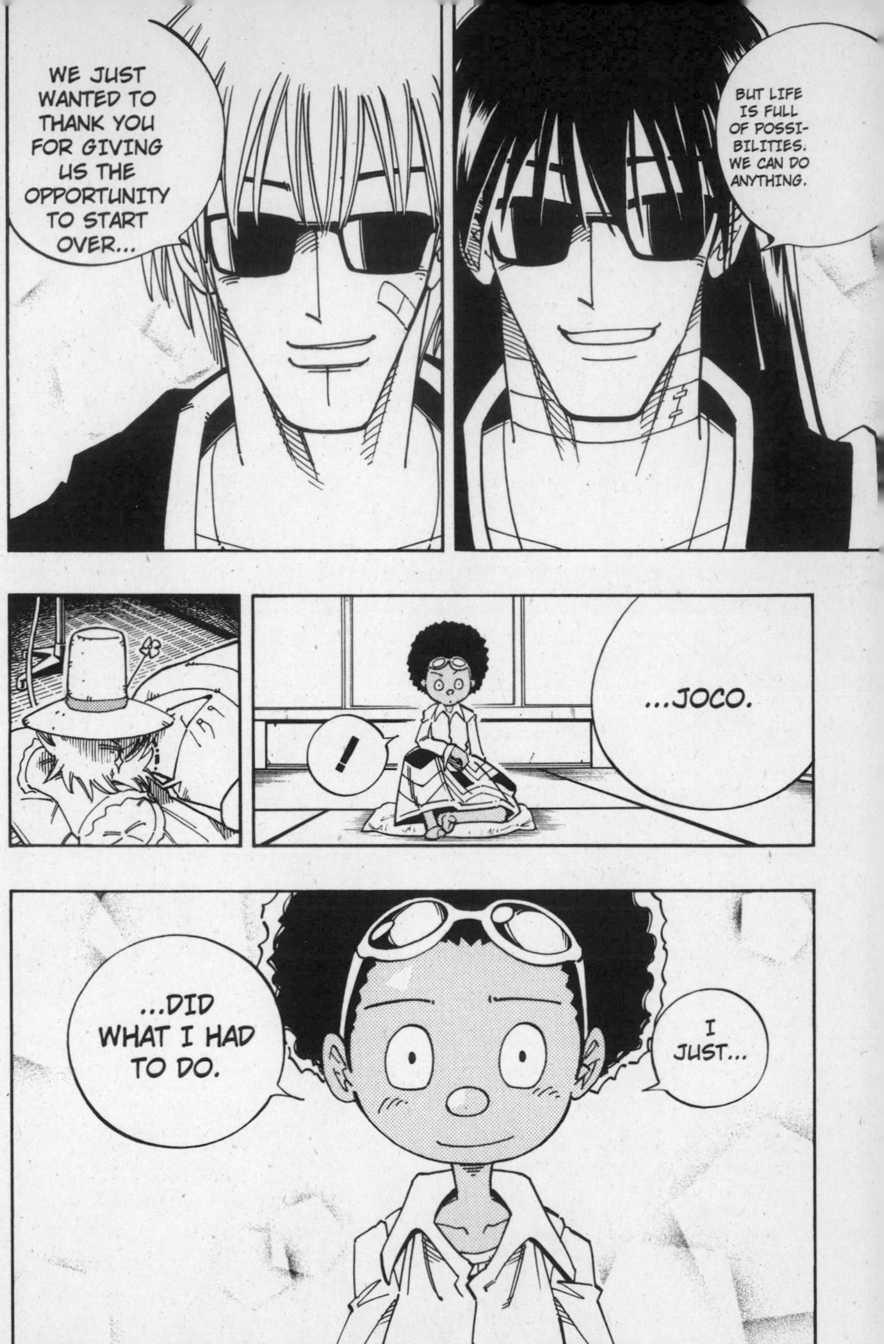
BUT LIFE IS FULL OF POSSI-BILITIES. WE CAN DO ANYTHING.
WE JUST WANTED TO THANK YOU FOR GIVING US THE OPPORTUNITY TO START OVER...
...JOCO.
!
I JUST...
...DID WHAT I HAD TO DO.

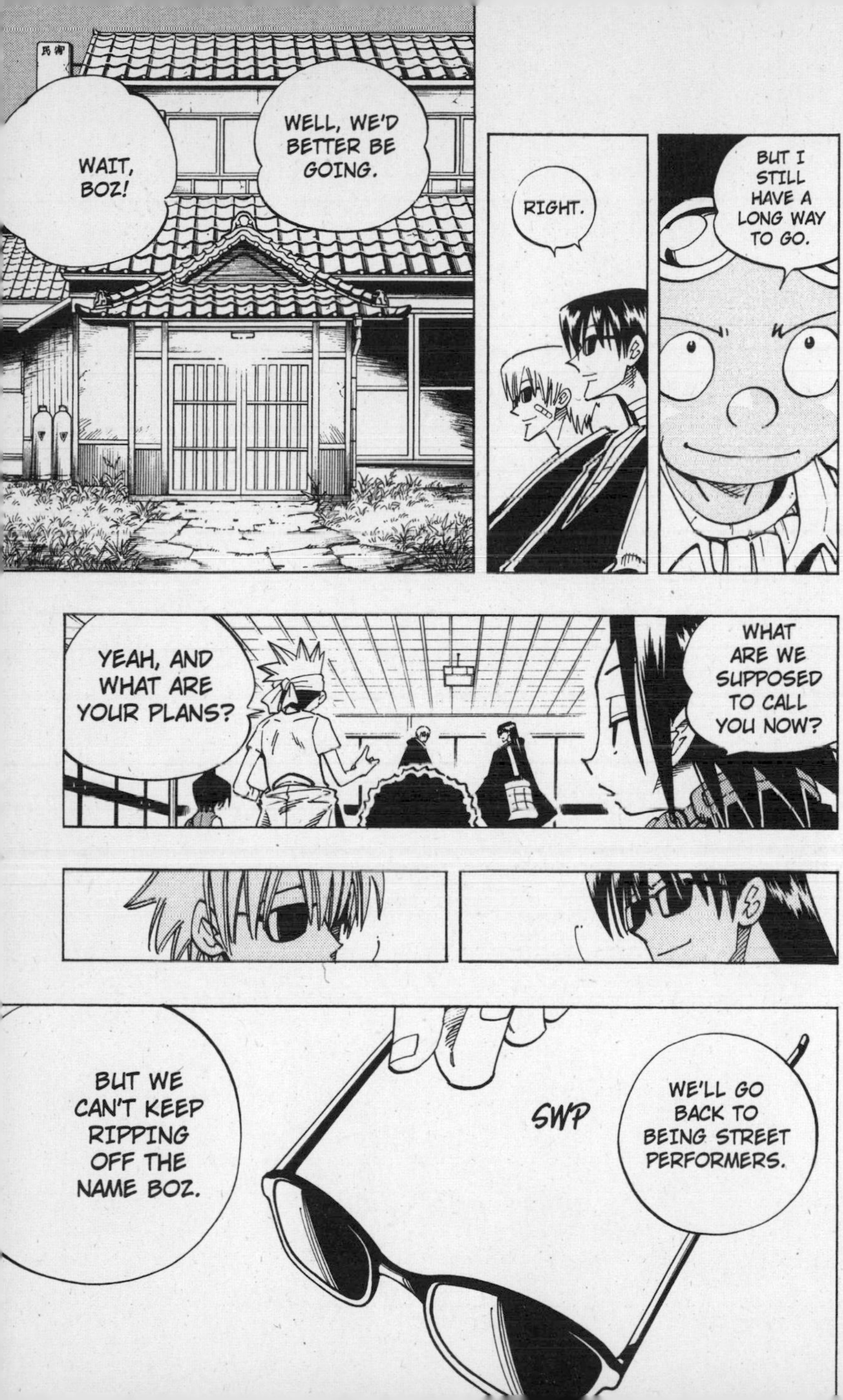
BUT I STILL HAVE A LONG WAY TO GO.
RIGHT.
WELL, WE'D BETTER BE GOING.
WAIT, BOZ!
WHAT ARE WE SUPPOSED TO CALL YOU NOW?
YEAH, AND WHAT ARE YOUR PLANS?
WE'LL GO BACK TO BEING STREET PERFORMERS.
SWP
BUT WE CAN'T KEEP RIPPING OFF THE NAME BOZ.

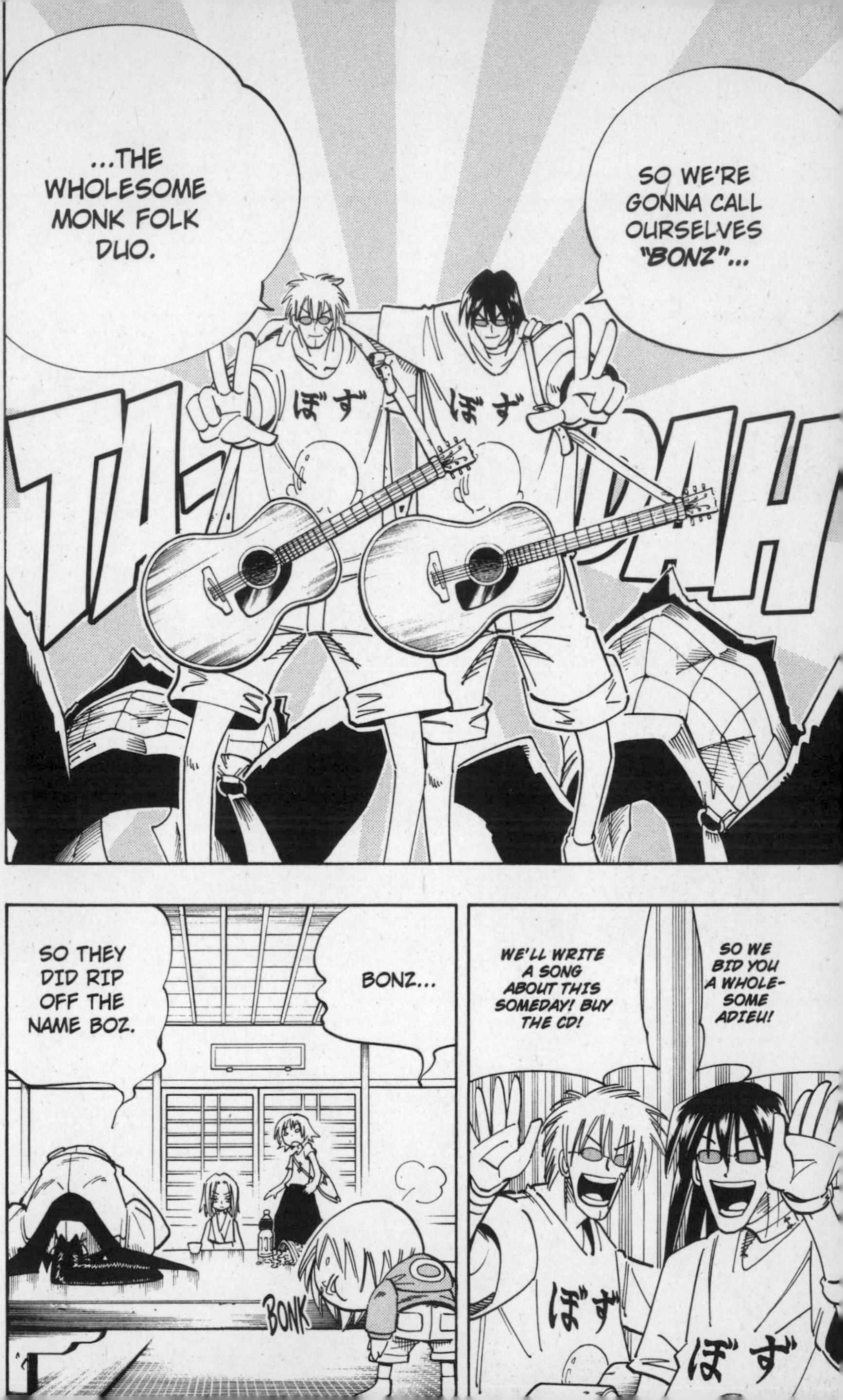
SO WE'RE GONNA CALL OURSELVES "BONZ"...
...THE WHOLESOME MONK FOLK DUO.
TA-DAH
ぼず
ぼず
SO WE BID YOU A WHOLE-SOME ADIEU!
WE'LL WRITE A SONG ABOUT THIS SOMEDAY! BUY THE CD!
ぼず
ぼず
BONZ...
SO THEY DID RIP OFF THE NAME BOZ.
BONK

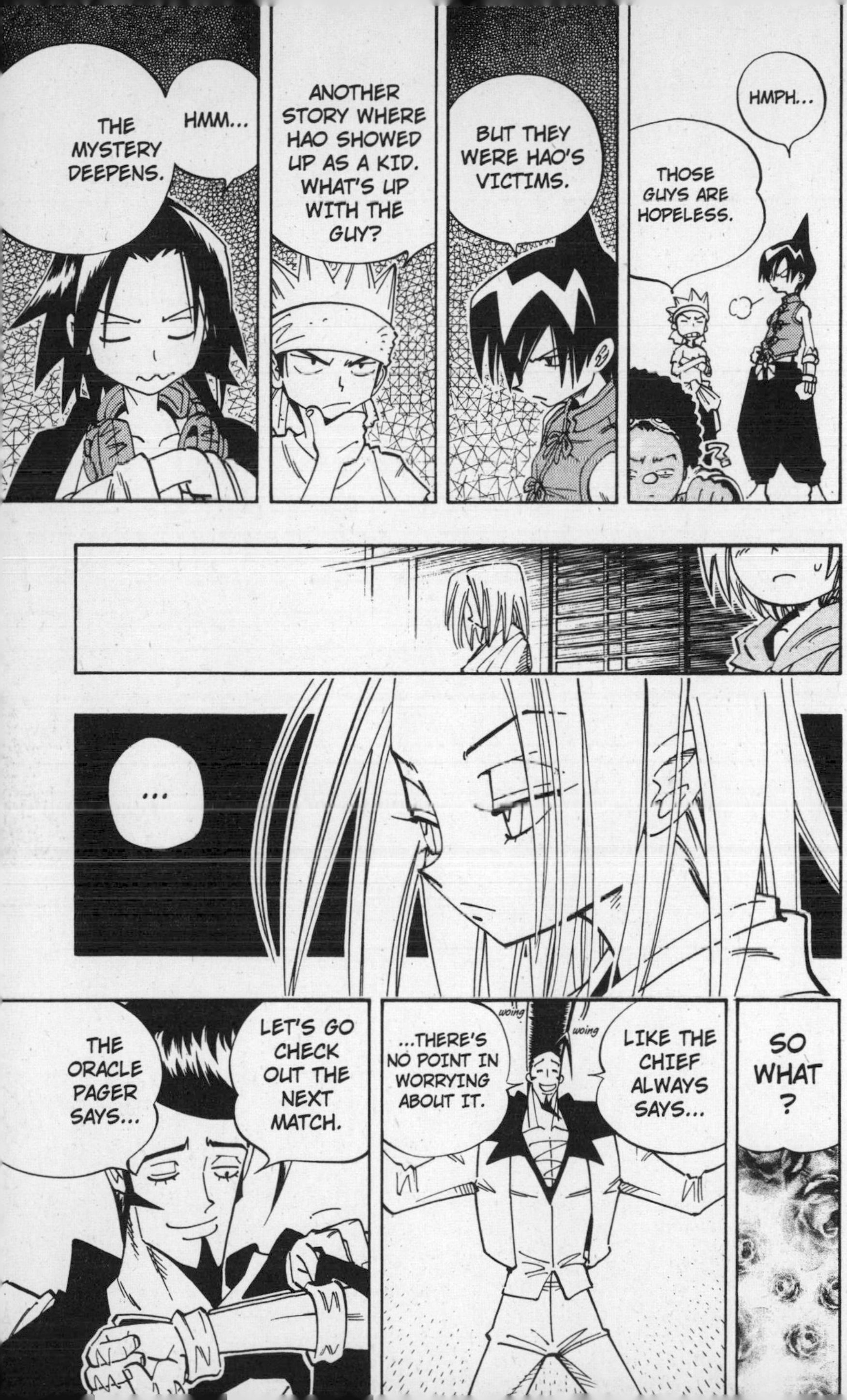
HMPH...
THOSE GUYS ARE HOPELESS.
BUT THEY WERE HAO'S VICTIMS.
ANOTHER STORY WHERE HAO SHOWED UP AS A KID. WHAT'S UP WITH THE GUY?
HMM...
THE MYSTERY DEEPENS.
...
SO WHAT?
LIKE THE CHIEF ALWAYS SAYS...
woing
woing
...THERE'S NO POINT IN WORRYING ABOUT IT.
LET'S GO CHECK OUT THE NEXT MATCH.
THE ORACLE PAGER SAYS...

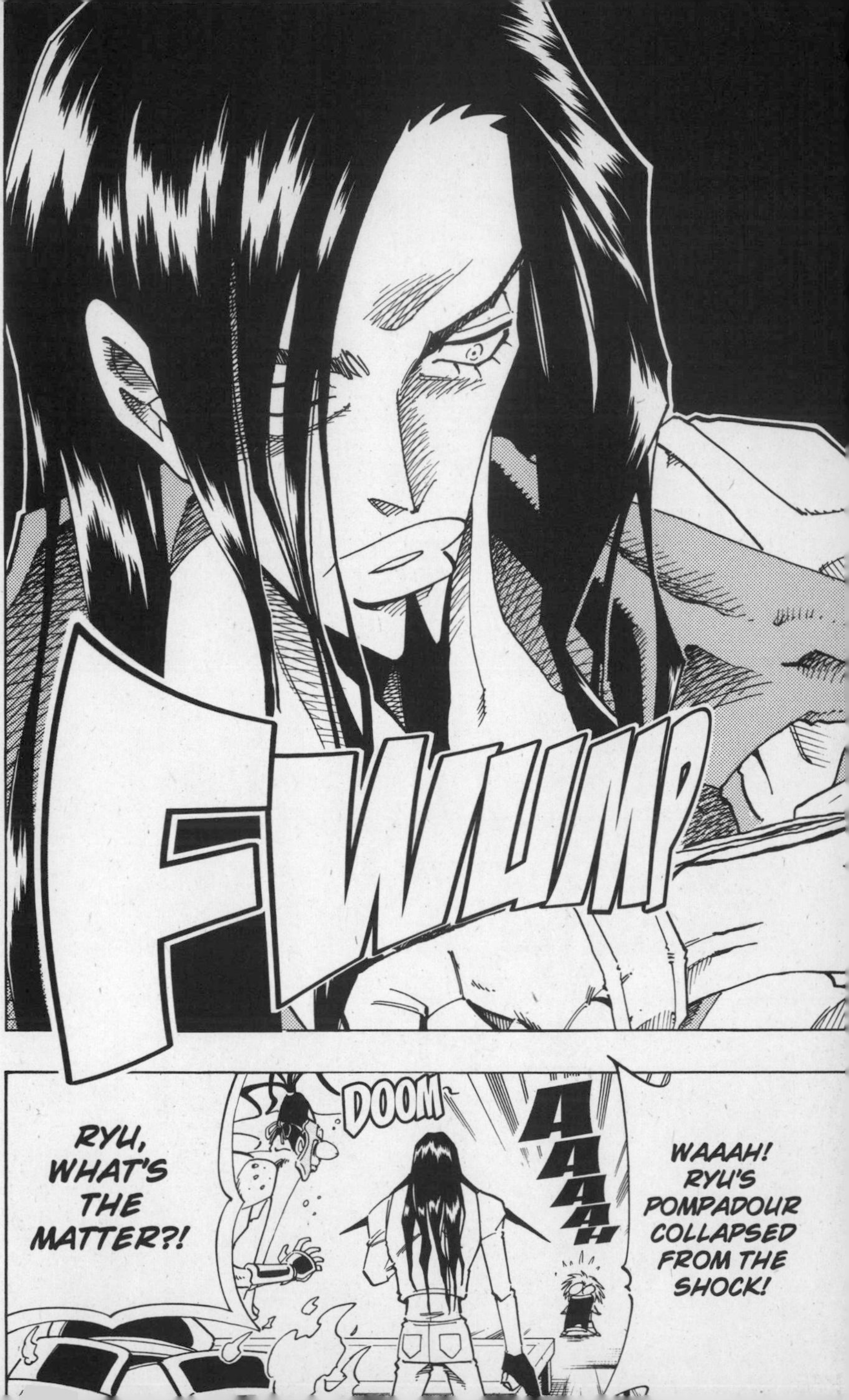
FWUMP
WAAAH! RYU'S POMPADOUR COLLAPSED FROM THE SHOCK!
AAAAH
DOOM
RYU, WHAT'S THE MATTER?!

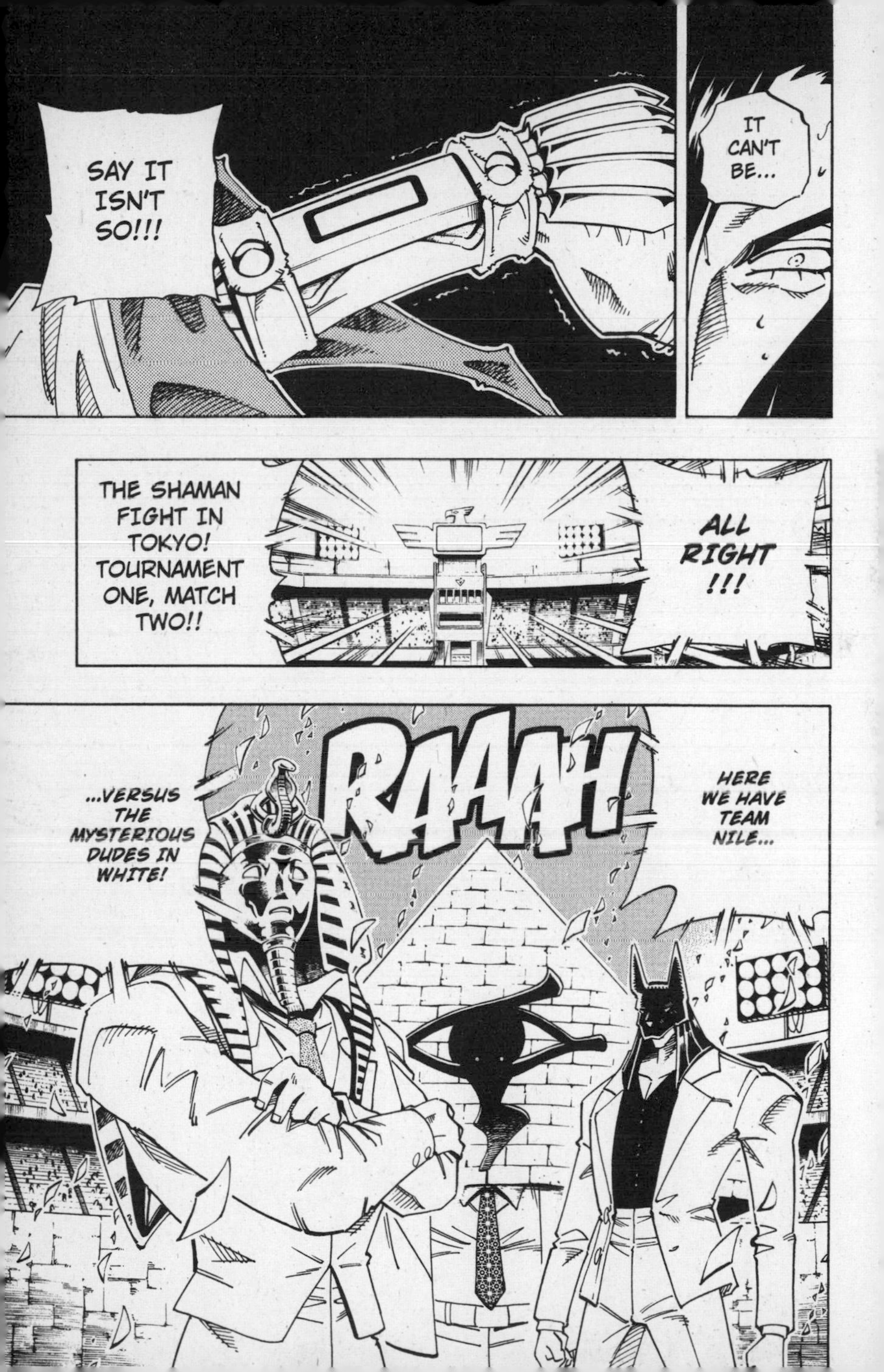

IT CAN'T BE...
SAY IT ISN'T SO!!!
ALL RIGHT!!!
THE SHAMAN FIGHT IN TOKYO! TOURNAMENT ONE, MATCH TWO!!
HERE WE HAVE TEAM NILE...
RAAAH
...VERSUS THE MYSTERIOUS DUDES IN WHITE!

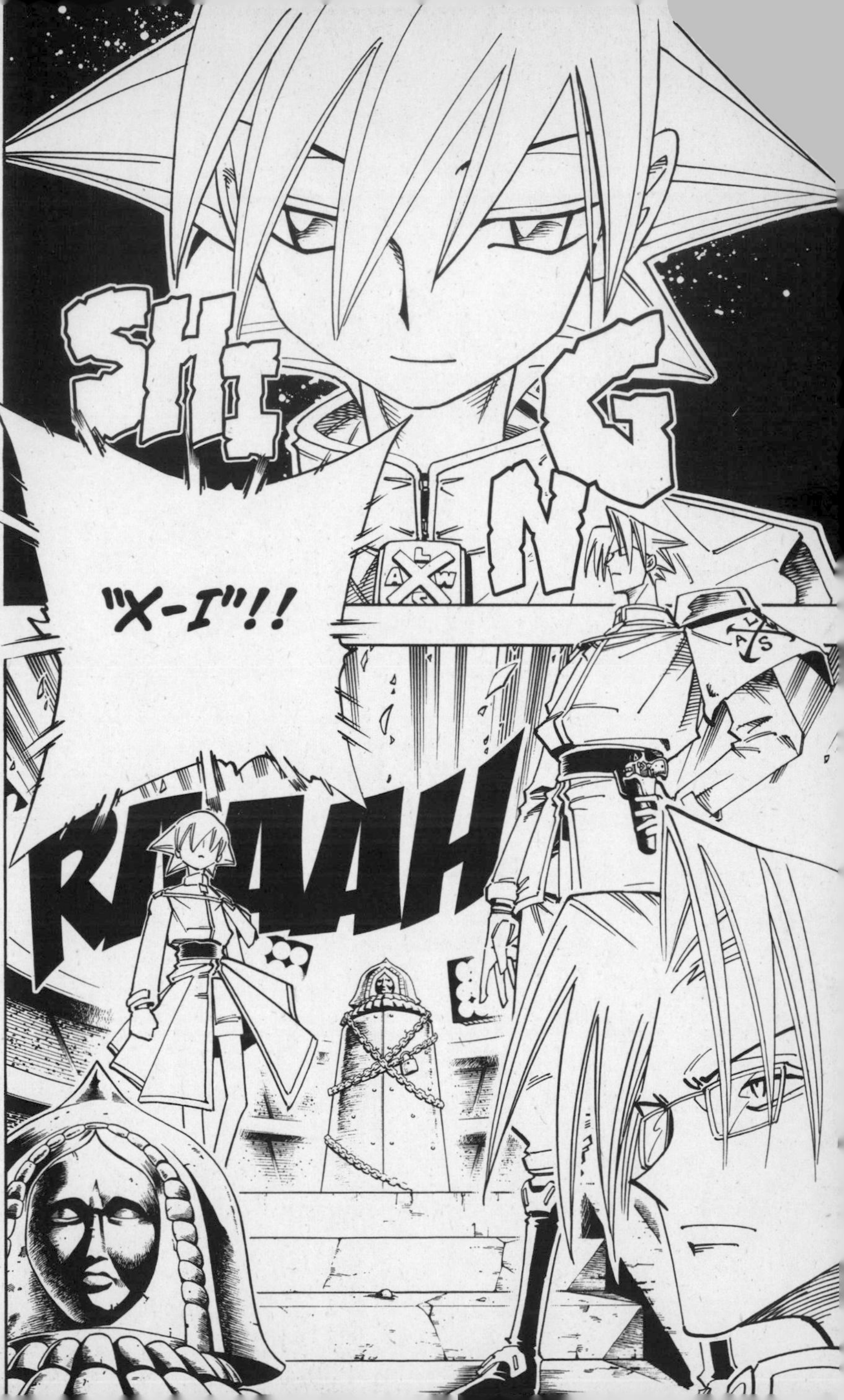
SHING
"X-I"!!
RAAH

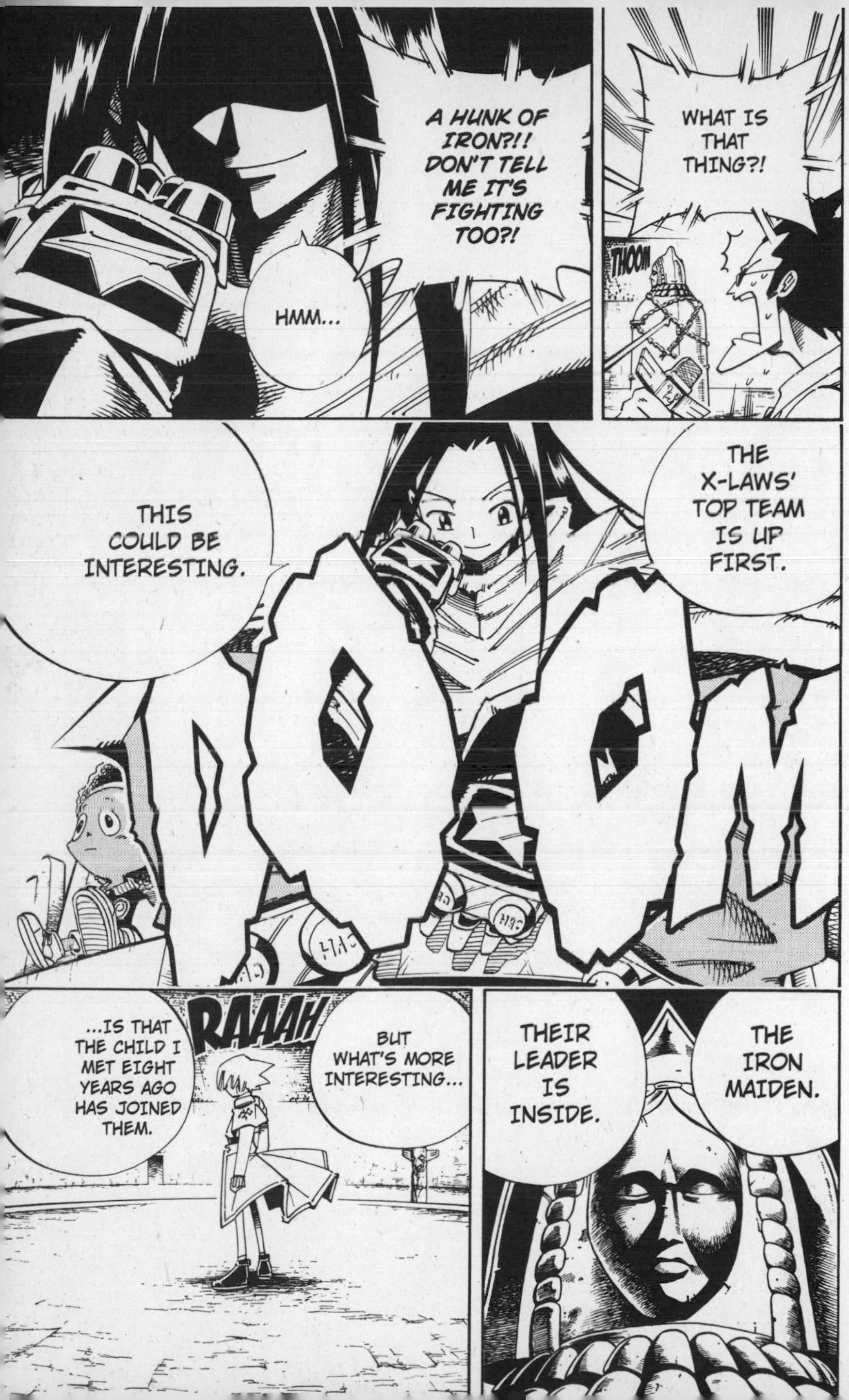
WHAT IS THAT THING?!
THOOM
A HUNK OF IRON?!! DON'T TELL ME IT'S FIGHTING TOO?!
HMM...
THE X-LAWS' TOP TEAM IS UP FIRST.
THIS COULD BE INTERESTING.
DOOM
THE IRON MAIDEN.
THEIR LEADER IS INSIDE.
BUT WHAT'S MORE INTERESTING...
RAAAH
...IS THAT THE CHILD I MET EIGHT YEARS AGO HAS JOINED THEM.

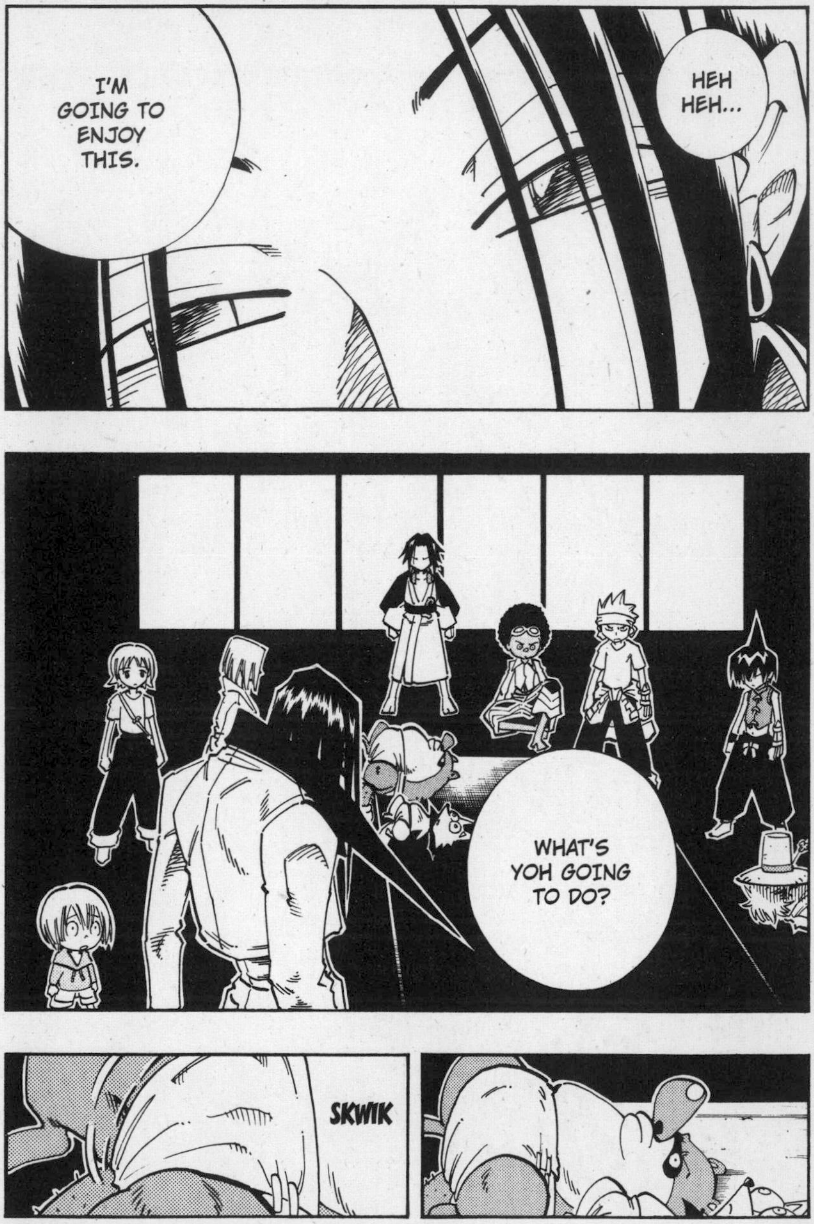
HEH HEH...
I'M GOING TO ENJOY THIS.
WHAT'S YOH GOING TO DO?
SKWIK

Shaman King™

SHAMAN KING ITEM FILE No.43

ナイルズ媒介(ばいかい)

TEAM NILE'S SPIRIT MEDIA

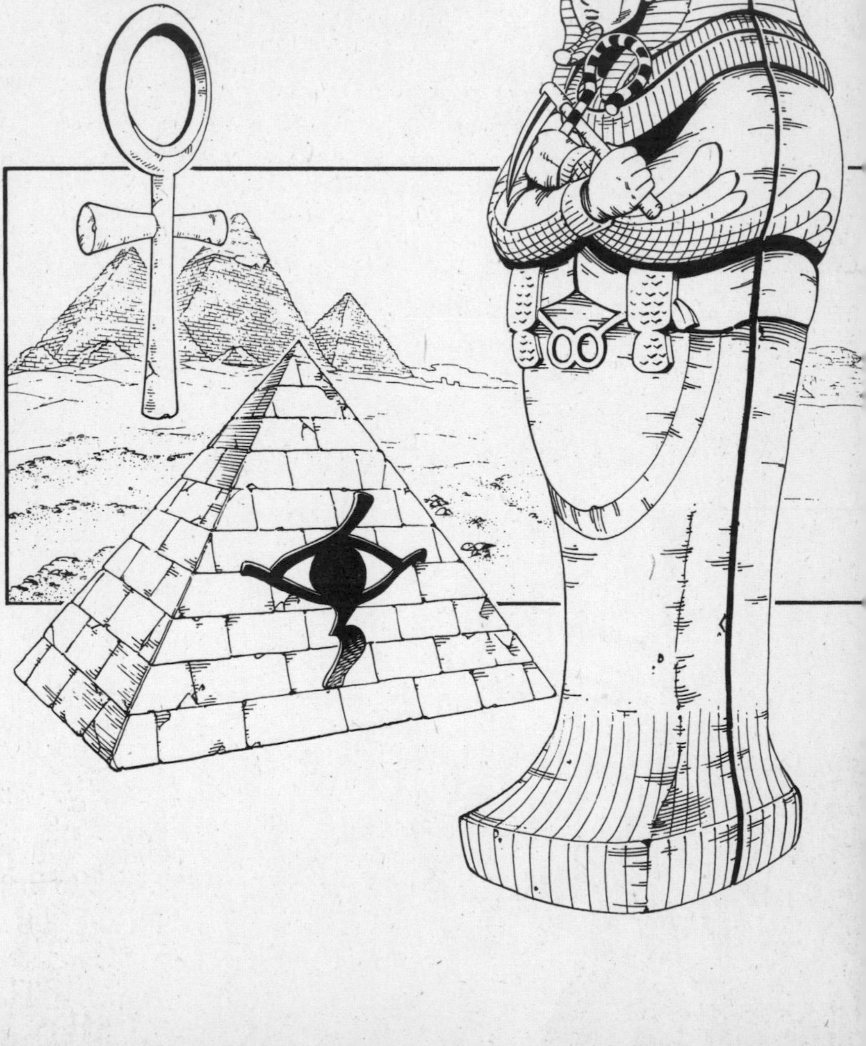

Reincarnation 121: Justice X

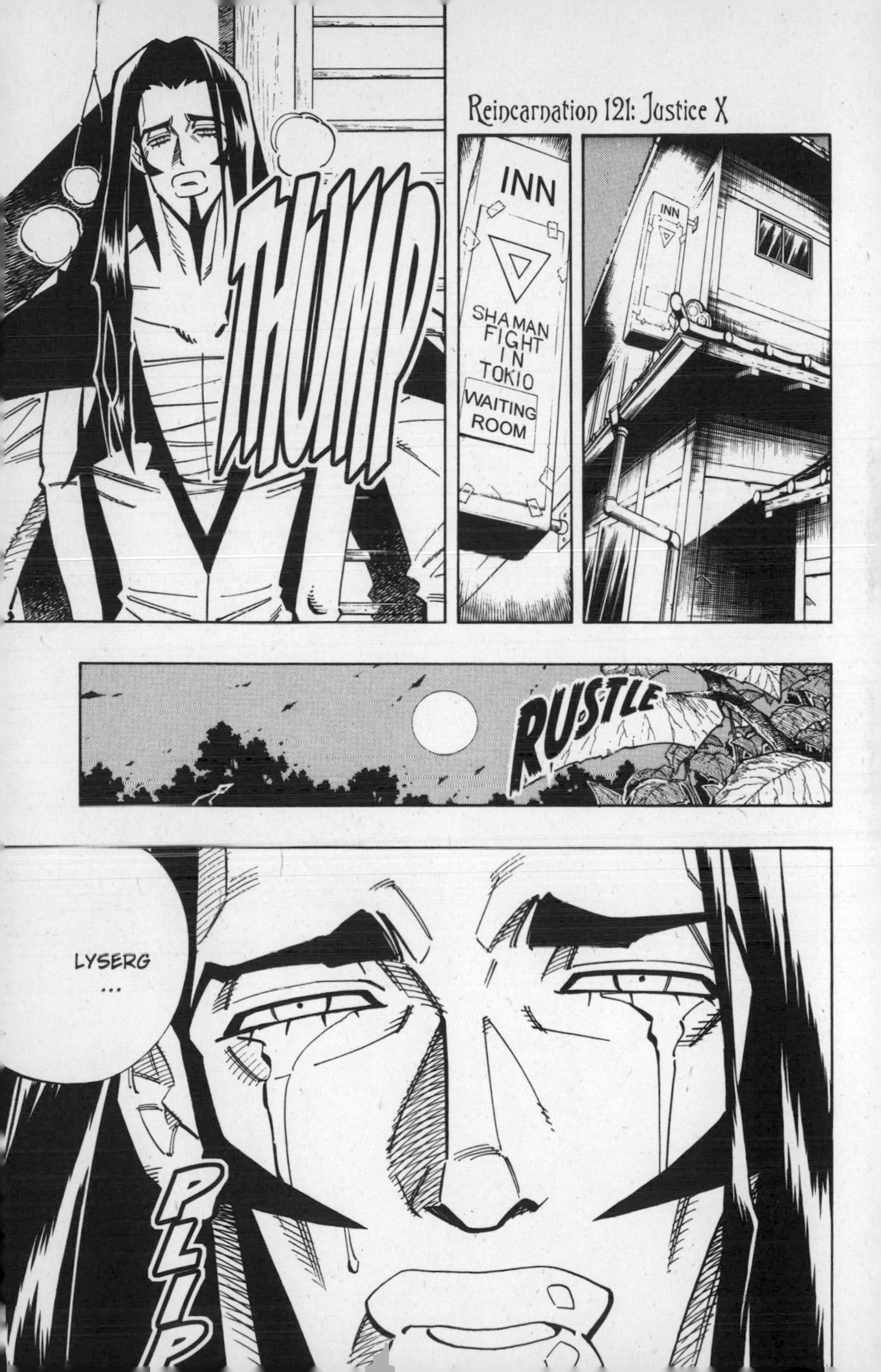
INN
INN
SHAMAN FIGHT IN TOKIO
WAITING ROOM
THUMP
RUSTLE
LYSERG ...
PLIP

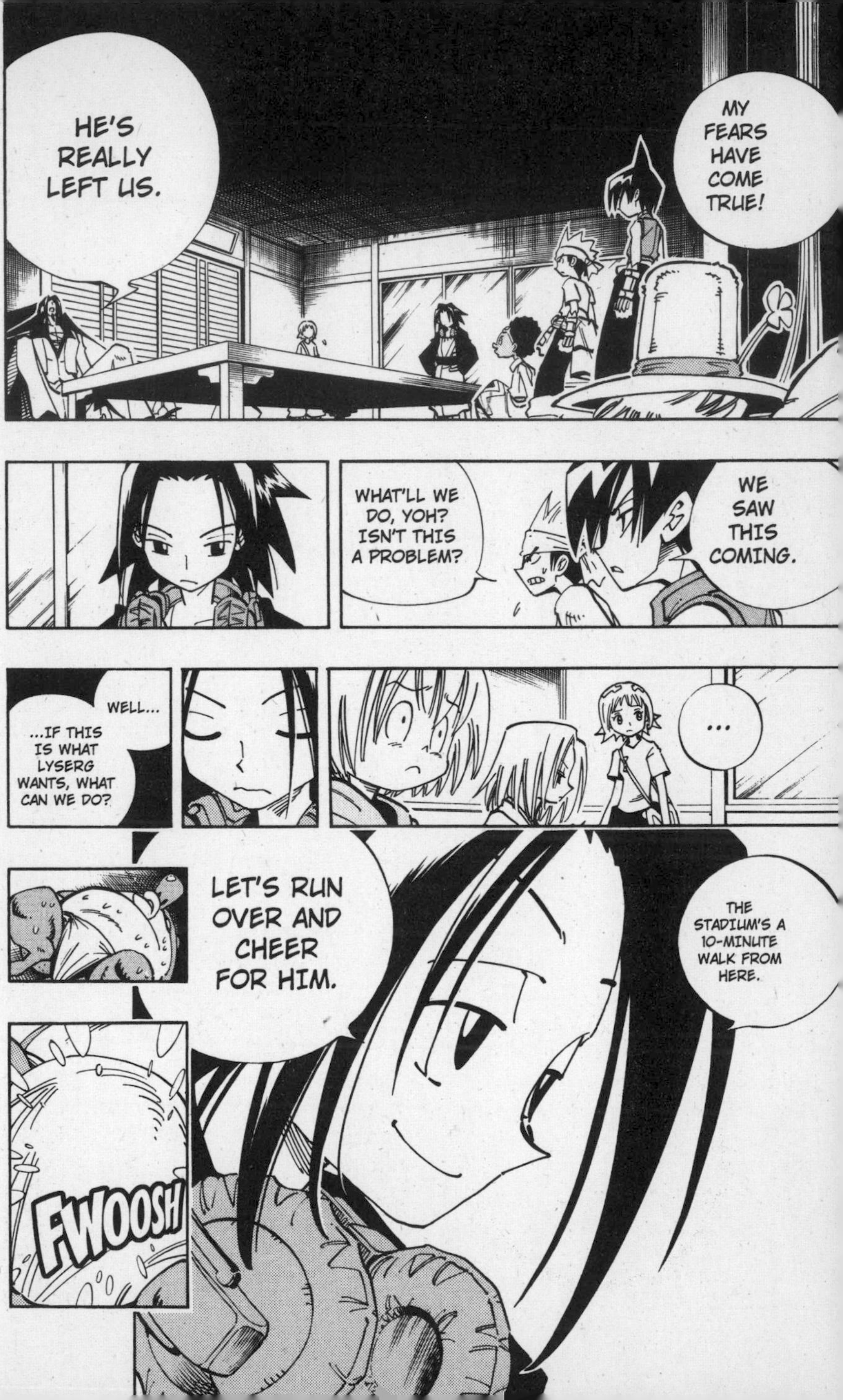
MY FEARS HAVE COME TRUE!
HE'S REALLY LEFT US.
WE SAW THIS COMING.
WHAT'LL WE DO, YOH? ISN'T THIS A PROBLEM?
...
WELL...
...IF THIS IS WHAT LYSERG WANTS, WHAT CAN WE DO?
THE STADIUM'S A 10-MINUTE WALK FROM HERE.
LET'S RUN OVER AND CHEER FOR HIM.
FWOOSH

Reincarnation 121:
Justice X

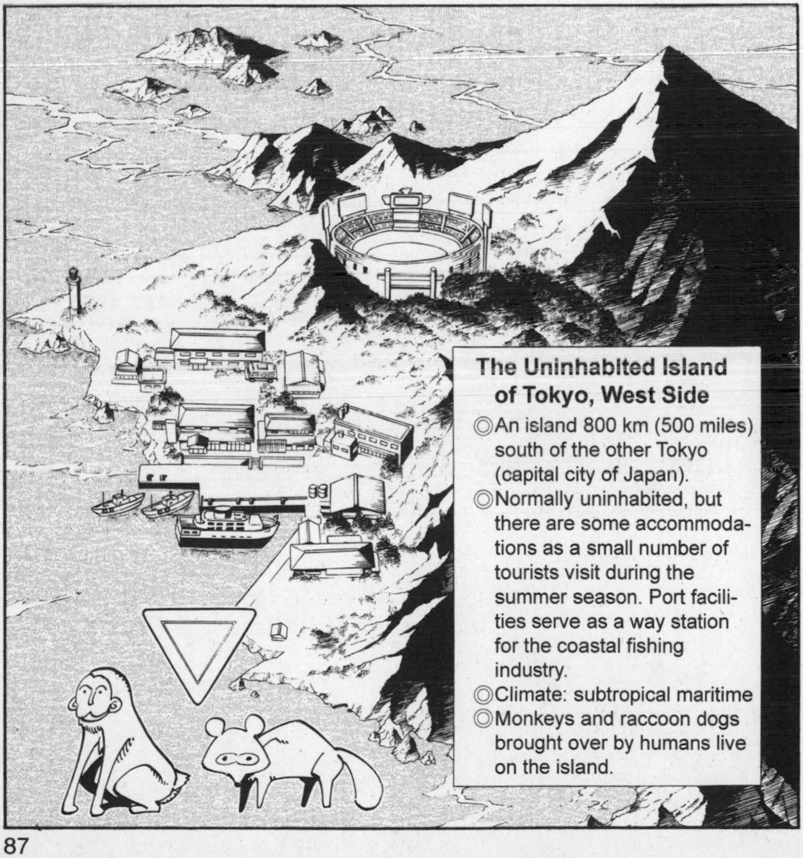
The Uninhabited Island of Tokyo, West Side
◎An island 800 km (500 miles) south of the other Tokyo (capital city of Japan).
◎Normally uninhabited, but there are some accommodations as a small number of tourists visit during the summer season. Port facilities serve as a way station for the coastal fishing industry.
◎Climate: subtropical maritime
◎Monkeys and raccoon dogs brought over by humans live on the island.

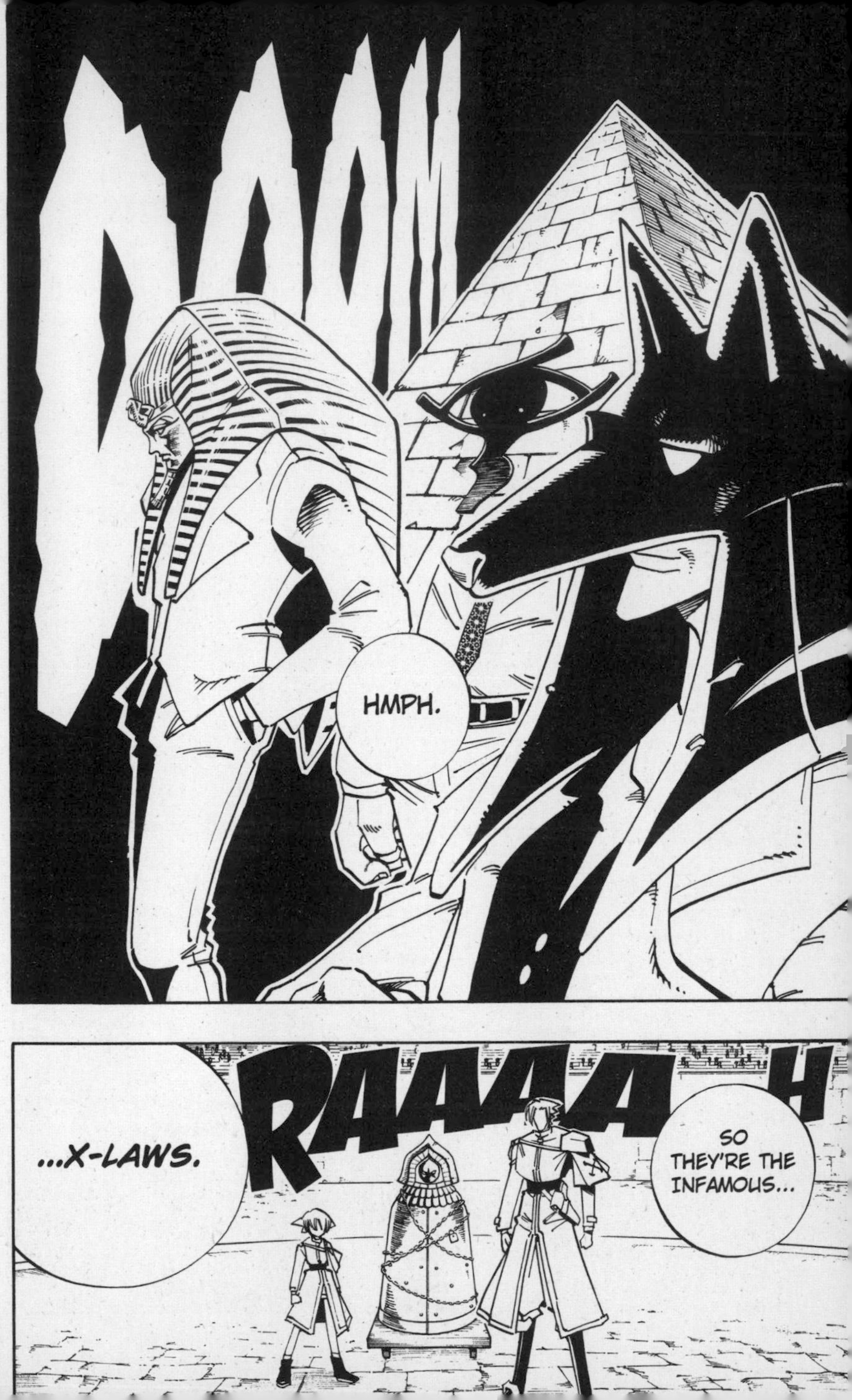
DOOM
HMPH.
RAAAAH
SO THEY'RE THE INFAMOUS...
...X-LAWS.

READ THIS WAY

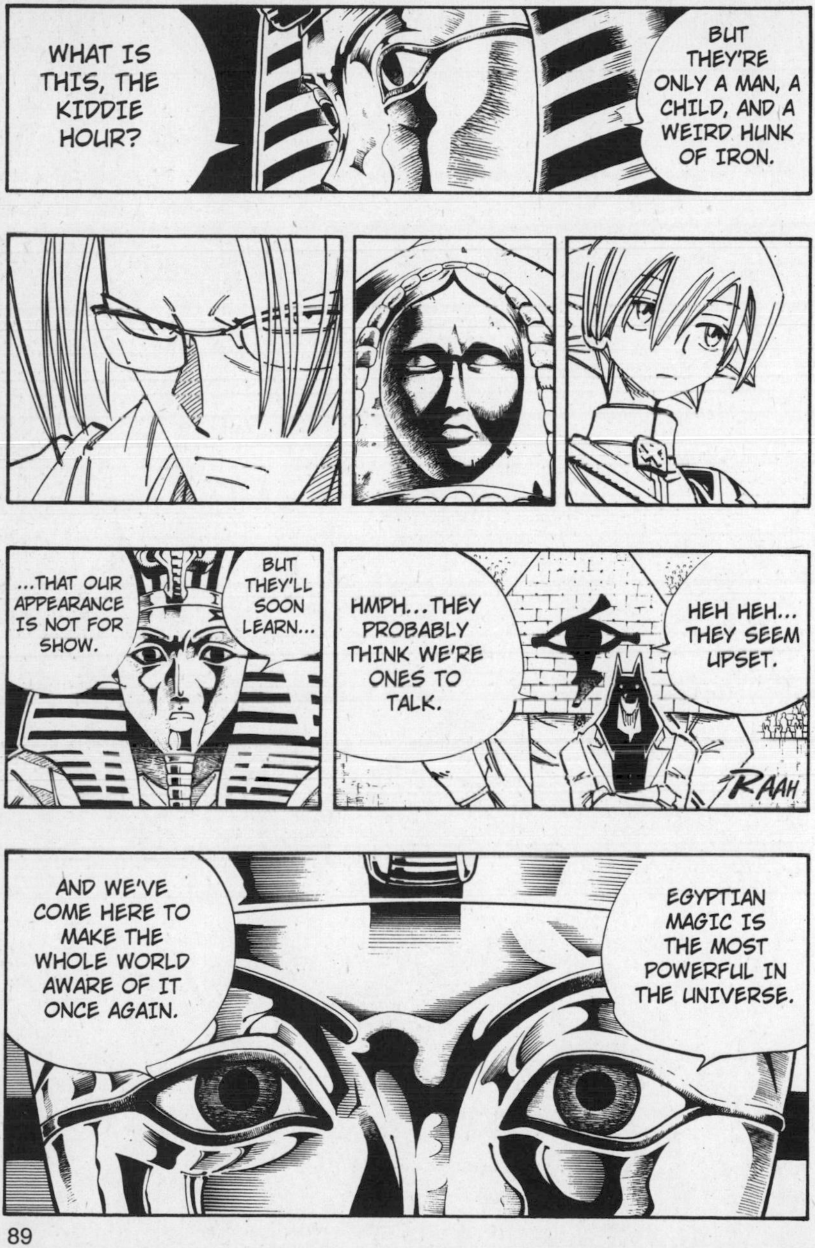
BUT THEY'RE ONLY A MAN, A CHILD, AND A WEIRD HUNK OF IRON.
WHAT IS THIS, THE KIDDIE HOUR?
HEH HEH... THEY SEEM UPSET.
HMPH...THEY PROBABLY THINK WE'RE ONES TO TALK.
RAAH
BUT THEY'LL SOON LEARN...
...THAT OUR APPEARANCE IS NOT FOR SHOW.
EGYPTIAN MAGIC IS THE MOST POWERFUL IN THE UNIVERSE.
AND WE'VE COME HERE TO MAKE THE WHOLE WORLD AWARE OF IT ONCE AGAIN.

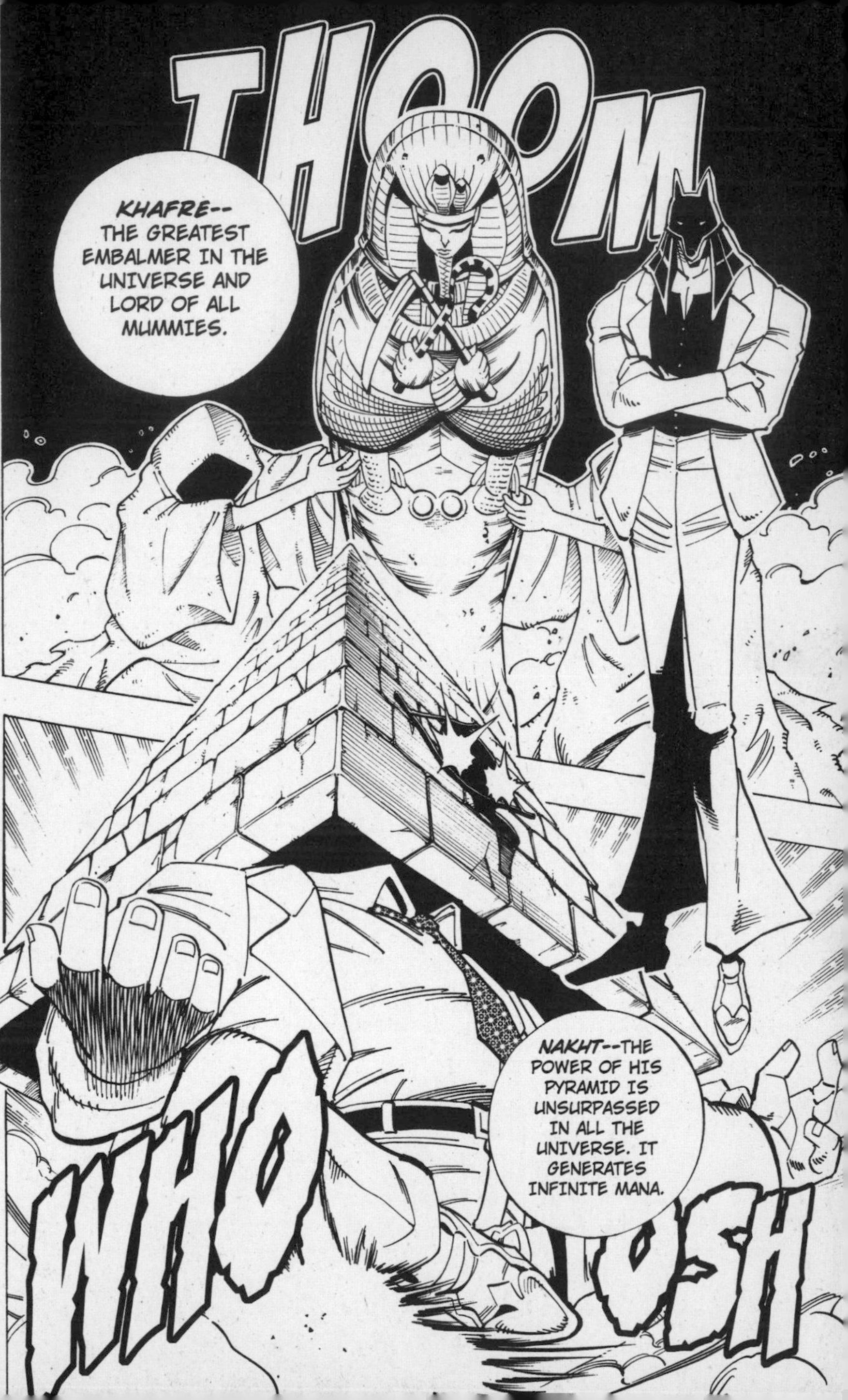
THOOM
KHAFRE-- THE GREATEST EMBALMER IN THE UNIVERSE AND LORD OF ALL MUMMIES.
NAKHT--THE POWER OF HIS PYRAMID IS UNSURPASSED IN ALL THE UNIVERSE. IT GENERATES INFINITE MANA.
WHOOSH

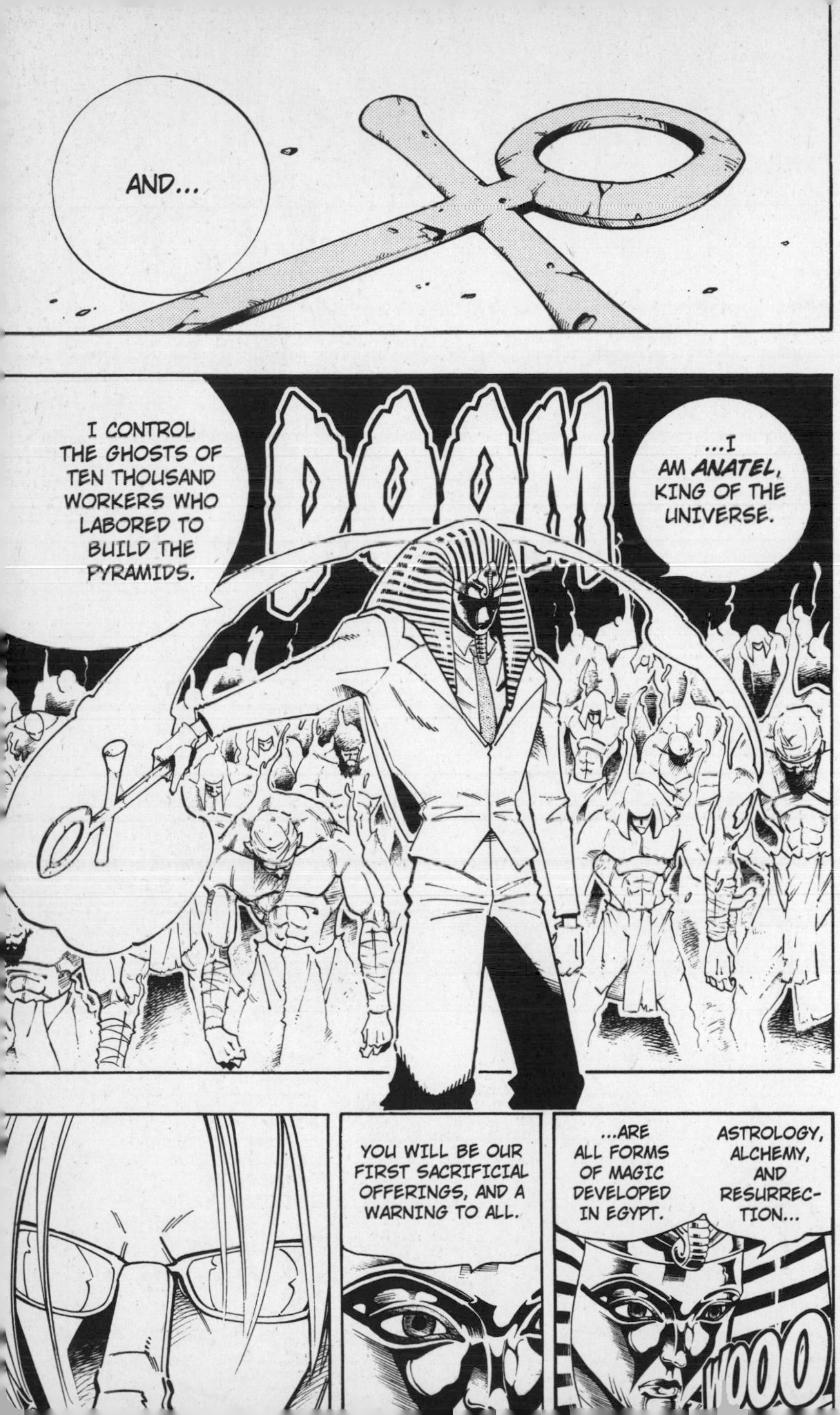
AND...
...I AM *ANATEL*, KING OF THE UNIVERSE.
DOOM
I CONTROL THE GHOSTS OF TEN THOUSAND WORKERS WHO LABORED TO BUILD THE PYRAMIDS.
ASTROLOGY, ALCHEMY, AND RESURREC-TION...
...ARE ALL FORMS OF MAGIC DEVELOPED IN EGYPT.
WOOO
YOU WILL BE OUR FIRST SACRIFICIAL OFFERINGS, AND A WARNING TO ALL.

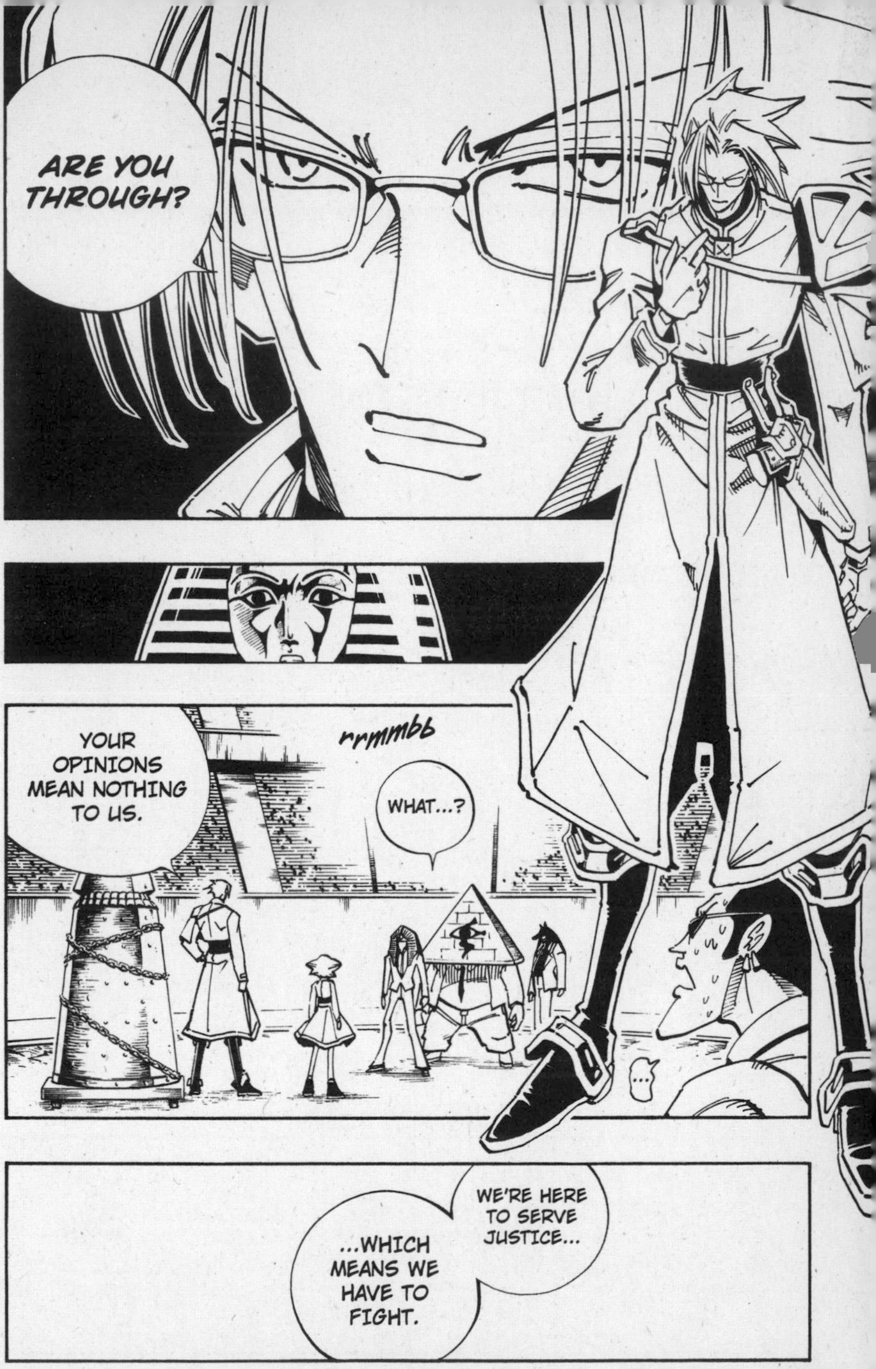
ARE YOU THROUGH?
rrmmbb
WHAT...?
YOUR OPINIONS MEAN NOTHING TO US.
...
WE'RE HERE TO SERVE JUSTICE...
...WHICH MEANS WE HAVE TO FIGHT.

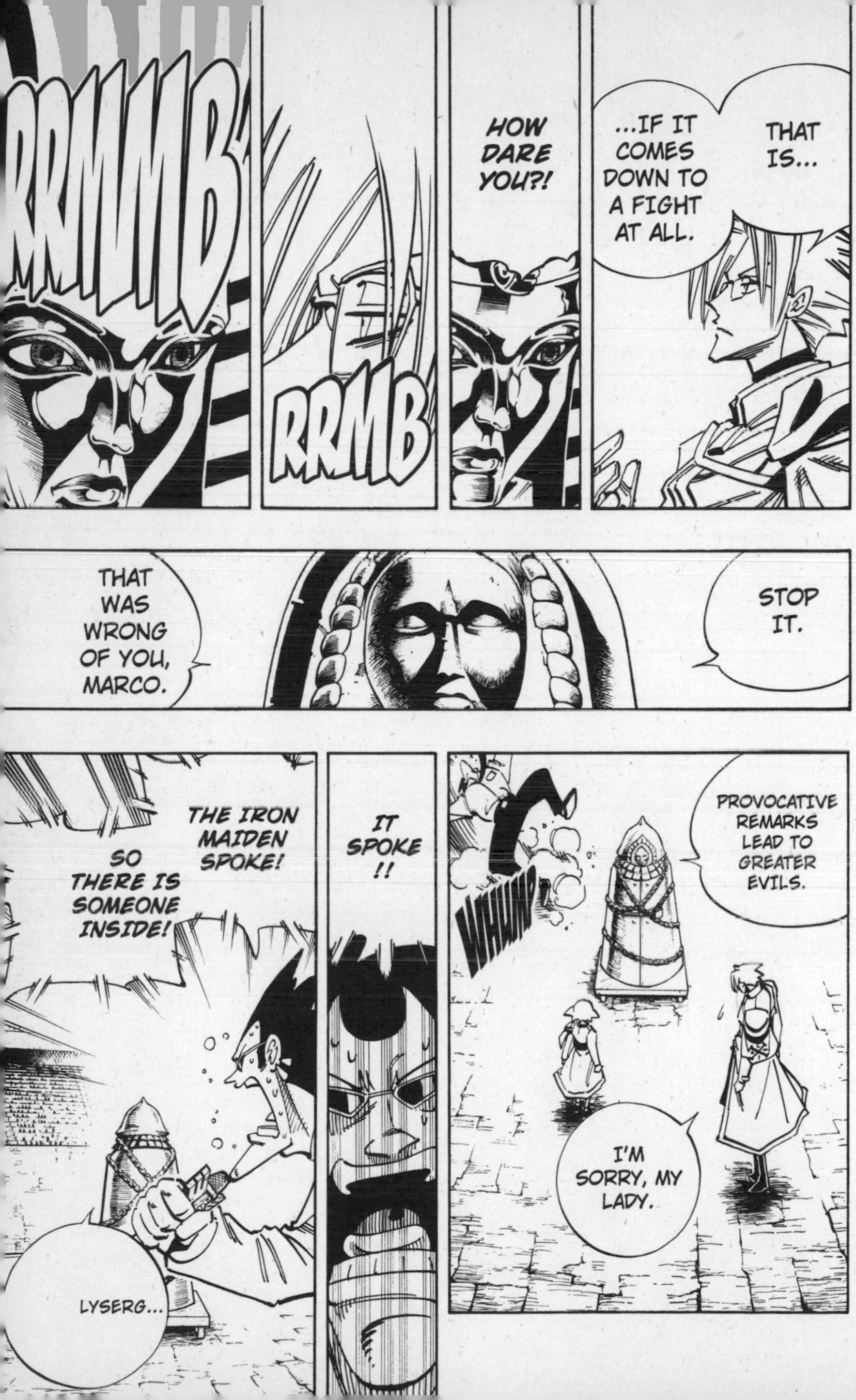
THAT IS...
...IF IT COMES DOWN TO A FIGHT AT ALL.
HOW DARE YOU?!
RRMB
RRMMB
STOP IT.
THAT WAS WRONG OF YOU, MARCO.
PROVOCATIVE REMARKS LEAD TO GREATER EVILS.
WHUMP
I'M SORRY, MY LADY.
IT SPOKE !!
THE IRON MAIDEN SPOKE!
SO THERE IS SOMEONE INSIDE!
LYSERG...

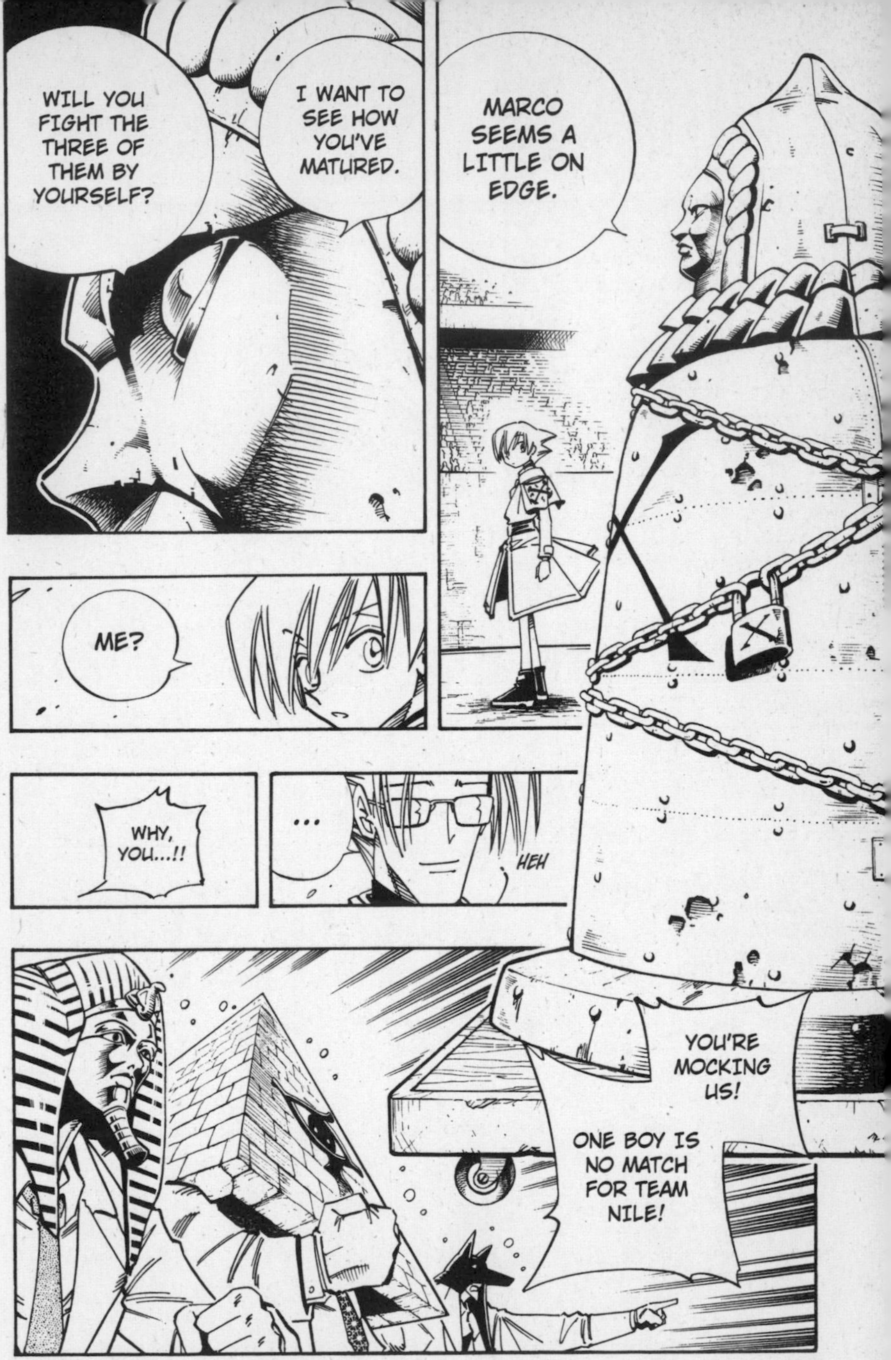
MARCO SEEMS A LITTLE ON EDGE.
I WANT TO SEE HOW YOU'VE MATURED.
WILL YOU FIGHT THE THREE OF THEM BY YOURSELF?
ME?
...
HEH
WHY, YOU...!!
YOU'RE MOCKING US!
ONE BOY IS NO MATCH FOR TEAM NILE!

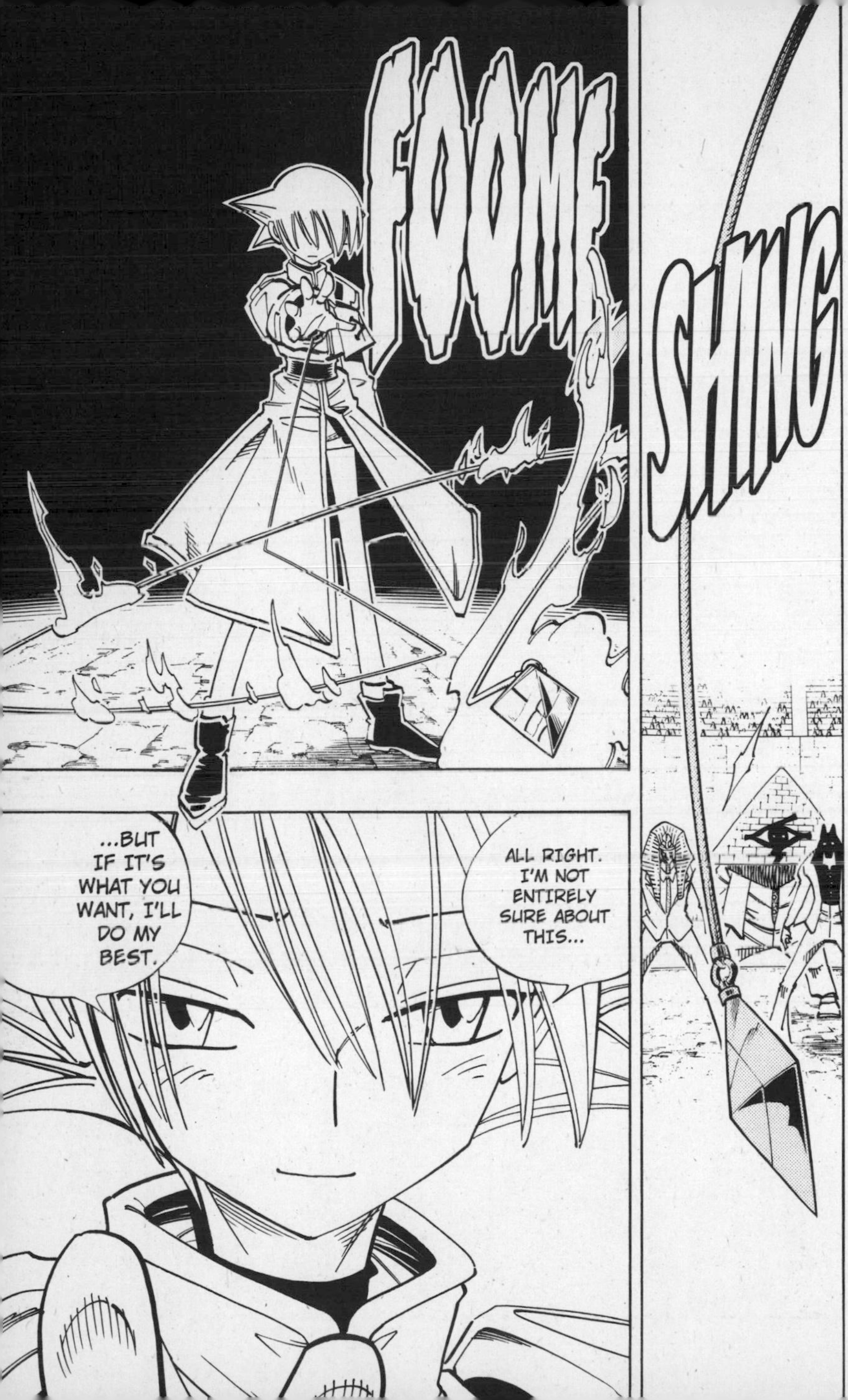
SHING
FOOME
ALL RIGHT. I'M NOT ENTIRELY SURE ABOUT THIS...
...BUT IF IT'S WHAT YOU WANT, I'LL DO MY BEST.

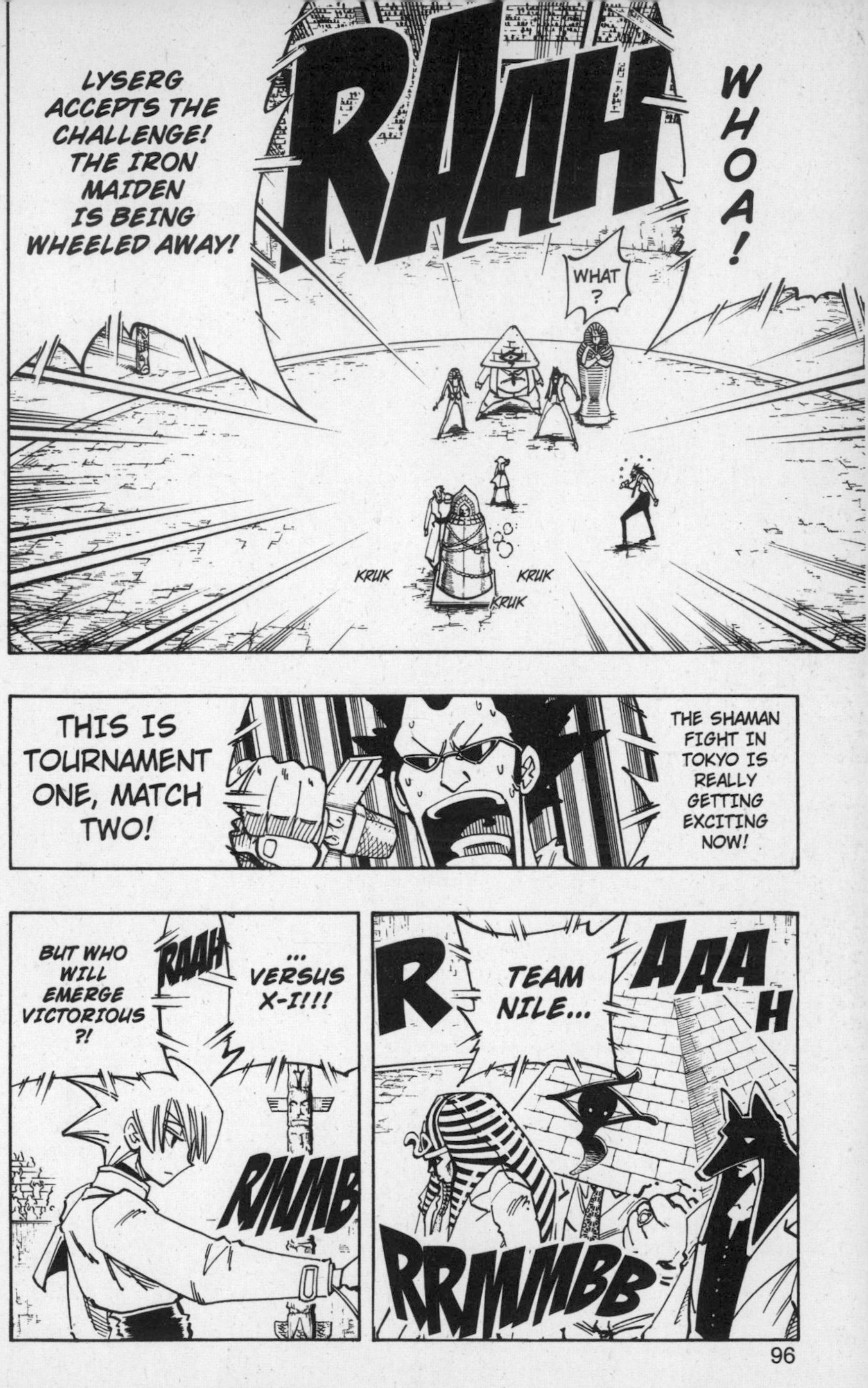

WHOA!
RAAH
WHAT?
LYSERG ACCEPTS THE CHALLENGE! THE IRON MAIDEN IS BEING WHEELED AWAY!
KRUK
KRUK
KRUK
THE SHAMAN FIGHT IN TOKYO IS REALLY GETTING EXCITING NOW!
THIS IS TOURNAMENT ONE, MATCH TWO!
AAAH
R
TEAM NILE...
RRMMBB
... VERSUS X-I!!!
RAAH
BUT WHO WILL EMERGE VICTORIOUS?!
RMMB

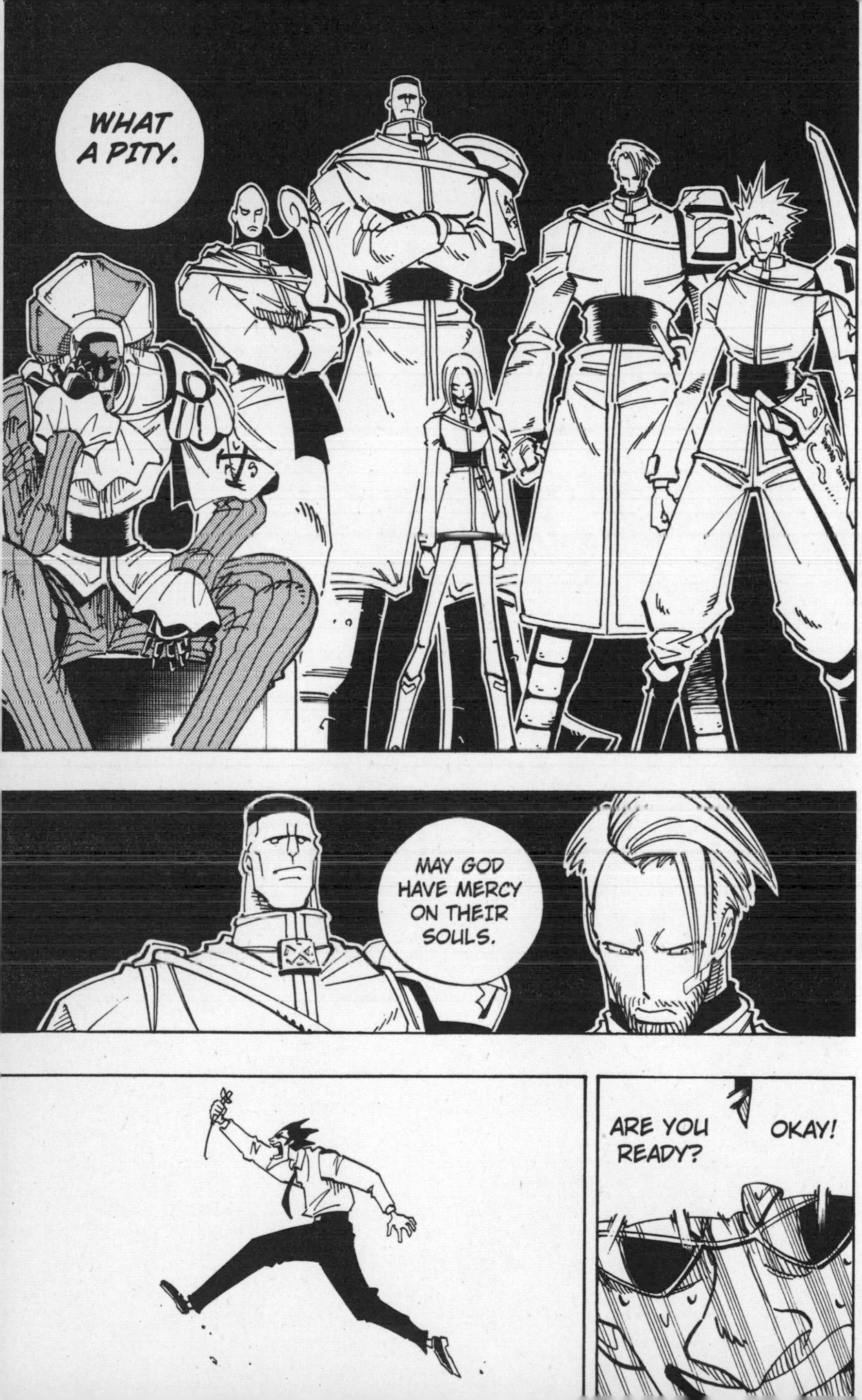
WHAT A PITY.
MAY GOD HAVE MERCY ON THEIR SOULS.
OKAY!
ARE YOU READY?

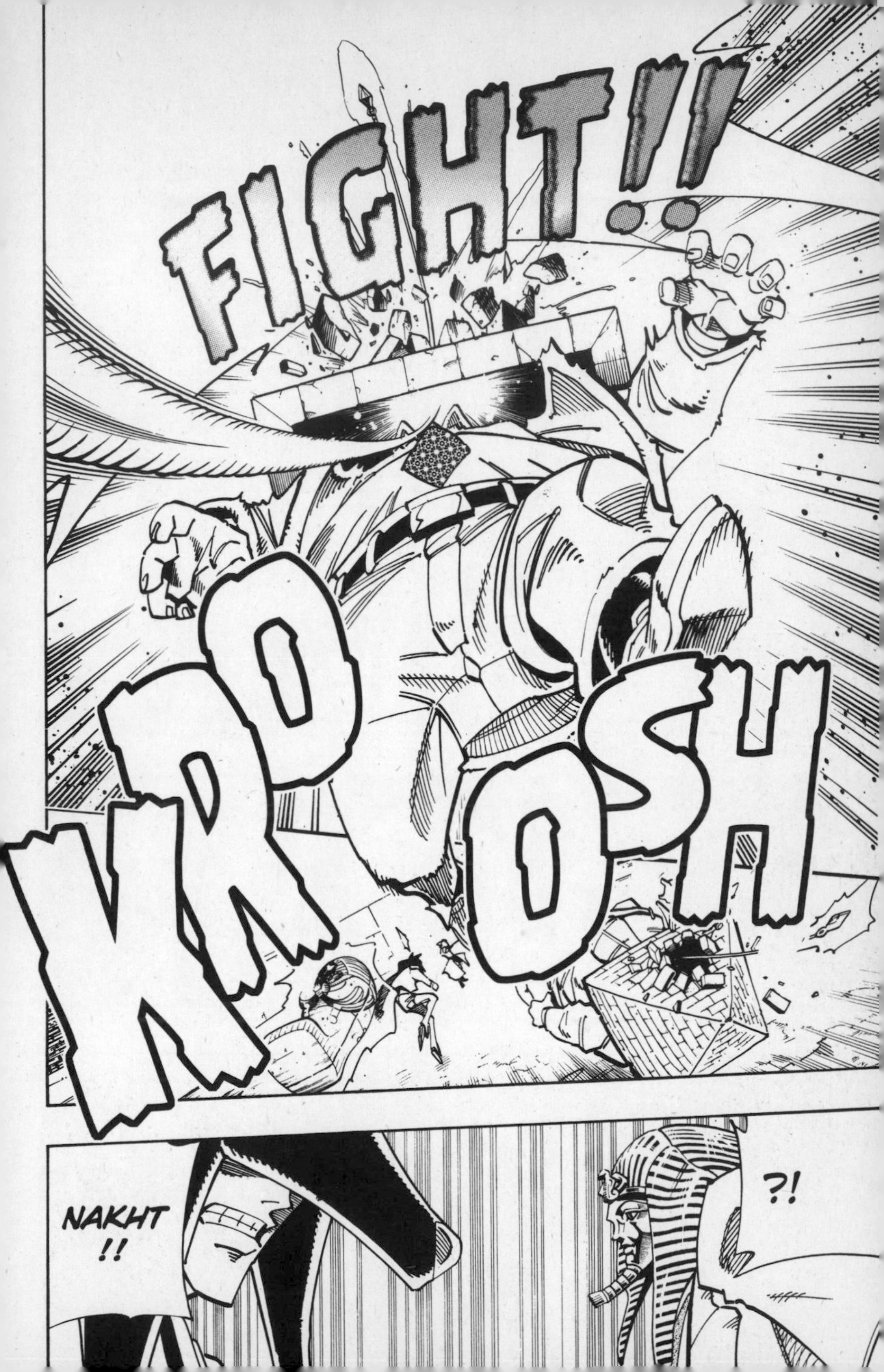
FIGHT!!
KROOSH
?!
NAKHT !!

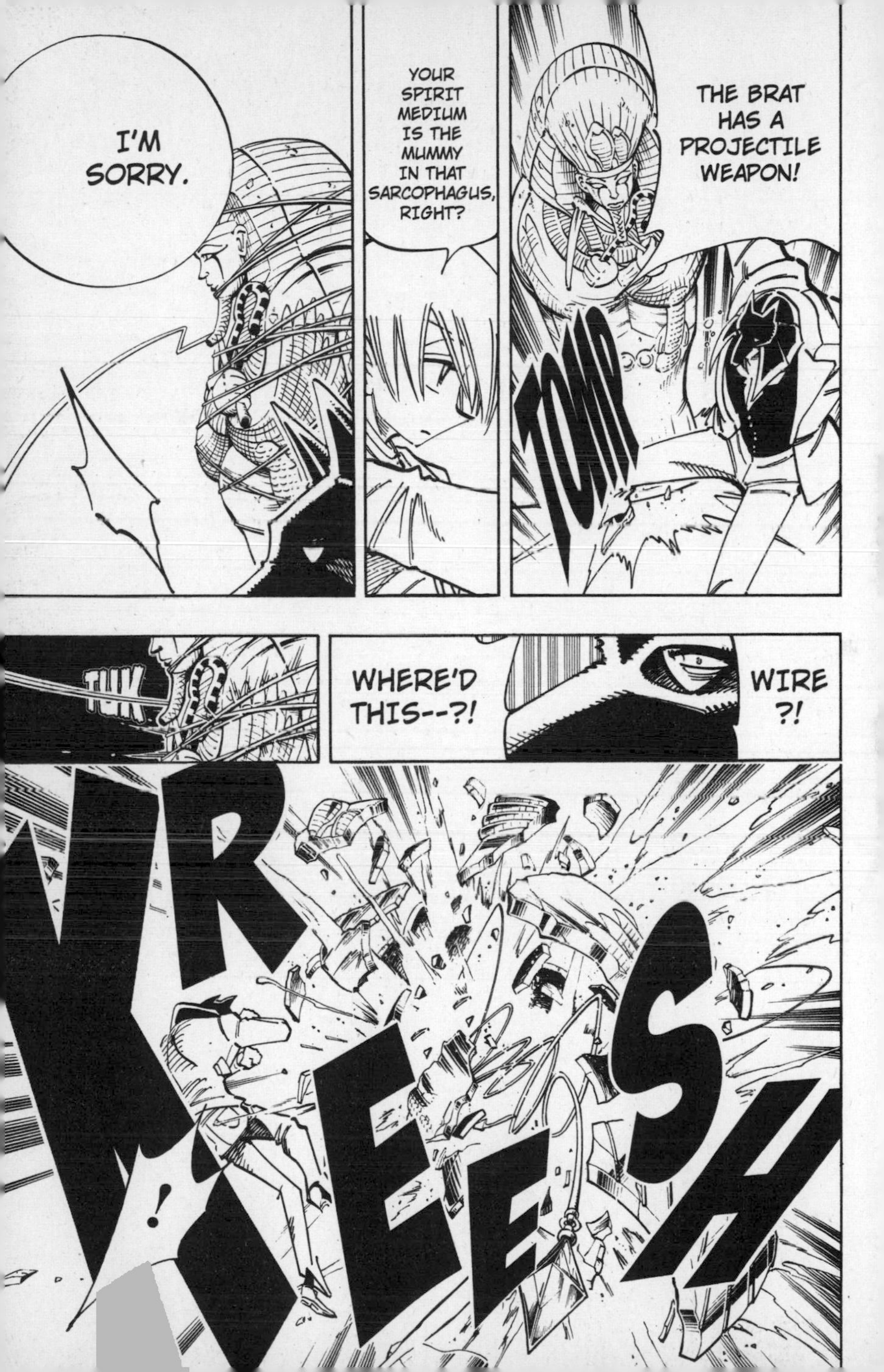
THE BRAT HAS A PROJECTILE WEAPON!
TOMP
YOUR SPIRIT MEDIUM IS THE MUMMY IN THAT SARCOPHAGUS, RIGHT?
I'M SORRY.
WIRE ?!
WHERE'D THIS--?!
TUK
WREESH
!

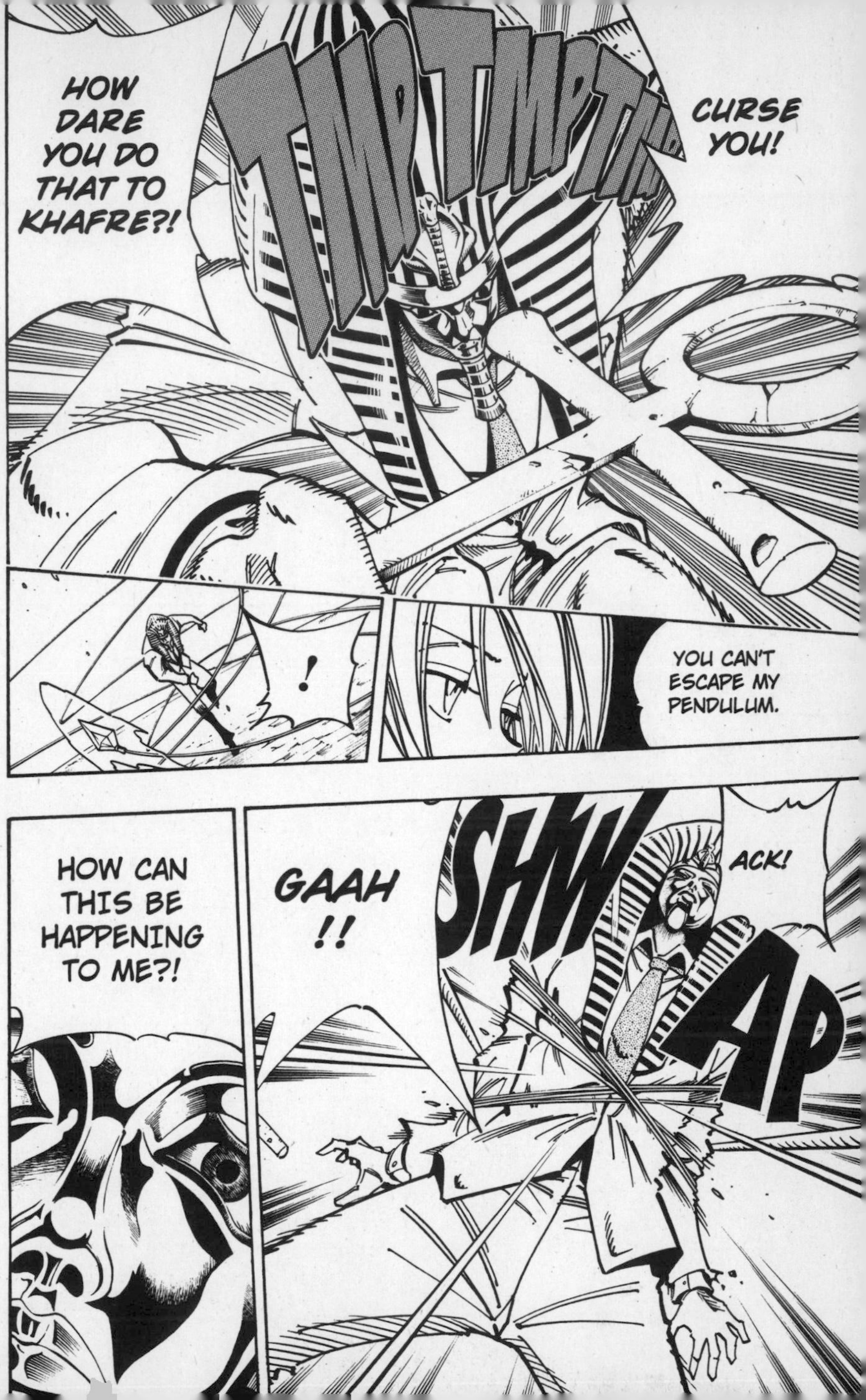
CURSE YOU!
HOW DARE YOU DO THAT TO KHAFRE?!
YOU CAN'T ESCAPE MY PENDULUM.
!
ACK!
SHWAP
GAAH !!
HOW CAN THIS BE HAPPENING TO ME?!

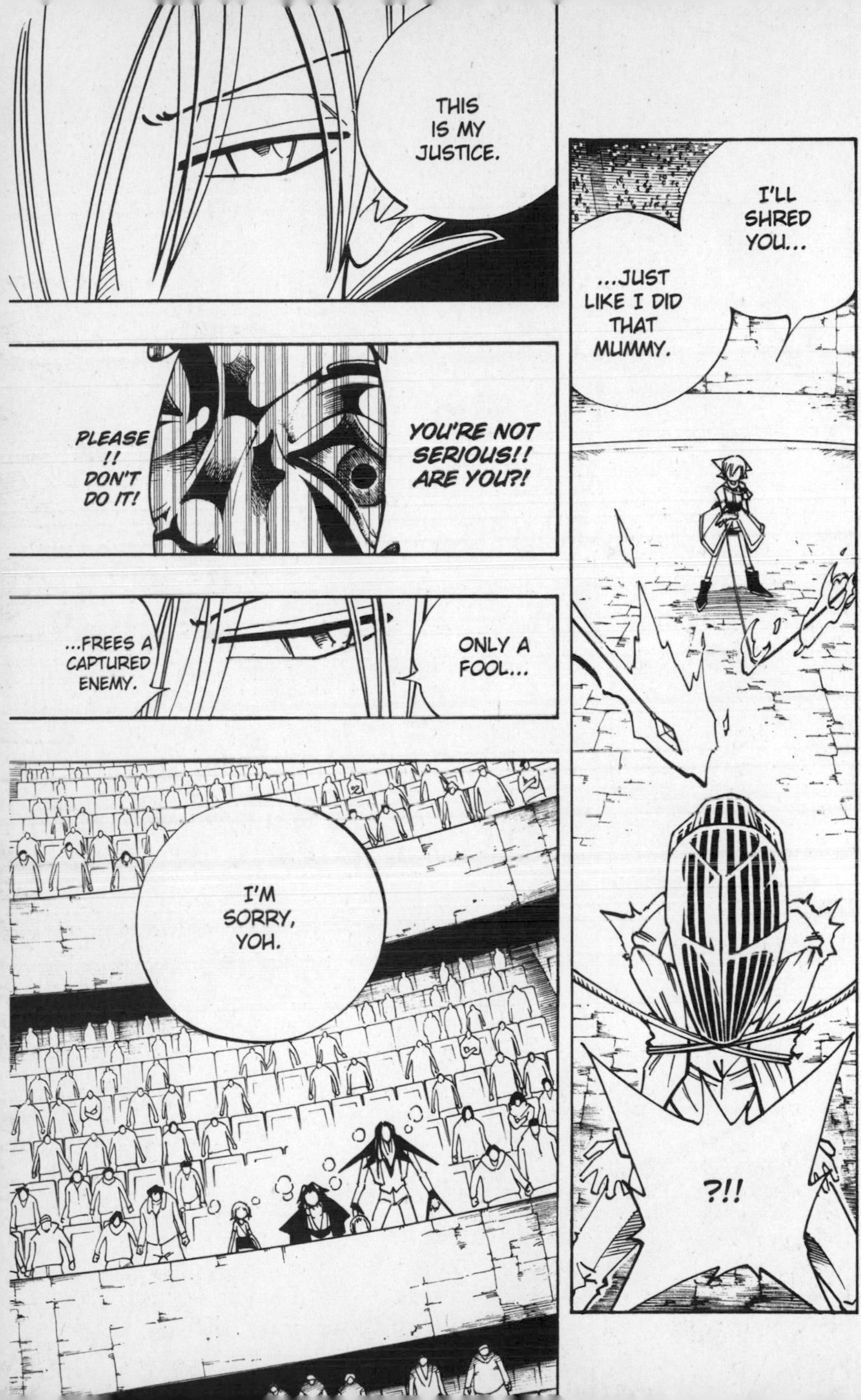

I'LL SHRED YOU...
...JUST LIKE I DID THAT MUMMY.
?!!
THIS IS MY JUSTICE.
YOU'RE NOT SERIOUS!! ARE YOU?!
PLEASE!! DON'T DO IT!
ONLY A FOOL...
...FREES A CAPTURED ENEMY.
I'M SORRY, YOH.

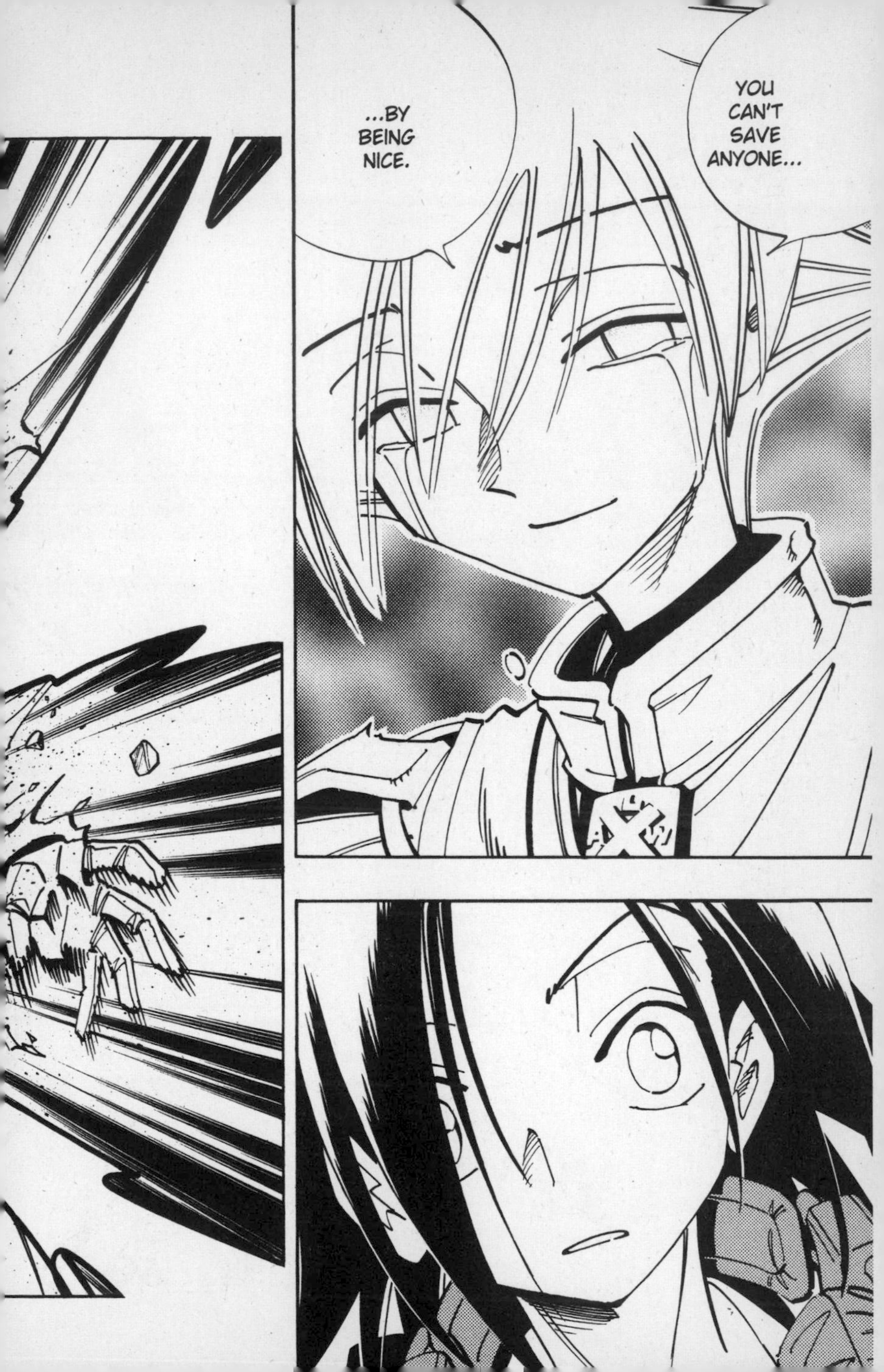
YOU CAN'T SAVE ANYONE...
...BY BEING NICE.

READ THIS WAY

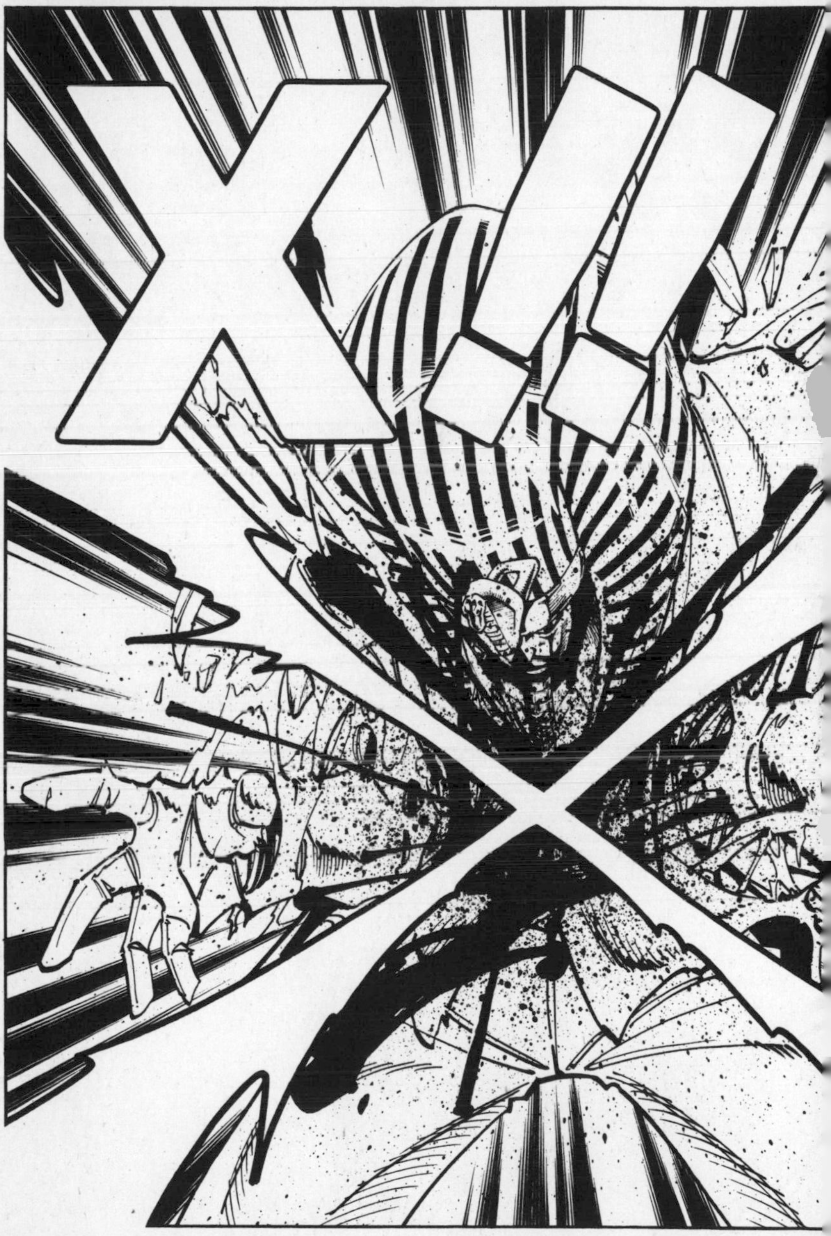
X!!

SHAMAN KING CHARACTER FILE No.67

マルコ
MARCO

2001
(JUNE)

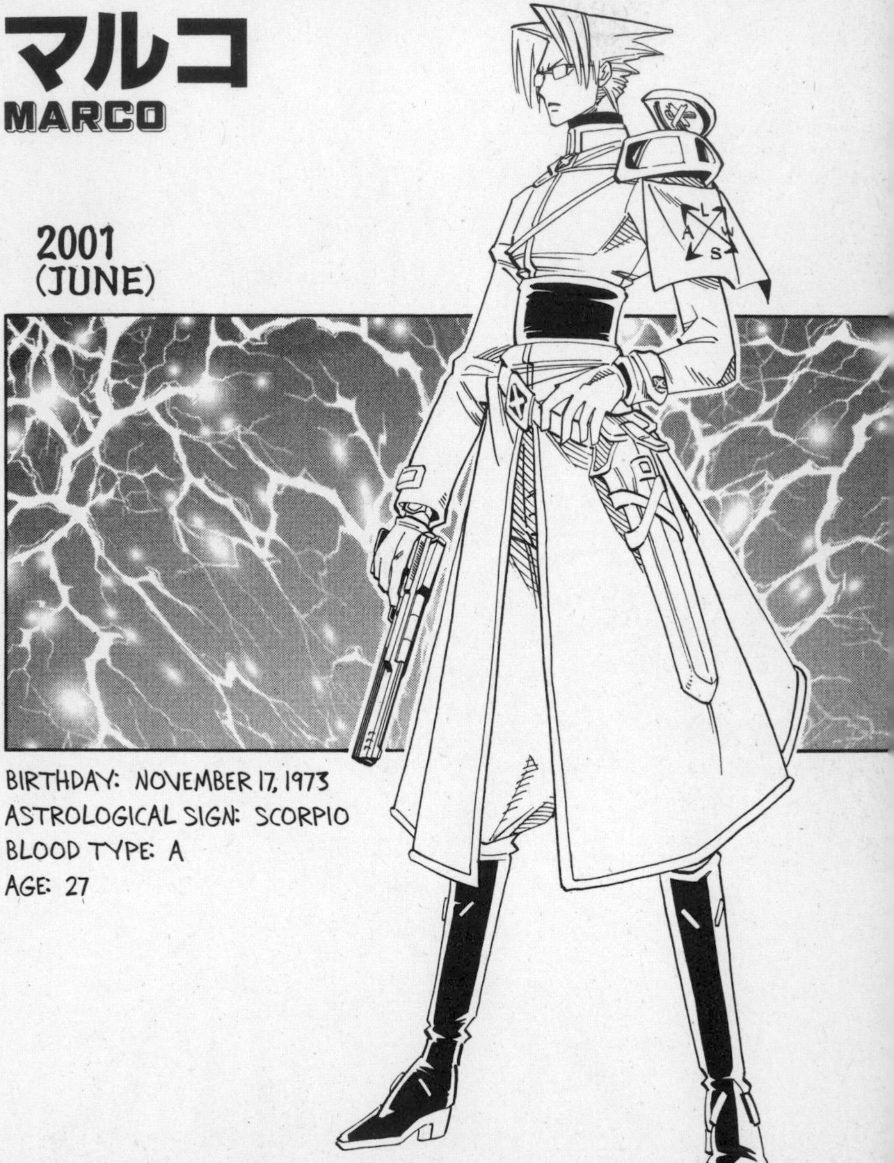

L
A
W
S

BIRTHDAY: NOVEMBER 17, 1973
ASTROLOGICAL SIGN: SCORPIO
BLOOD TYPE: A
AGE: 27

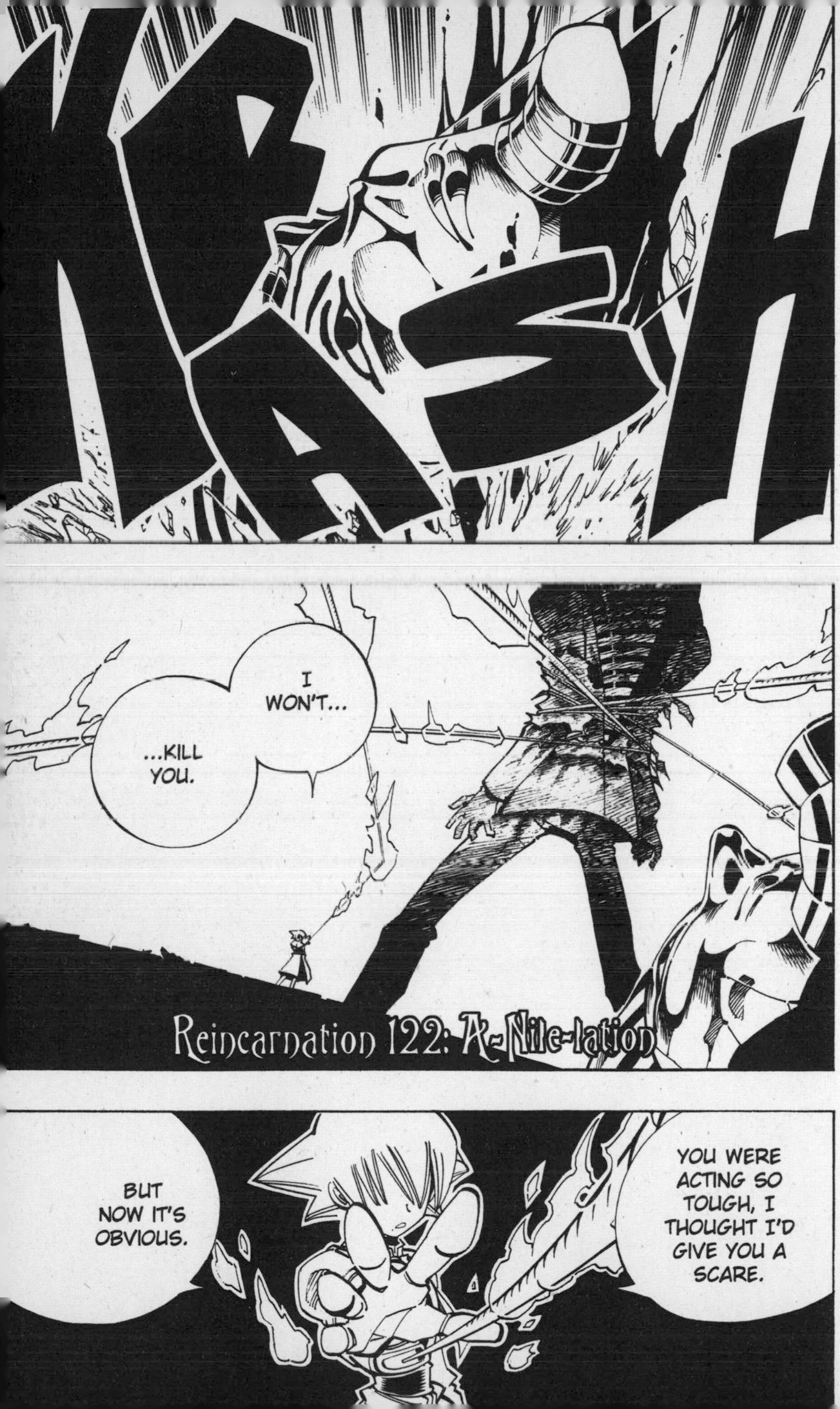
I WON'T...
...KILL YOU.
Reincarnation 122: A-Nile-lation
YOU WERE ACTING SO TOUGH, I THOUGHT I'D GIVE YOU A SCARE.
BUT NOW IT'S OBVIOUS.

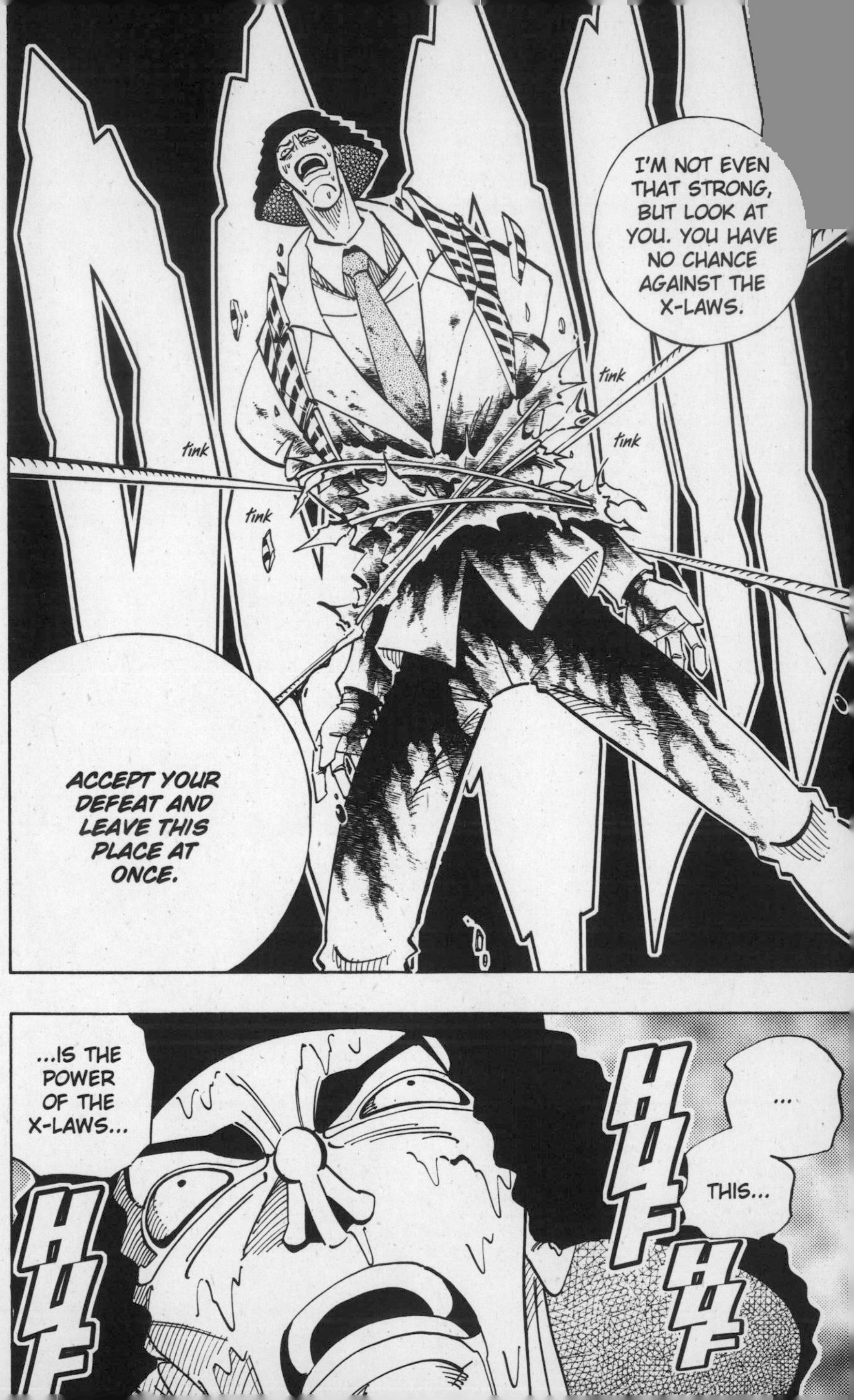

I'M NOT EVEN THAT STRONG, BUT LOOK AT YOU. YOU HAVE NO CHANCE AGAINST THE X-LAWS.
tink
tink
tink
tink
ACCEPT YOUR DEFEAT AND LEAVE THIS PLACE AT ONCE.
...
THIS...
HUF
HUF
...IS THE POWER OF THE X-LAWS...
HUF

Reincarnation 122:
A-Nile-lation

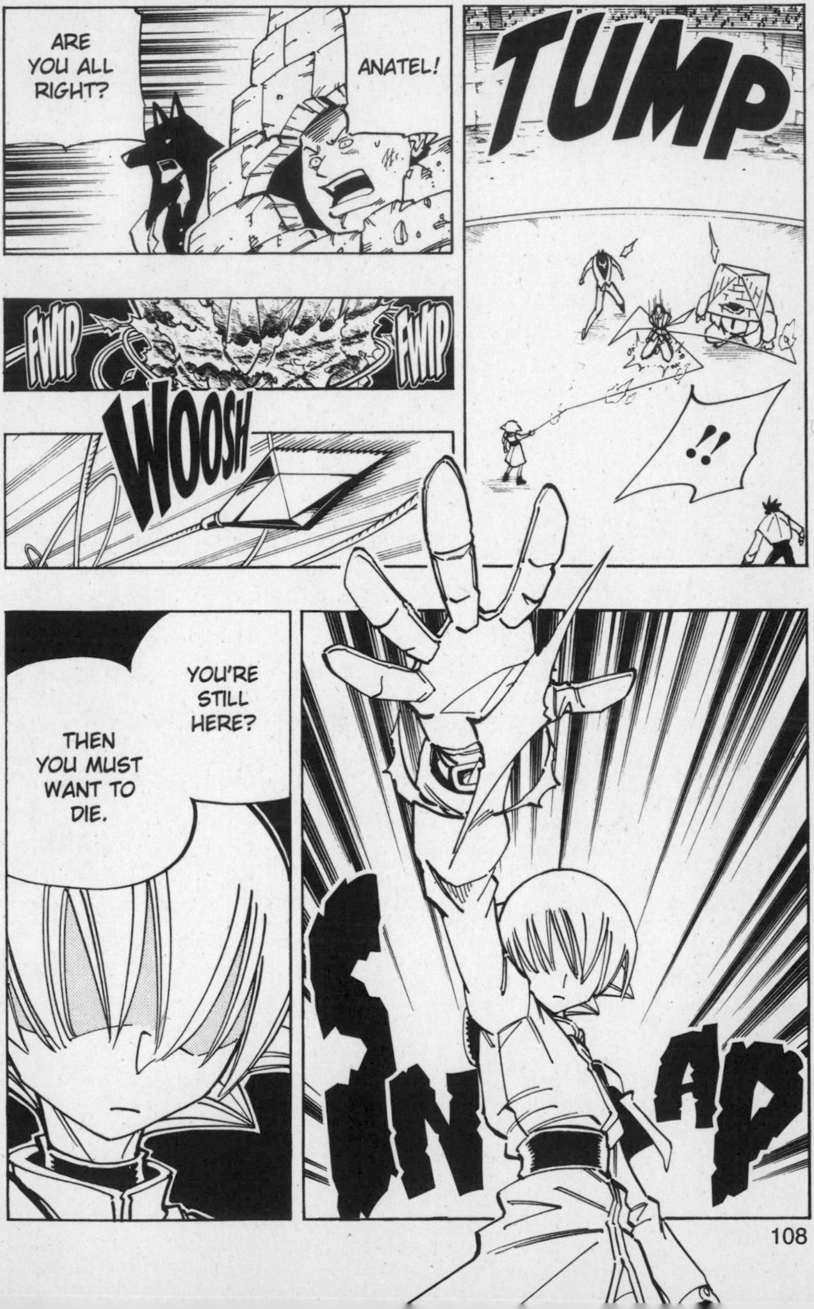
TUMP
!!
ANATEL!
ARE YOU ALL RIGHT?
FWIP
FWIP
WOOSH
SNAP
YOU'RE STILL HERE?
THEN YOU MUST WANT TO DIE.

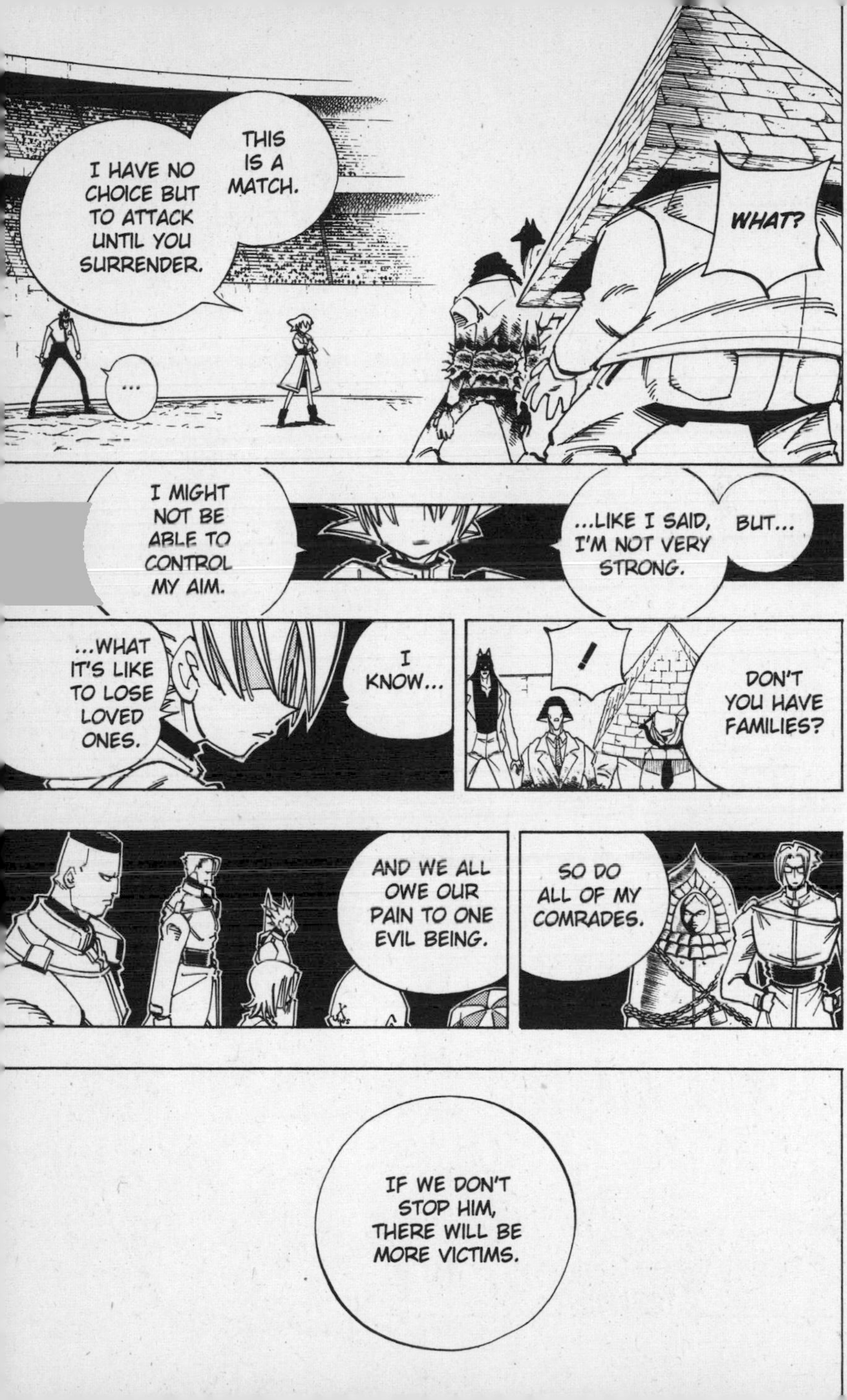
WHAT?
THIS IS A MATCH.
I HAVE NO CHOICE BUT TO ATTACK UNTIL YOU SURRENDER.
...
BUT...
...LIKE I SAID, I'M NOT VERY STRONG.
I MIGHT NOT BE ABLE TO CONTROL MY AIM.
!
DON'T YOU HAVE FAMILIES?
I KNOW...
...WHAT IT'S LIKE TO LOSE LOVED ONES.
SO DO ALL OF MY COMRADES.
AND WE ALL OWE OUR PAIN TO ONE EVIL BEING.
IF WE DON'T STOP HIM, THERE WILL BE MORE VICTIMS.

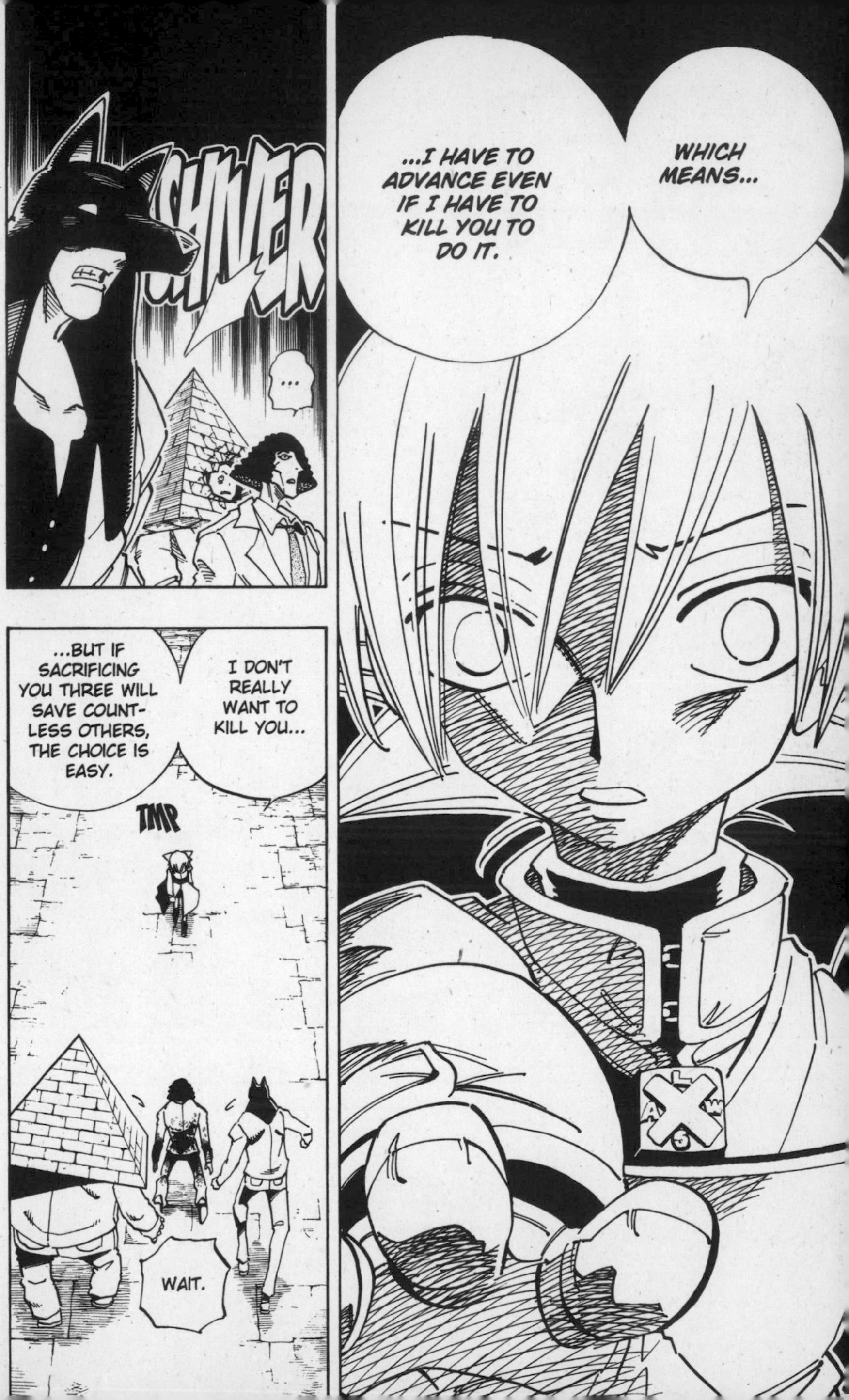
WHICH MEANS...
...I HAVE TO ADVANCE EVEN IF I HAVE TO KILL YOU TO DO IT.
SHIVER
...
I DON'T REALLY WANT TO KILL YOU...
...BUT IF SACRIFICING YOU THREE WILL SAVE COUNT-LESS OTHERS, THE CHOICE IS EASY.
TMP
WAIT.

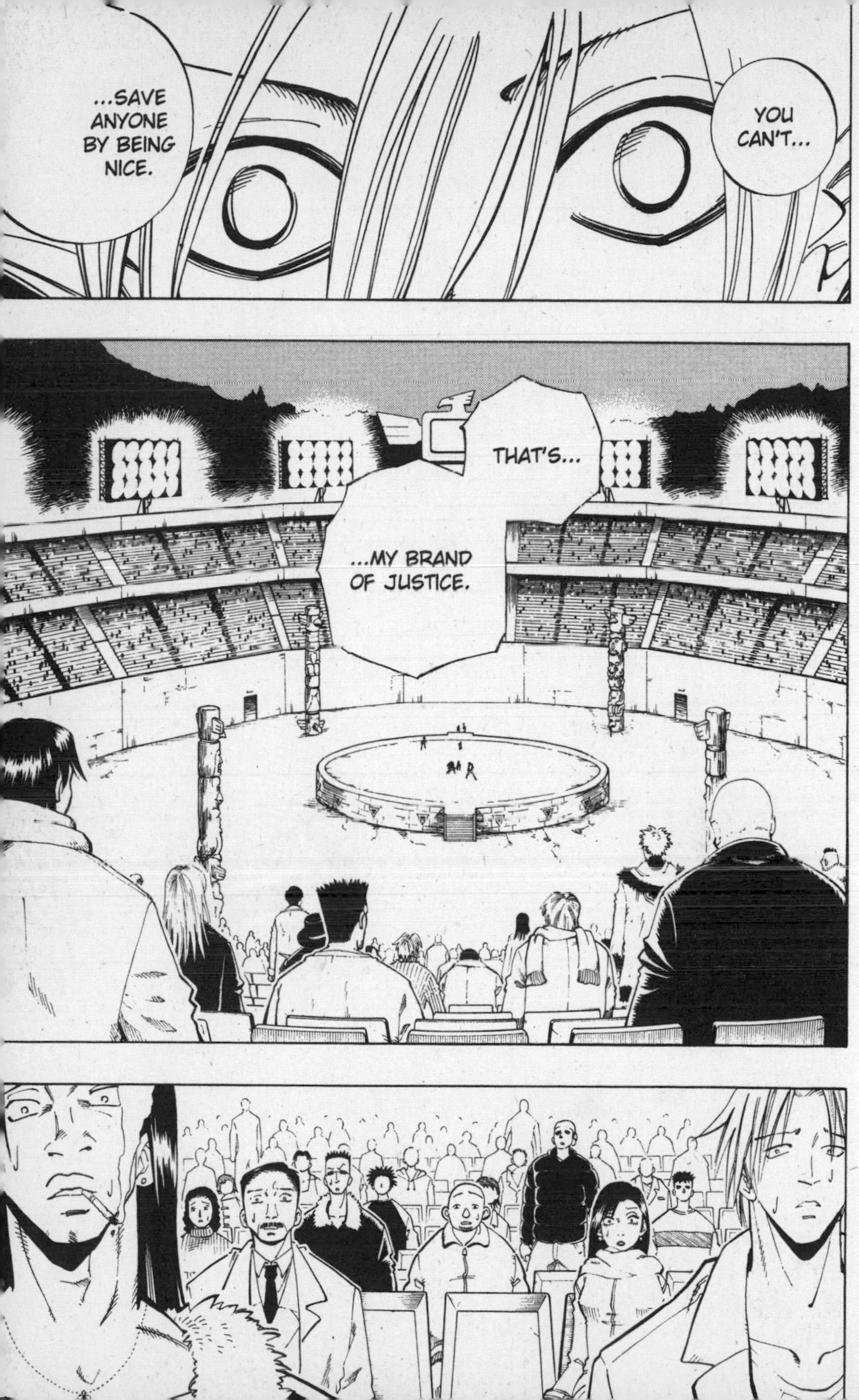
YOU CAN'T...
...SAVE ANYONE BY BEING NICE.
THAT'S...
...MY BRAND OF JUSTICE.

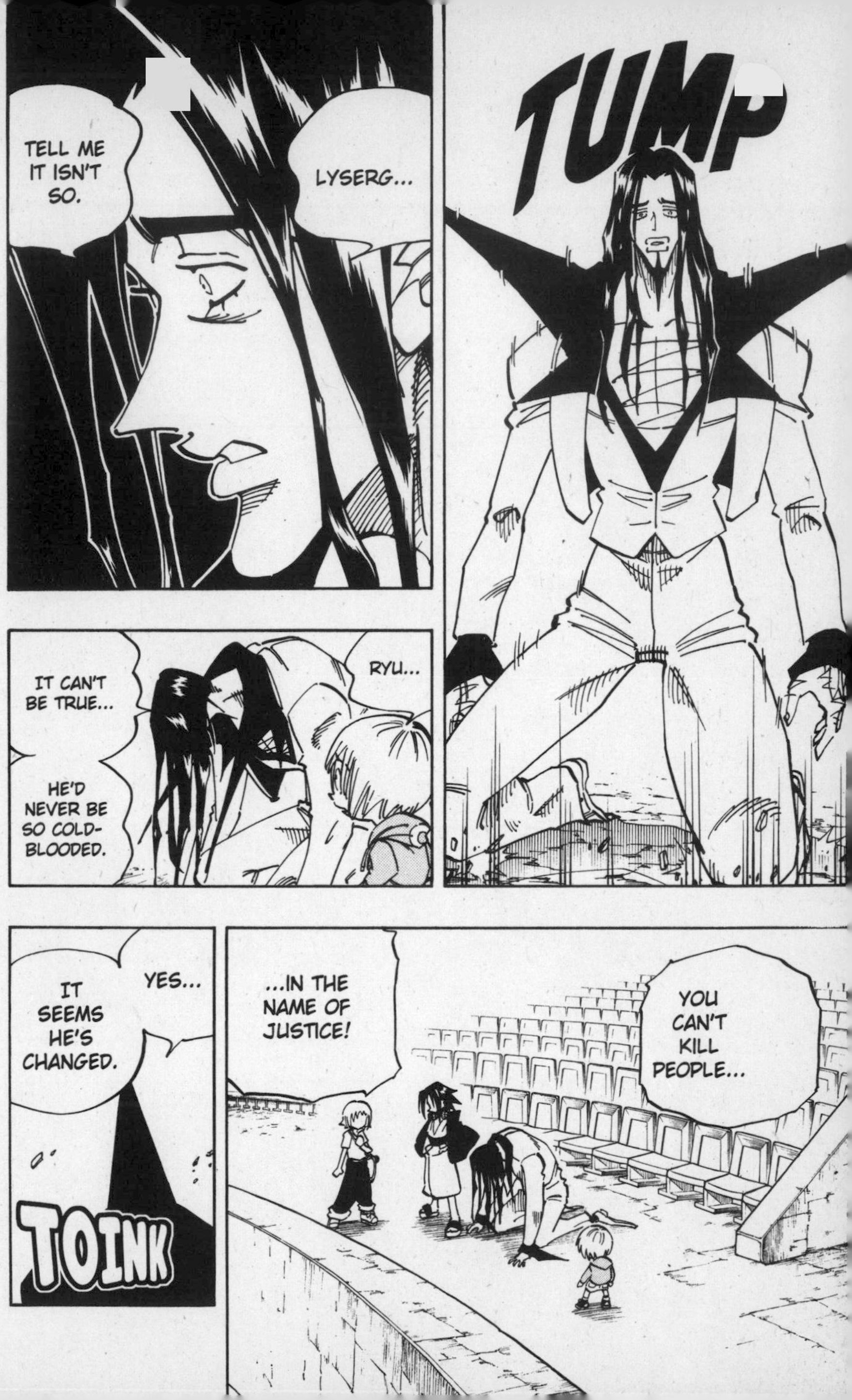
TUMP
LYSERG...
TELL ME IT ISN'T SO.
RYU...
IT CAN'T BE TRUE...
HE'D NEVER BE SO COLD-BLOODED.
YOU CAN'T KILL PEOPLE...
...IN THE NAME OF JUSTICE!
YES...
IT SEEMS HE'S CHANGED.
TOINK

READ THIS WAY

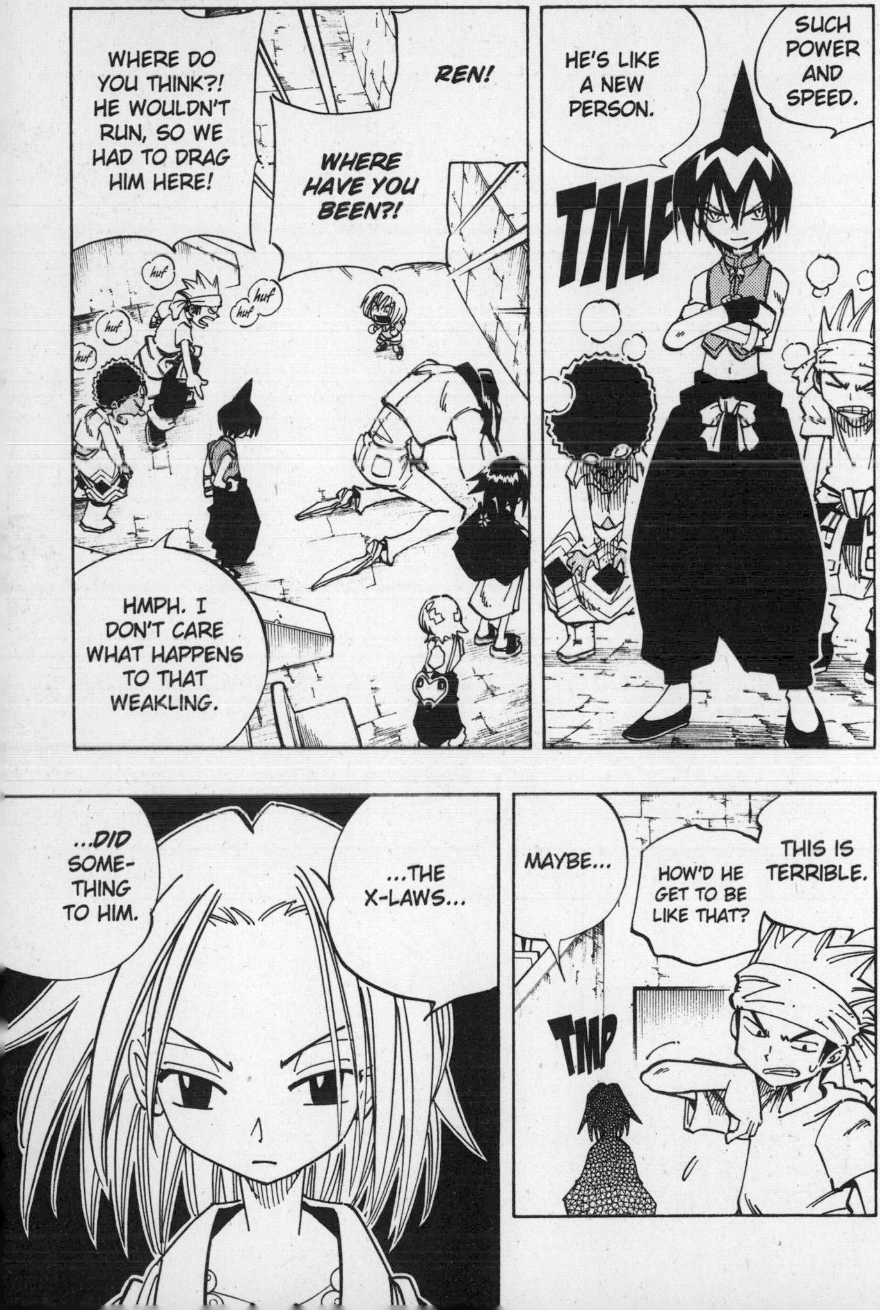
SUCH POWER AND SPEED.
HE'S LIKE A NEW PERSON.
TMP
REN!
WHERE HAVE YOU BEEN?!
WHERE DO YOU THINK?! HE WOULDN'T RUN, SO WE HAD TO DRAG HIM HERE!
huf
huf
huf
huf
huf
HMPH. I DON'T CARE WHAT HAPPENS TO THAT WEAKLING.
THIS IS TERRIBLE.
HOW'D HE GET TO BE LIKE THAT?
MAYBE...
TMP
...THE X-LAWS...
...DID SOMETHING TO HIM.

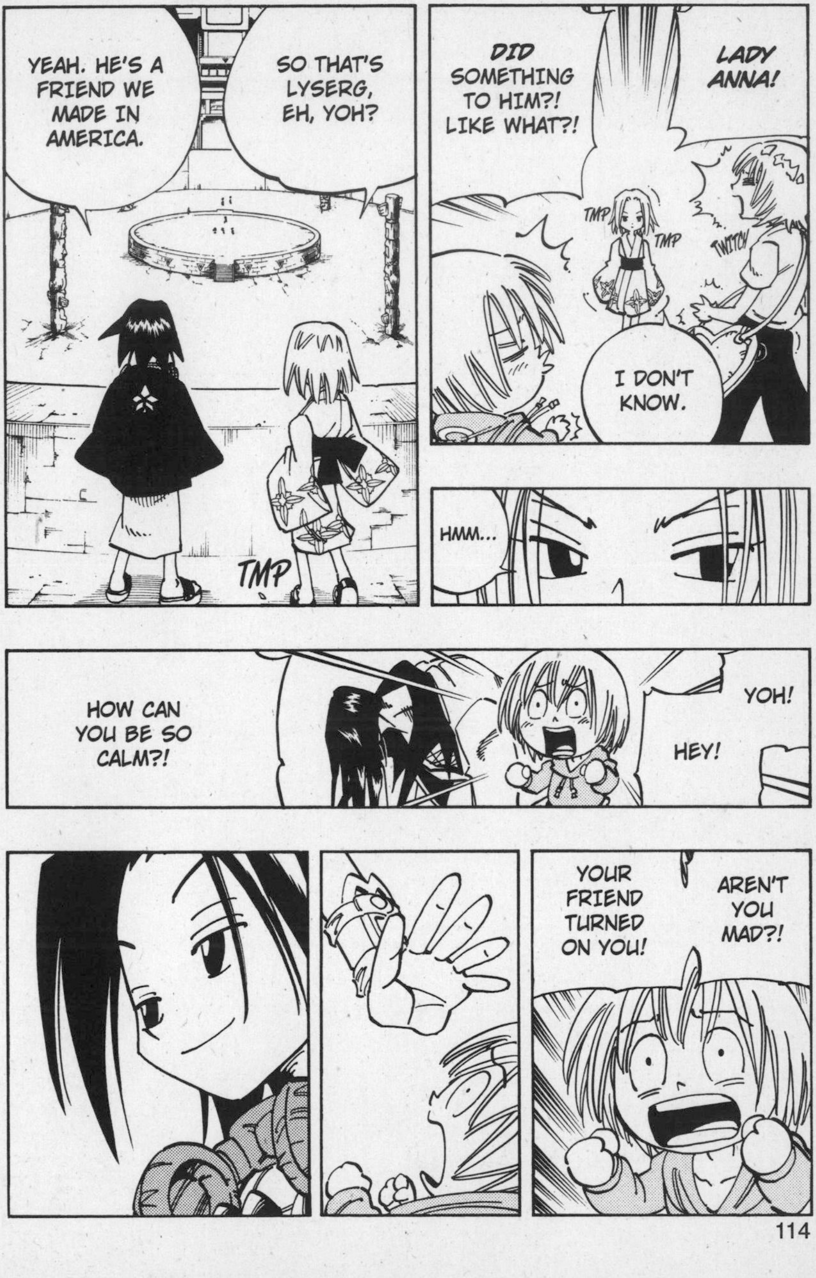
LADY ANNA!
DID SOMETHING TO HIM?! LIKE WHAT?!
TMP
TMP
TWITCH
I DON'T KNOW.
HMM...
SO THAT'S LYSERG, EH, YOH?
YEAH. HE'S A FRIEND WE MADE IN AMERICA.
TMP
YOH!
HEY!
HOW CAN YOU BE SO CALM?!
AREN'T YOU MAD?!
YOUR FRIEND TURNED ON YOU!

READ THIS WAY

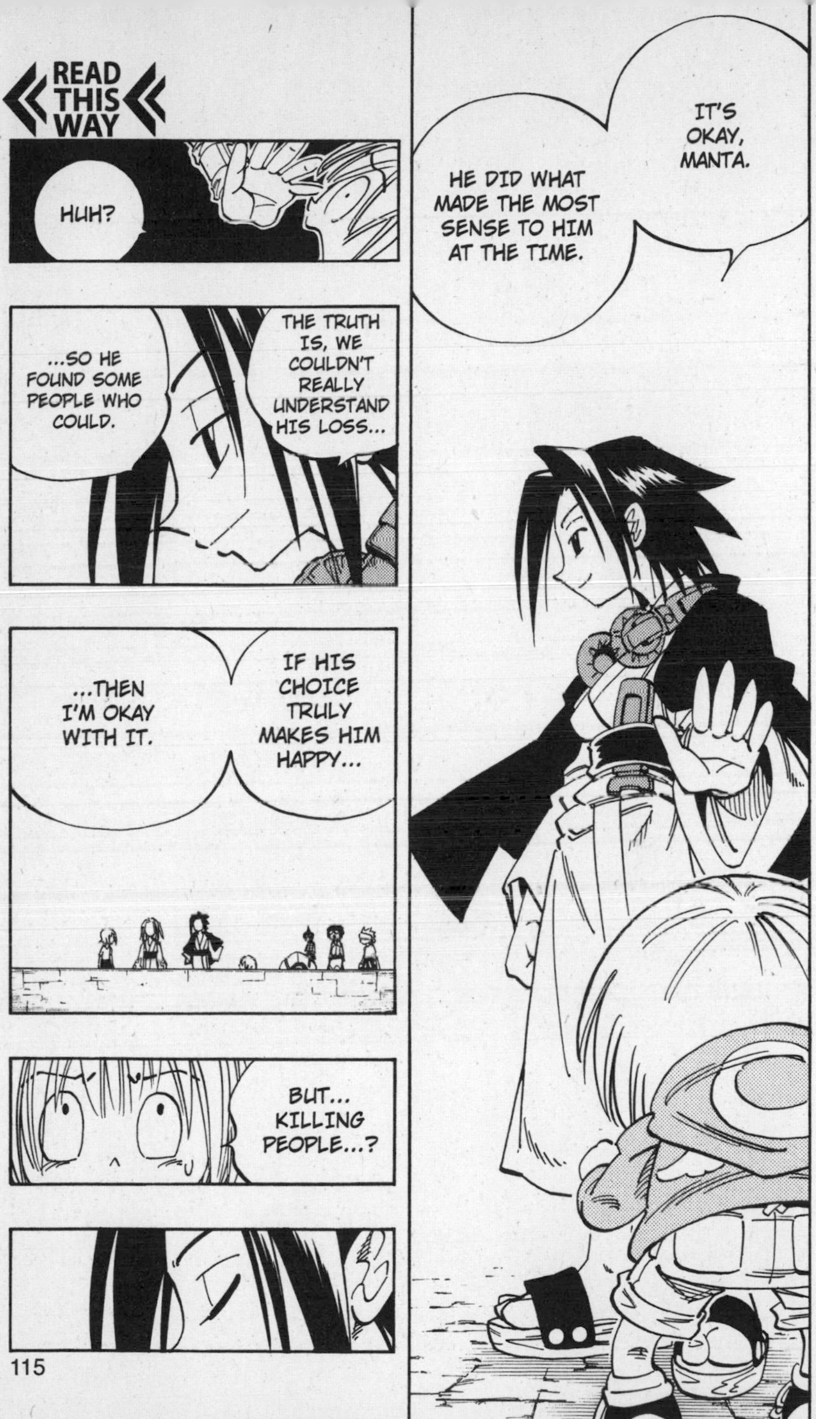
IT'S OKAY, MANTA.
HE DID WHAT MADE THE MOST SENSE TO HIM AT THE TIME.
HUH?
THE TRUTH IS, WE COULDN'T REALLY UNDERSTAND HIS LOSS...
...SO HE FOUND SOME PEOPLE WHO COULD.
IF HIS CHOICE TRULY MAKES HIM HAPPY...
...THEN I'M OKAY WITH IT.
BUT... KILLING PEOPLE...?

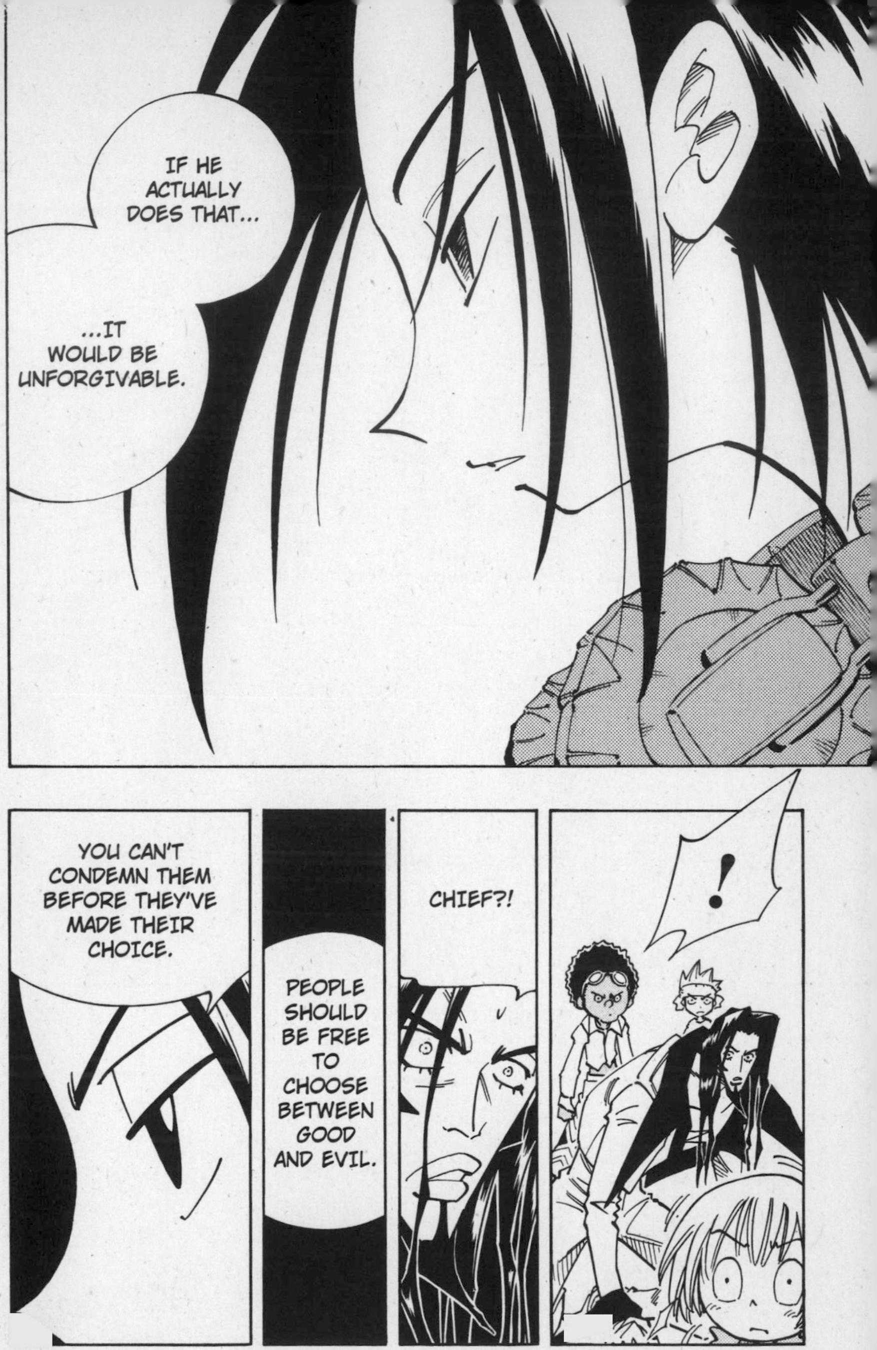
IF HE ACTUALLY DOES THAT...
...IT WOULD BE UNFORGIVABLE.
!
CHIEF?!
PEOPLE SHOULD BE FREE TO CHOOSE BETWEEN GOOD AND EVIL.
YOU CAN'T CONDEMN THEM BEFORE THEY'VE MADE THEIR CHOICE.

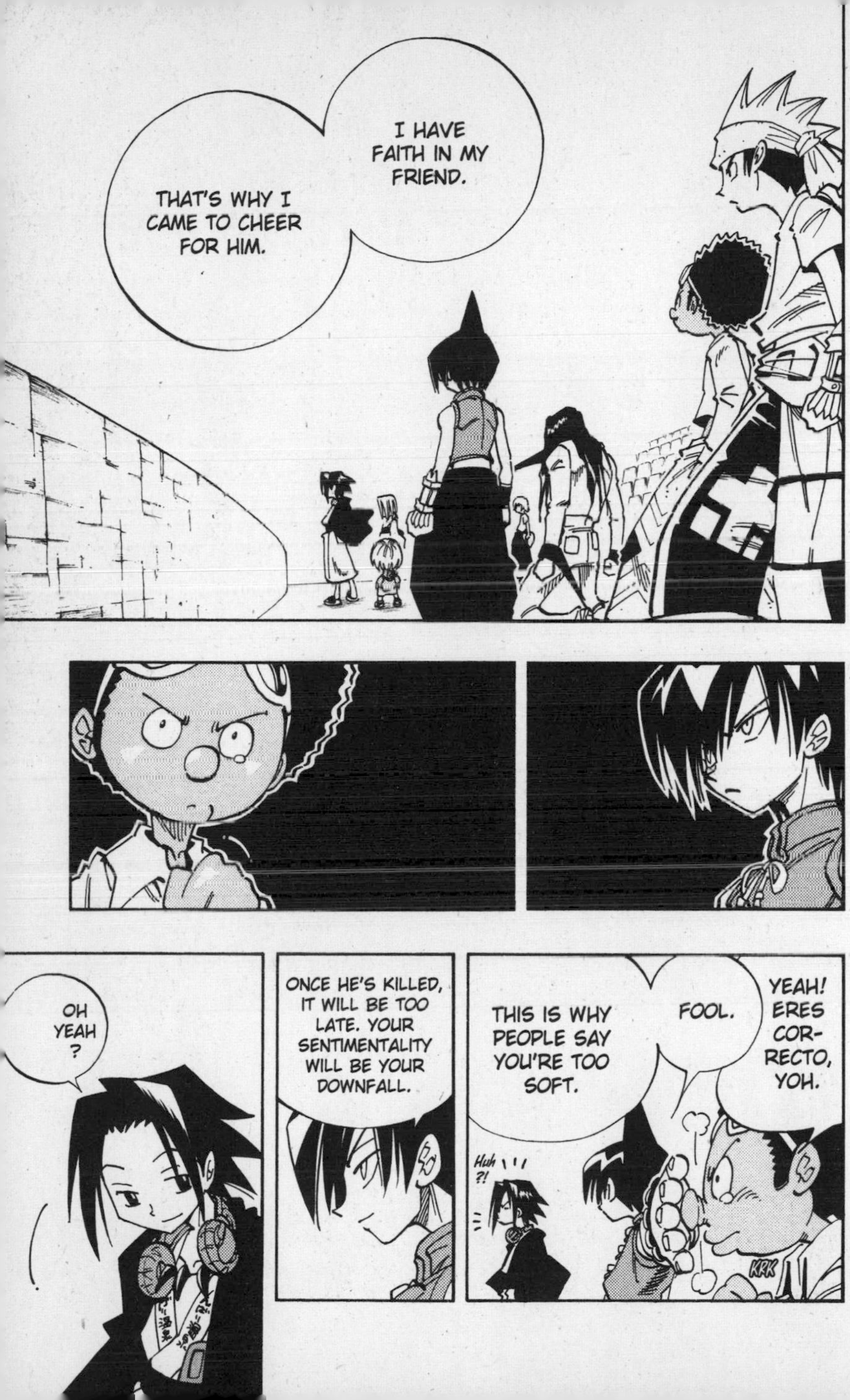
I HAVE FAITH IN MY FRIEND.
THAT'S WHY I CAME TO CHEER FOR HIM.
YEAH! ERES COR-RECTO, YOH.
FOOL.
THIS IS WHY PEOPLE SAY YOU'RE TOO SOFT.
Huh ?!
KRK
ONCE HE'S KILLED, IT WILL BE TOO LATE. YOUR SENTIMENTALITY WILL BE YOUR DOWNFALL.
OH YEAH ?

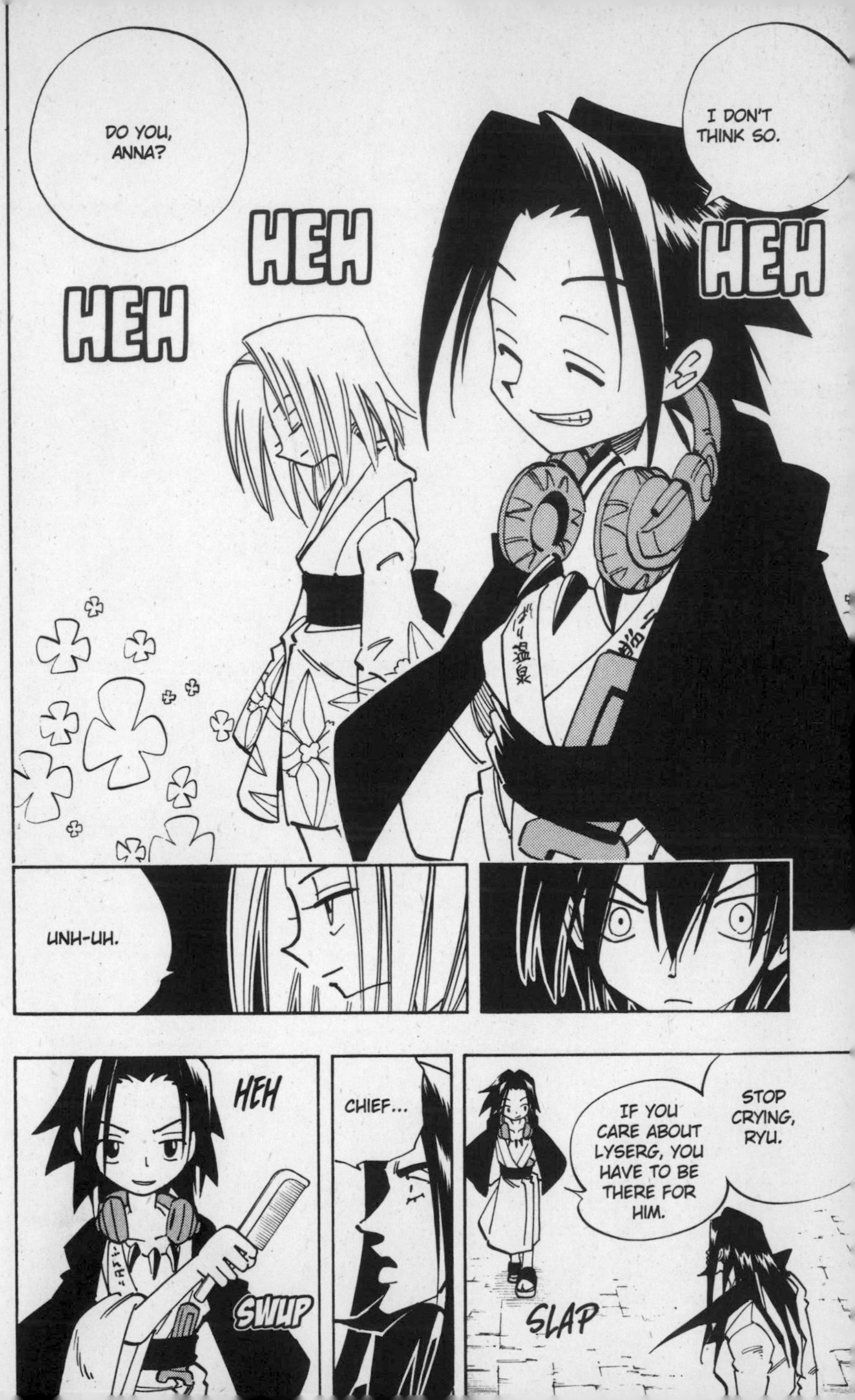
I DON'T THINK SO.
HEH
DO YOU, ANNA?
HEH
HEH
UNH-UH.
STOP CRYING, RYU.
IF YOU CARE ABOUT LYSERG, YOU HAVE TO BE THERE FOR HIM.
SLAP
CHIEF...
HEH
SWUP

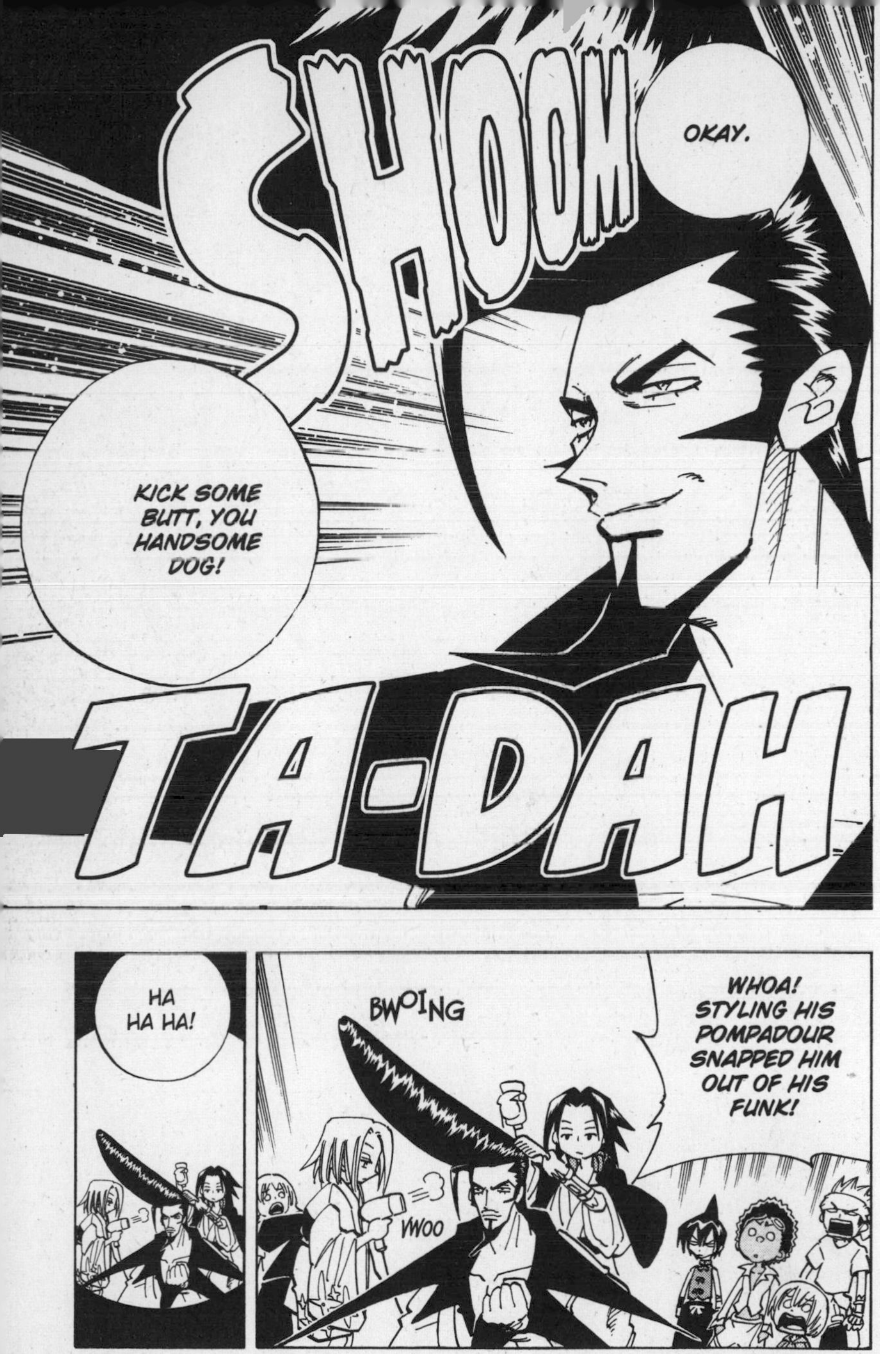
OKAY.
SHOOM
KICK SOME BUTT, YOU HANDSOME DOG!
T-A-DAH
WHOA! STYLING HIS POMPADOUR SNAPPED HIM OUT OF HIS FUNK!
BWOING
VWOO
HA HA HA!

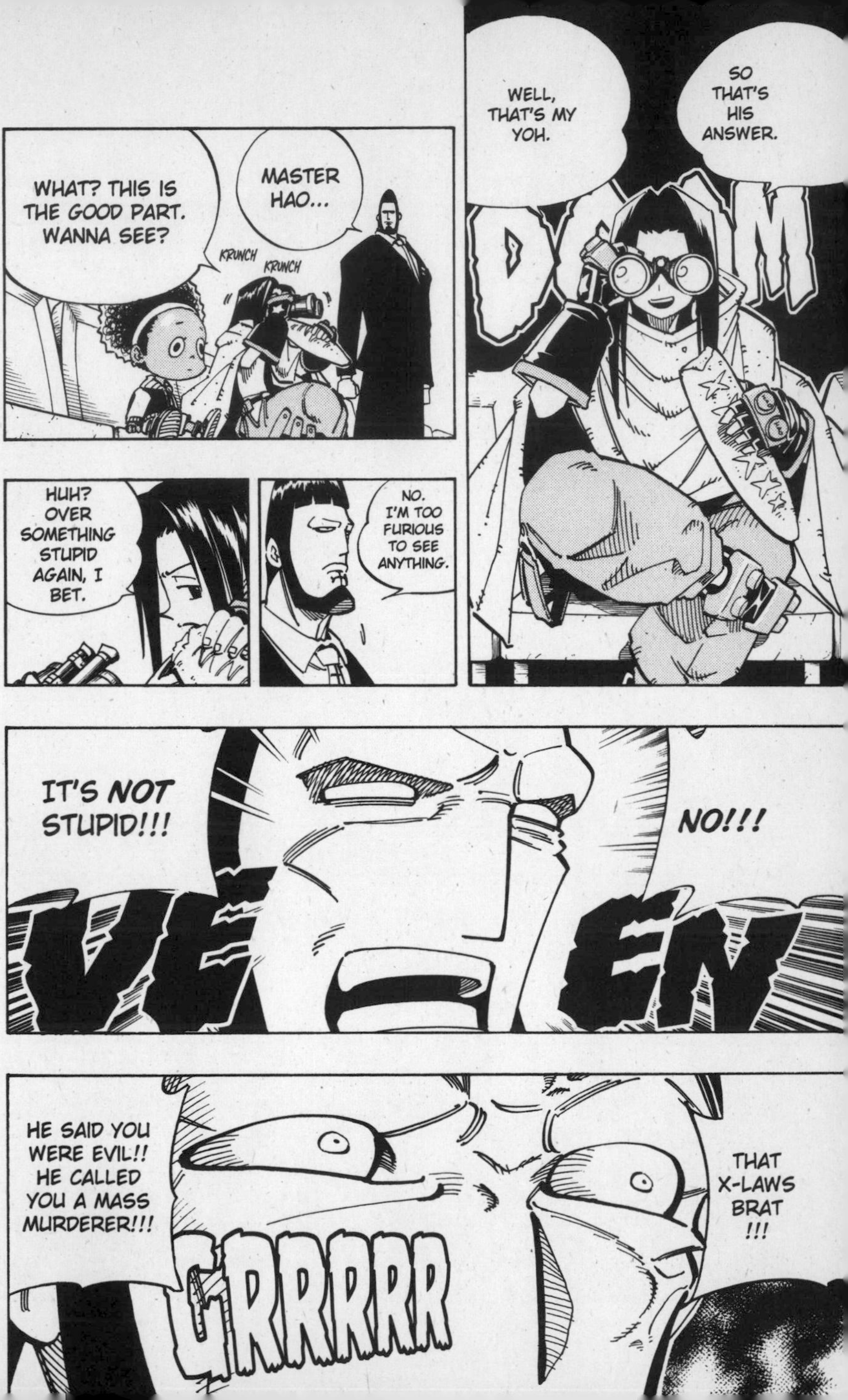
SO THAT'S HIS ANSWER.
WELL, THAT'S MY YOH.
MASTER HAO...
WHAT? THIS IS THE GOOD PART. WANNA SEE?
KRUNCH
KRUNCH
NO. I'M TOO FURIOUS TO SEE ANYTHING.
HUH? OVER SOMETHING STUPID AGAIN, I BET.
NO!!!
IT'S NOT STUPID!!!
THAT X-LAWS BRAT!!!
HE SAID YOU WERE EVIL!! HE CALLED YOU A MASS MURDERER!!!
GRRRRR

READ THIS WAY

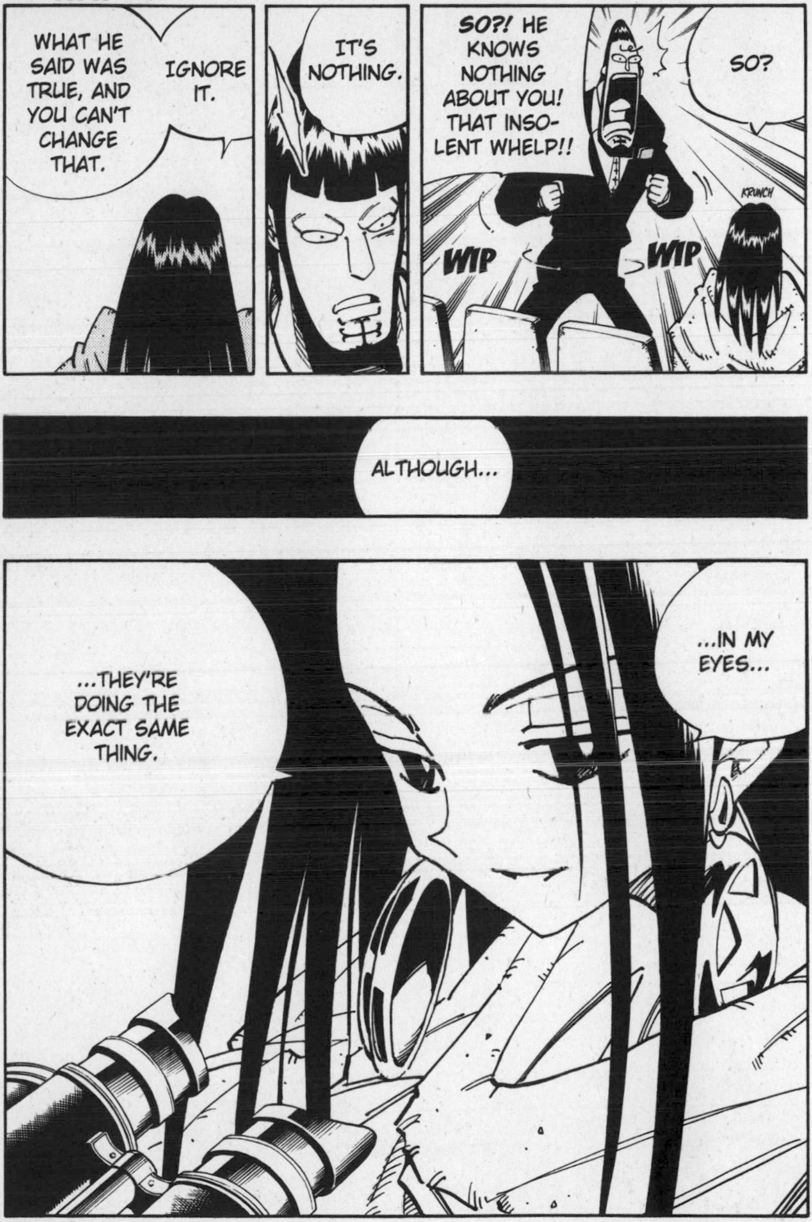

SO?
KRUNCH
SO?! HE KNOWS NOTHING ABOUT YOU! THAT INSOLENT WHELP!!
WIP
WIP
IT'S NOTHING.
IGNORE IT.
WHAT HE SAID WAS TRUE, AND YOU CAN'T CHANGE THAT.
ALTHOUGH...
...IN MY EYES...
...THEY'RE DOING THE EXACT SAME THING.

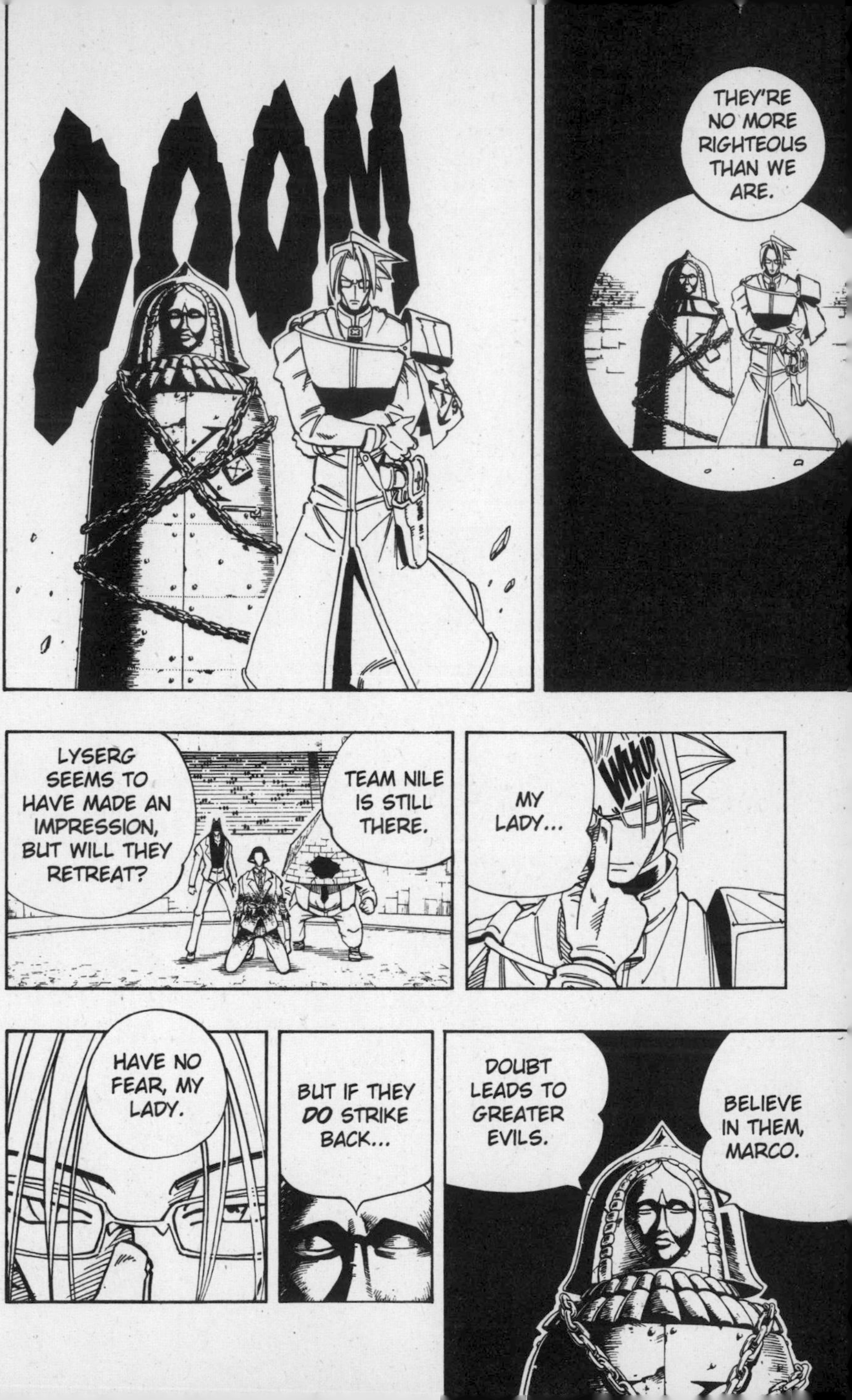
THEY'RE NO MORE RIGHTEOUS THAN WE ARE.
DOOM
WHUP
MY LADY...
TEAM NILE IS STILL THERE.
LYSERG SEEMS TO HAVE MADE AN IMPRESSION, BUT WILL THEY RETREAT?
BELIEVE IN THEM, MARCO.
DOUBT LEADS TO GREATER EVILS.
BUT IF THEY *DO* STRIKE BACK...
HAVE NO FEAR, MY LADY.

READ THIS WAY

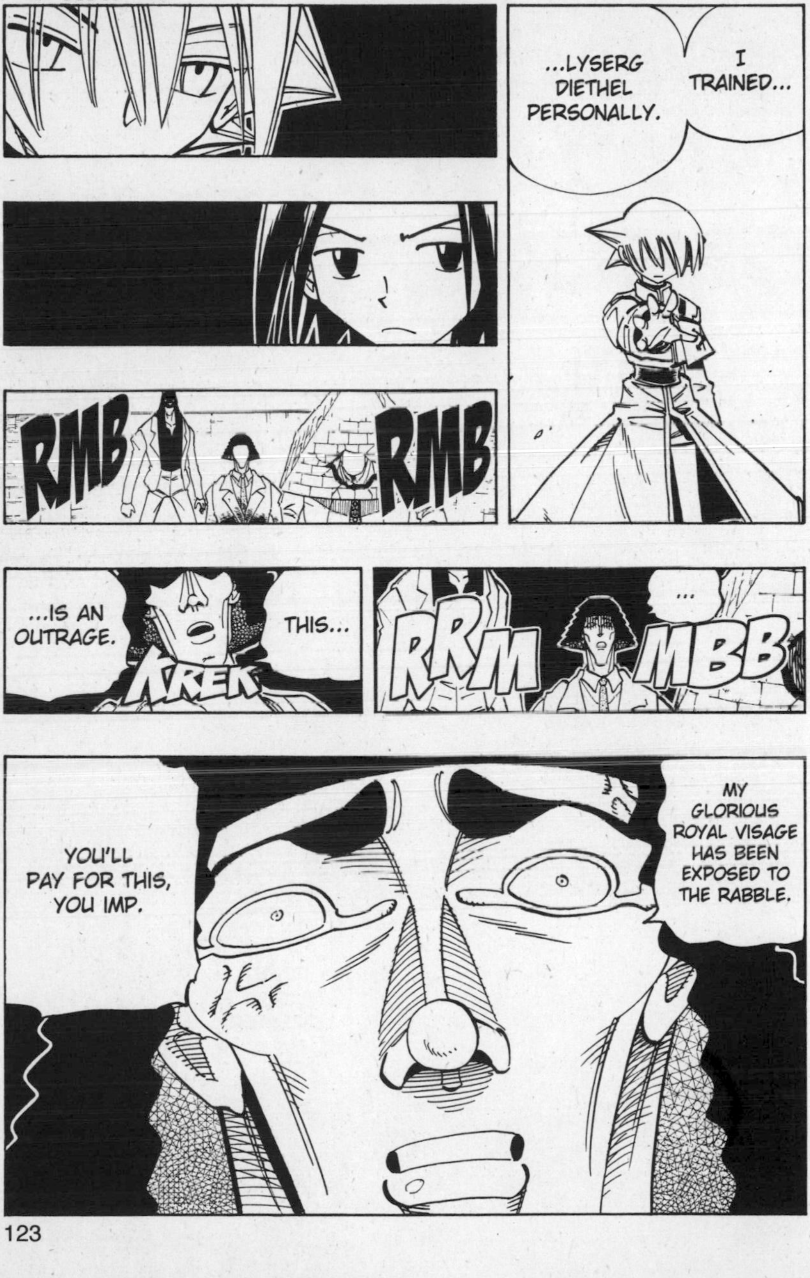
I TRAINED...
...LYSERG DIETHEL PERSONALLY.
RMB
RMB
...
RRM
MBB
THIS...
...IS AN OUTRAGE.
KREK
MY GLORIOUS ROYAL VISAGE HAS BEEN EXPOSED TO THE RABBLE.
YOU'LL PAY FOR THIS, YOU IMP.

SHAMAN KING CHARACTER FILE No.68

聖(せい)・少(しょう)・女(じょ)アイアンメイデン・ジャンヌ

HOLY GIRL IRON MAIDEN・JEANNE

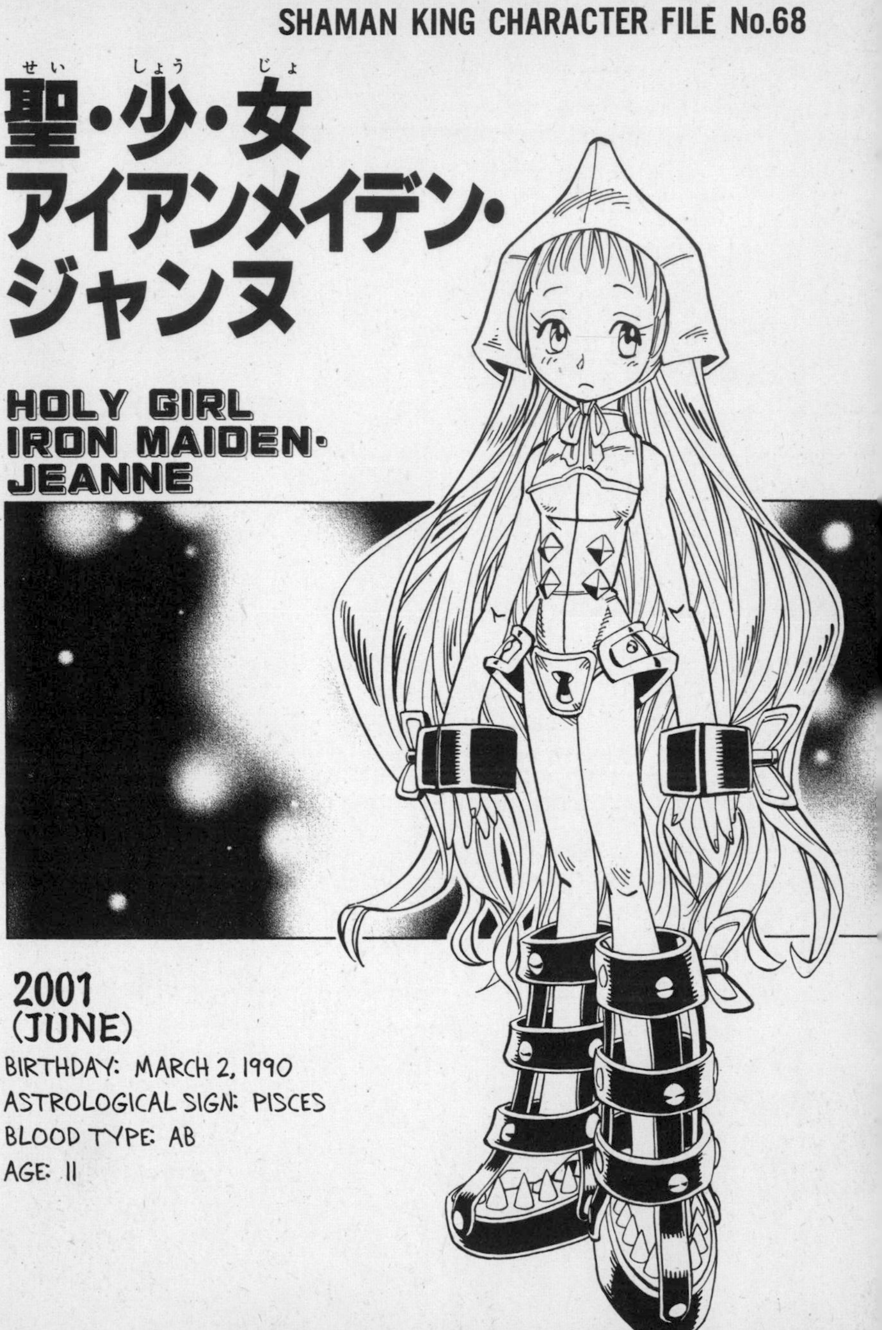

2001 (JUNE)

BIRTHDAY: MARCH 2, 1990

ASTROLOGICAL SIGN: PISCES

BLOOD TYPE: AB

AGE: 11

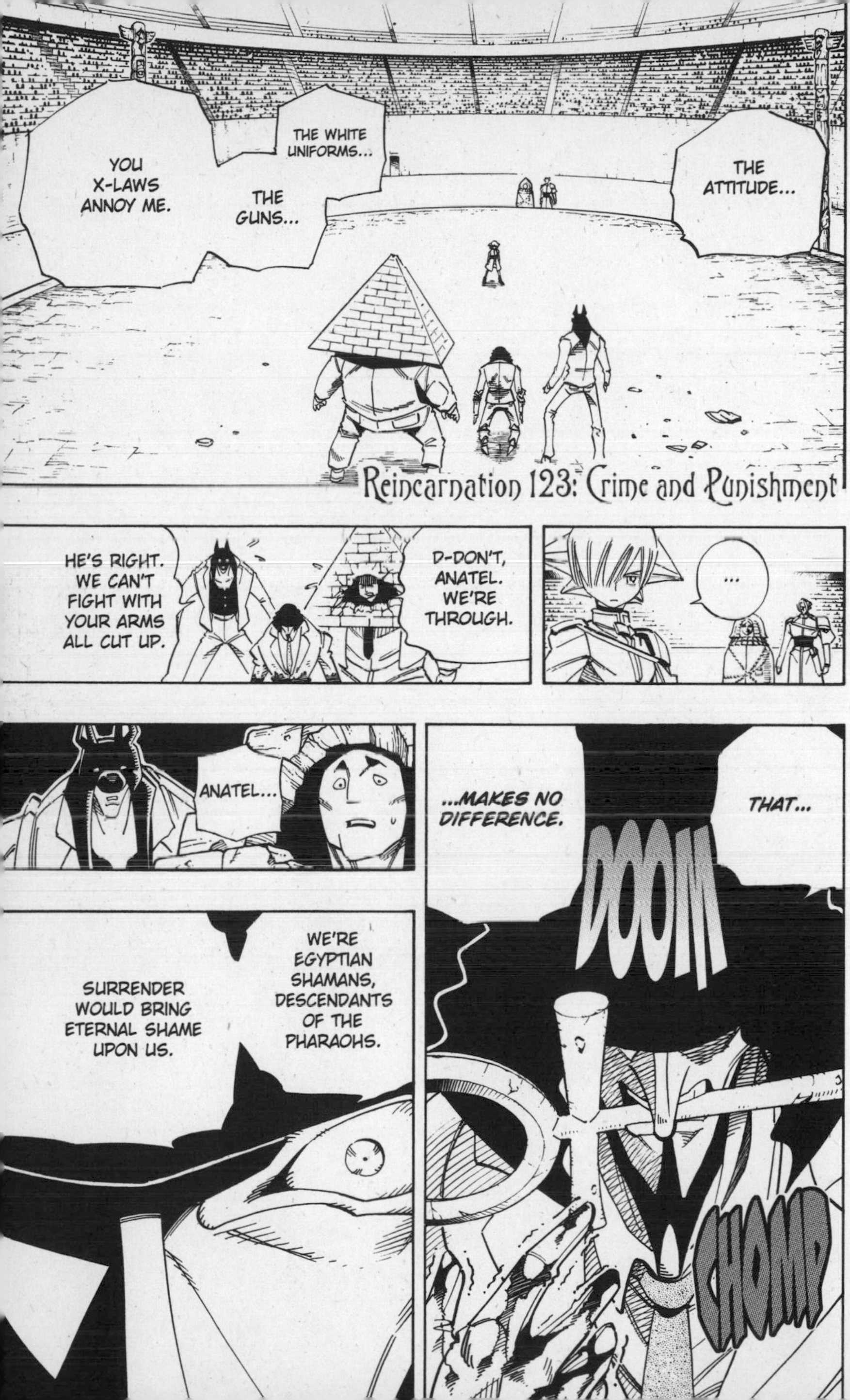
THE ATTITUDE...
THE WHITE UNIFORMS...
THE GUNS...
YOU X-LAWS ANNOY ME.
Reincarnation 123: Crime and Punishment
...
D-DON'T, ANATEL. WE'RE THROUGH.
HE'S RIGHT. WE CAN'T FIGHT WITH YOUR ARMS ALL CUT UP.
THAT...
...MAKES NO DIFFERENCE.
DOOM
CHOMP
ANATEL...
WE'RE EGYPTIAN SHAMANS, DESCENDANTS OF THE PHARAOHS.
SURRENDER WOULD BRING ETERNAL SHAME UPON US.

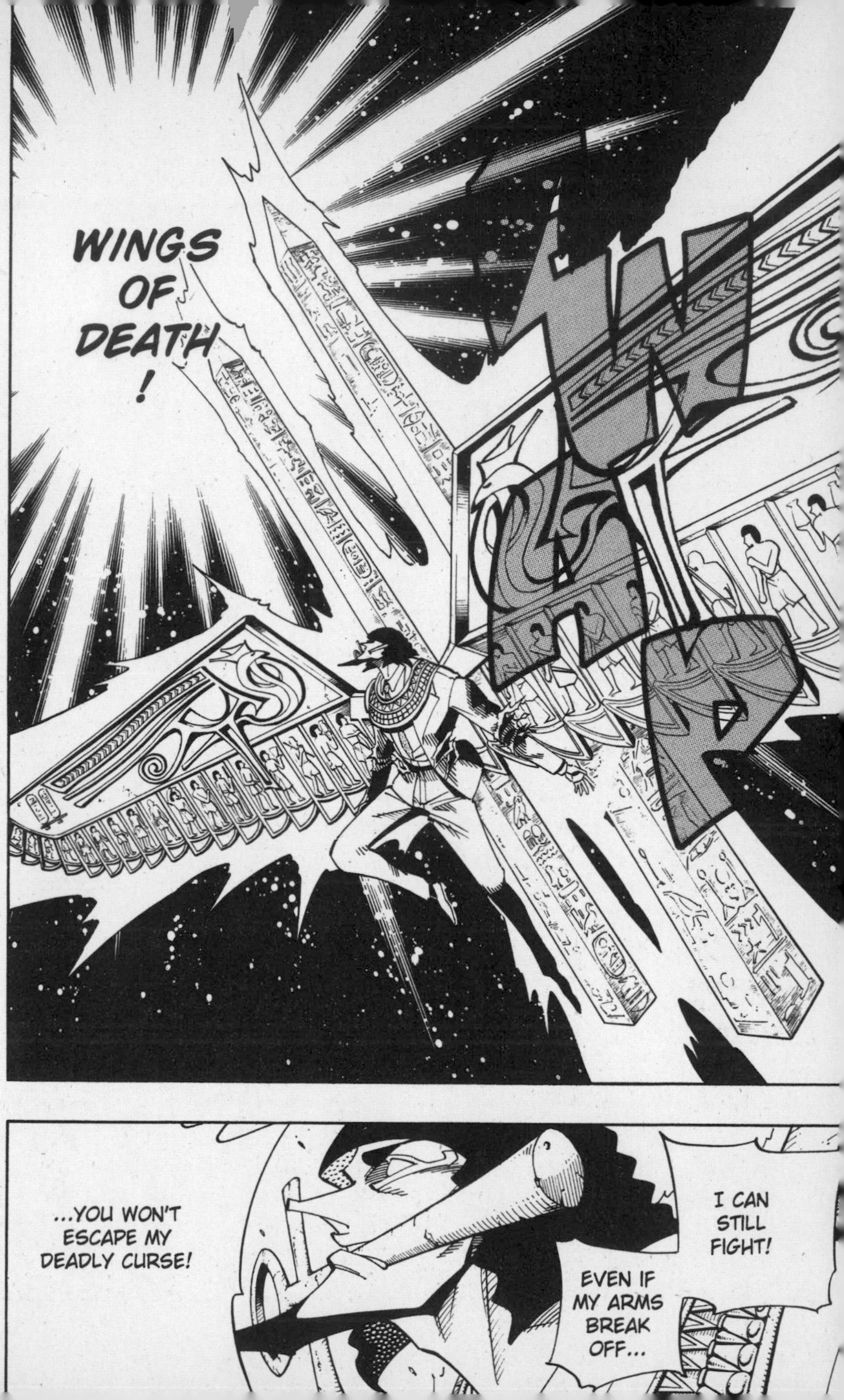
WINGS OF DEATH!
I CAN STILL FIGHT!
EVEN IF MY ARMS BREAK OFF...
...YOU WON'T ESCAPE MY DEADLY CURSE!

Reincarnation 123:
Crime and Punishment

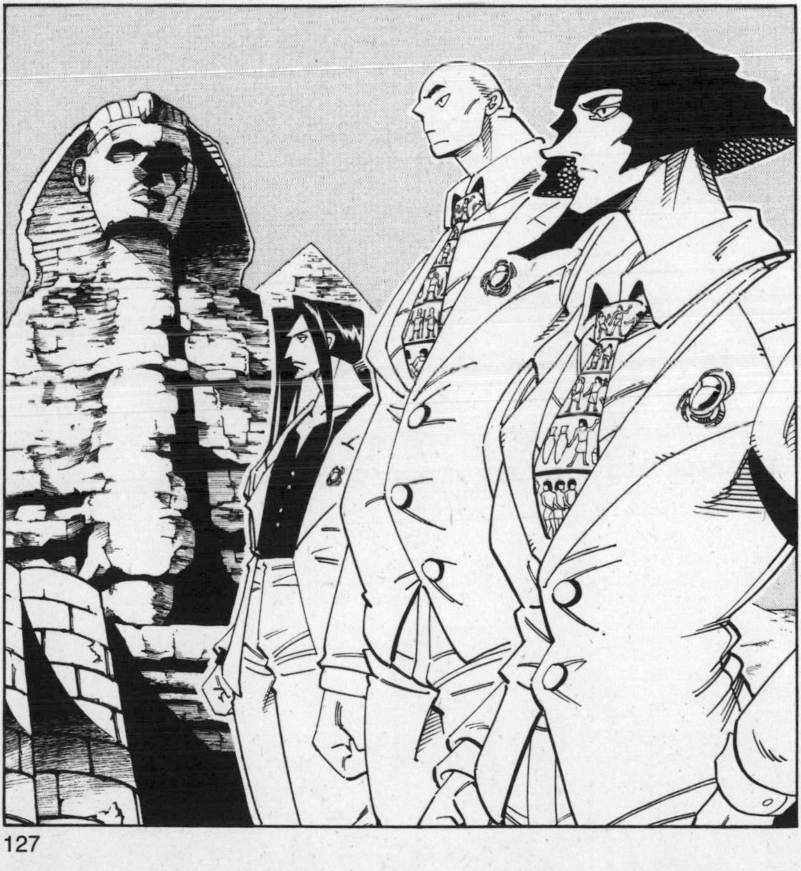

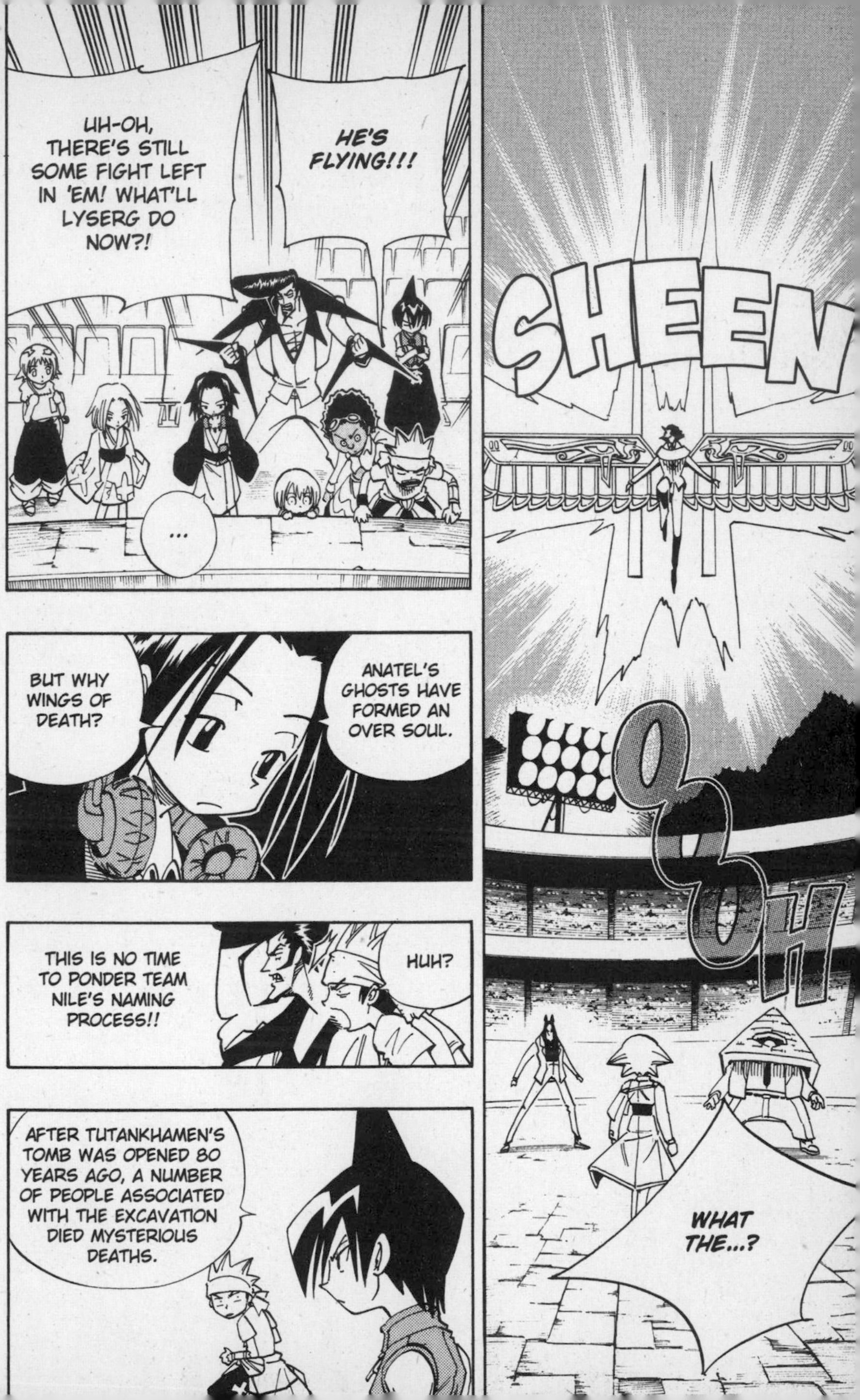
SHEEN
OOOH
WHAT THE...?
HE'S FLYING!!!
UH-OH, THERE'S STILL SOME FIGHT LEFT IN 'EM! WHAT'LL LYSERG DO NOW?!
...
ANATEL'S GHOSTS HAVE FORMED AN OVER SOUL.
BUT WHY WINGS OF DEATH?
HUH?
THIS IS NO TIME TO PONDER TEAM NILE'S NAMING PROCESS!!
AFTER TUTANKHAMEN'S TOMB WAS OPENED 80 YEARS AGO, A NUMBER OF PEOPLE ASSOCIATED WITH THE EXCAVATION DIED MYSTERIOUS DEATHS.

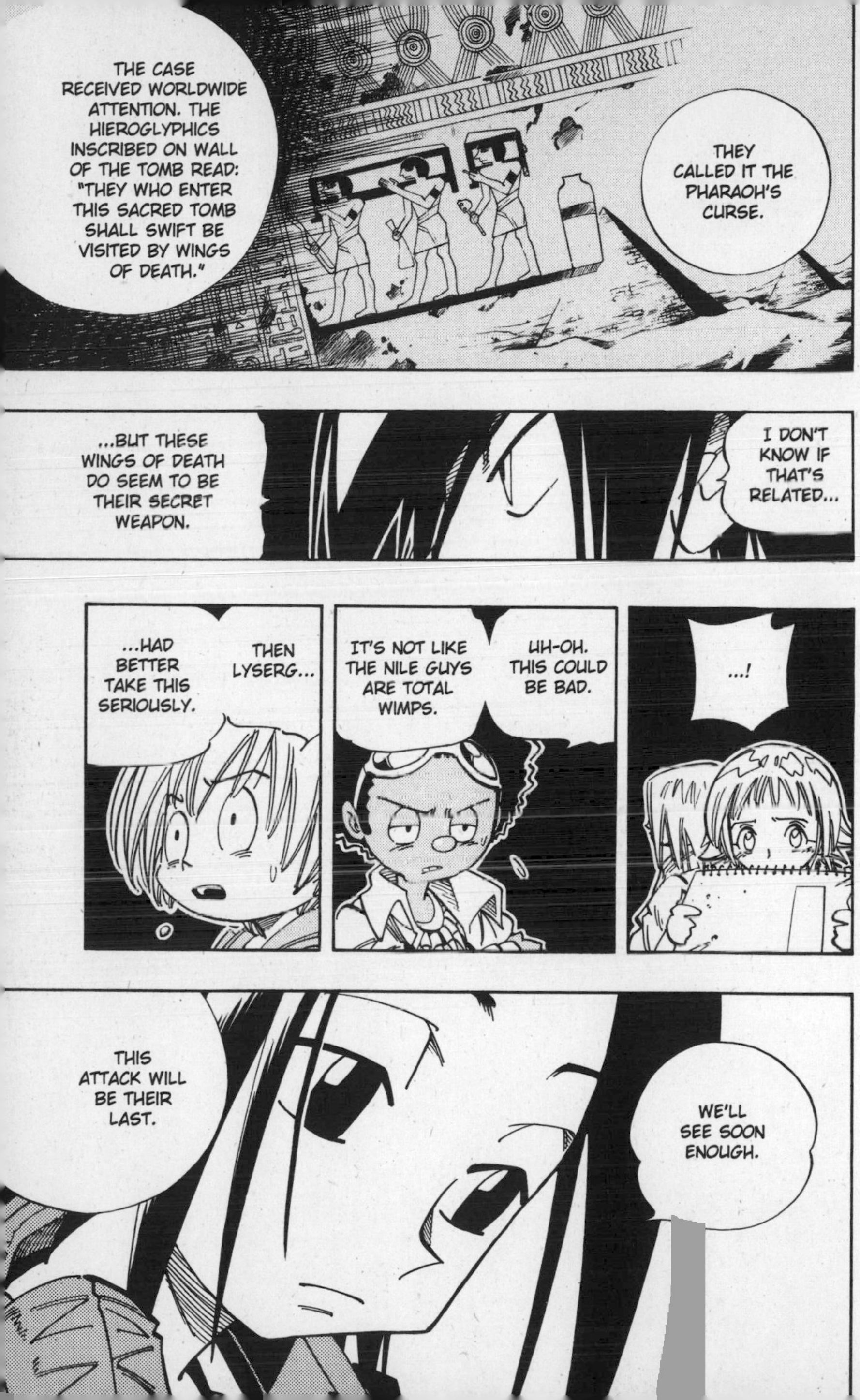
THE CASE RECEIVED WORLDWIDE ATTENTION. THE HIEROGLYPHICS INSCRIBED ON WALL OF THE TOMB READ: "THEY WHO ENTER THIS SACRED TOMB SHALL SWIFT BE VISITED BY WINGS OF DEATH."
THEY CALLED IT THE PHARAOH'S CURSE.
I DON'T KNOW IF THAT'S RELATED...
...BUT THESE WINGS OF DEATH DO SEEM TO BE THEIR SECRET WEAPON.
...!
UH-OH. THIS COULD BE BAD.
IT'S NOT LIKE THE NILE GUYS ARE TOTAL WIMPS.
THEN LYSERG...
...HAD BETTER TAKE THIS SERIOUSLY.
THIS ATTACK WILL BE THEIR LAST.
WE'LL SEE SOON ENOUGH.

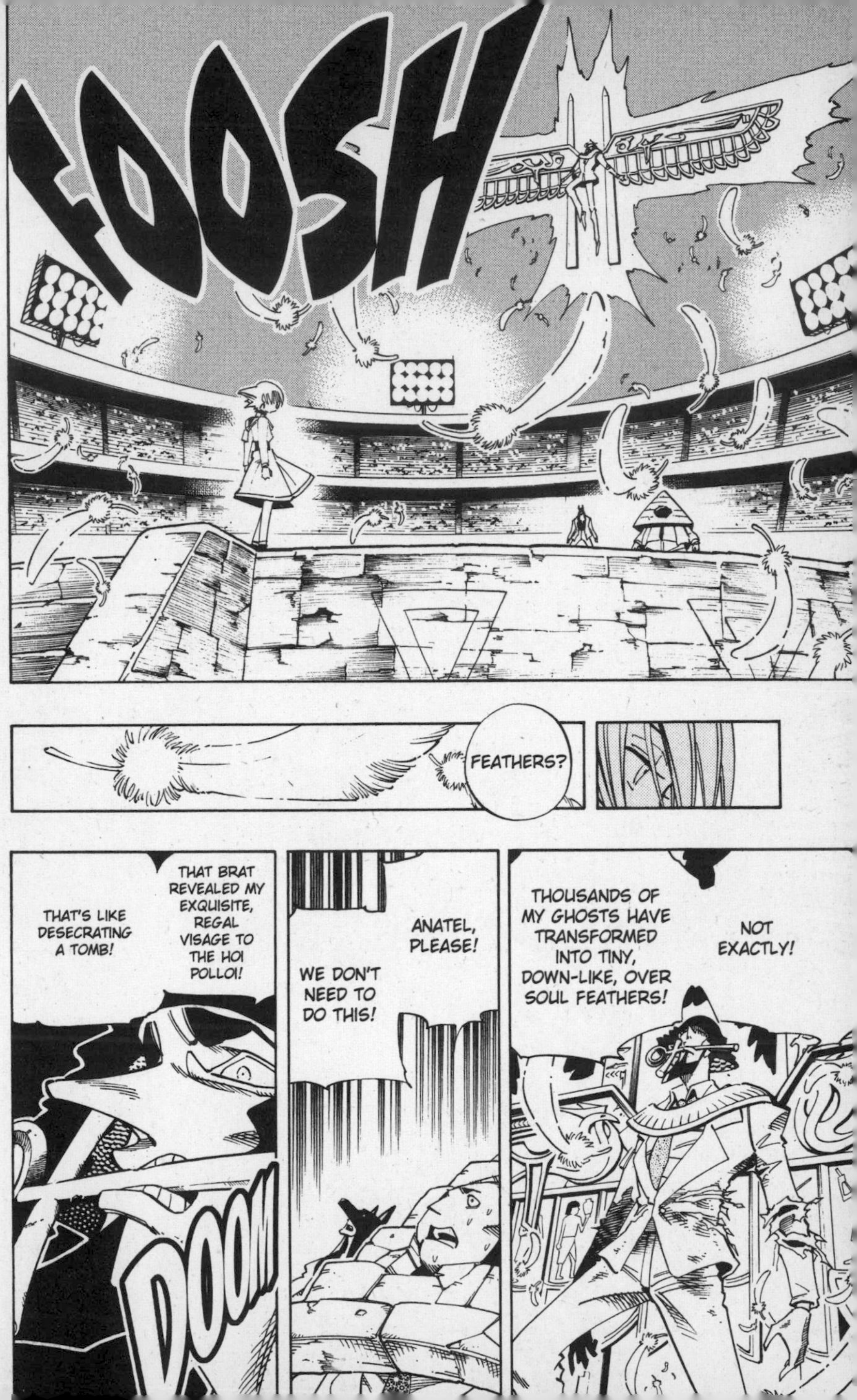
FOOSH
FEATHERS?
NOT EXACTLY!
THOUSANDS OF MY GHOSTS HAVE TRANSFORMED INTO TINY, DOWN-LIKE, OVER SOUL FEATHERS!
ANATEL, PLEASE!
WE DON'T NEED TO DO THIS!
THAT BRAT REVEALED MY EXQUISITE, REGAL VISAGE TO THE HOI POLLOI!
THAT'S LIKE DESECRATING A TOMB!
DOOM

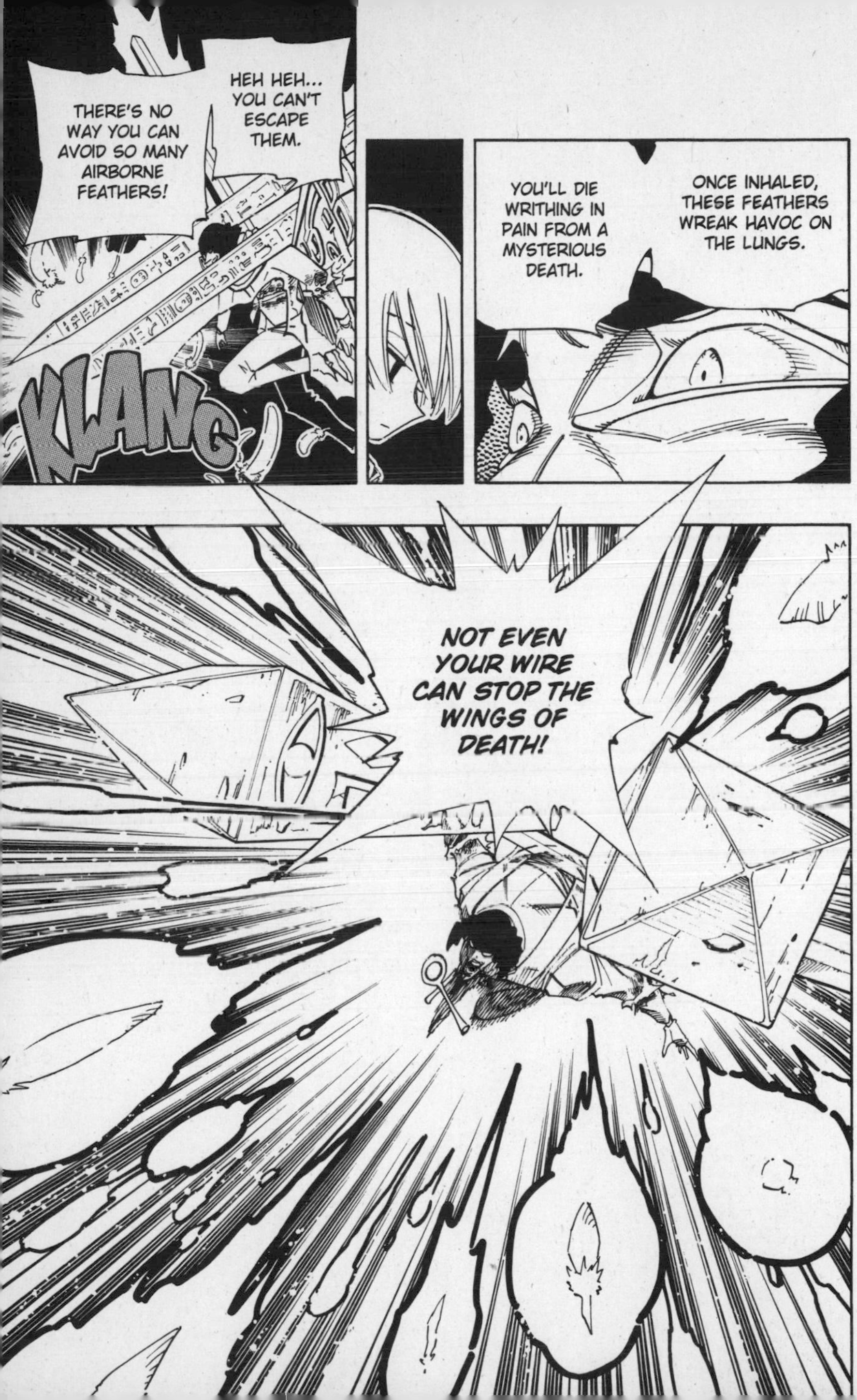
ONCE INHALED, THESE FEATHERS WREAK HAVOC ON THE LUNGS.
YOU'LL DIE WRITHING IN PAIN FROM A MYSTERIOUS DEATH.
HEH HEH... YOU CAN'T ESCAPE THEM.
THERE'S NO WAY YOU CAN AVOID SO MANY AIRBORNE FEATHERS!
KLANG
NOT EVEN YOUR WIRE CAN STOP THE WINGS OF DEATH!

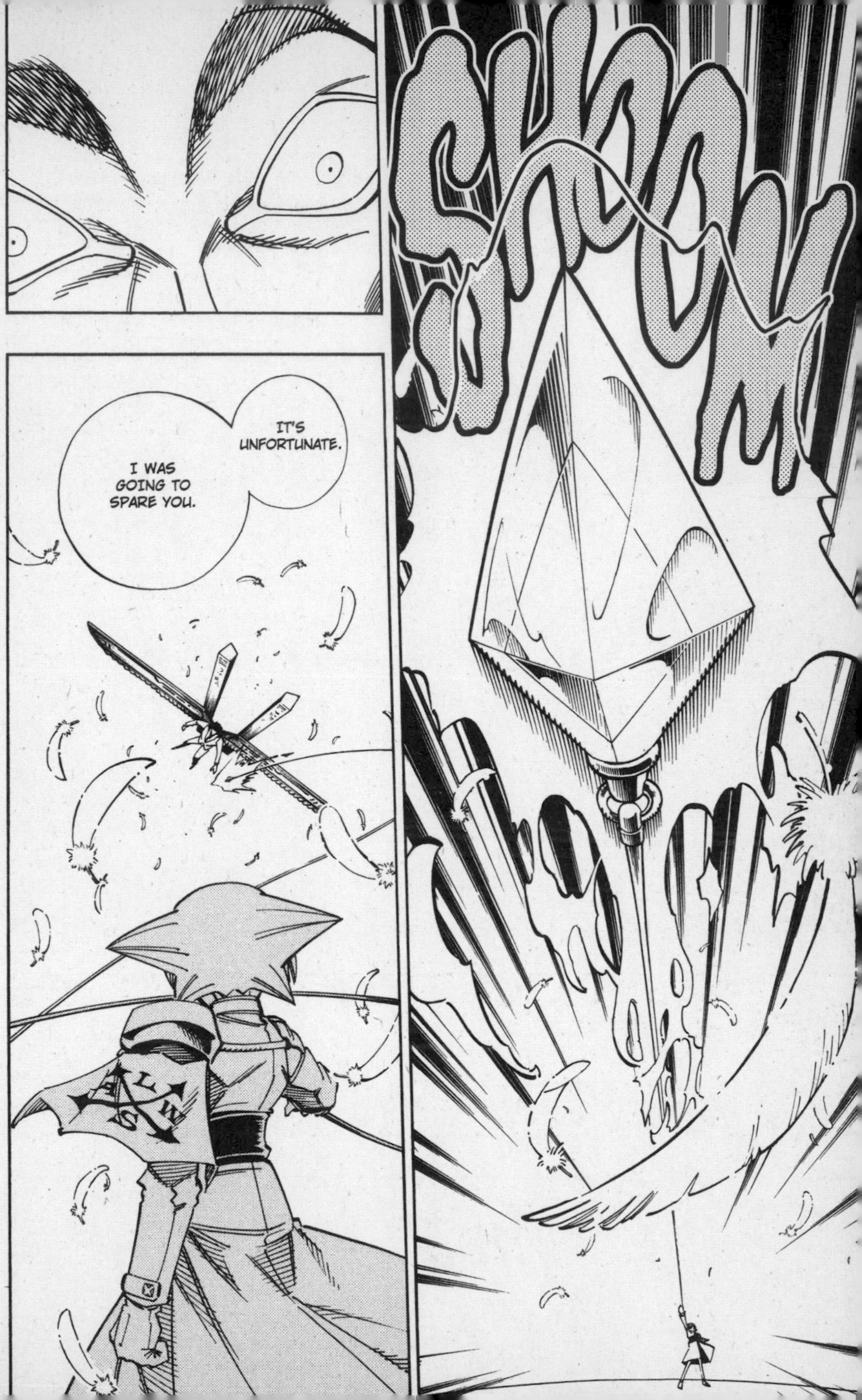
SHOOM
IT'S UNFORTUNATE.
I WAS GOING TO SPARE YOU.

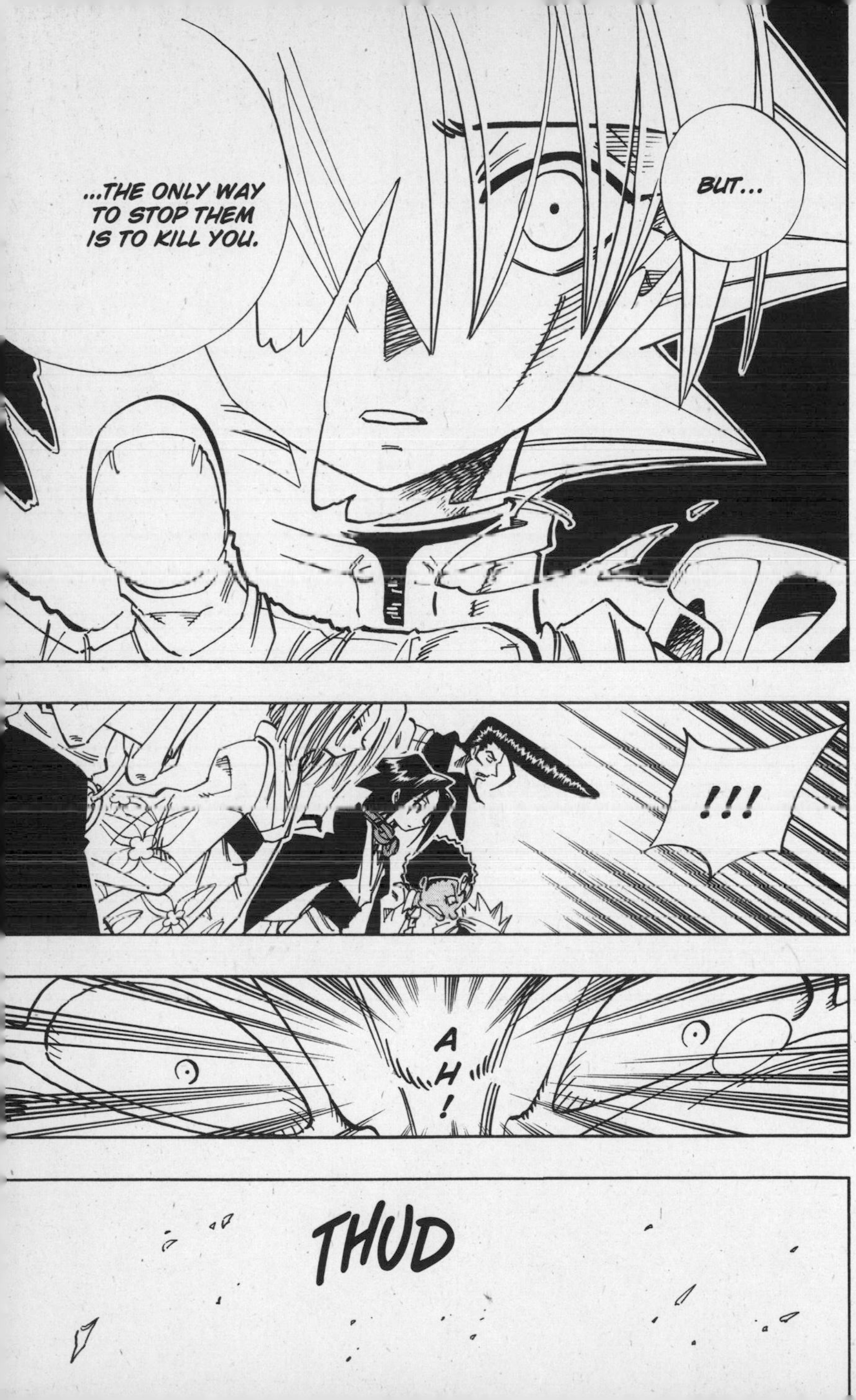
BUT...
...THE ONLY WAY TO STOP THEM IS TO KILL YOU.
!!!
AH!
THUD

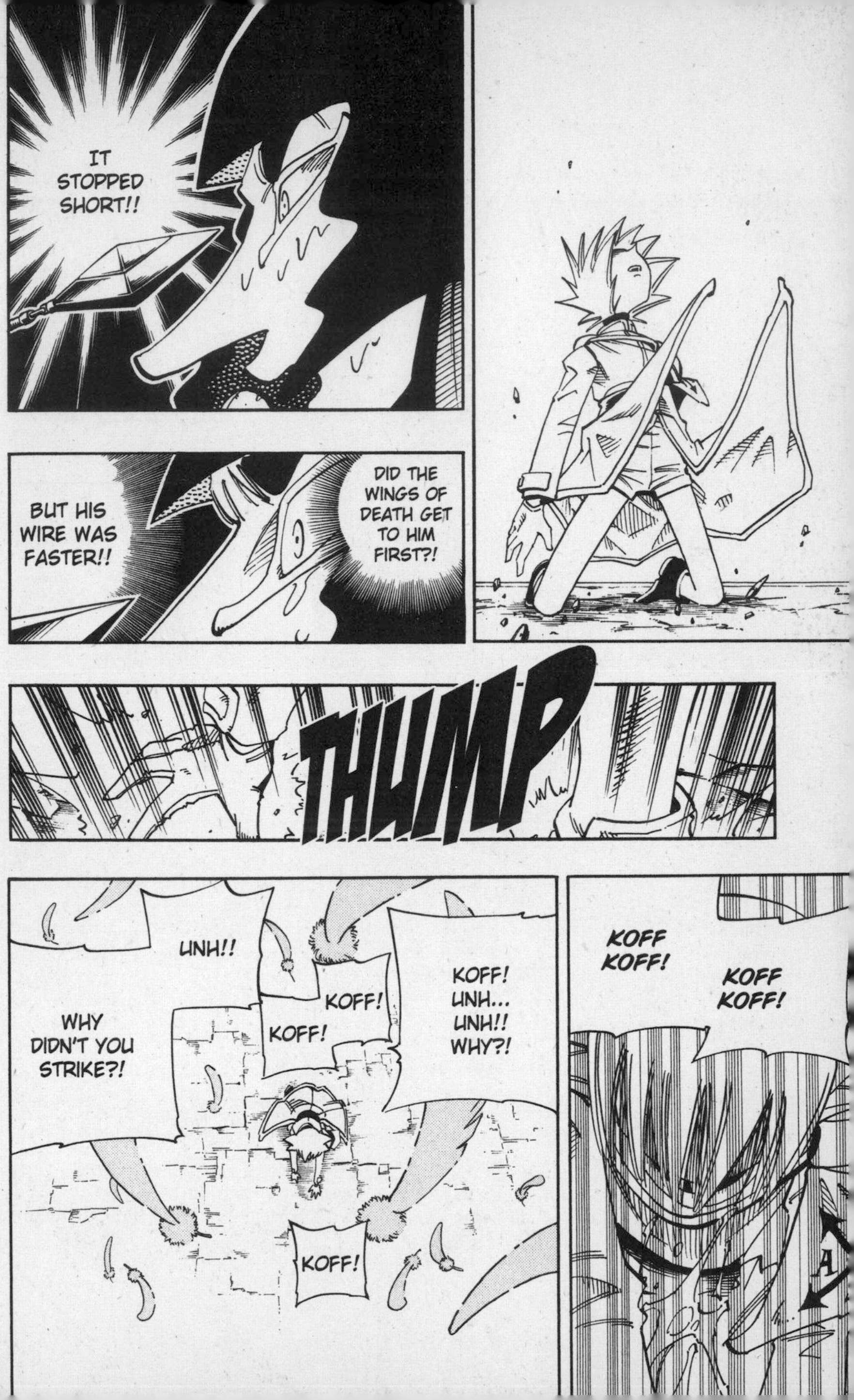
IT STOPPED SHORT!!
DID THE WINGS OF DEATH GET TO HIM FIRST?!
BUT HIS WIRE WAS FASTER!!
THUMP
KOFF KOFF!
KOFF KOFF!
KOFF! UNH... UNH!! WHY?!
UNH!!
KOFF!
KOFF!
WHY DIDN'T YOU STRIKE?!
KOFF!

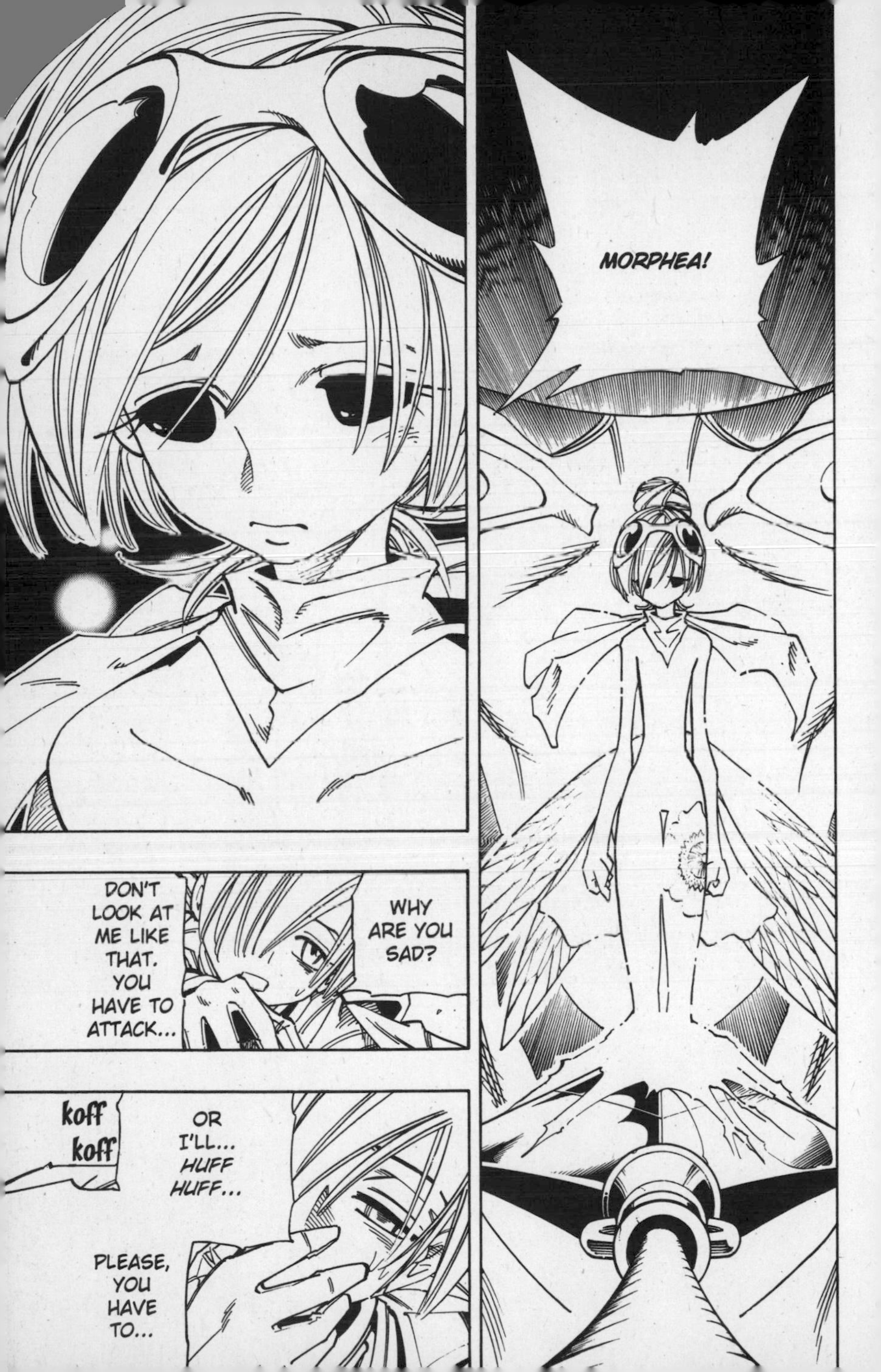
MORPHEA!
WHY ARE YOU SAD?
DON'T LOOK AT ME LIKE THAT. YOU HAVE TO ATTACK...
OR I'LL... HUFF HUFF...
koff koff
PLEASE, YOU HAVE TO...

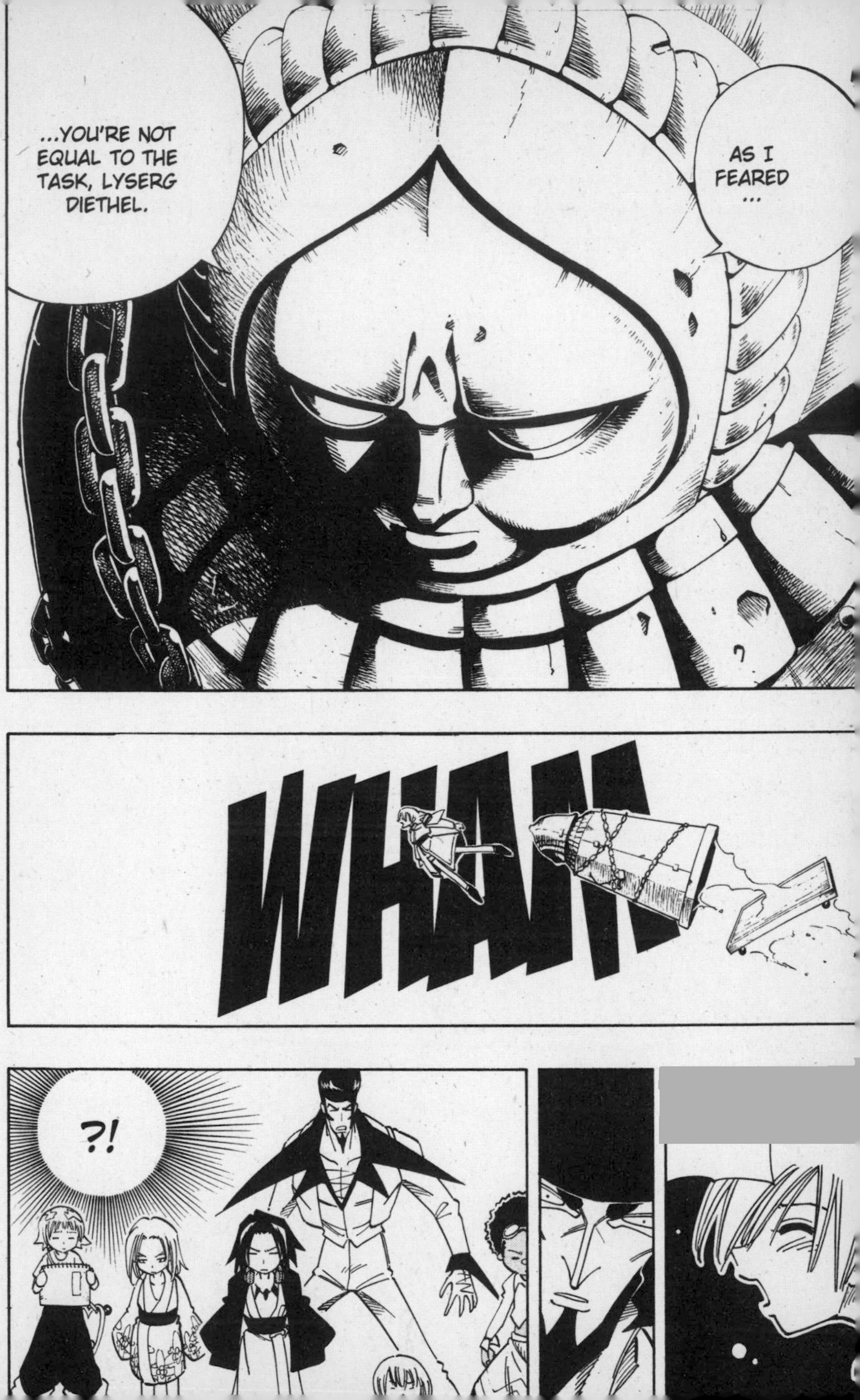
AS I FEARED ...
...YOU'RE NOT EQUAL TO THE TASK, LYSERG DIETHEL.
WHAM
?!

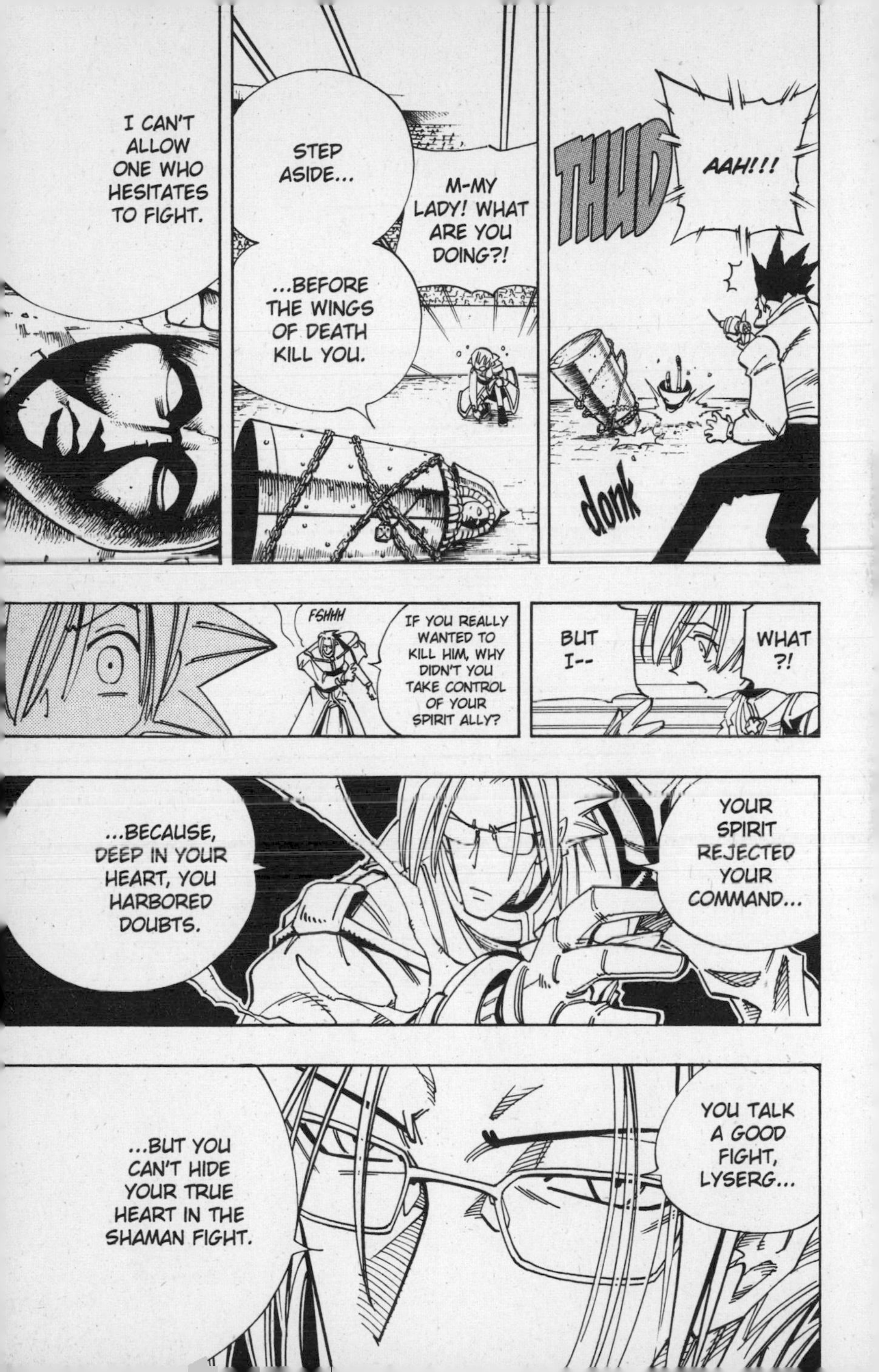
THUD
AAH!!!
donk
STEP ASIDE...
M-MY LADY! WHAT ARE YOU DOING?!
...BEFORE THE WINGS OF DEATH KILL YOU.
I CAN'T ALLOW ONE WHO HESITATES TO FIGHT.
WHAT?!
BUT I--
IF YOU REALLY WANTED TO KILL HIM, WHY DIDN'T YOU TAKE CONTROL OF YOUR SPIRIT ALLY?
FSHHH
YOUR SPIRIT REJECTED YOUR COMMAND...
...BECAUSE, DEEP IN YOUR HEART, YOU HARBORED DOUBTS.
YOU TALK A GOOD FIGHT, LYSERG...
...BUT YOU CAN'T HIDE YOUR TRUE HEART IN THE SHAMAN FIGHT.

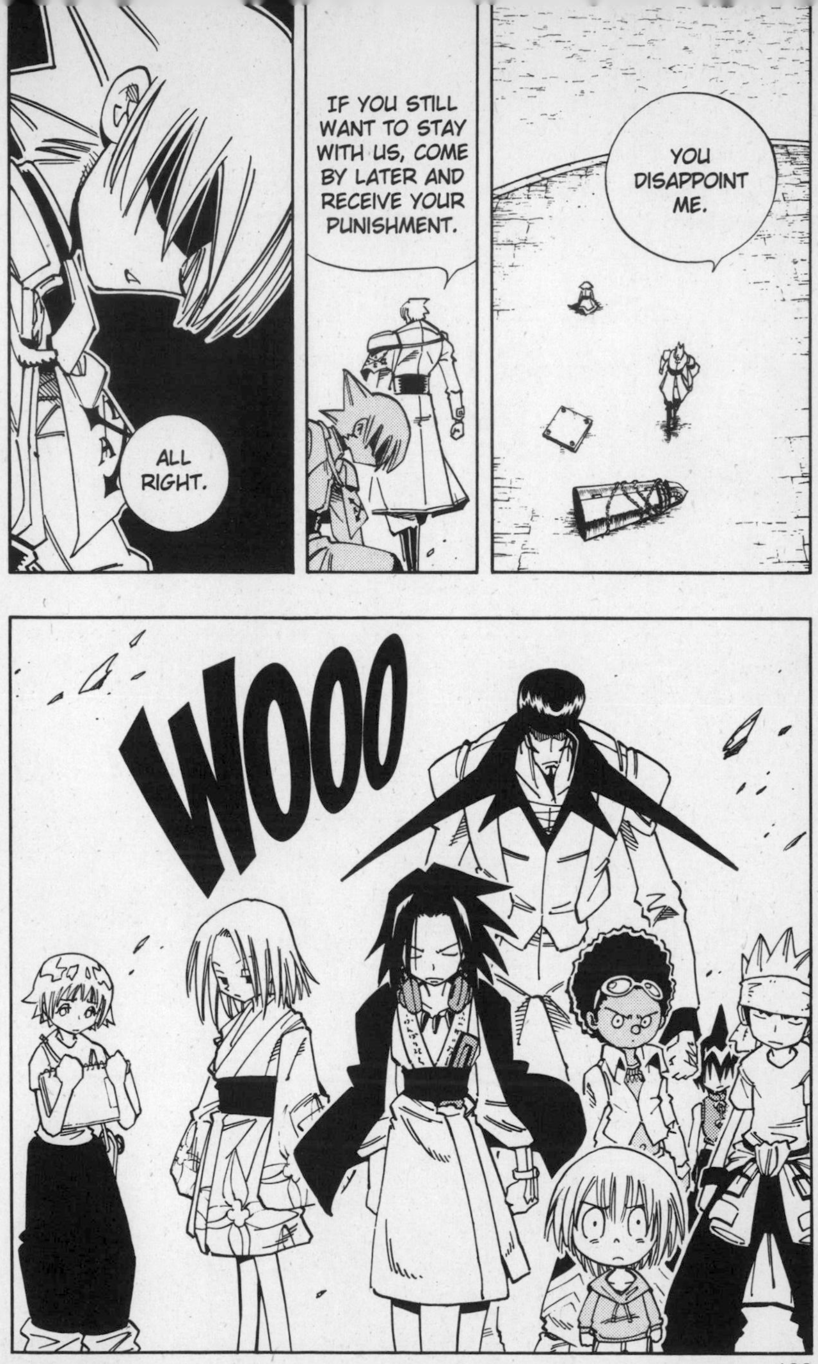
YOU DISAPPOINT ME.
IF YOU STILL WANT TO STAY WITH US, COME BY LATER AND RECEIVE YOUR PUNISHMENT.
ALL RIGHT.
WOOO

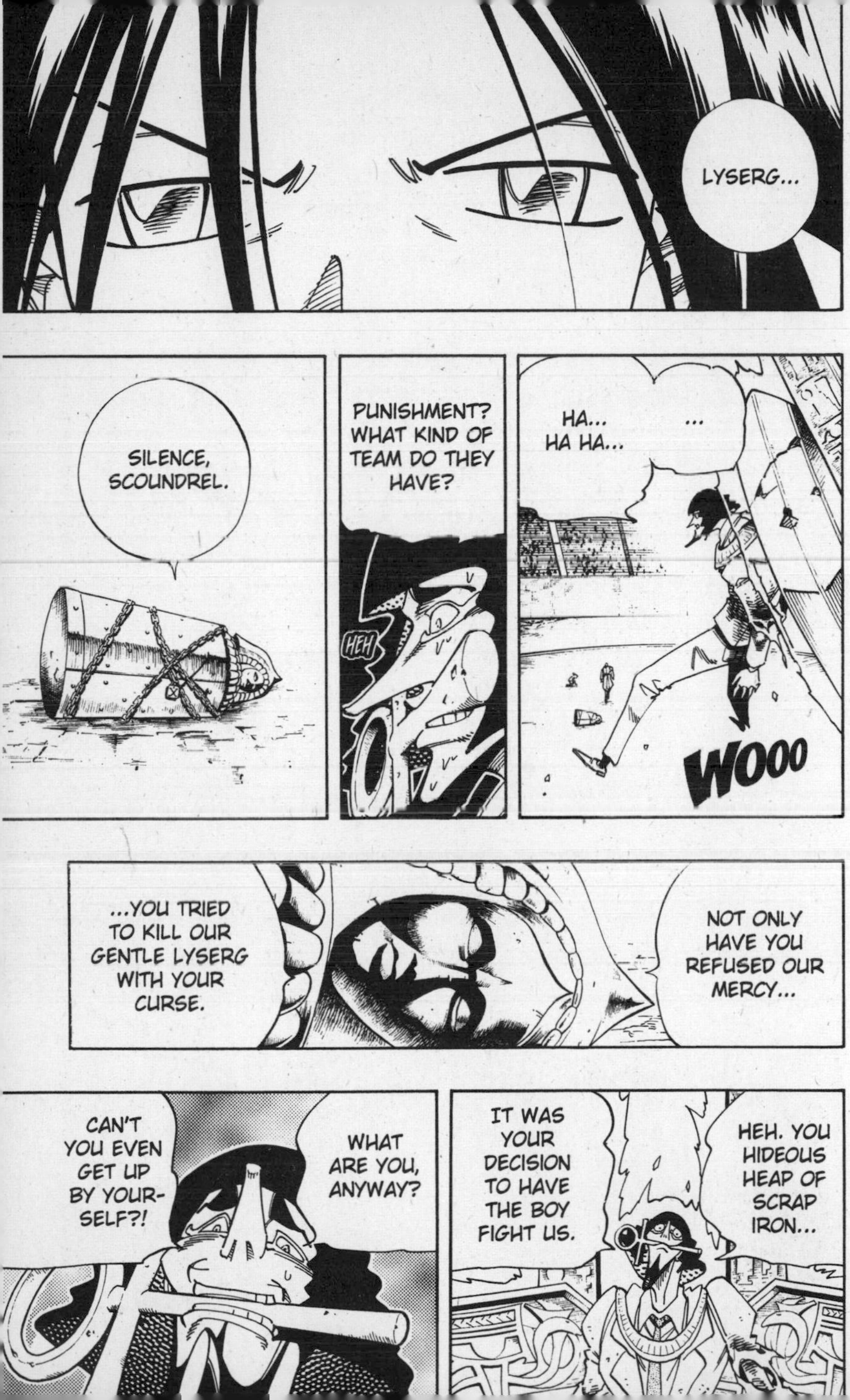
LYSERG...
...
HA... HA HA...
WOOO
PUNISHMENT? WHAT KIND OF TEAM DO THEY HAVE?
HEH
SILENCE, SCOUNDREL.
NOT ONLY HAVE YOU REFUSED OUR MERCY...
...YOU TRIED TO KILL OUR GENTLE LYSERG WITH YOUR CURSE.
HEH. YOU HIDEOUS HEAP OF SCRAP IRON...
IT WAS YOUR DECISION TO HAVE THE BOY FIGHT US.
WHAT ARE YOU, ANYWAY?
CAN'T YOU EVEN GET UP BY YOUR-SELF?!

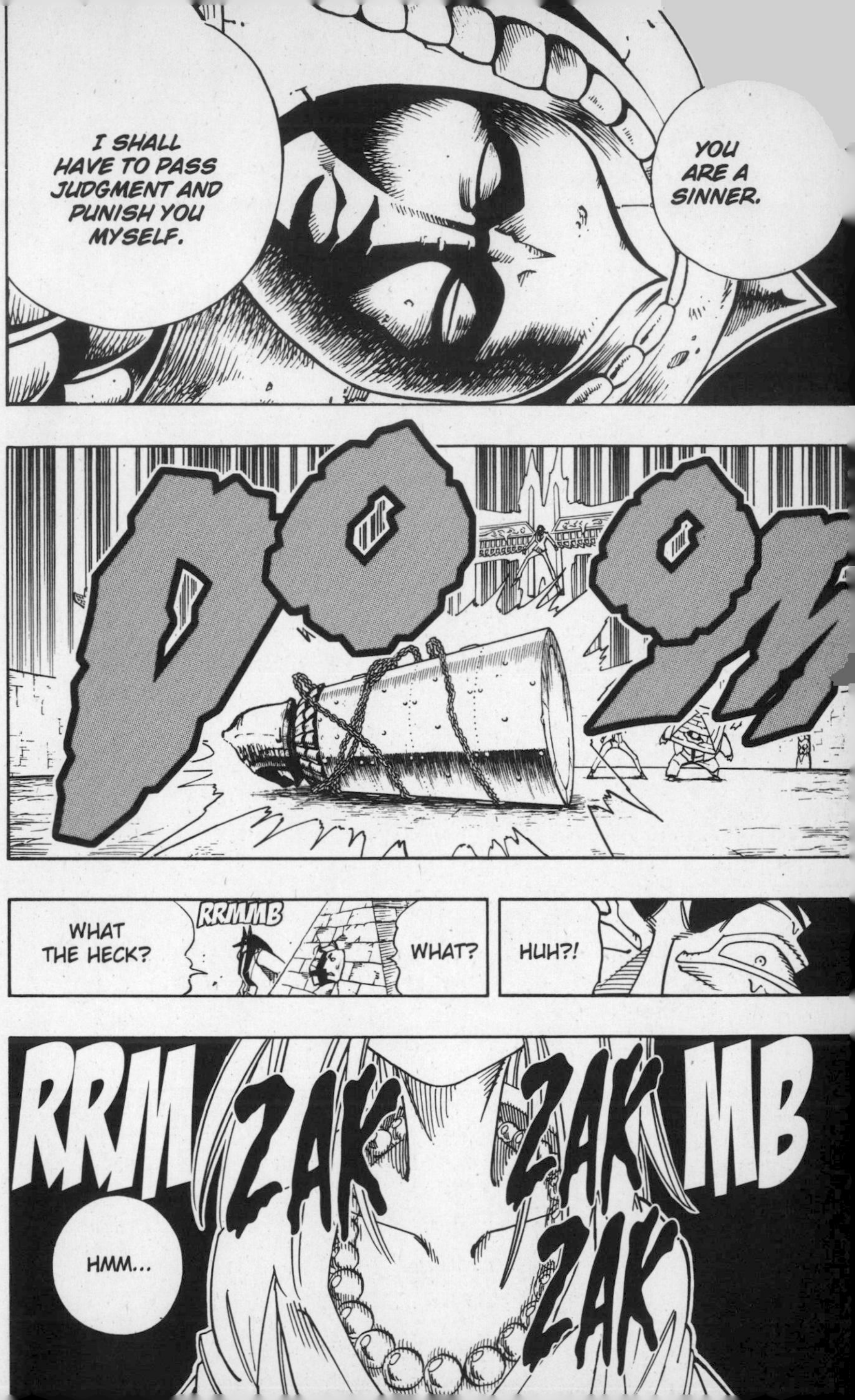
YOU ARE A SINNER.
I SHALL HAVE TO PASS JUDGMENT AND PUNISH YOU MYSELF.
DOOM
HUH?!
WHAT?
RRMMB
WHAT THE HECK?
RRM
MB
ZAK
ZAK
ZAK
ZAK
HMM...

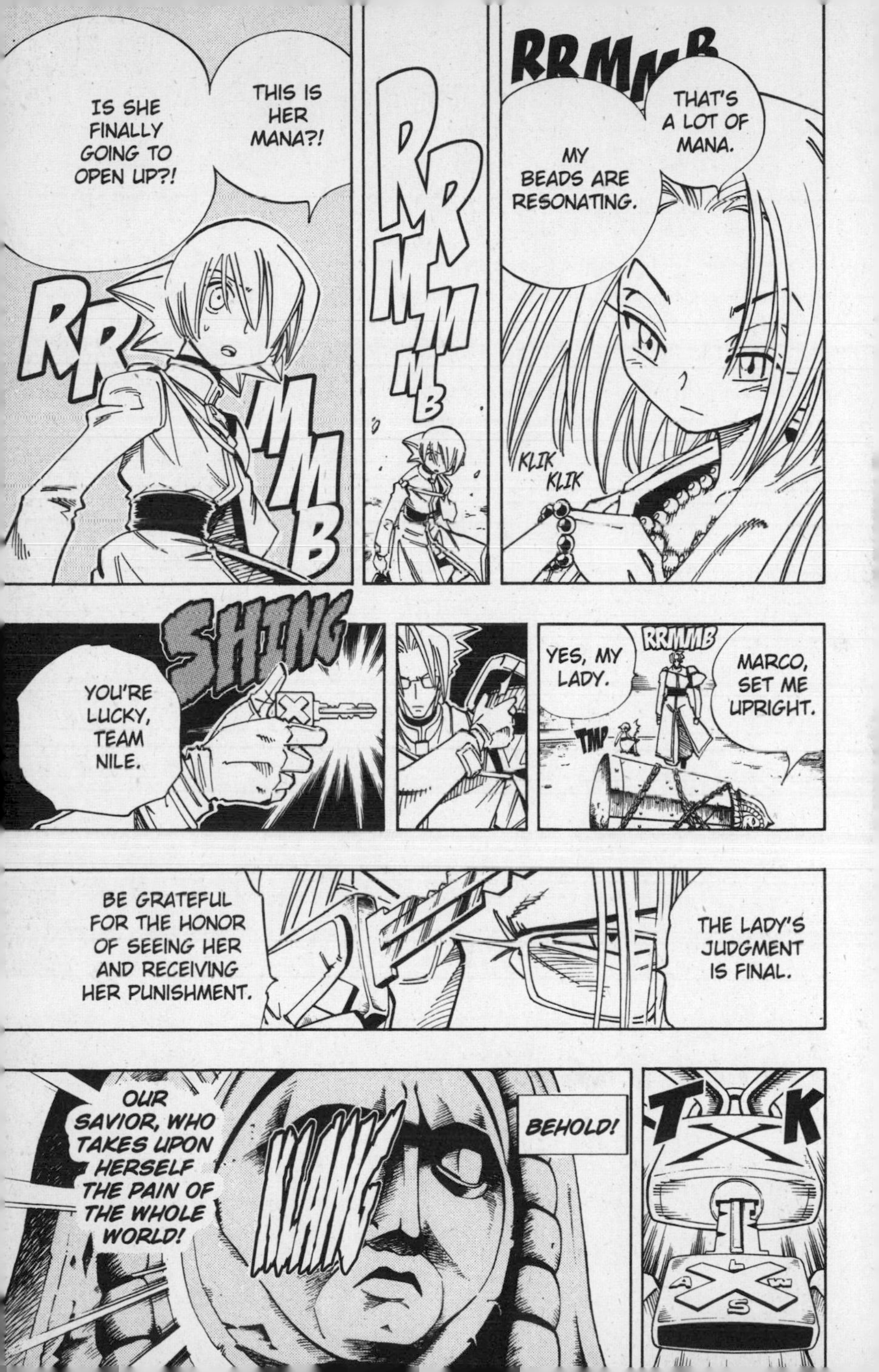
RRMMB
THAT'S A LOT OF MANA.
MY BEADS ARE RESONATING.
KLIK KLIK
RRMMMMB
THIS IS HER MANA?!
IS SHE FINALLY GOING TO OPEN UP?!
RRMMMB
RRMMB
MARCO, SET ME UPRIGHT.
YES, MY LADY.
TMP
SHING
YOU'RE LUCKY, TEAM NILE.
THE LADY'S JUDGMENT IS FINAL.
BE GRATEFUL FOR THE HONOR OF SEEING HER AND RECEIVING HER PUNISHMENT.
TK
BEHOLD!
OUR SAVIOR, WHO TAKES UPON HERSELF THE PAIN OF THE WHOLE WORLD!

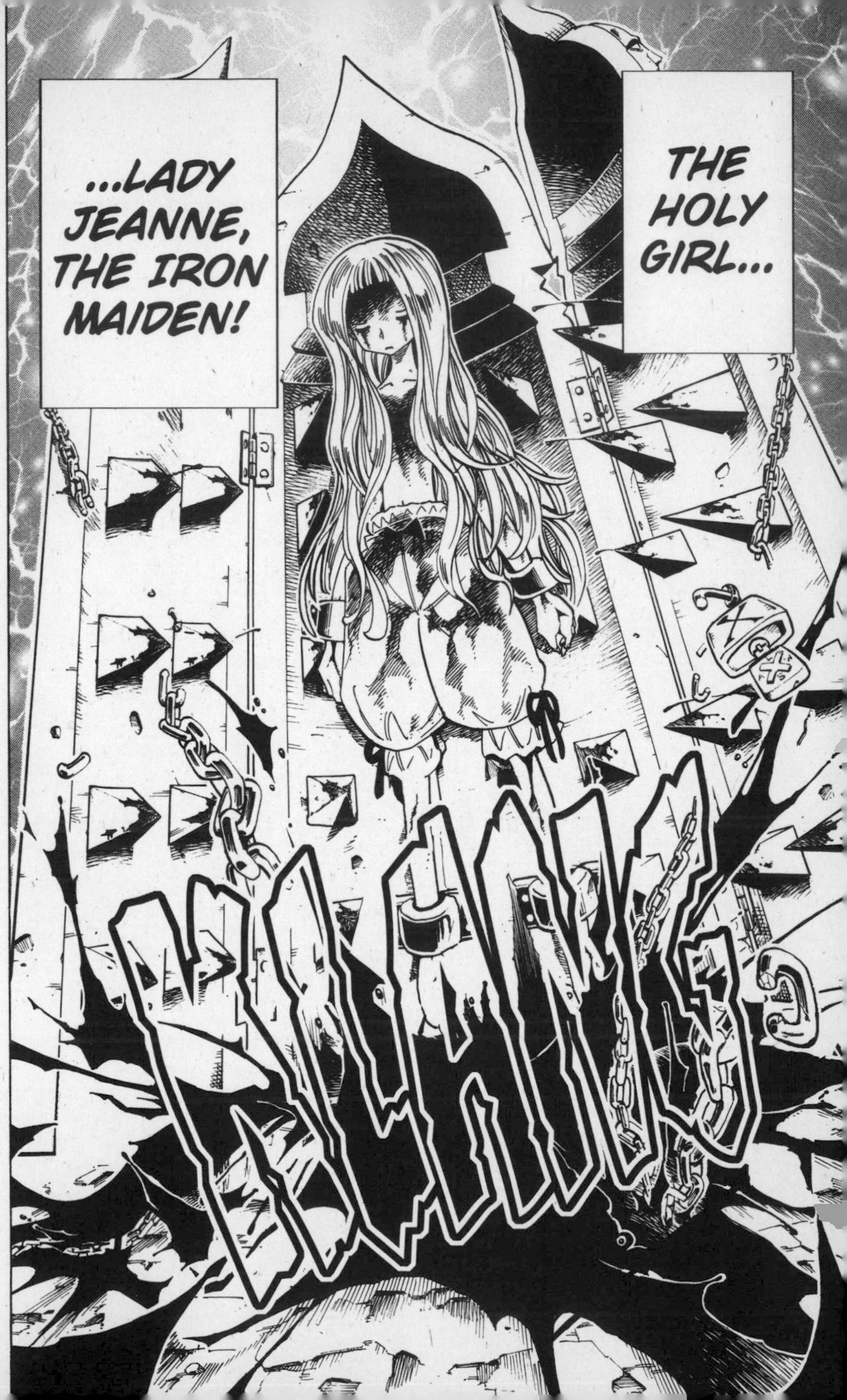
THE HOLY GIRL...
...LADY JEANNE, THE IRON MAIDEN!

Shaman King™

SHAMAN KING CHARACTER FILE No.69

シャマシュ
SHAMASH

2001
(JUNE)

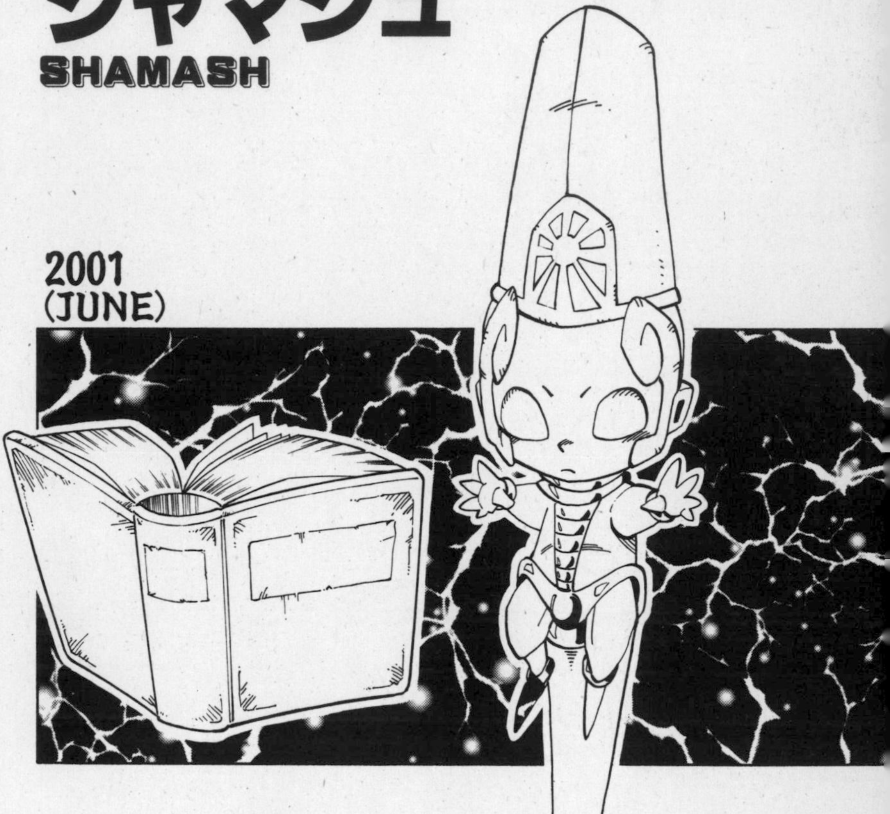

?

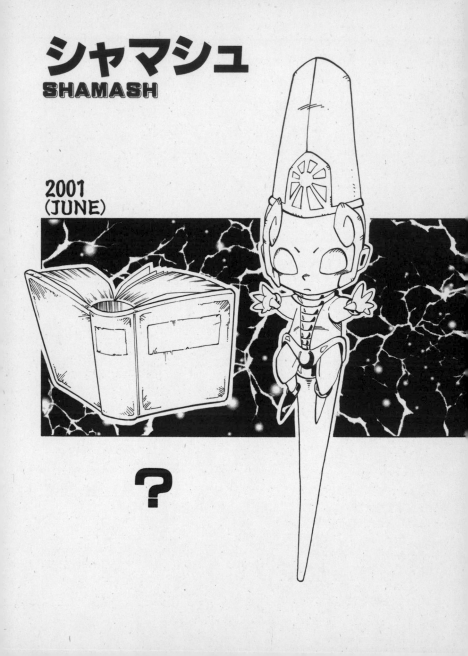

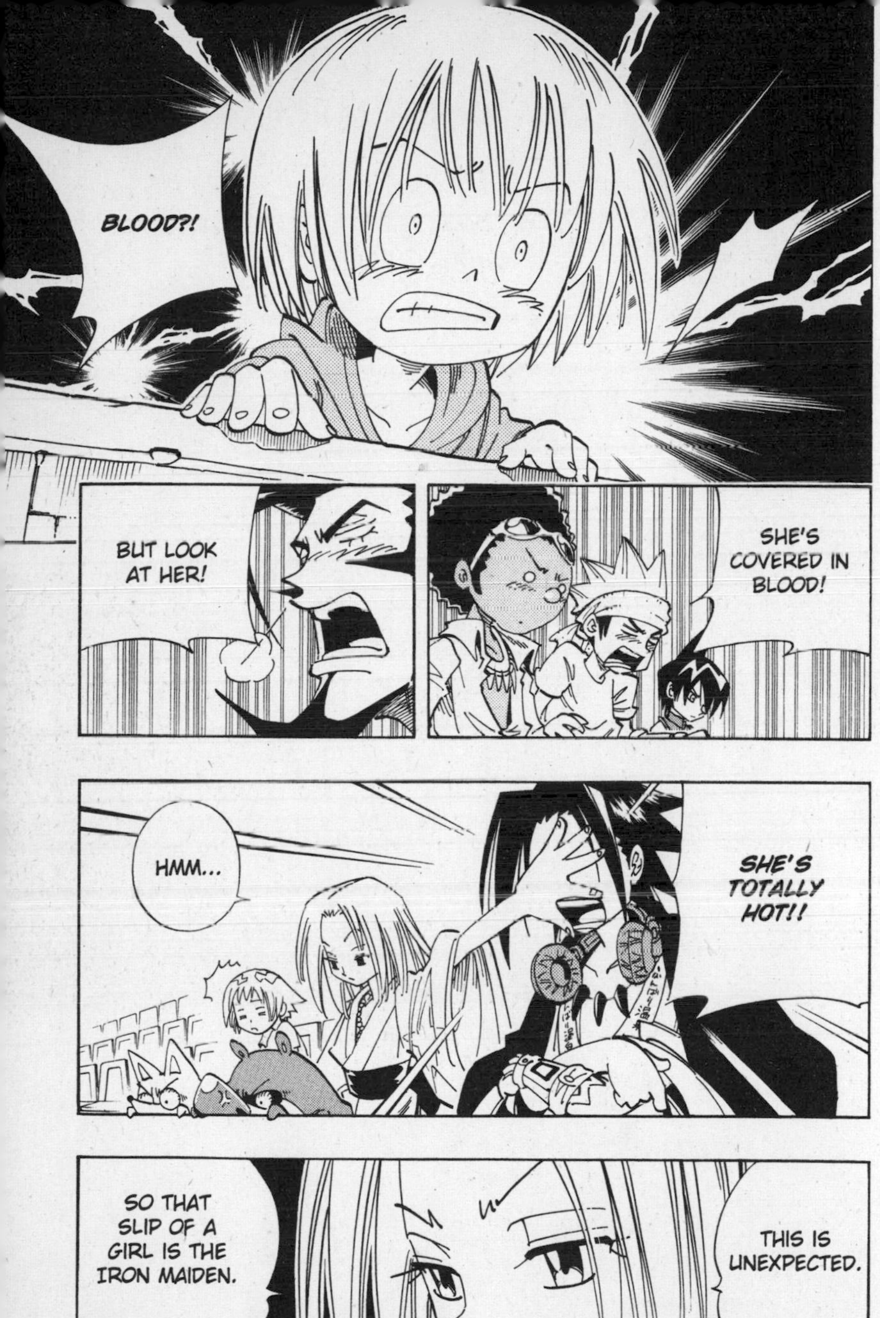
BLOOD?!
SHE'S COVERED IN BLOOD!
BUT LOOK AT HER!
SHE'S TOTALLY HOT!!
HMM...
THIS IS UNEXPECTED.
SO THAT SLIP OF A GIRL IS THE IRON MAIDEN.

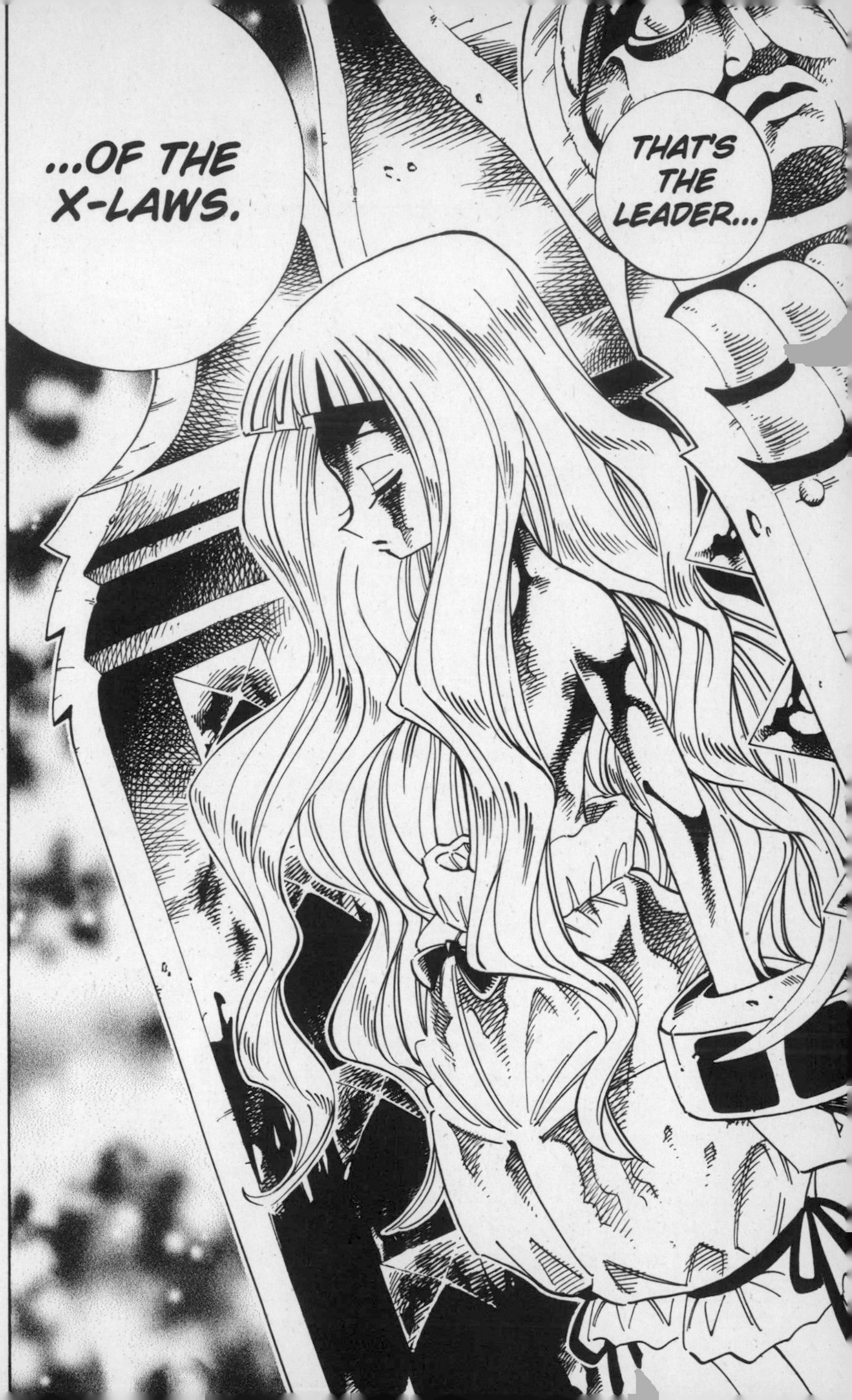
THAT'S THE LEADER...
...OF THE X-LAWS.

Reincarnation 124:
Holy Girl

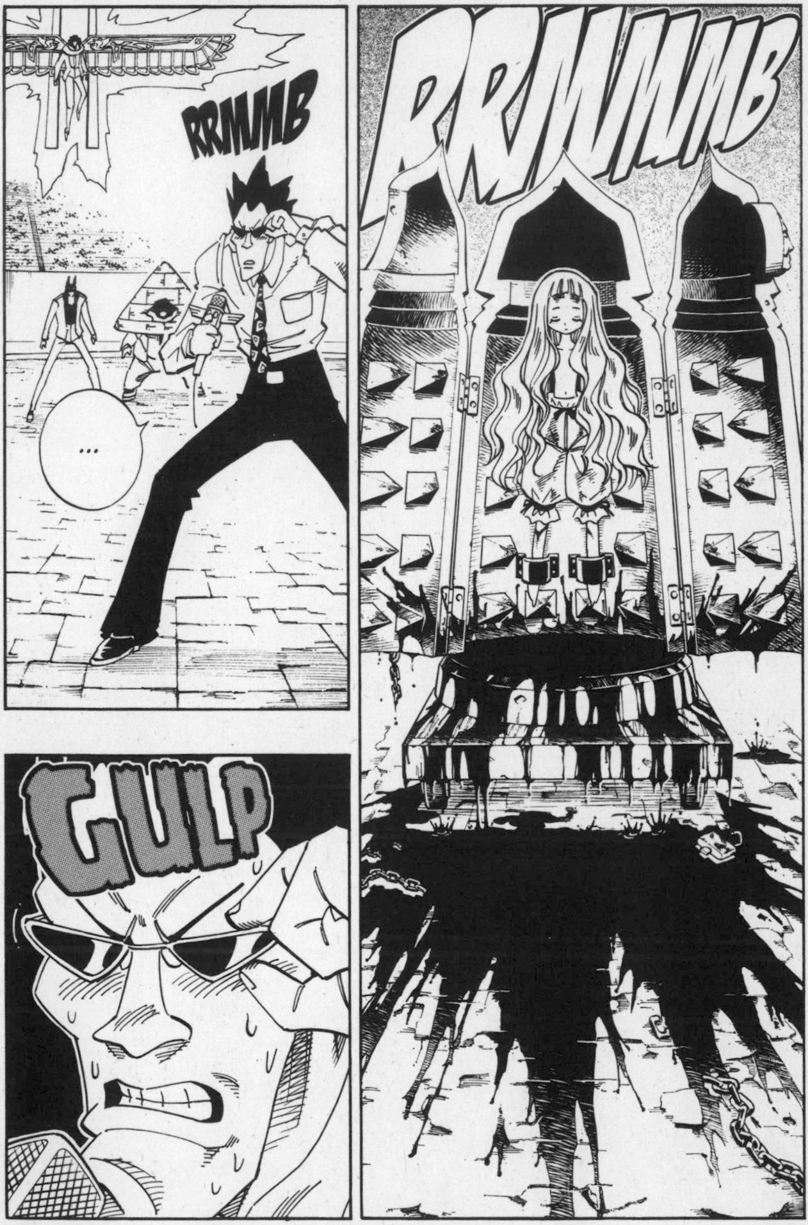
RRMMMB
RRMMB
...
GULP

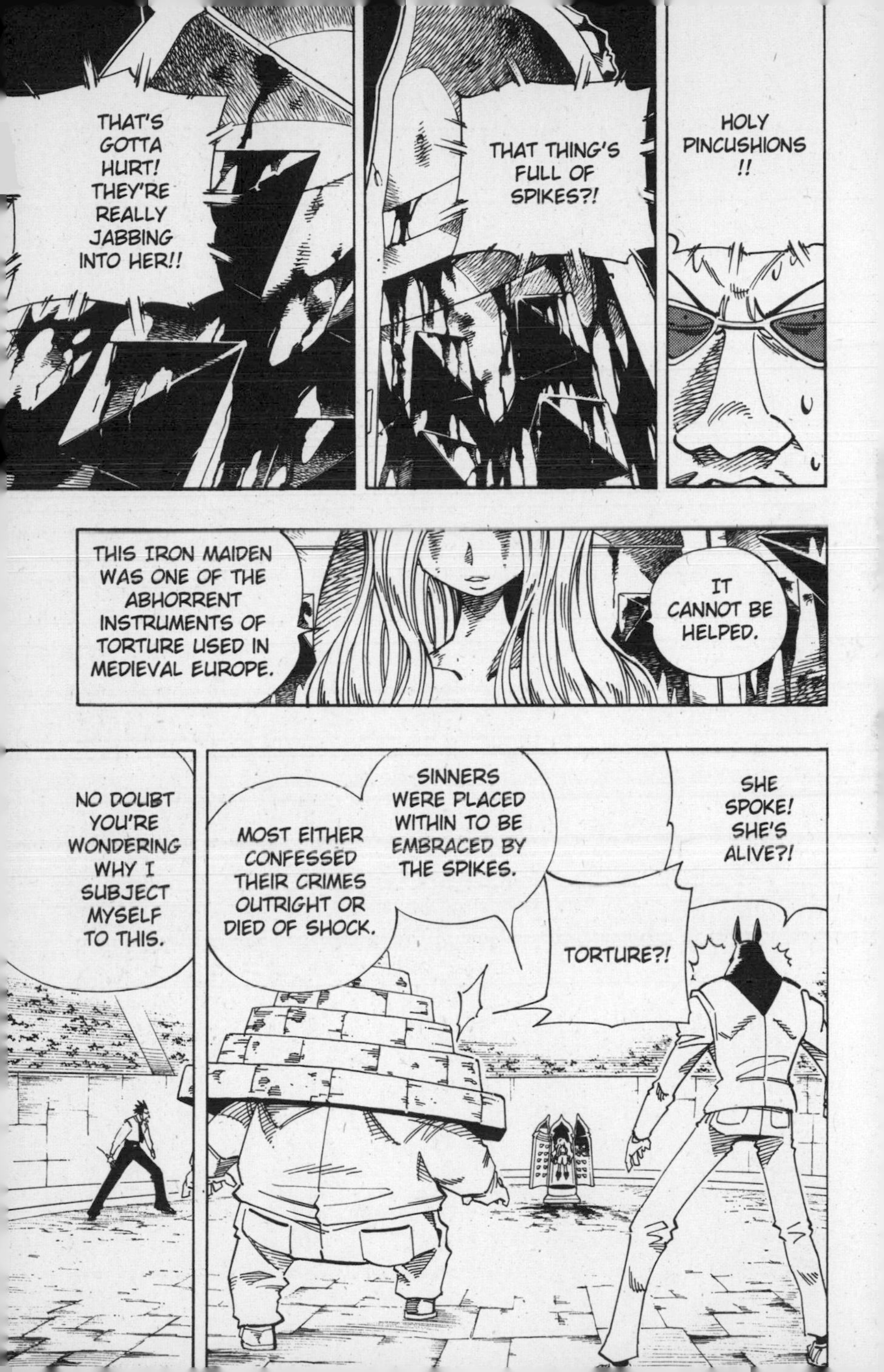
HOLY PINCUSHIONS !!
THAT THING'S FULL OF SPIKES?!
THAT'S GOTTA HURT! THEY'RE REALLY JABBING INTO HER!!
IT CANNOT BE HELPED.
THIS IRON MAIDEN WAS ONE OF THE ABHORRENT INSTRUMENTS OF TORTURE USED IN MEDIEVAL EUROPE.
SHE SPOKE! SHE'S ALIVE?!
SINNERS WERE PLACED WITHIN TO BE EMBRACED BY THE SPIKES.
TORTURE?!
MOST EITHER CONFESSED THEIR CRIMES OUTRIGHT OR DIED OF SHOCK.
NO DOUBT YOU'RE WONDERING WHY I SUBJECT MYSELF TO THIS.

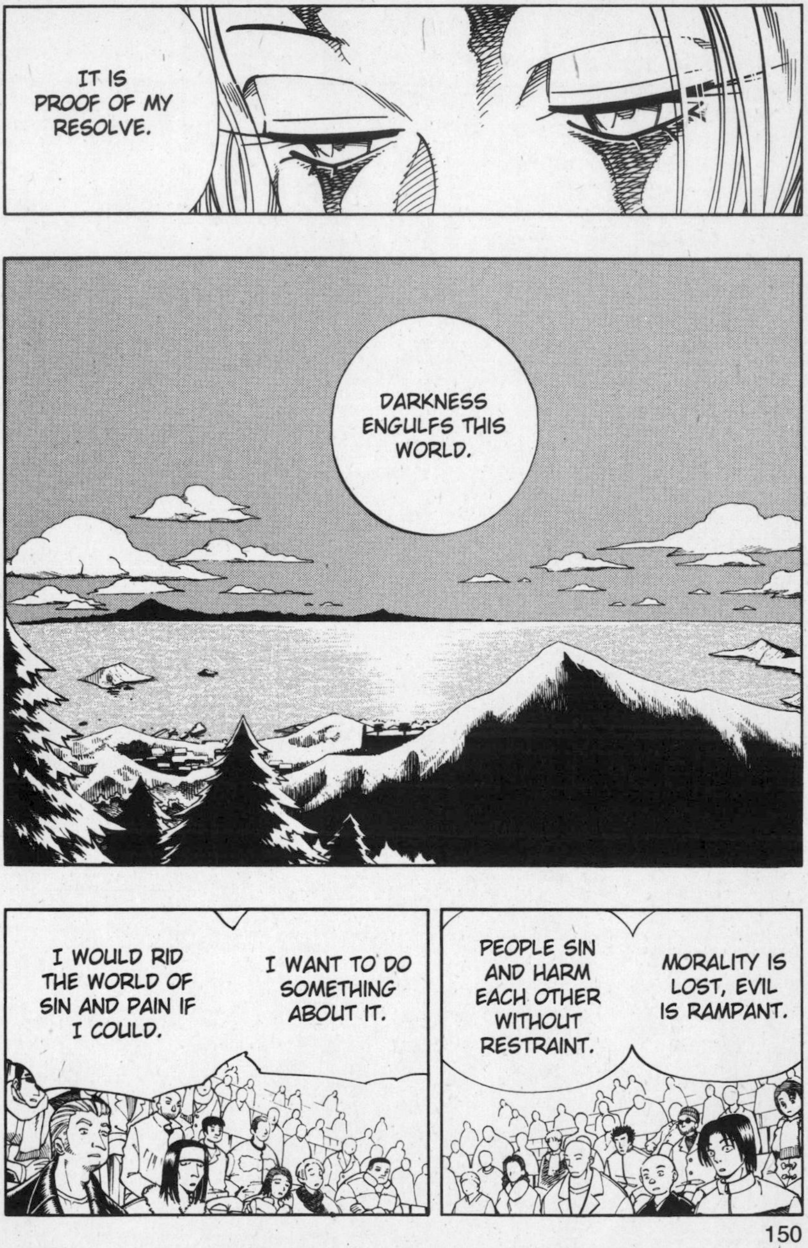
IT IS PROOF OF MY RESOLVE.
DARKNESS ENGULFS THIS WORLD.
MORALITY IS LOST, EVIL IS RAMPANT.
PEOPLE SIN AND HARM EACH OTHER WITHOUT RESTRAINT.
I WANT TO DO SOMETHING ABOUT IT.
I WOULD RID THE WORLD OF SIN AND PAIN IF I COULD.

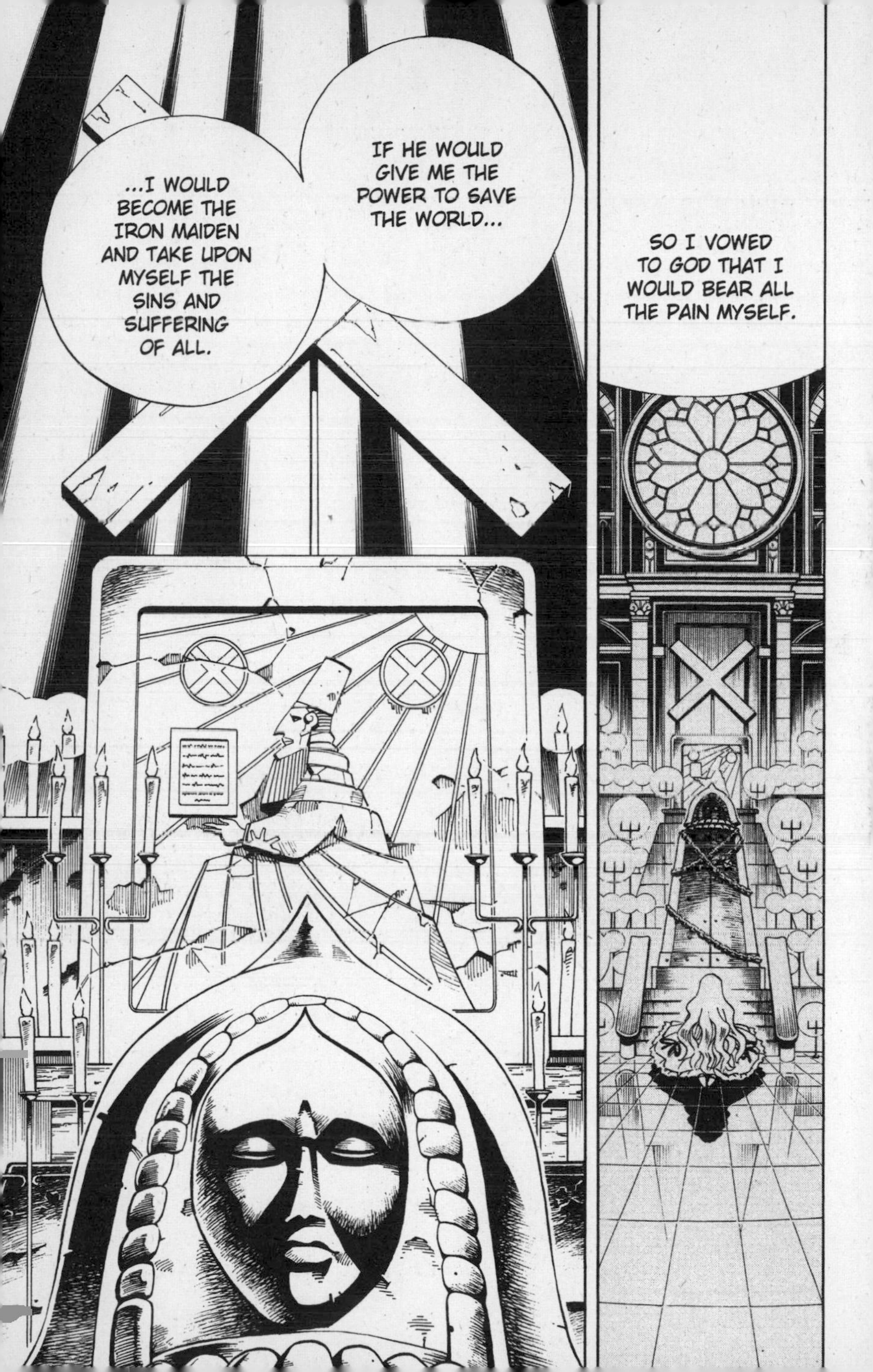
SO I VOWED TO GOD THAT I WOULD BEAR ALL THE PAIN MYSELF.
IF HE WOULD GIVE ME THE POWER TO SAVE THE WORLD...
...I WOULD BECOME THE IRON MAIDEN AND TAKE UPON MYSELF THE SINS AND SUFFERING OF ALL.

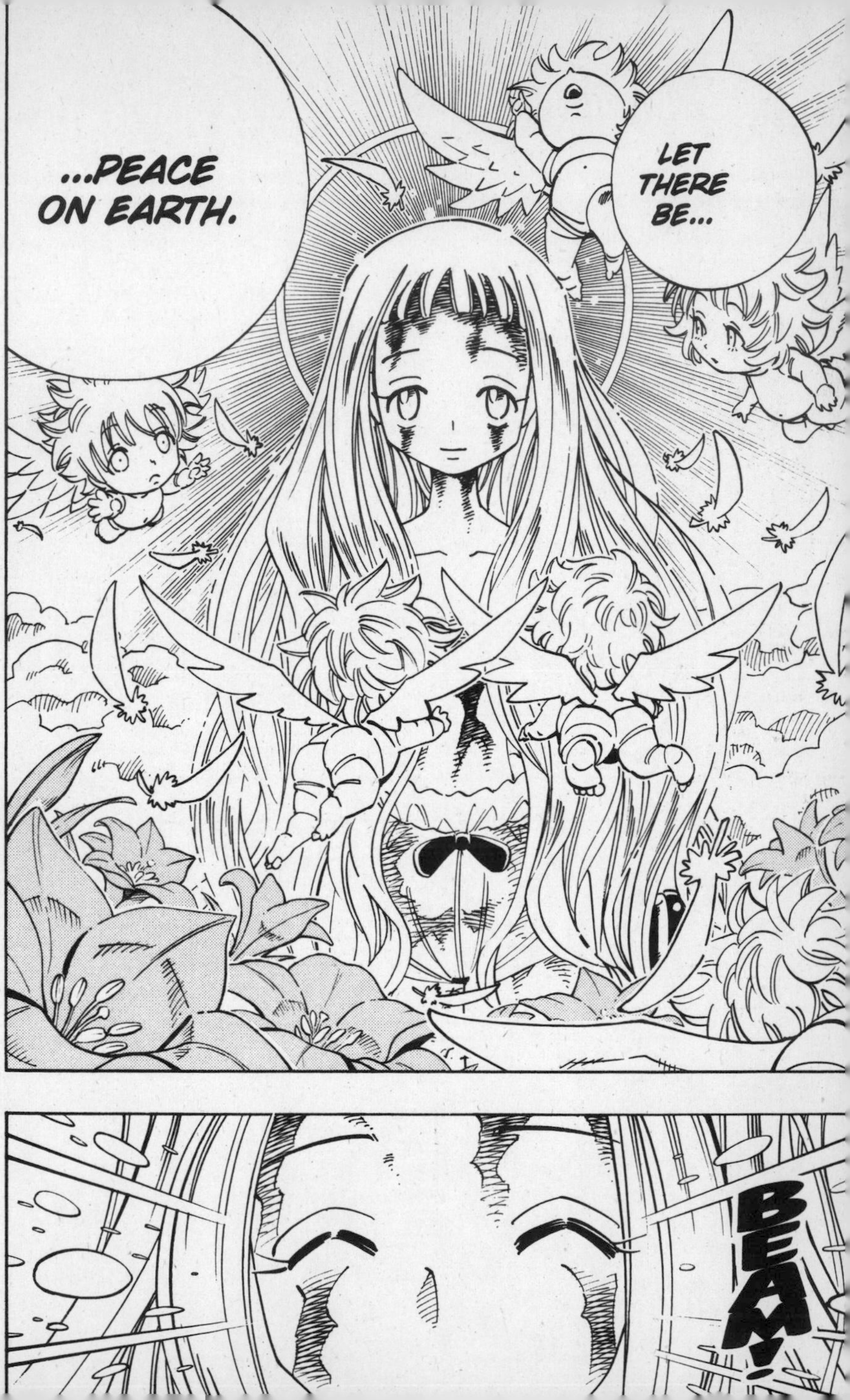
LET THERE BE...
...PEACE ON EARTH.
BEAM!

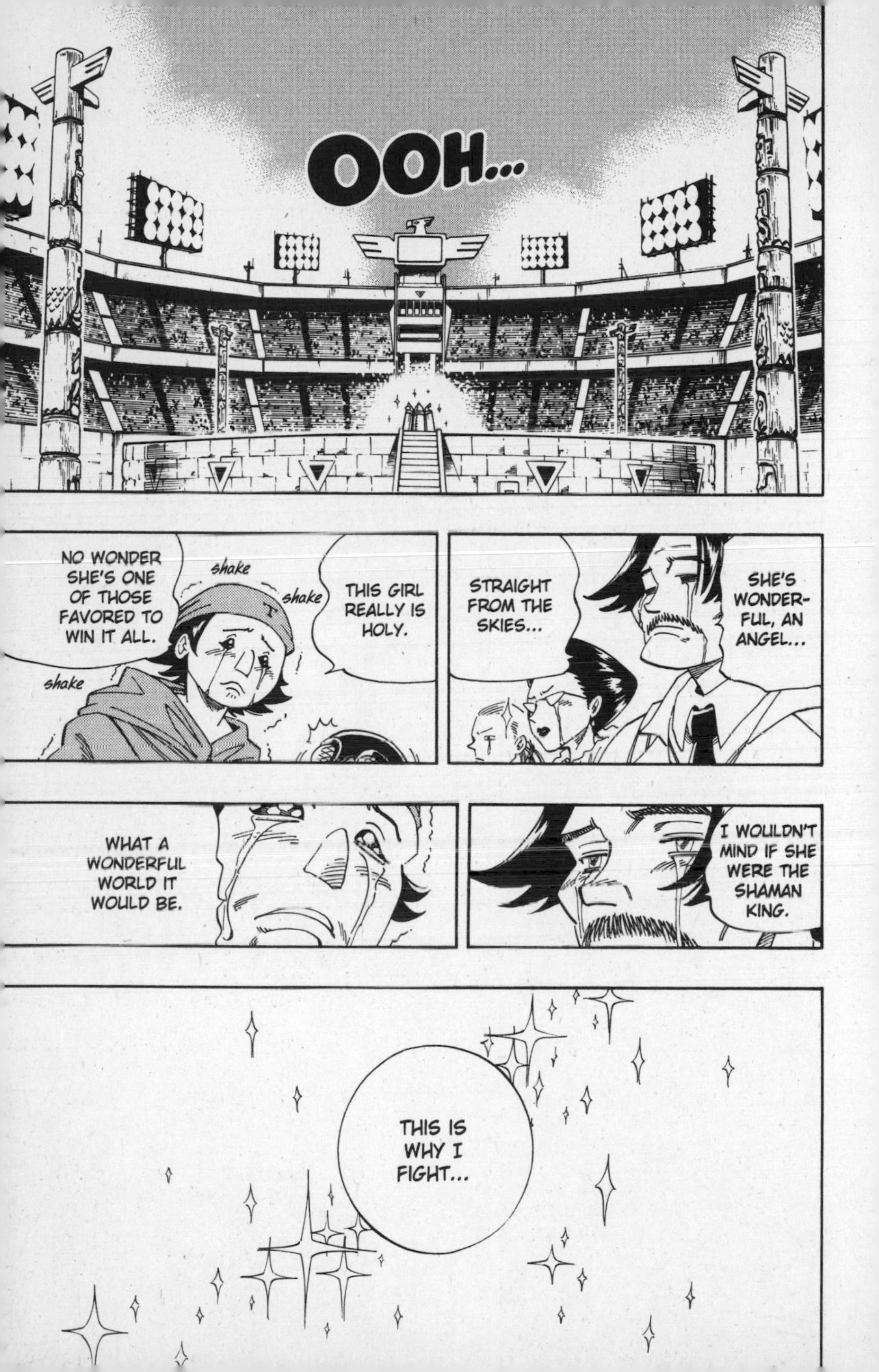
OOH...
SHE'S WONDERFUL, AN ANGEL...
STRAIGHT FROM THE SKIES...
THIS GIRL REALLY IS HOLY.
shake
shake
NO WONDER SHE'S ONE OF THOSE FAVORED TO WIN IT ALL.
shake
I WOULDN'T MIND IF SHE WERE THE SHAMAN KING.
WHAT A WONDERFUL WORLD IT WOULD BE.
THIS IS WHY I FIGHT...

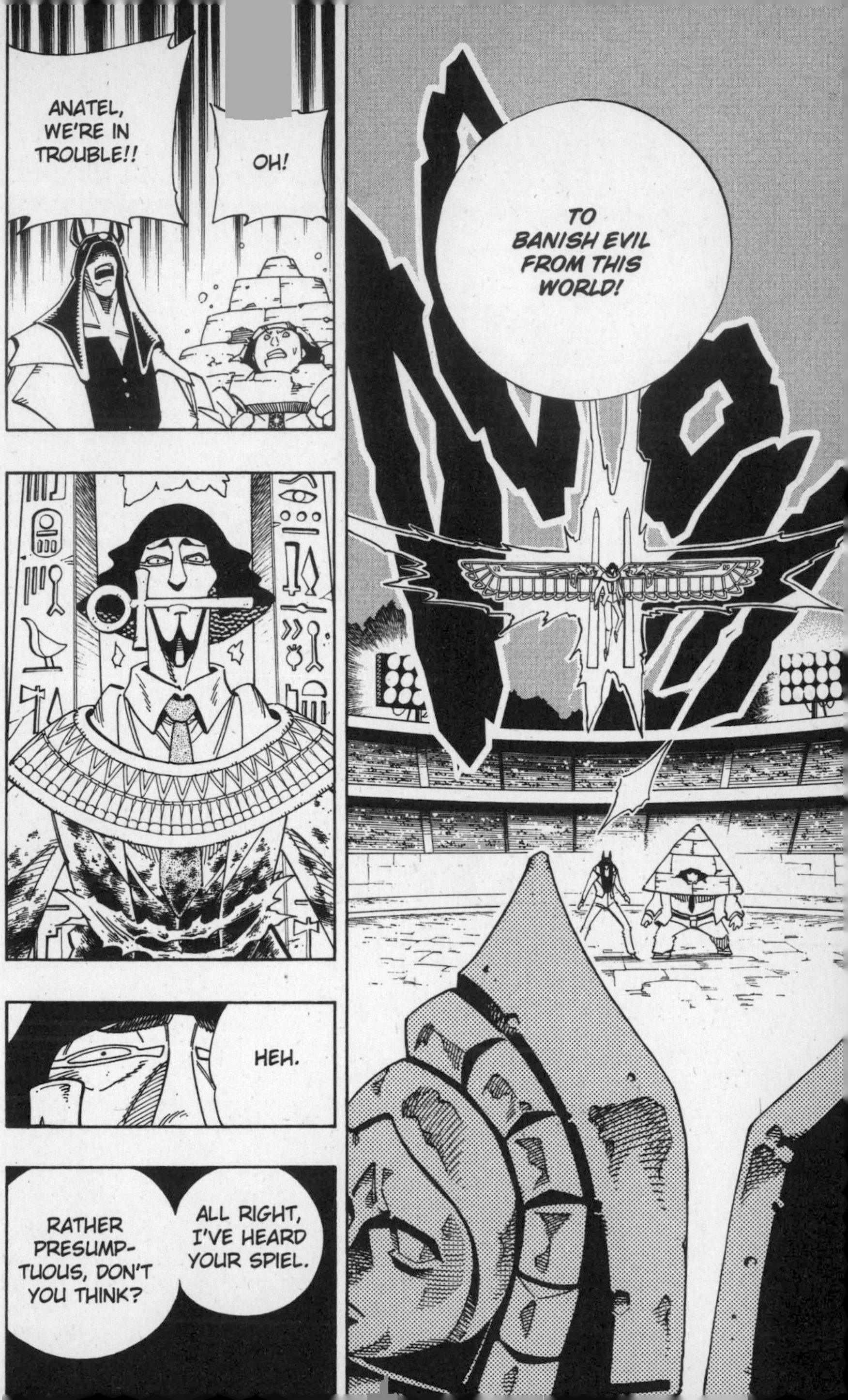
TO BANISH EVIL FROM THIS WORLD!
OH!
ANATEL, WE'RE IN TROUBLE!!
HEH.
ALL RIGHT, I'VE HEARD YOUR SPIEL.
RATHER PRESUMP-TUOUS, DON'T YOU THINK?

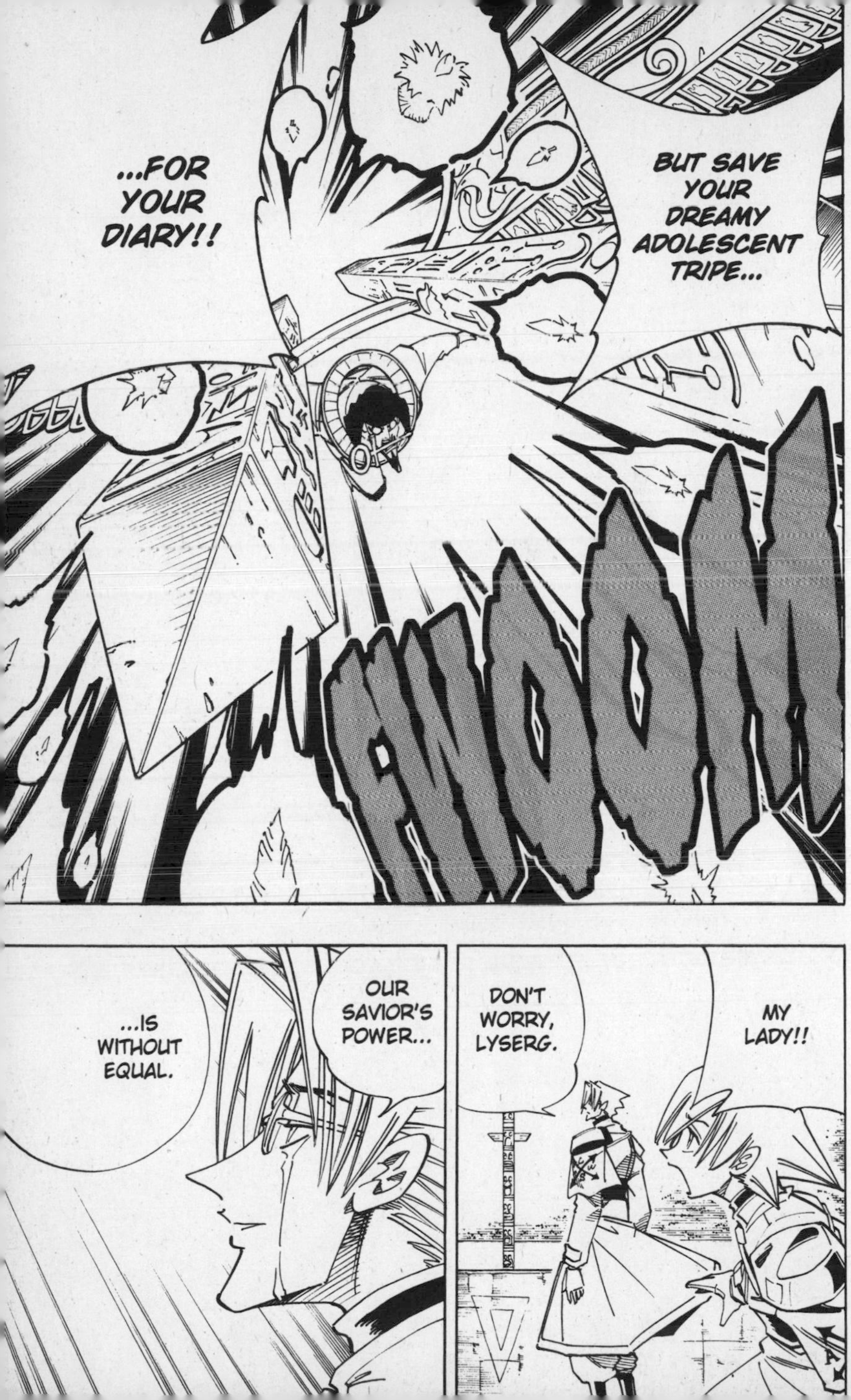
BUT SAVE YOUR DREAMY ADOLESCENT TRIPE...
...FOR YOUR DIARY!!
FWOOM
MY LADY!!
DON'T WORRY, LYSERG.
OUR SAVIOR'S POWER...
...IS WITHOUT EQUAL.

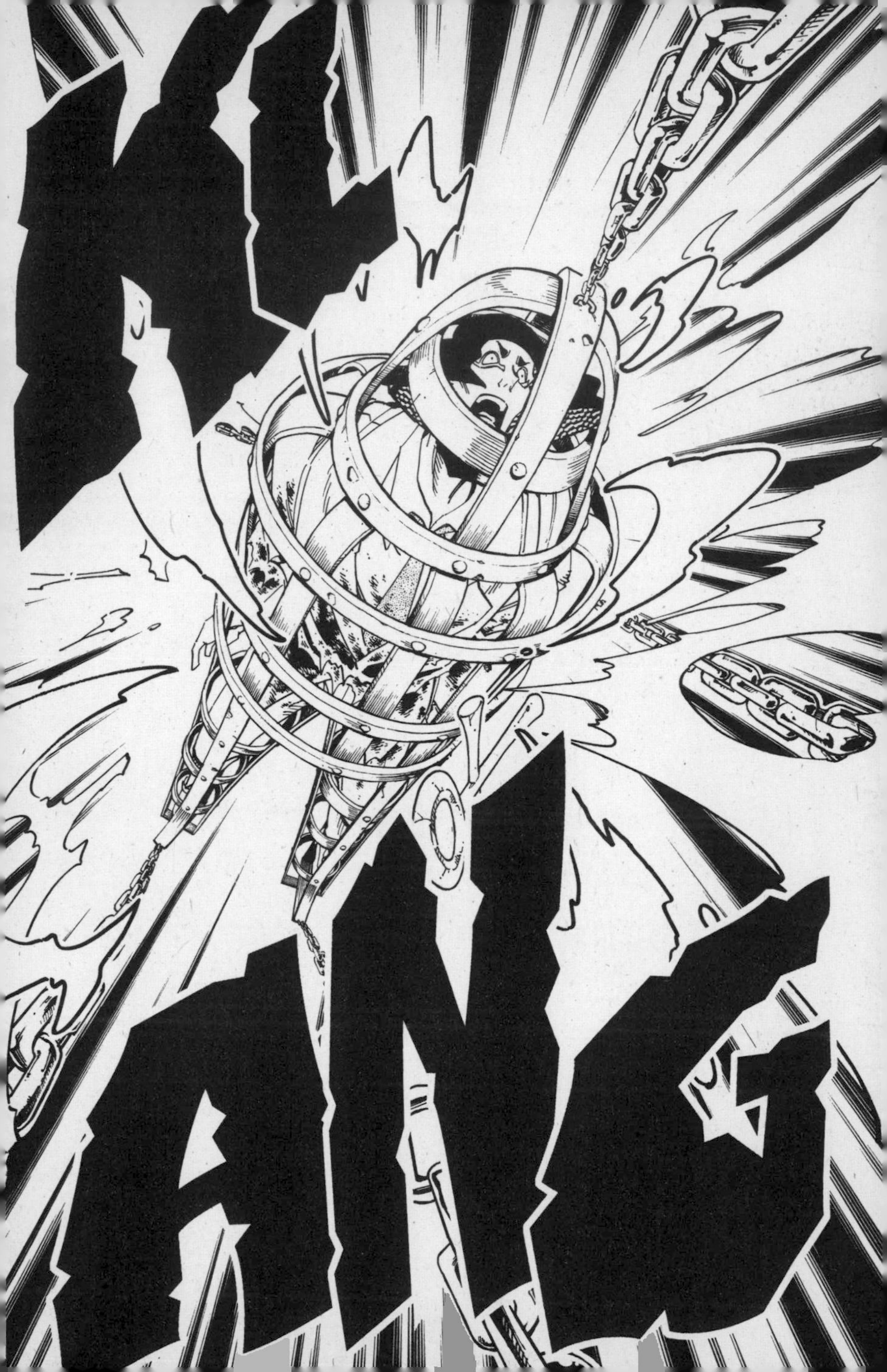
KLANG

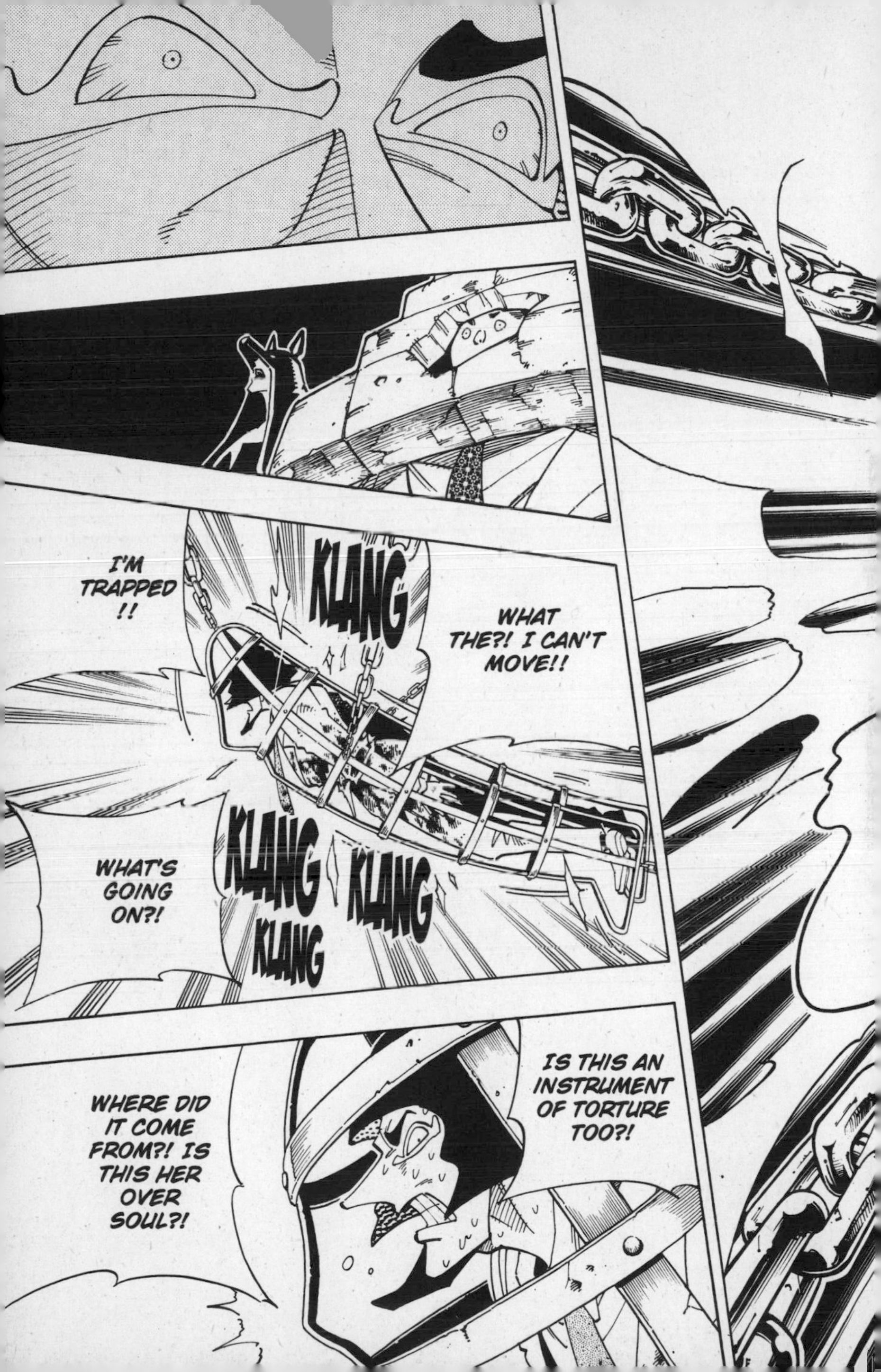
KLANG
WHAT THE?! I CAN'T MOVE!!
I'M TRAPPED!!
KLANG
KLANG
KLANG
WHAT'S GOING ON?!
IS THIS AN INSTRUMENT OF TORTURE TOO?!
WHERE DID IT COME FROM?! IS THIS HER OVER SOUL?!

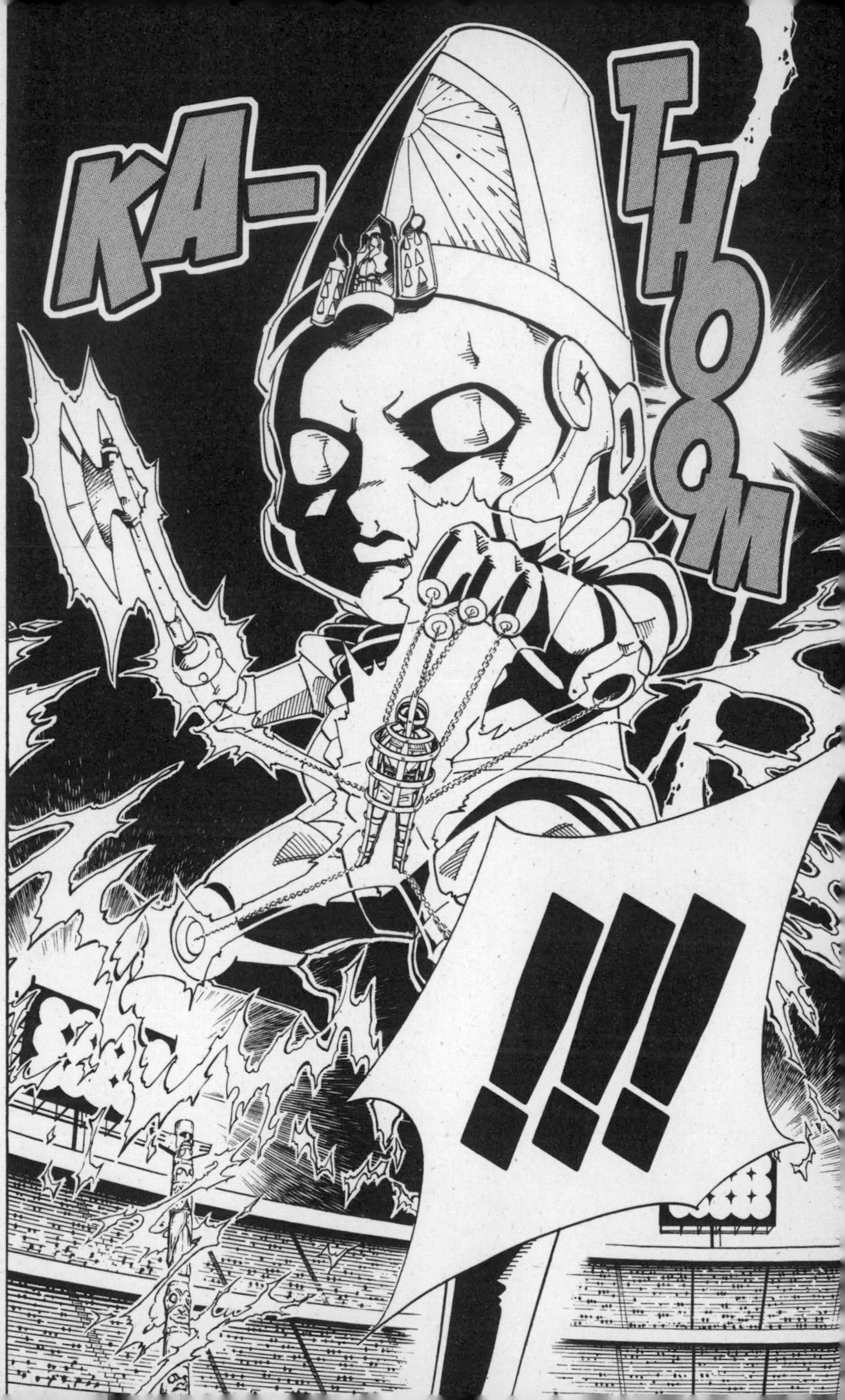
KA-
THOOM
!!!

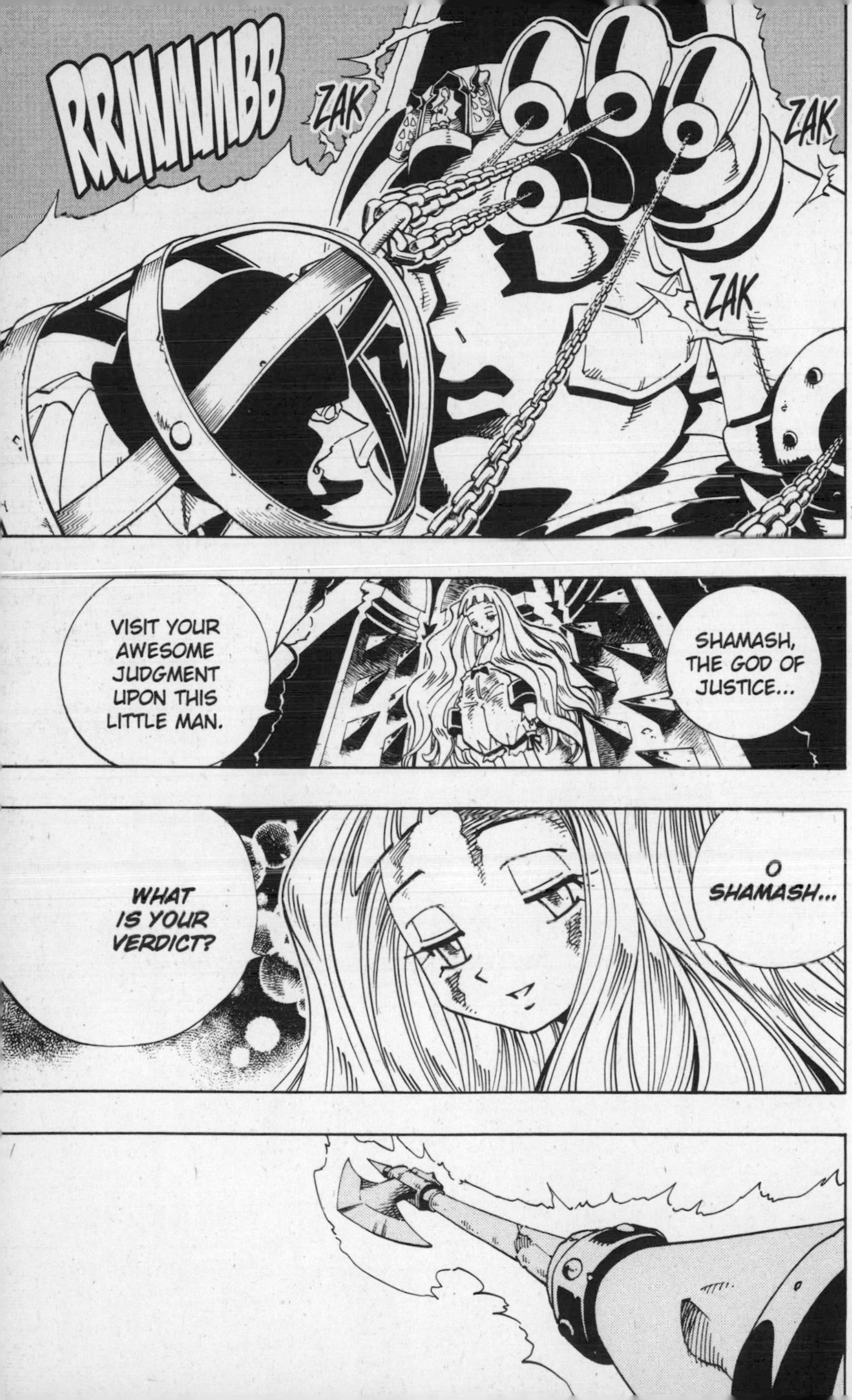
ZAK
ZAK
ZAK
RRMMMBB
SHAMASH, THE GOD OF JUSTICE...
VISIT YOUR AWESOME JUDGMENT UPON THIS LITTLE MAN.
O SHAMASH...
WHAT IS YOUR VERDICT?

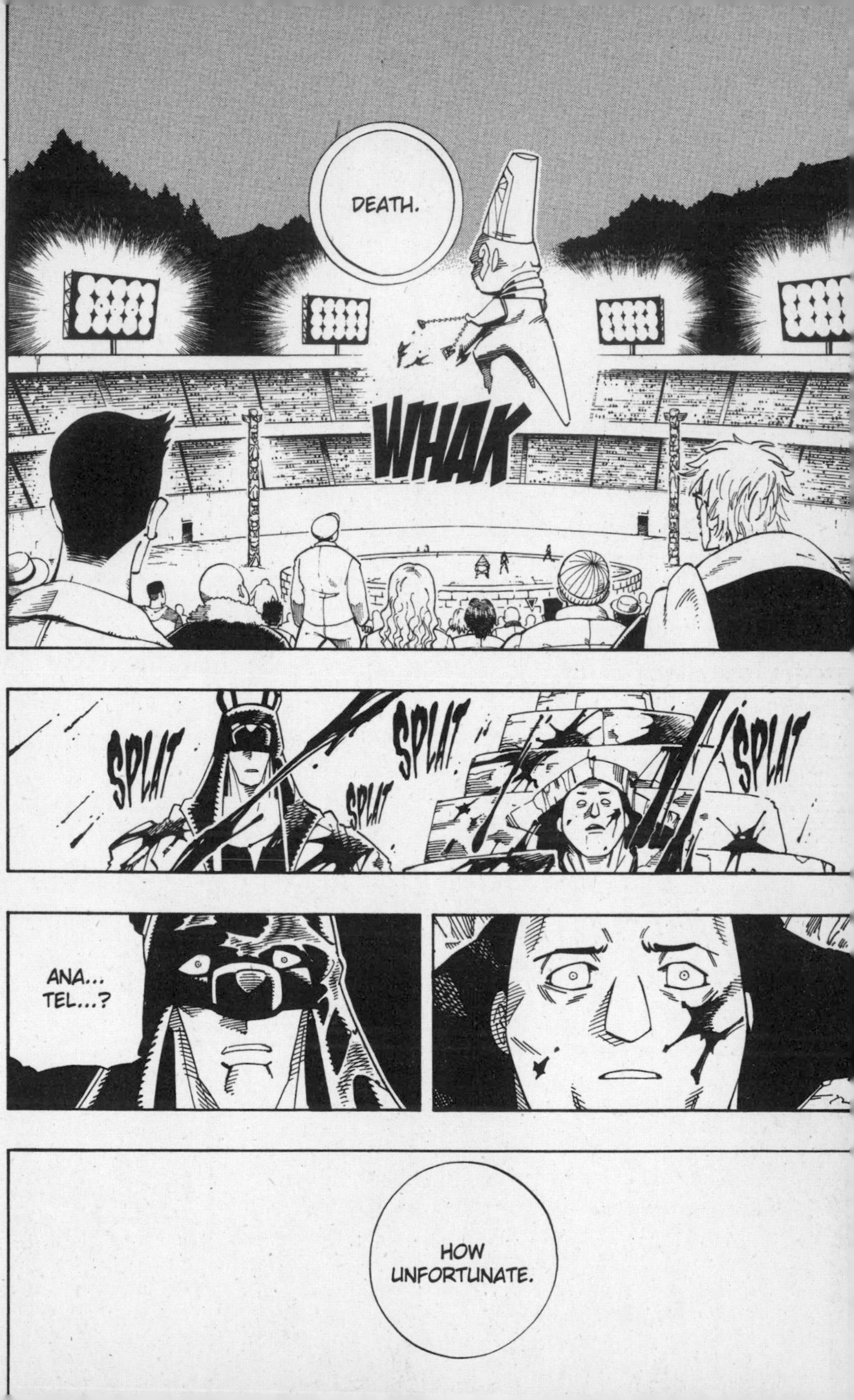
DEATH.
WHAK
SPLAT
SPLAT
SPLAT
SPLAT
ANA... TEL...?
HOW UNFORTUNATE.

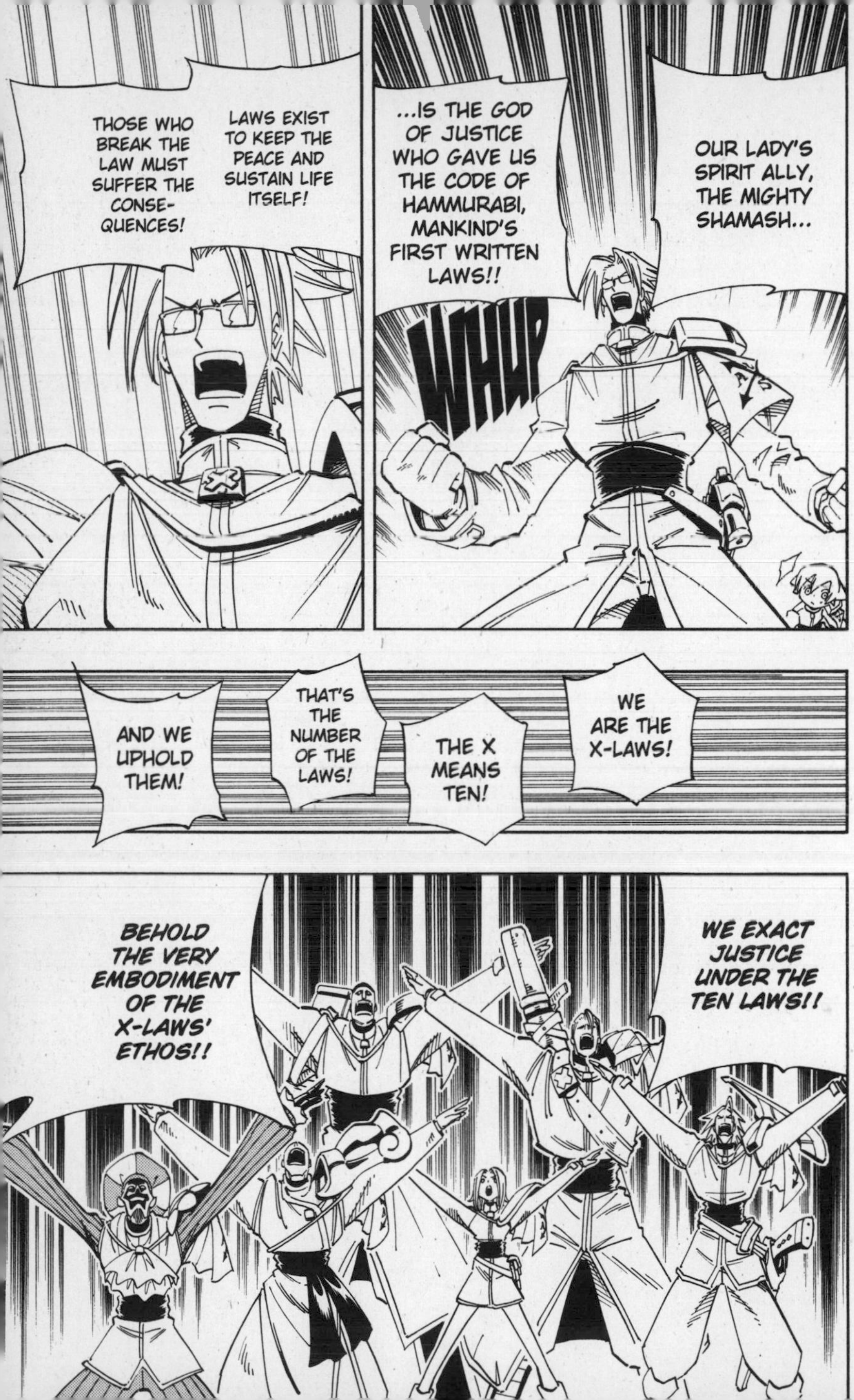
OUR LADY'S SPIRIT ALLY, THE MIGHTY SHAMASH...
...IS THE GOD OF JUSTICE WHO GAVE US THE CODE OF HAMMURABI, MANKIND'S FIRST WRITTEN LAWS!!
WHUP
LAWS EXIST TO KEEP THE PEACE AND SUSTAIN LIFE ITSELF!
THOSE WHO BREAK THE LAW MUST SUFFER THE CONSE-QUENCES!
WE ARE THE X-LAWS!
THE X MEANS TEN!
THAT'S THE NUMBER OF THE LAWS!
AND WE UPHOLD THEM!
WE EXACT JUSTICE UNDER THE TEN LAWS!!
BEHOLD THE VERY EMBODIMENT OF THE X-LAWS' ETHOS!!

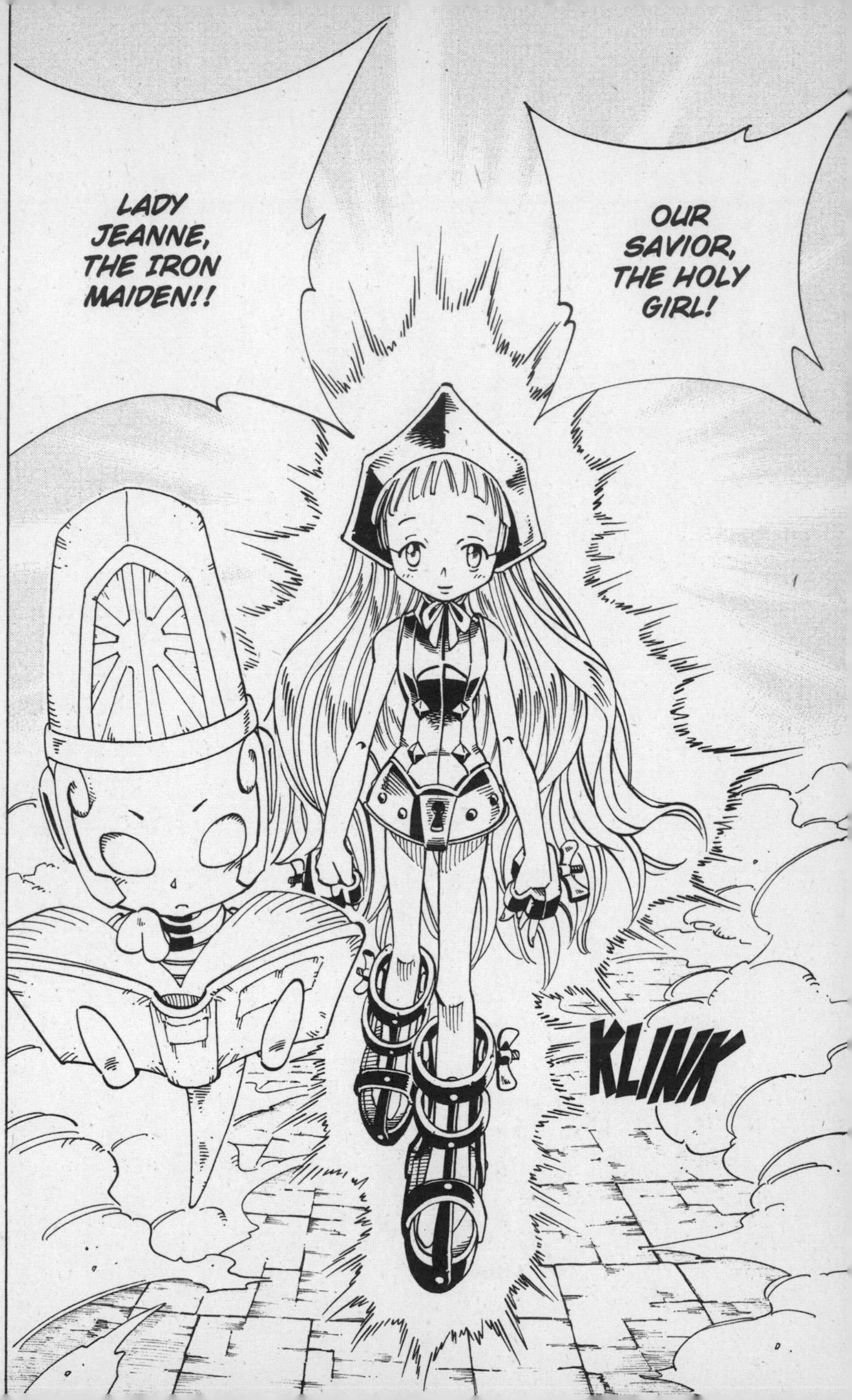
OUR SAVIOR, THE HOLY GIRL!
LADY JEANNE, THE IRON MAIDEN!!
KLINK

Shaman King™

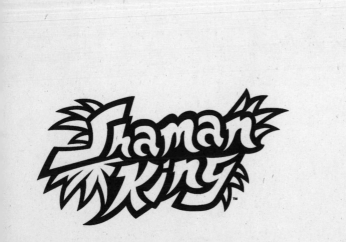

SHAMAN KING ITEM FILE No.44

拷問器具アイアンメイデン(ジャンヌ専用)

INSTRUMENT OF TORTURE: THE IRON MAIDEN (FOR JEANNE'S PRIVATE USE)

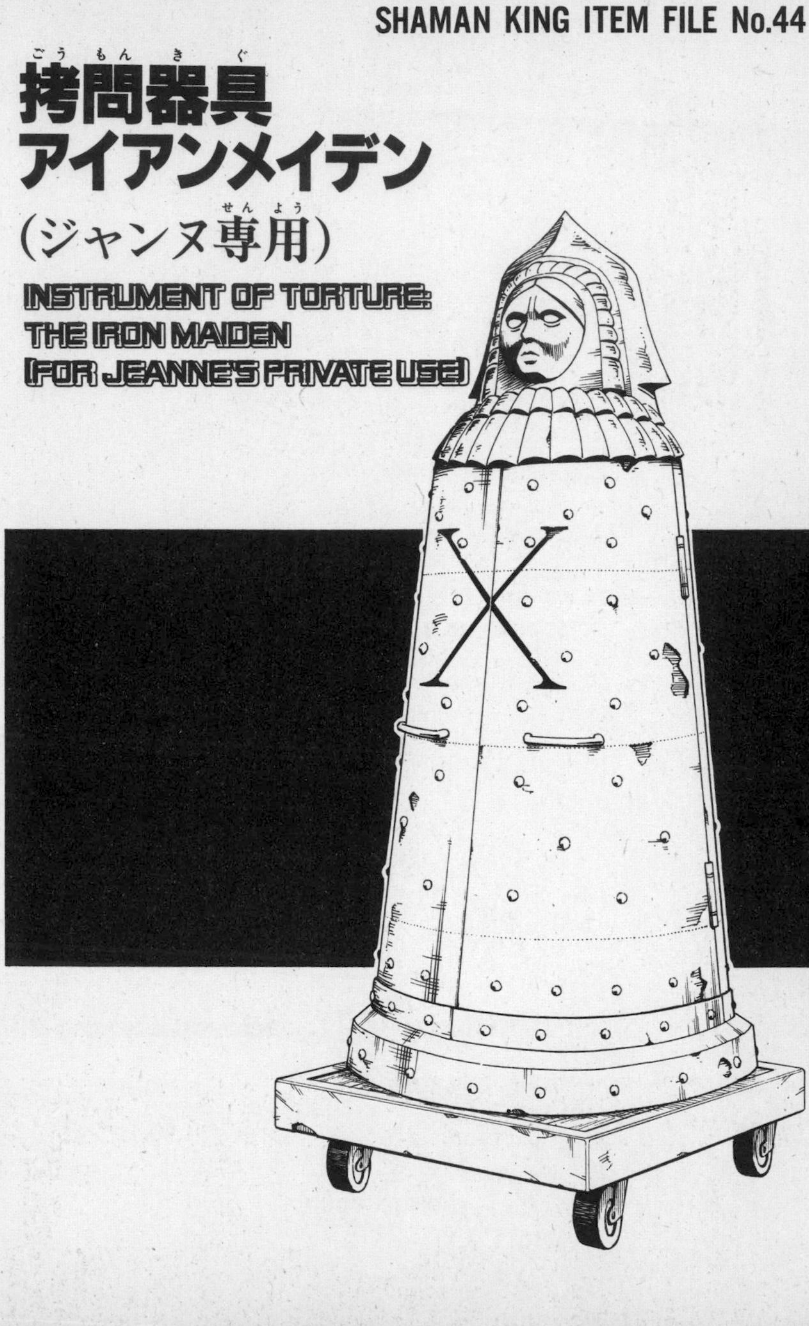
X

Reincarnation 125: The Tortured Princess: The Cheeky Iron Maiden

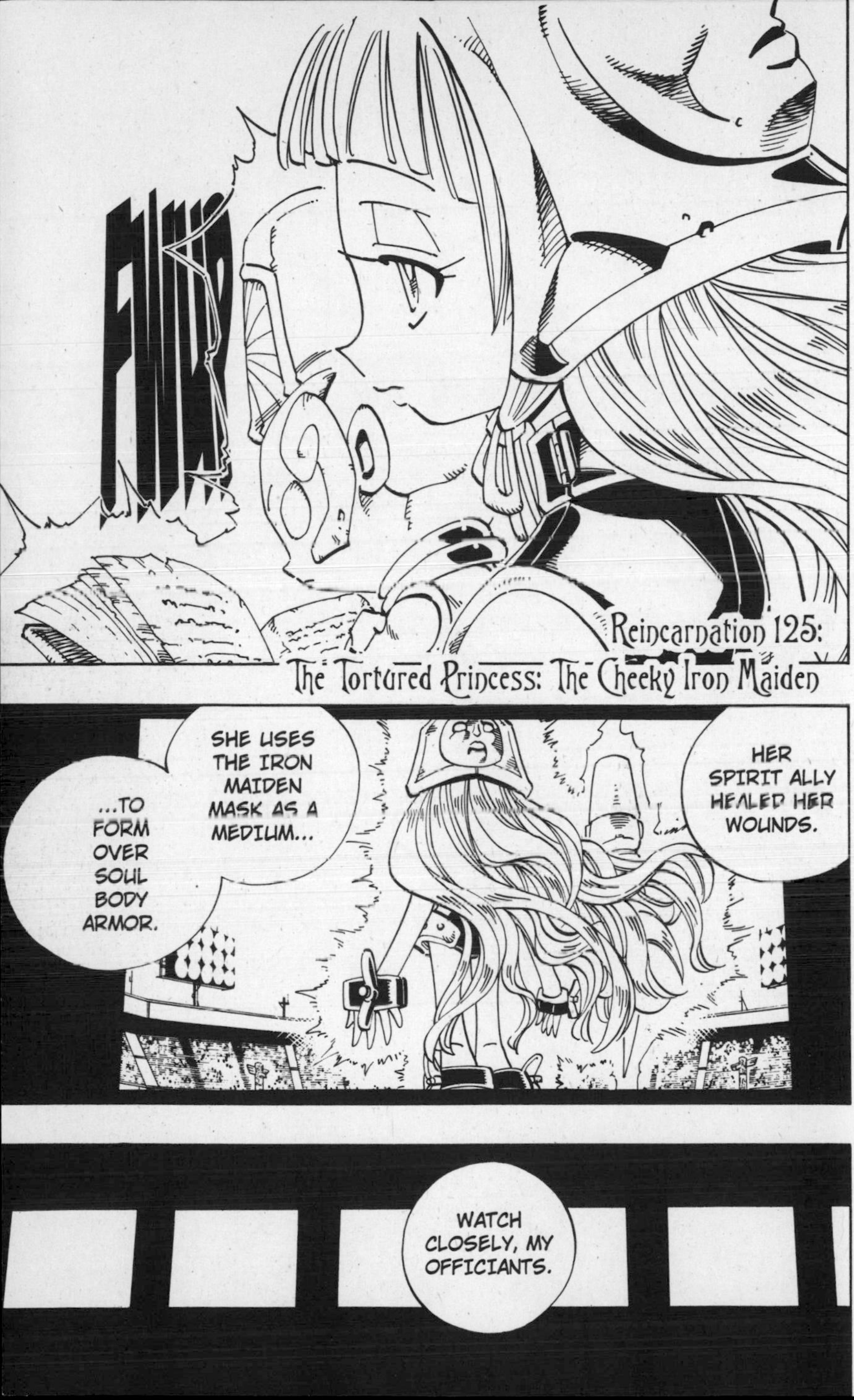
HER SPIRIT ALLY HEALED HER WOUNDS.
SHE USES THE IRON MAIDEN MASK AS A MEDIUM...
...TO FORM OVER SOUL BODY ARMOR.
WATCH CLOSELY, MY OFFICIANTS.

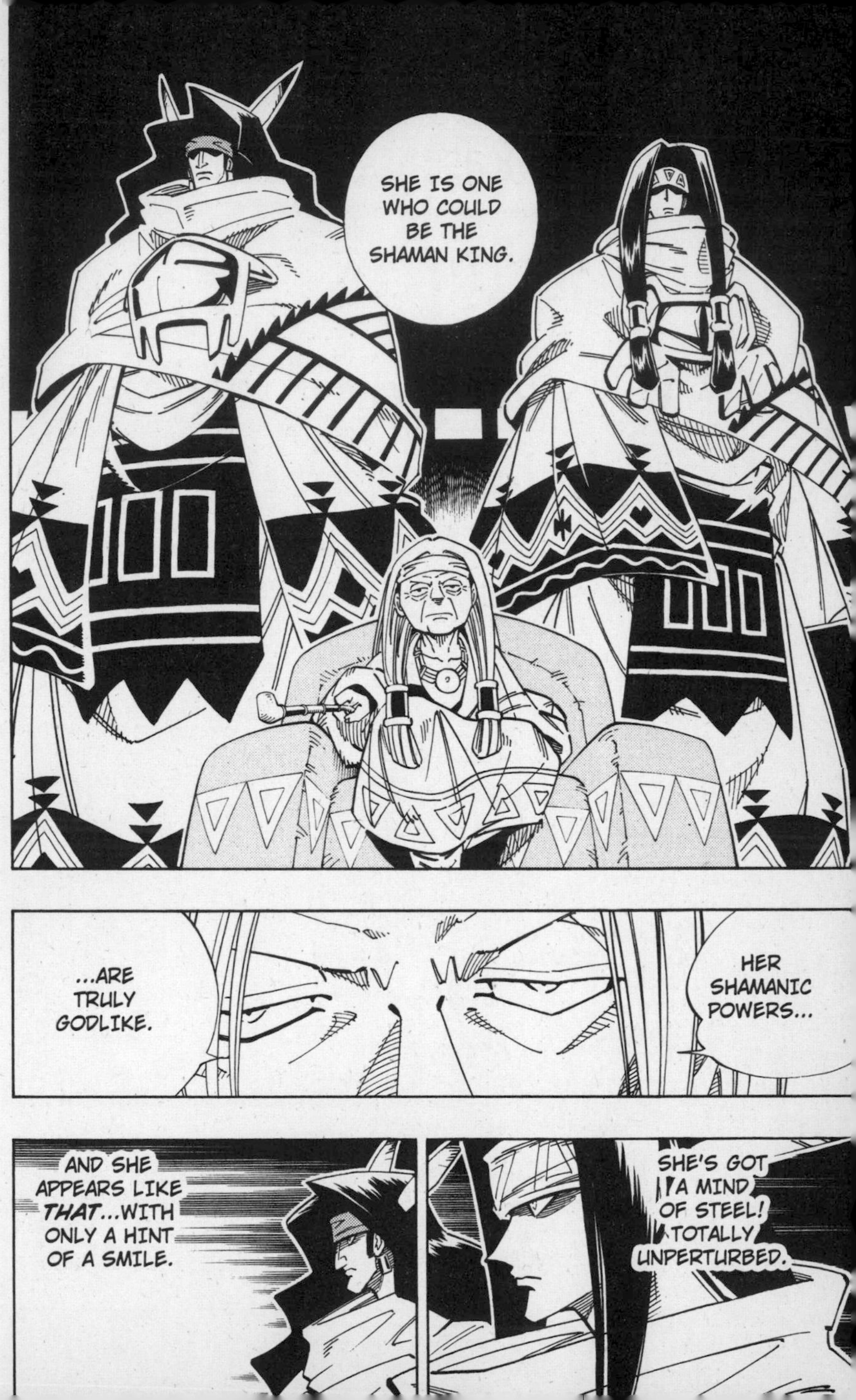
SHE IS ONE WHO COULD BE THE SHAMAN KING.
HER SHAMANIC POWERS...
...ARE TRULY GODLIKE.
SHE'S GOT A MIND OF STEEL! TOTALLY UNPERTURBED.
AND SHE APPEARS LIKE *THAT*...WITH ONLY A HINT OF A SMILE.

Reincarnation 125:
The Tortured Princess: Cheeky Iron Maiden

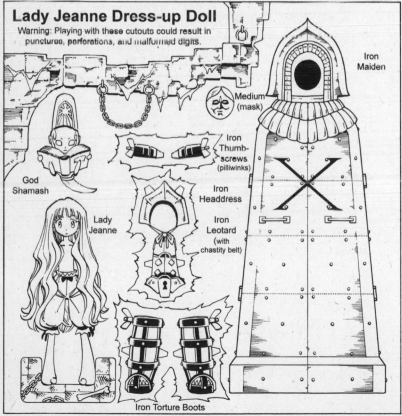

Lady Jeanne Dress-up Doll

Warning: Playing with these cutouts could result in punctures, perforations, and malformed digits.

Iron Maiden

Medium (mask)

God Shamash

Iron Thumb-screws (pilliwinks)

Iron Headdress

Lady Jeanne

Iron Leotard (with chastity belt)

Iron Torture Boots

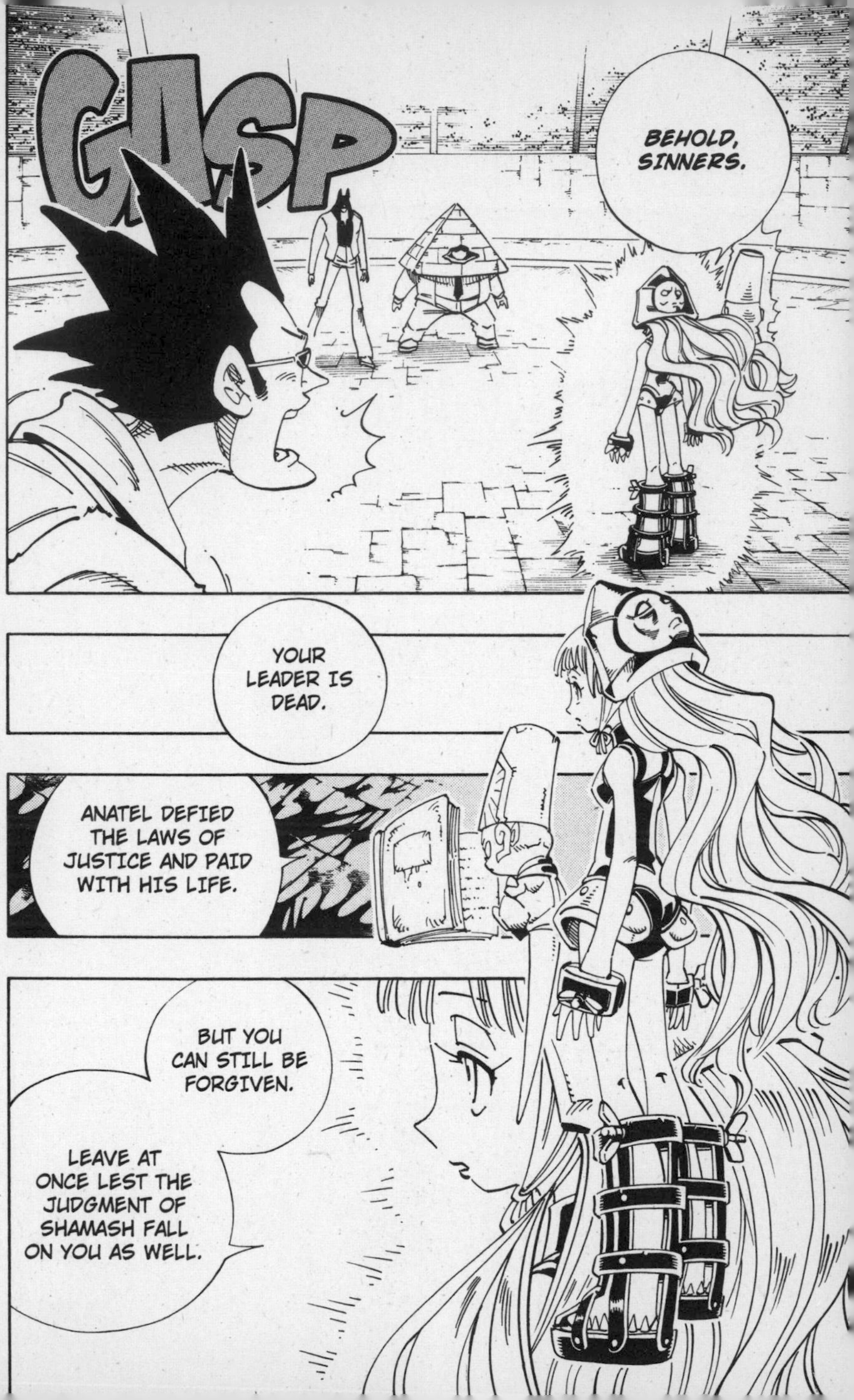
BEHOLD, SINNERS.
GASP
YOUR LEADER IS DEAD.
ANATEL DEFIED THE LAWS OF JUSTICE AND PAID WITH HIS LIFE.
BUT YOU CAN STILL BE FORGIVEN.
LEAVE AT ONCE LEST THE JUDGMENT OF SHAMASH FALL ON YOU AS WELL.

READ THIS WAY

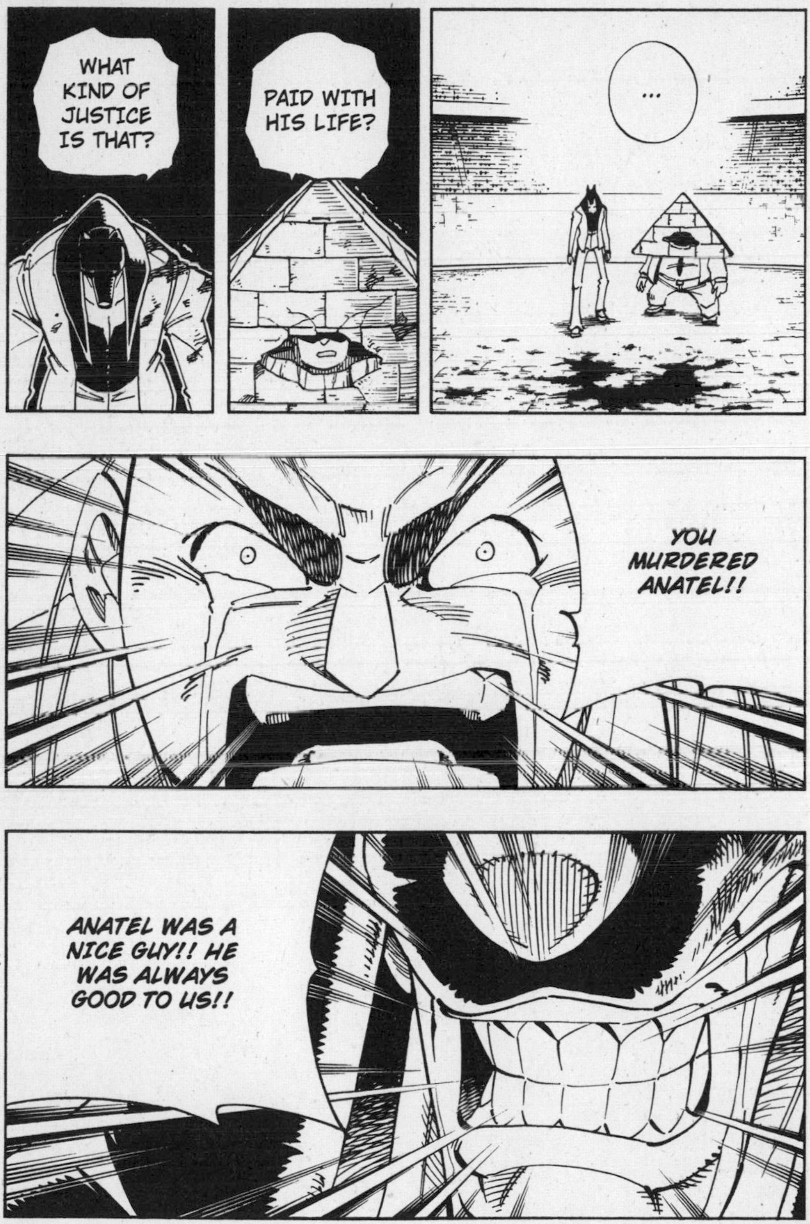
...
PAID WITH HIS LIFE?
WHAT KIND OF JUSTICE IS THAT?
YOU MURDERED ANATEL!!
ANATEL WAS A NICE GUY!! HE WAS ALWAYS GOOD TO US!!

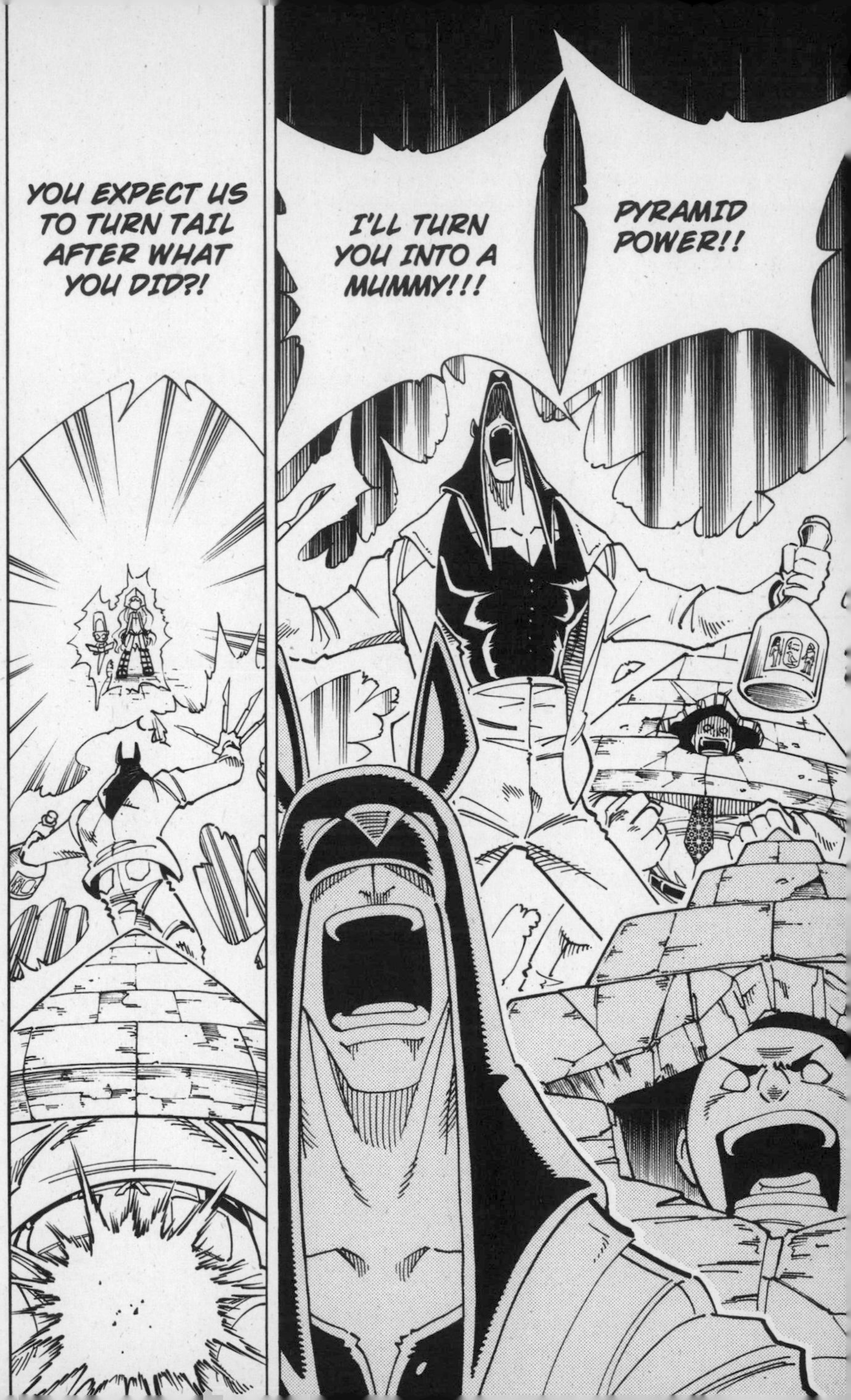
PYRAMID POWER!!
I'LL TURN YOU INTO A MUMMY!!!
YOU EXPECT US TO TURN TAIL AFTER WHAT YOU DID?!

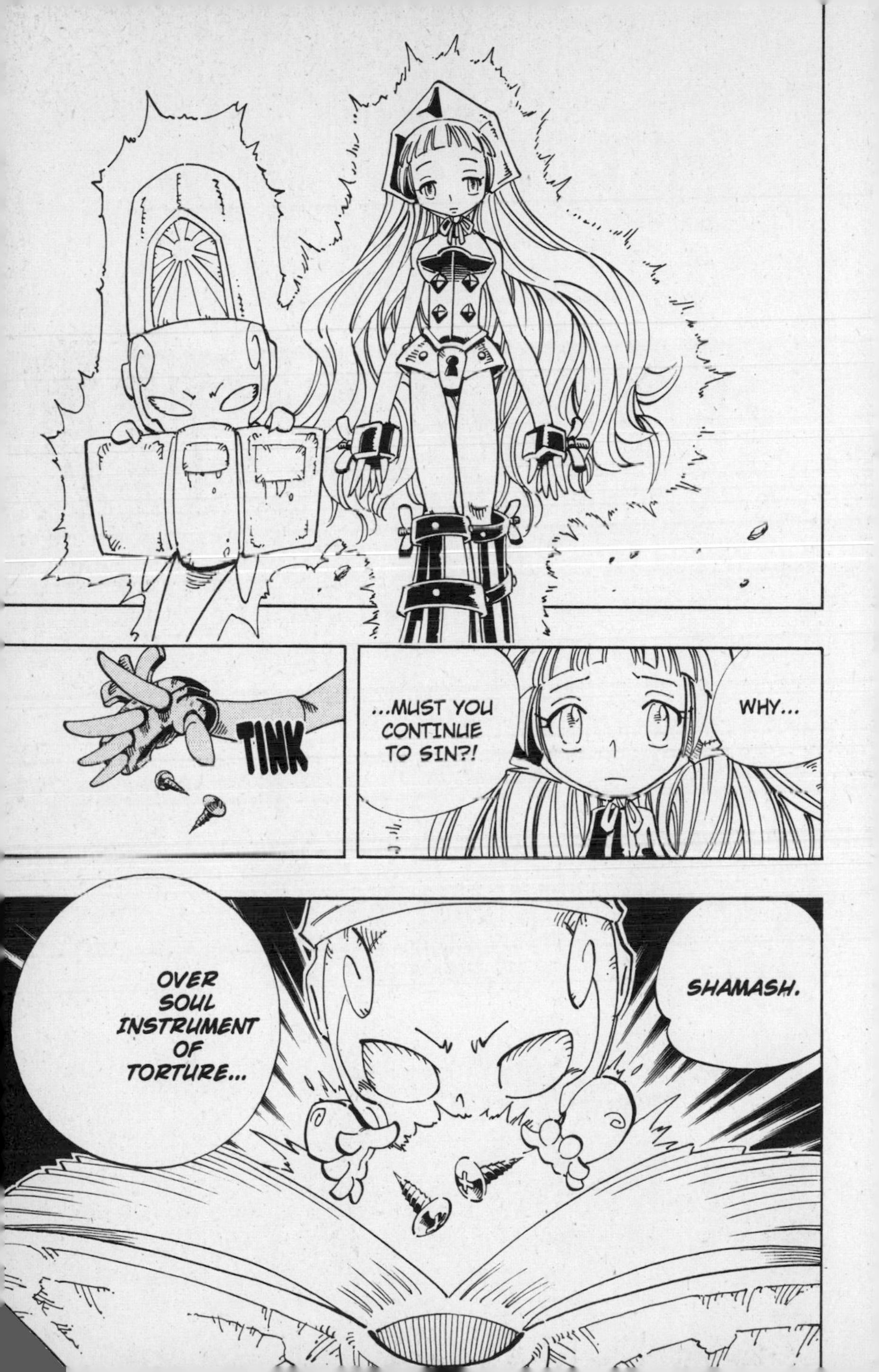
WHY...
...MUST YOU CONTINUE TO SIN?!
TINK
SHAMASH.
OVER SOUL INSTRUMENT OF TORTURE...

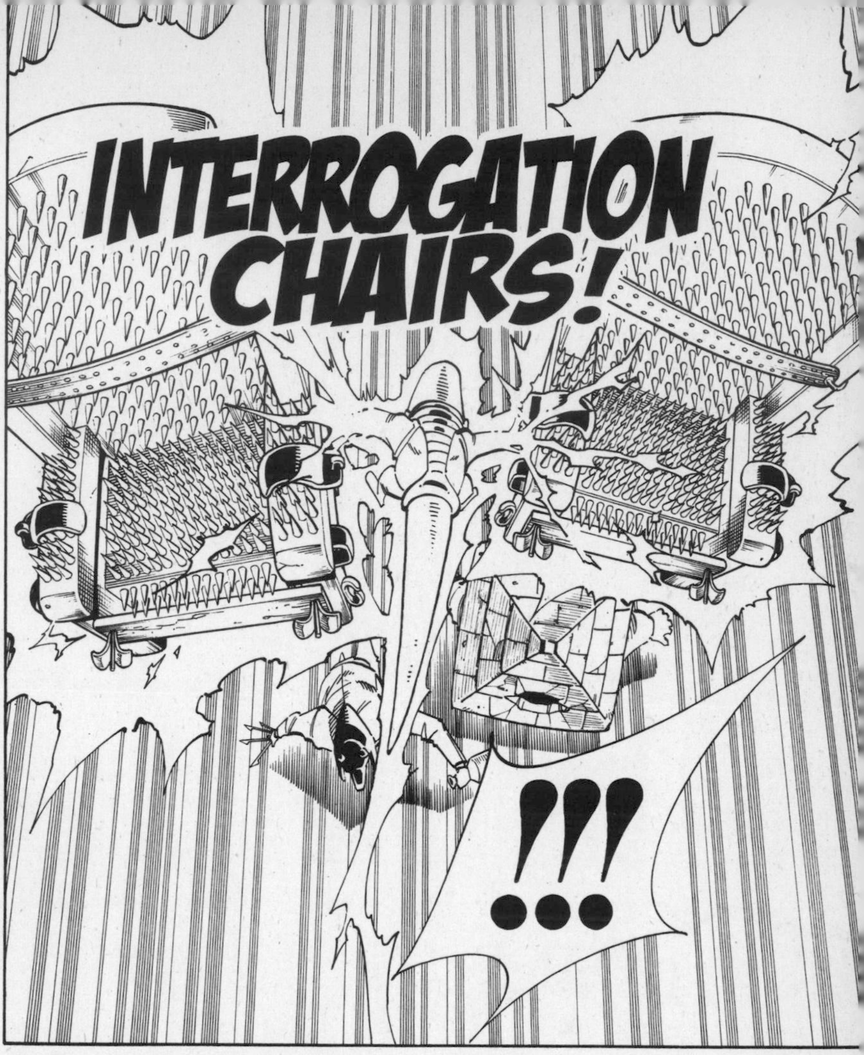
INTERROGATION CHAIRS!
!!!
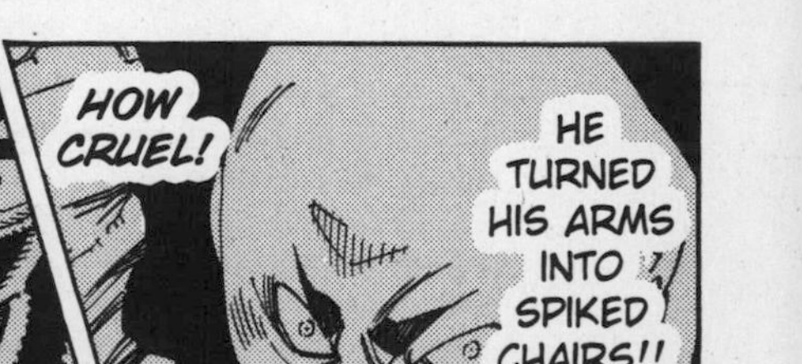
HE TURNED HIS ARMS INTO SPIKED CHAIRS!!
HOW CRUEL!
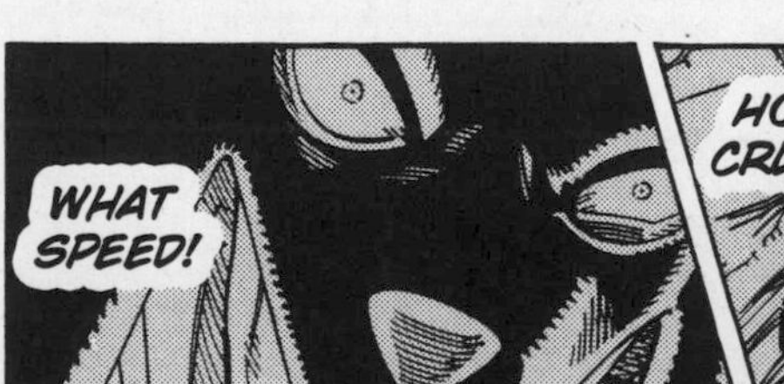
WHAT SPEED!

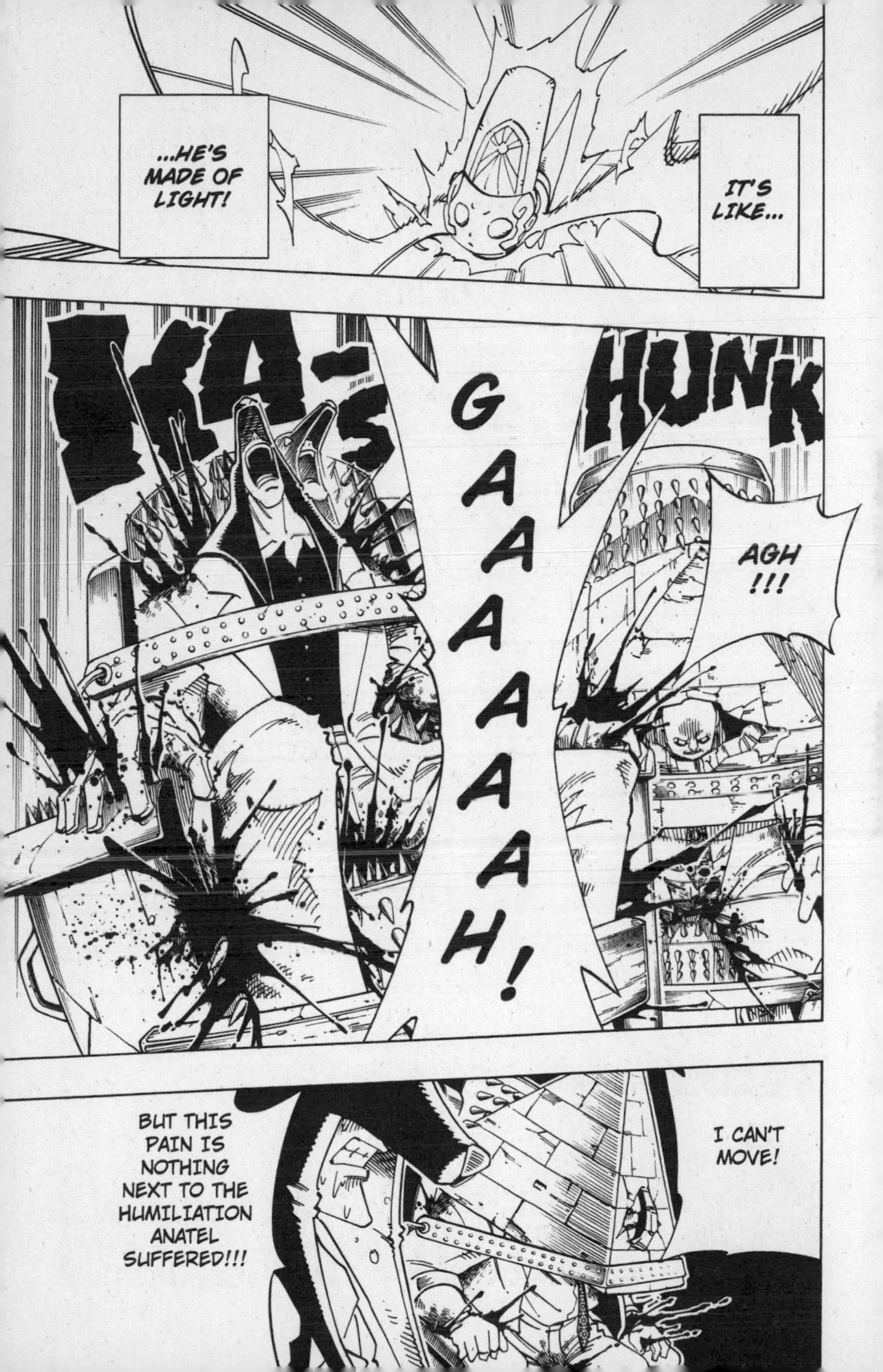
IT'S LIKE...
...HE'S MADE OF LIGHT!
KA-SHUNK
GAAAAAH!
AGH !!!
I CAN'T MOVE!
BUT THIS PAIN IS NOTHING NEXT TO THE HUMILIATION ANATEL SUFFERED!!!

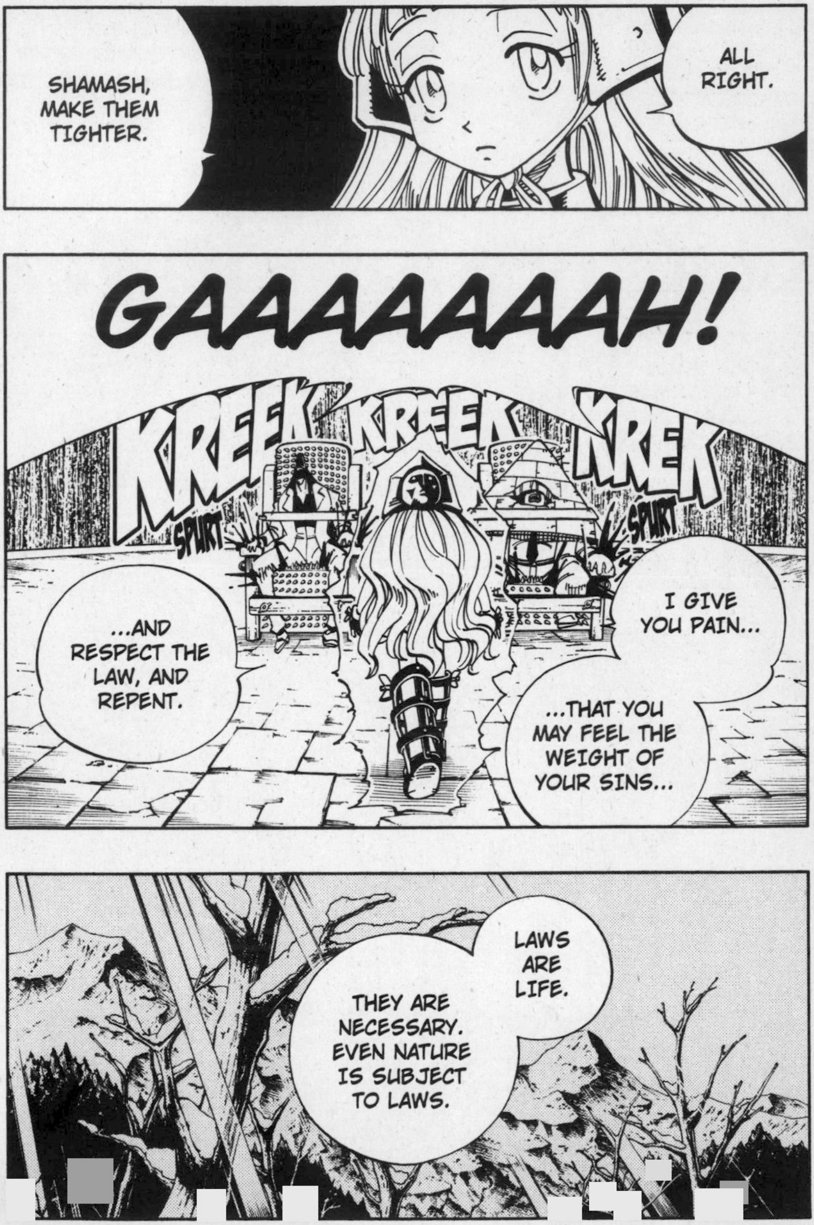
ALL RIGHT.
SHAMASH, MAKE THEM TIGHTER.
GAAAAAAH!
KREEK KREEK KREK
SPURT
SPURT
I GIVE YOU PAIN...
...THAT YOU MAY FEEL THE WEIGHT OF YOUR SINS...
...AND RESPECT THE LAW, AND REPENT.
LAWS ARE LIFE.
THEY ARE NECESSARY. EVEN NATURE IS SUBJECT TO LAWS.

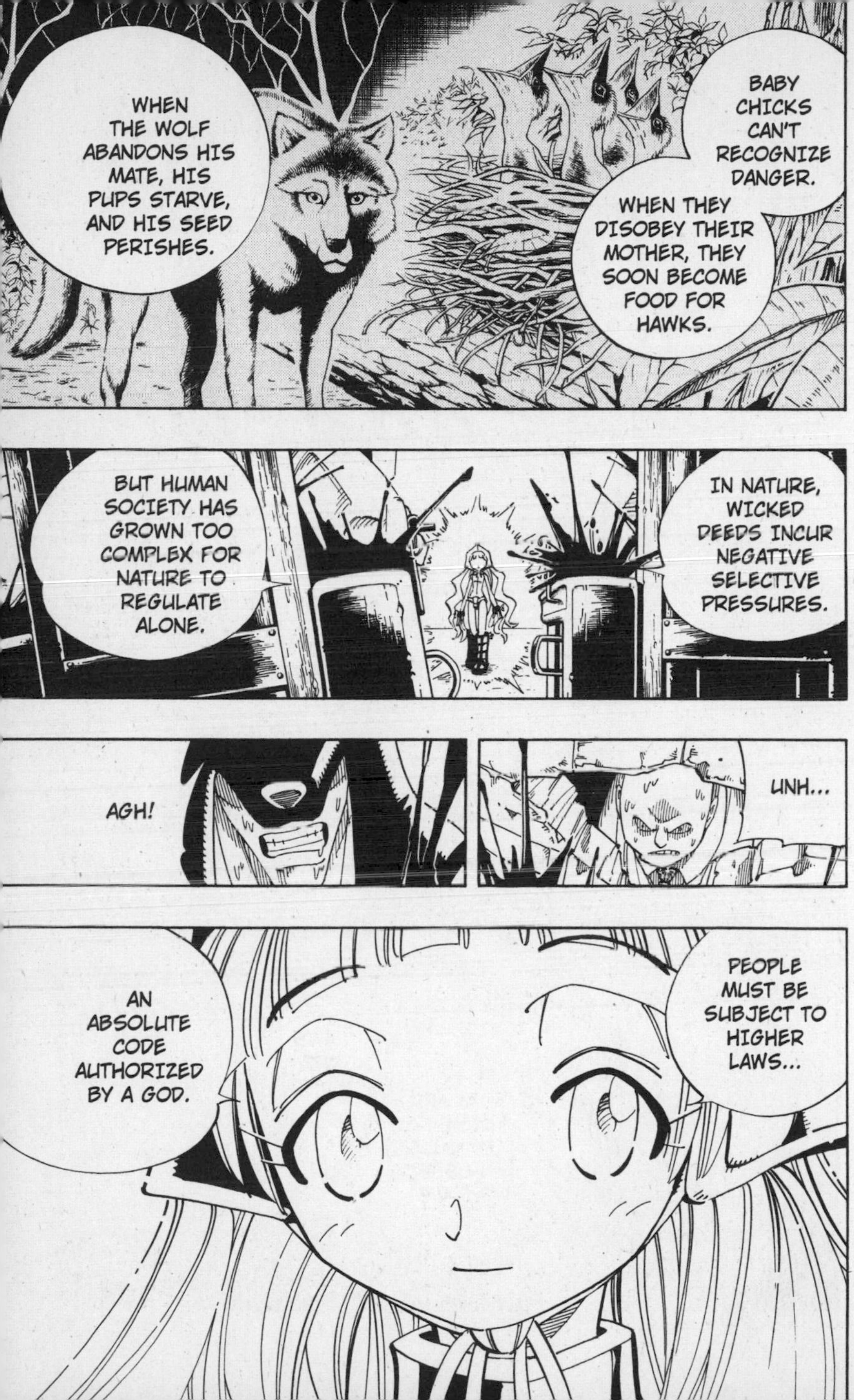
BABY CHICKS CAN'T RECOGNIZE DANGER.
WHEN THEY DISOBEY THEIR MOTHER, THEY SOON BECOME FOOD FOR HAWKS.
WHEN THE WOLF ABANDONS HIS MATE, HIS PUPS STARVE, AND HIS SEED PERISHES.
IN NATURE, WICKED DEEDS INCUR NEGATIVE SELECTIVE PRESSURES.
BUT HUMAN SOCIETY HAS GROWN TOO COMPLEX FOR NATURE TO REGULATE ALONE.
UNH...
AGH!
PEOPLE MUST BE SUBJECT TO HIGHER LAWS...
AN ABSOLUTE CODE AUTHORIZED BY A GOD.

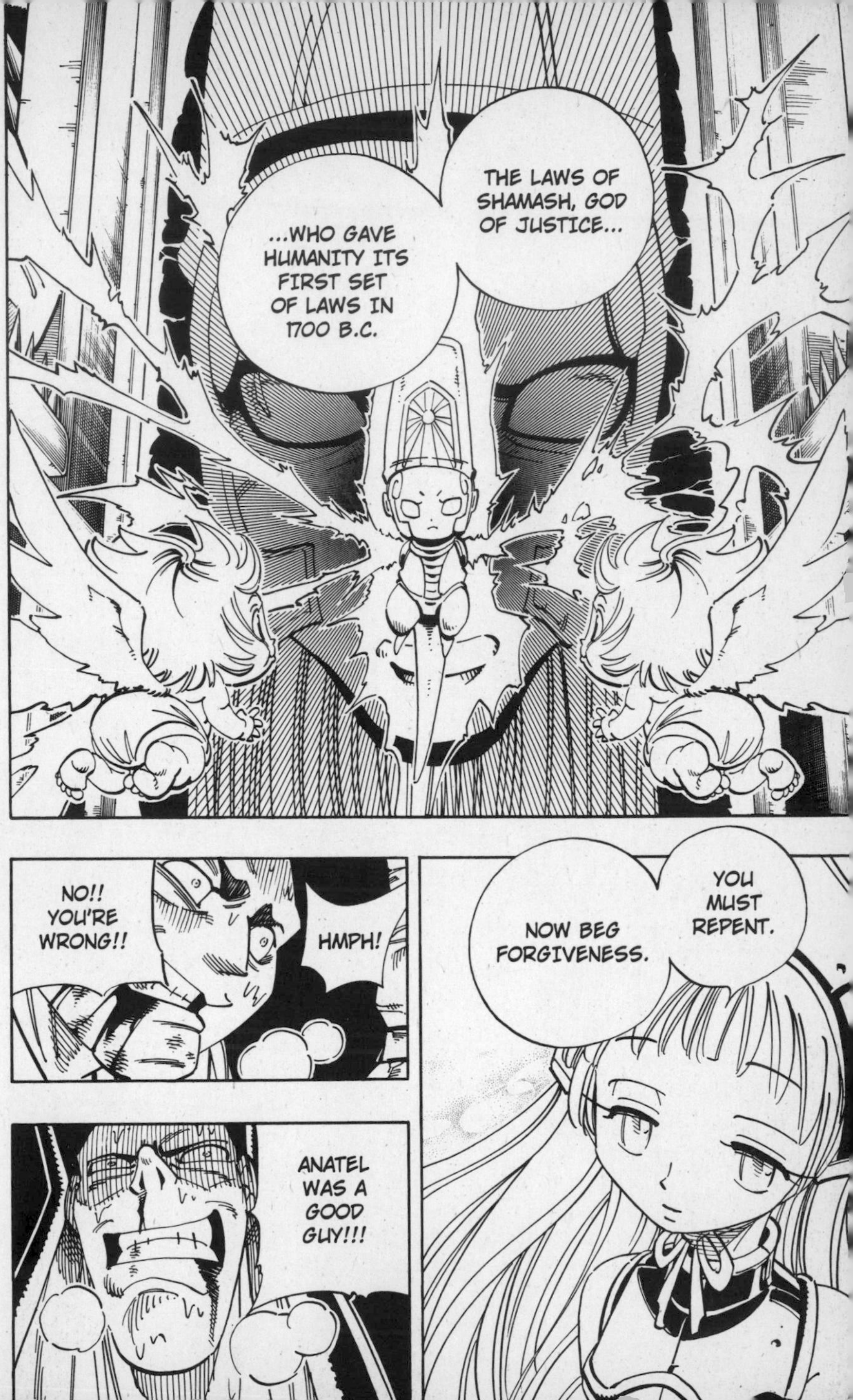
THE LAWS OF SHAMASH, GOD OF JUSTICE...
...WHO GAVE HUMANITY ITS FIRST SET OF LAWS IN 1700 B.C.
YOU MUST REPENT.
NOW BEG FORGIVENESS.
HMPH!
NO!! YOU'RE WRONG!!
ANATEL WAS A GOOD GUY!!!

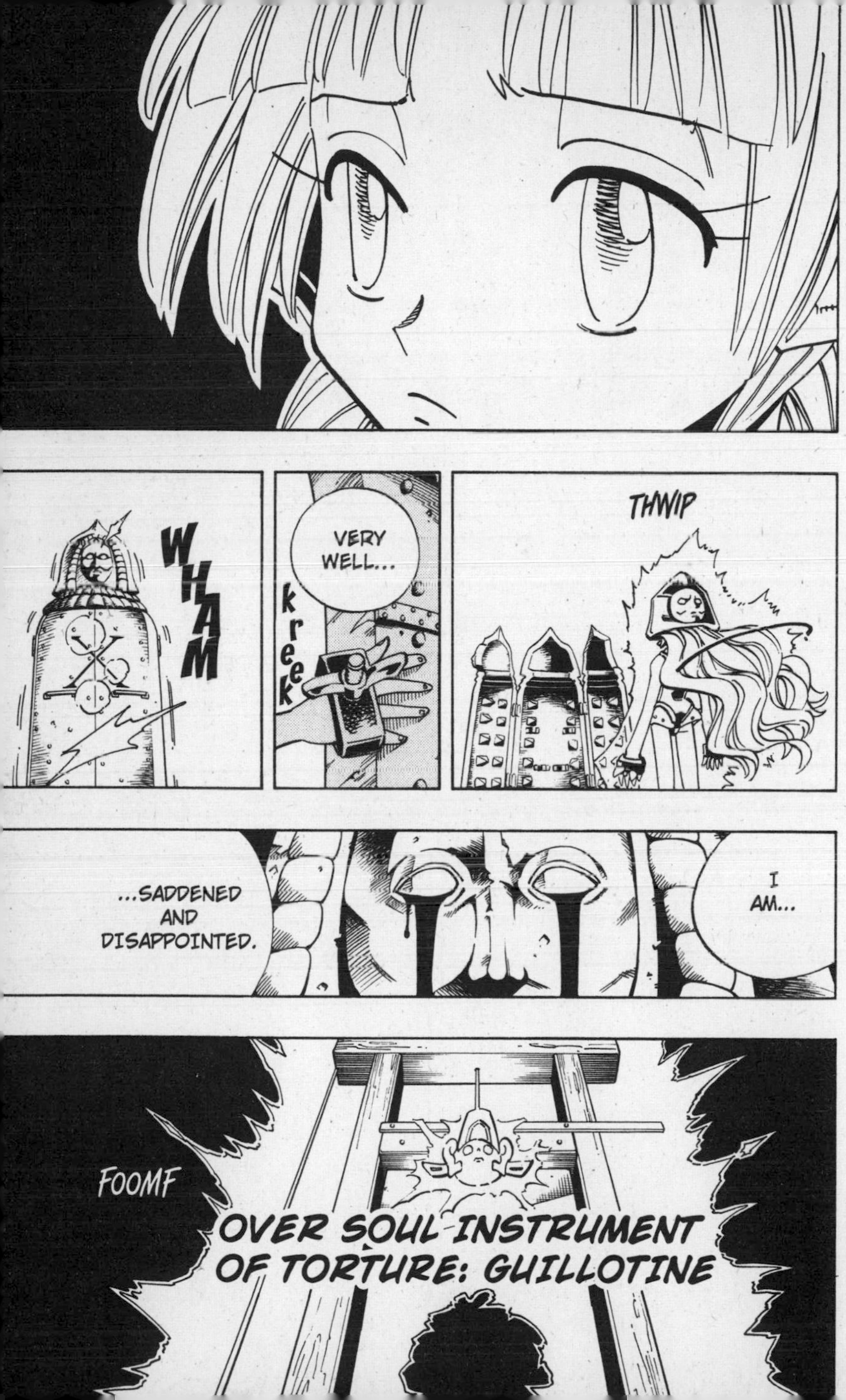
THWIP
VERY WELL...
kreek
WHAM
I AM...
...SADDENED AND DISAPPOINTED.
FOOMF
OVER SOUL INSTRUMENT OF TORTURE: GUILLOTINE

OVER SOUL
INSTRUMENT
OF TORTURE: STATUE OF
APEGA

NOTE: SIMILAR TO AN IRON MAIDEN, THIS DEVICE WAS USED BY THE SPARTAN TYRANT NABIS, WHO NAMED IT AFTER HIS WIFE, APEGA.

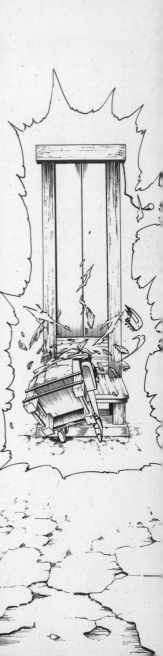

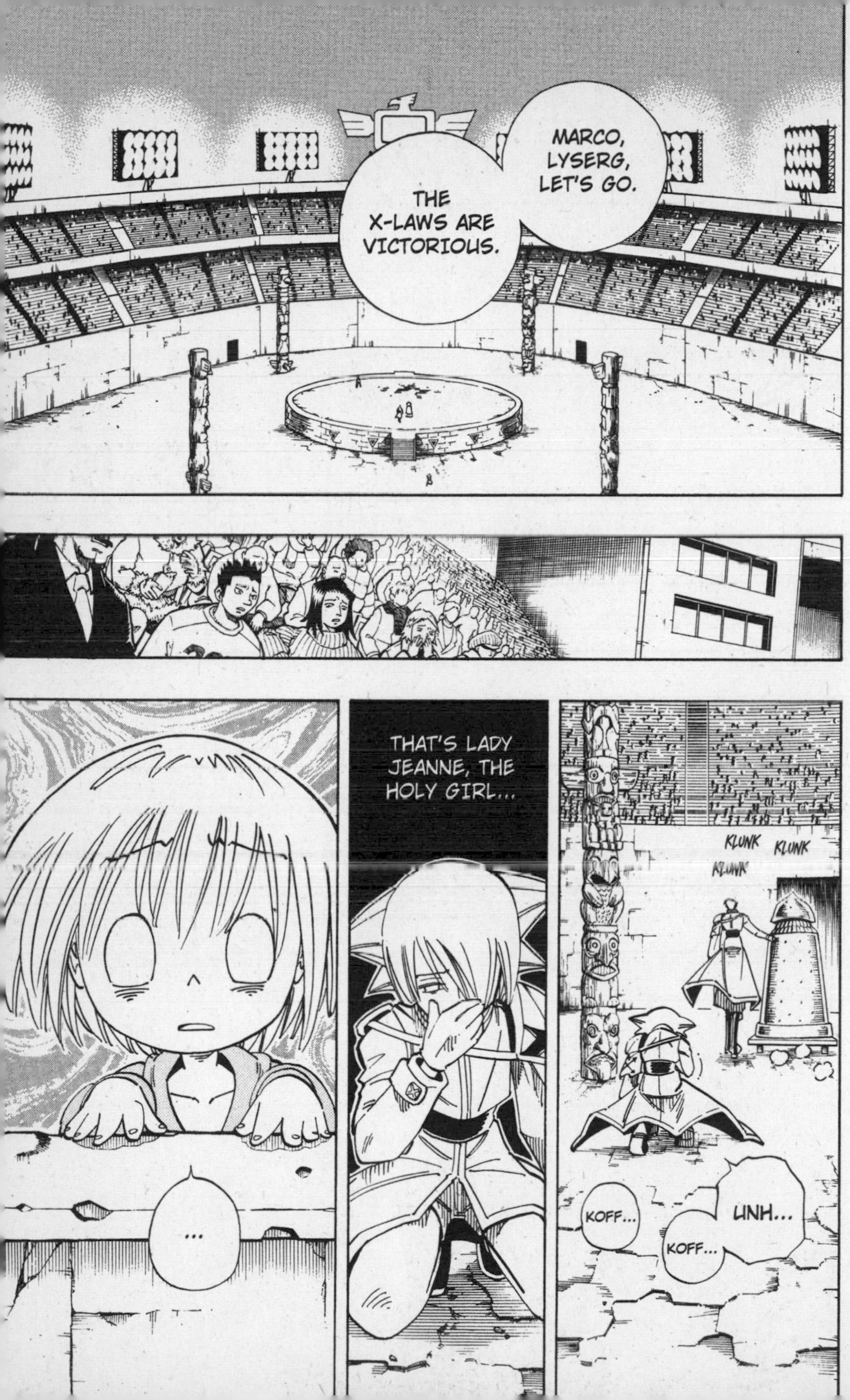
MARCO, LYSERG, LET'S GO.
THE X-LAWS ARE VICTORIOUS.
KLUNK KLUNK
KLUNK
UNH...
KOFF...
KOFF...
THAT'S LADY JEANNE, THE HOLY GIRL...
...

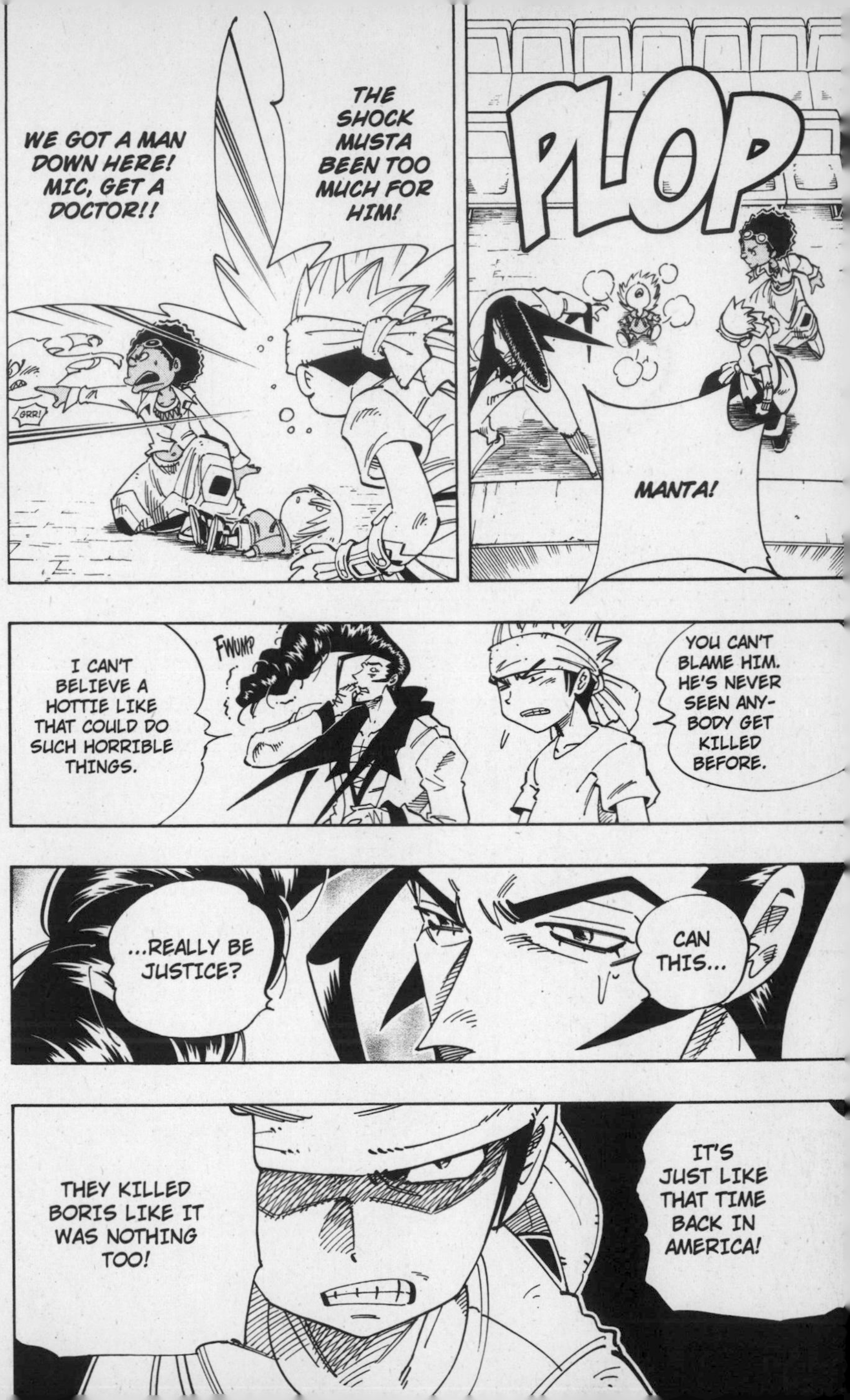
PLOP
MANTA!
THE SHOCK MUSTA BEEN TOO MUCH FOR HIM!
WE GOT A MAN DOWN HERE! MIC, GET A DOCTOR!!
GRR!
YOU CAN'T BLAME HIM. HE'S NEVER SEEN ANY-BODY GET KILLED BEFORE.
FWUMP
I CAN'T BELIEVE A HOTTIE LIKE THAT COULD DO SUCH HORRIBLE THINGS.
CAN THIS...
...REALLY BE JUSTICE?
IT'S JUST LIKE THAT TIME BACK IN AMERICA!
THEY KILLED BORIS LIKE IT WAS NOTHING TOO!

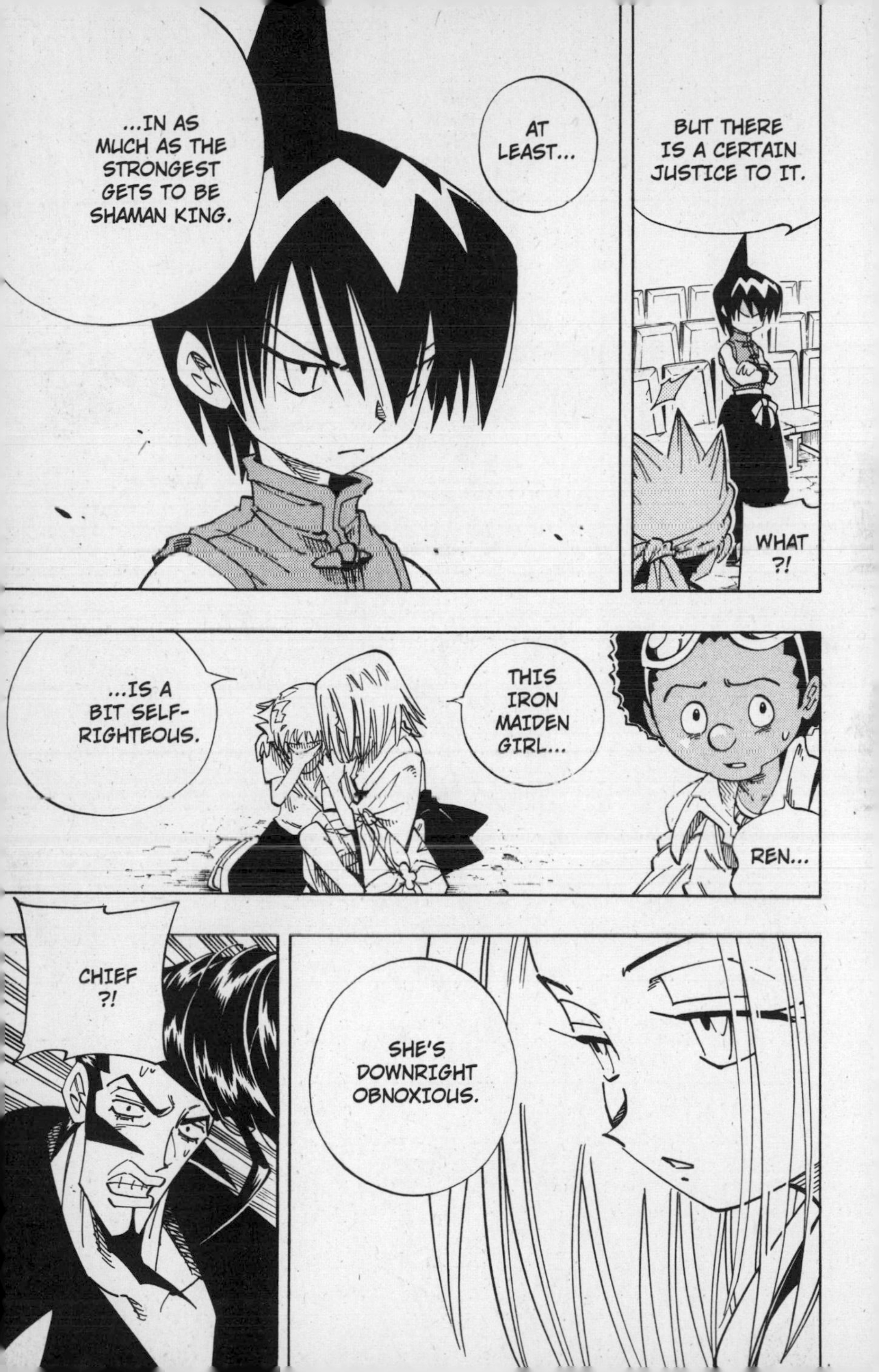
BUT THERE IS A CERTAIN JUSTICE TO IT.
WHAT ?!
AT LEAST...
...IN AS MUCH AS THE STRONGEST GETS TO BE SHAMAN KING.
REN...
THIS IRON MAIDEN GIRL...
...IS A BIT SELF-RIGHTEOUS.
SHE'S DOWNRIGHT OBNOXIOUS.
CHIEF ?!

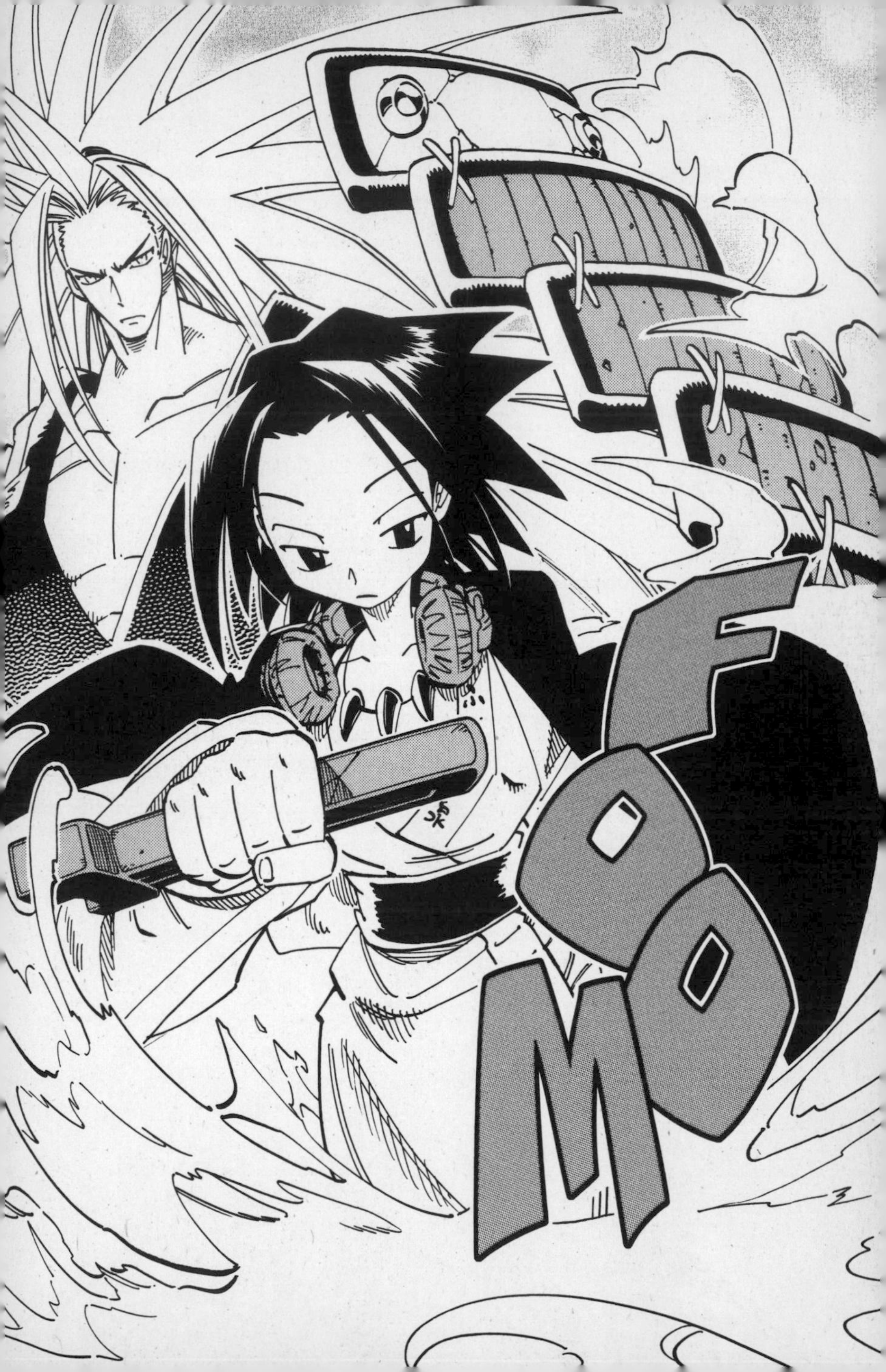
FOOM

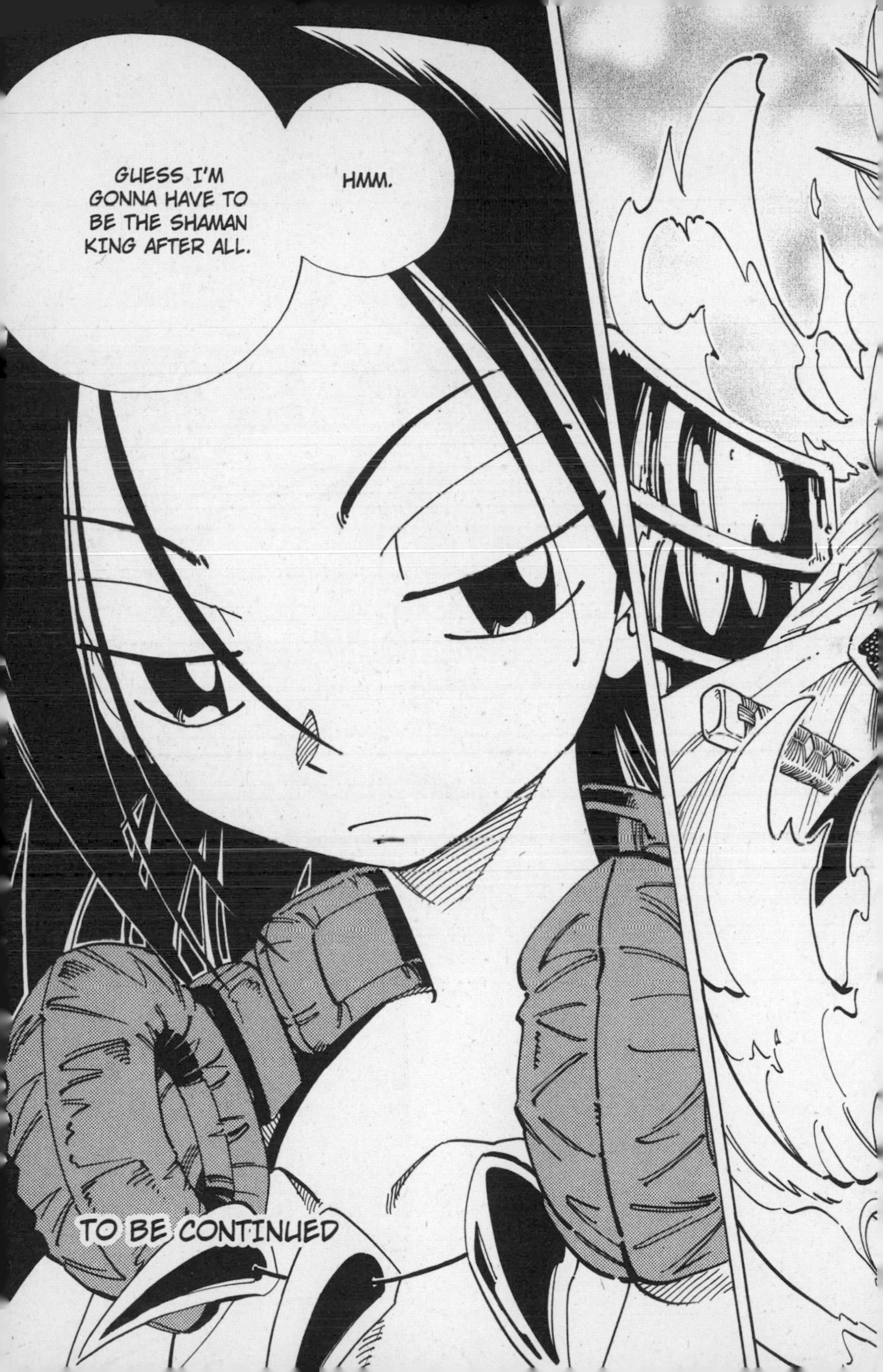
HMM.
GUESS I'M GONNA HAVE TO BE THE SHAMAN KING AFTER ALL.
TO BE CONTINUED

SHAMAN KING ITEM FILE No.45

拷問器具（ごうもんきぐ）ジベット

INSTRUMENTS OF TORTURE: GIBBET

[redacted]

Shaman King™

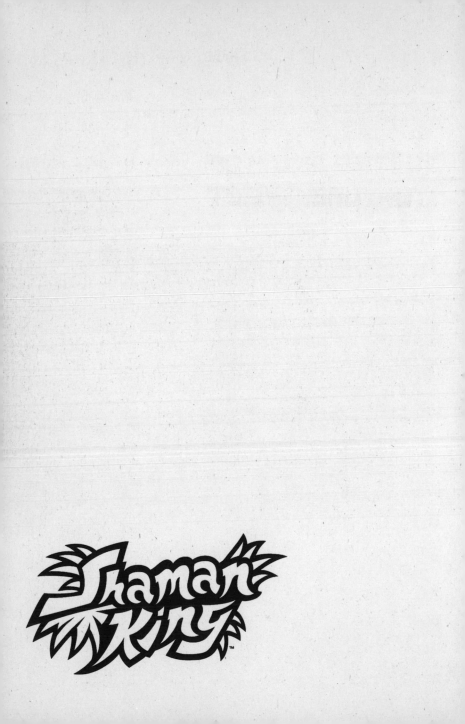

SHAMAN KING ITEM FILE No.46

拷問器具
審問椅子

INSTRUMENTS OF TORTURE: INTERROGATION CHAIR

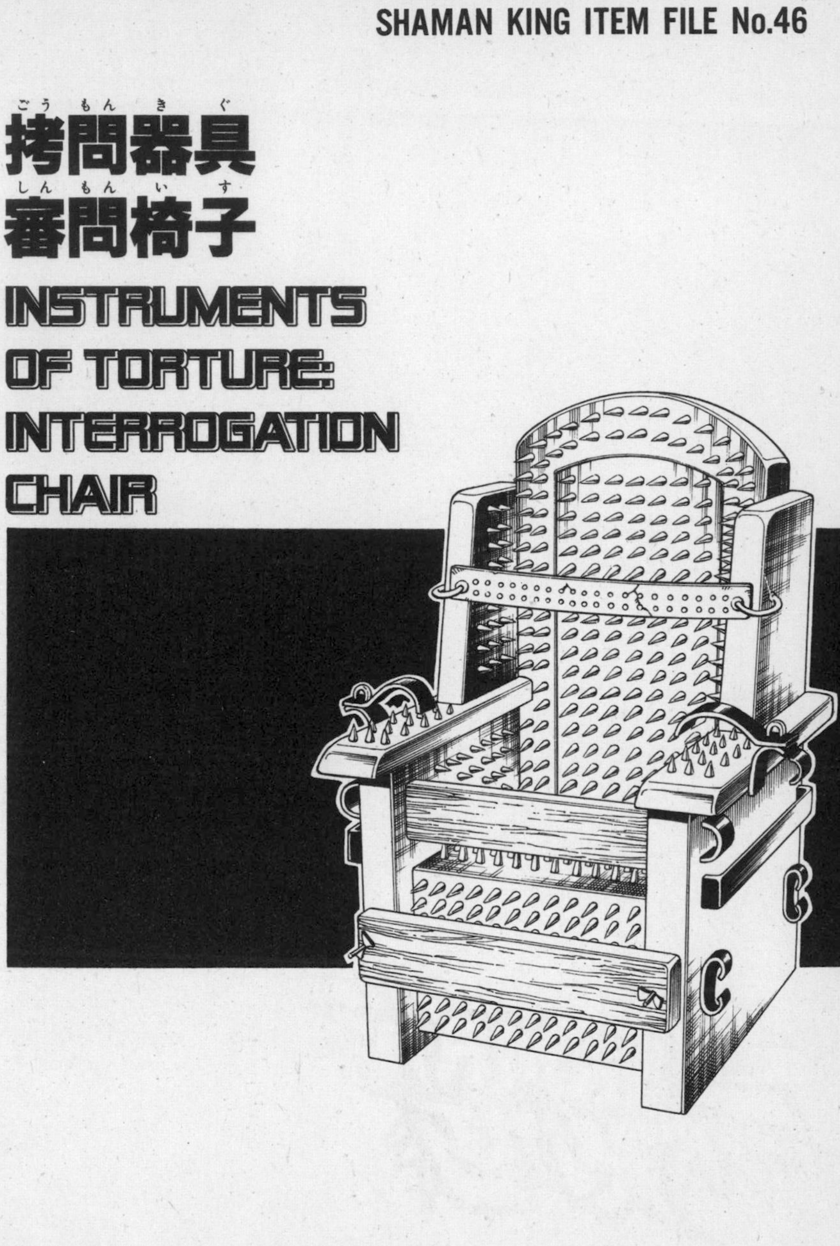

Shaman King™

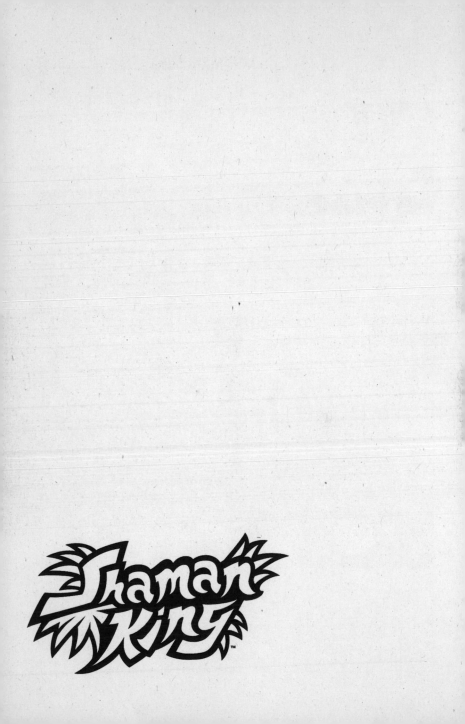

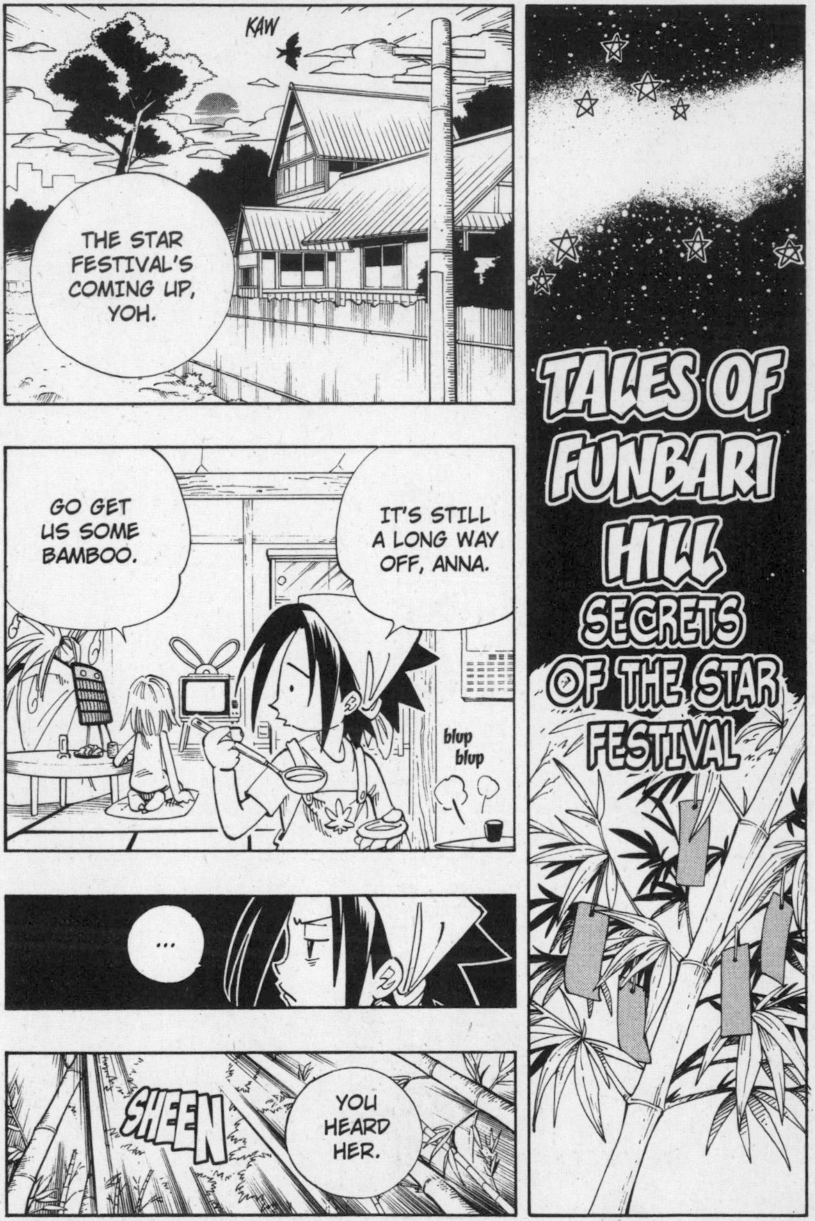
TALES OF FUNBARI HILL
SECRETS OF THE STAR FESTIVAL
KAW
THE STAR FESTIVAL'S COMING UP, YOH.
IT'S STILL A LONG WAY OFF, ANNA.
GO GET US SOME BAMBOO.
blup blup
...
SHEEN
YOU HEARD HER.

READ THIS WAY

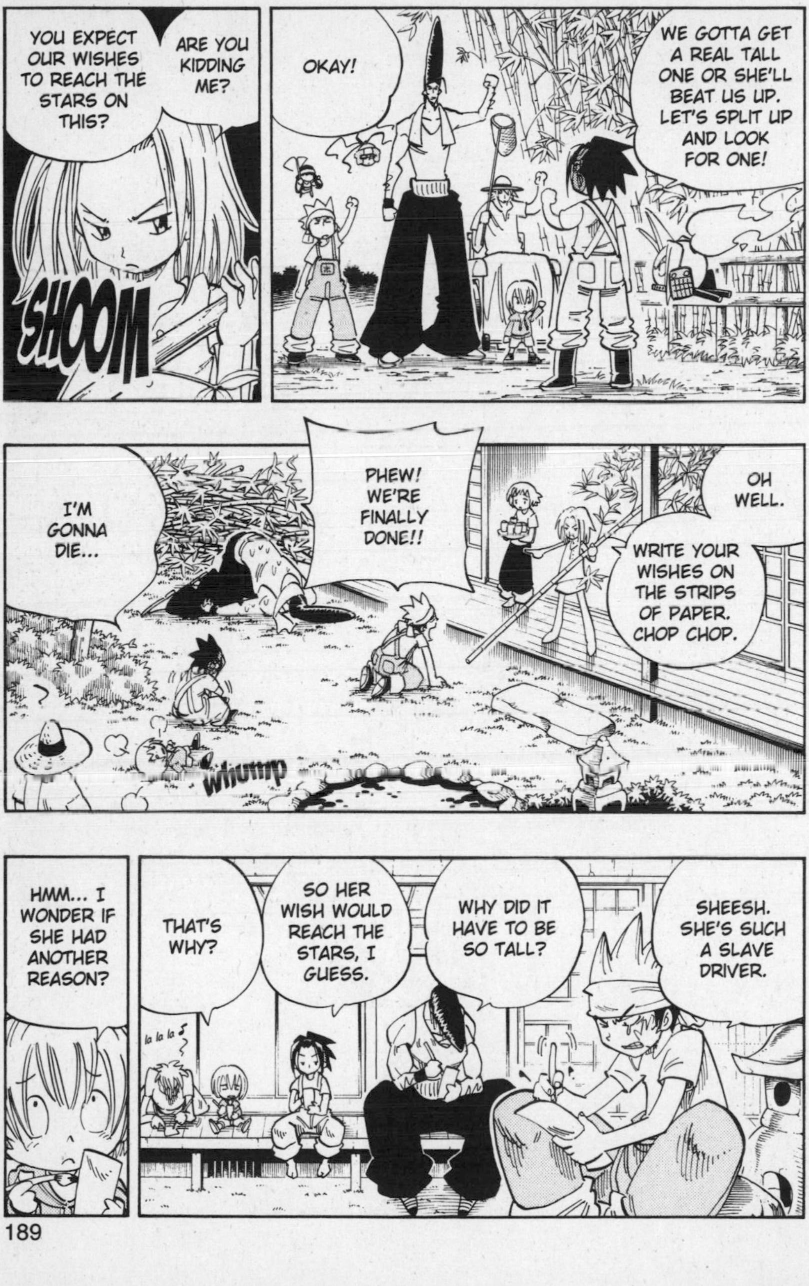

WE GOTTA GET A REAL TALL ONE OR SHE'LL BEAT US UP. LET'S SPLIT UP AND LOOK FOR ONE!
OKAY!
ARE YOU KIDDING ME?
YOU EXPECT OUR WISHES TO REACH THE STARS ON THIS?
SHOOM
OH WELL.
WRITE YOUR WISHES ON THE STRIPS OF PAPER. CHOP CHOP.
PHEW! WE'RE FINALLY DONE!!
I'M GONNA DIE...
whump
SHEESH. SHE'S SUCH A SLAVE DRIVER.
WHY DID IT HAVE TO BE SO TALL?
SO HER WISH WOULD REACH THE STARS, I GUESS.
THAT'S WHY?
la la la
HMM... I WONDER IF SHE HAD ANOTHER REASON?

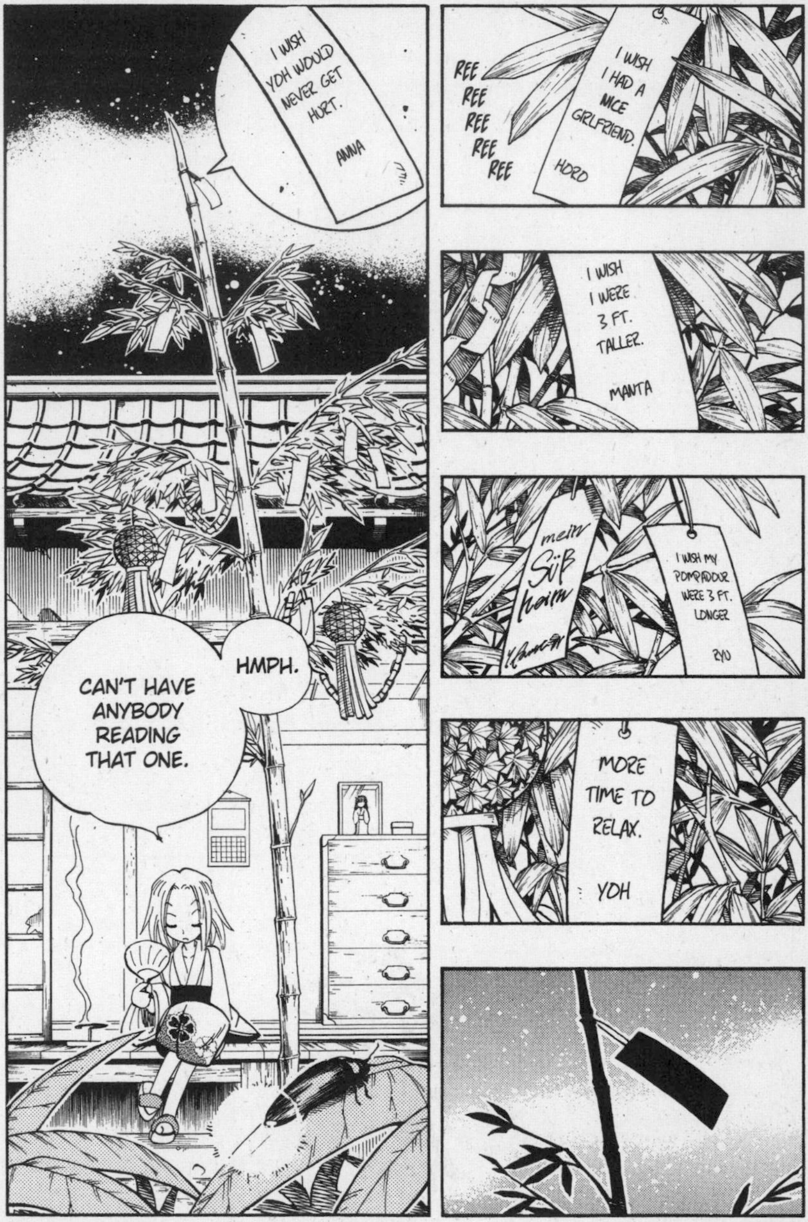
REE REE REE REE REE
I WISH I HAD A NICE GRLFRIEND. HORO
I WISH I WERE 3 FT. TALLER. MANTA
I WISH MY POMPADOUR WERE 3 FT. LONGER RYU
mein Süß heim
MORE TIME TO RELAX. YOH
I WISH YOH WOULD NEVER GET HURT. ANNA
HMPH.
CAN'T HAVE ANYBODY READING THAT ONE.

The End

Shaman King™

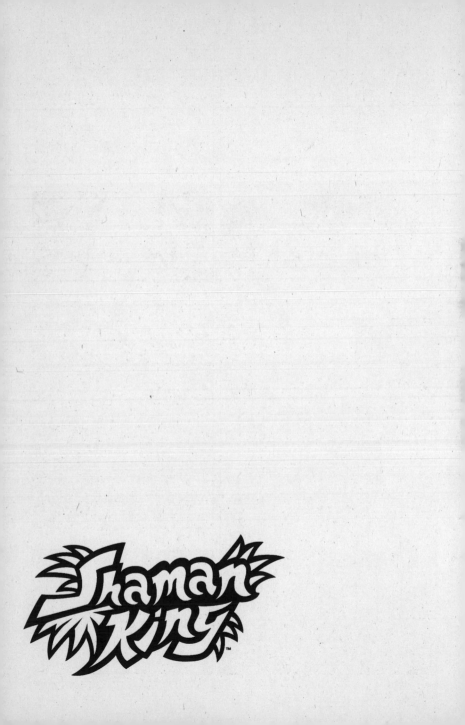

IN THE NEXT VOLUME...

Team Funbari Hot Springs' first match is about to begin!
Manta and Ryu are nervous, but Yoh is confident he will easily
crush his opponents...

Too bad his opponents are the tough-as-nails Icemen!

AVAILABLE NOW!

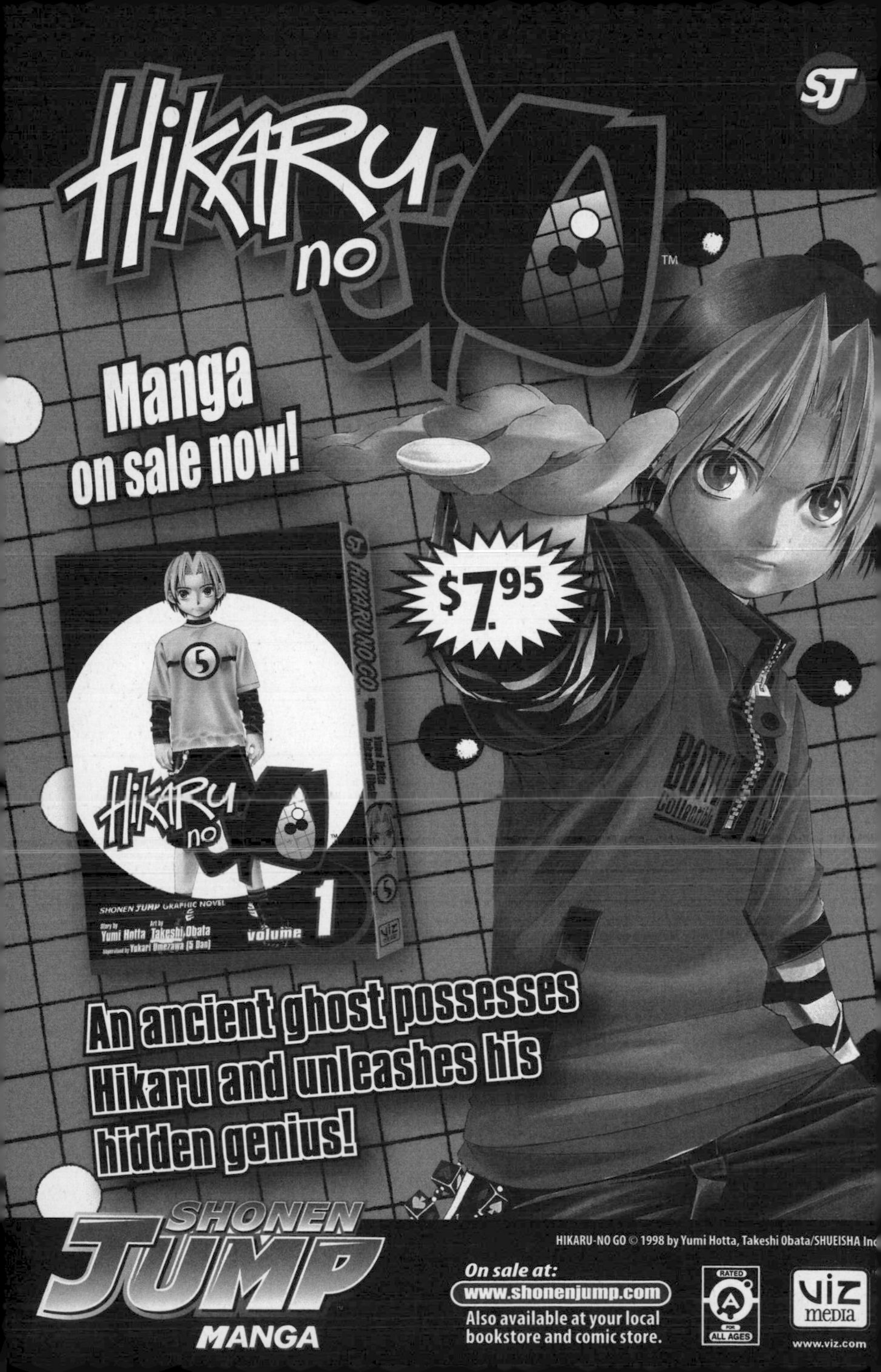

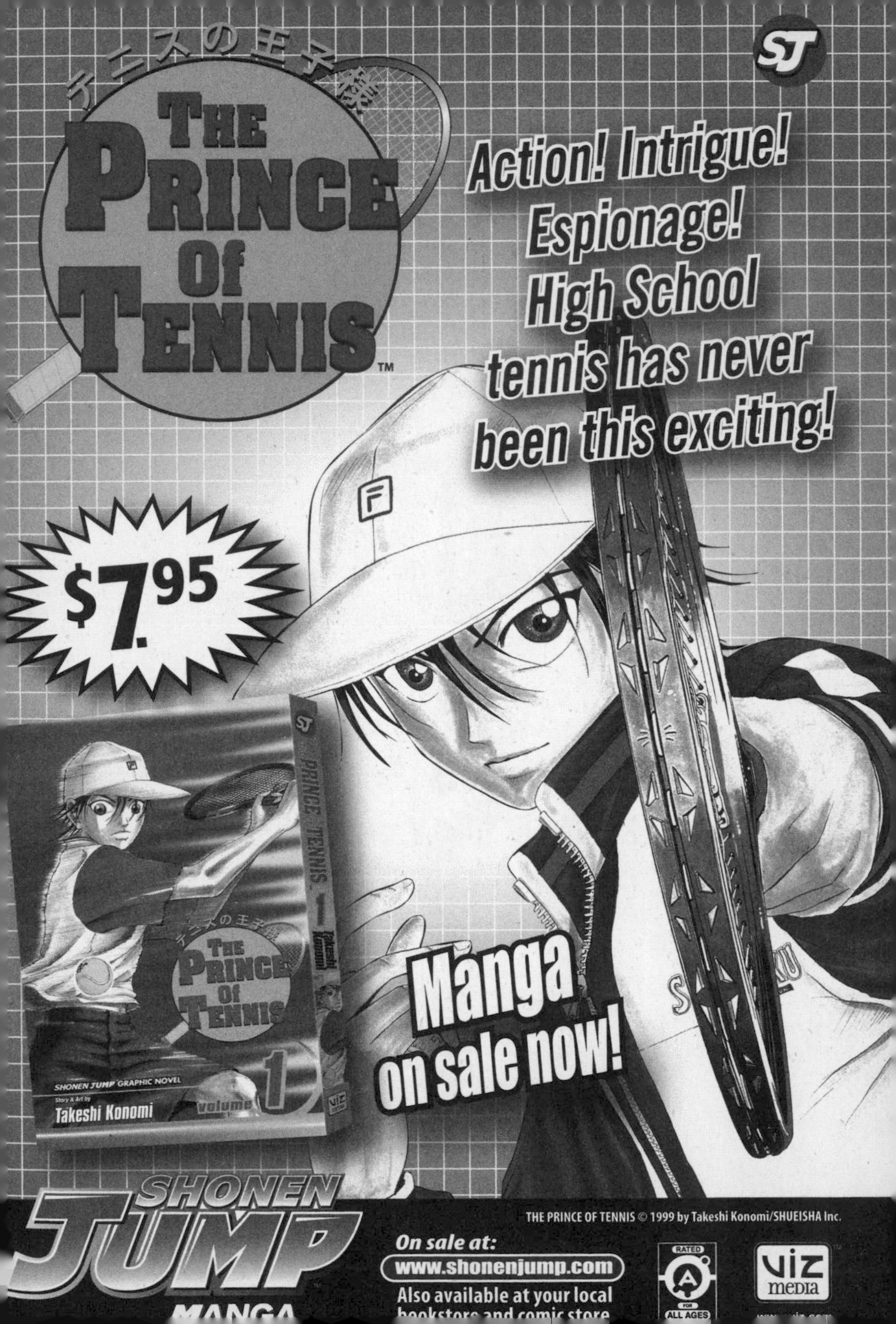

SJ
テニスの王子様
THE PRINCE Of TENNIS™
Action! Intrigue! Espionage! High School tennis has never been this exciting!
$7.95
SHONEN JUMP GRAPHIC NOVEL
Story & Art by
Takeshi Konomi
volume 1
Manga on sale now!
SHONEN JUMP MANGA
THE PRINCE OF TENNIS © 1999 by Takeshi Konomi/SHUEISHA Inc.
On sale at:
www.shonenjump.com
Also available at your local
RATED A FOR ALL AGES
viz media

WHISTLE!™

Manga
on sale now!

$7.99

When the whistle blows,
get ready for rip-roaring
soccer action!

WHISTLE! © 1998 by Daisuke Higuchi/SHUEISHA Inc

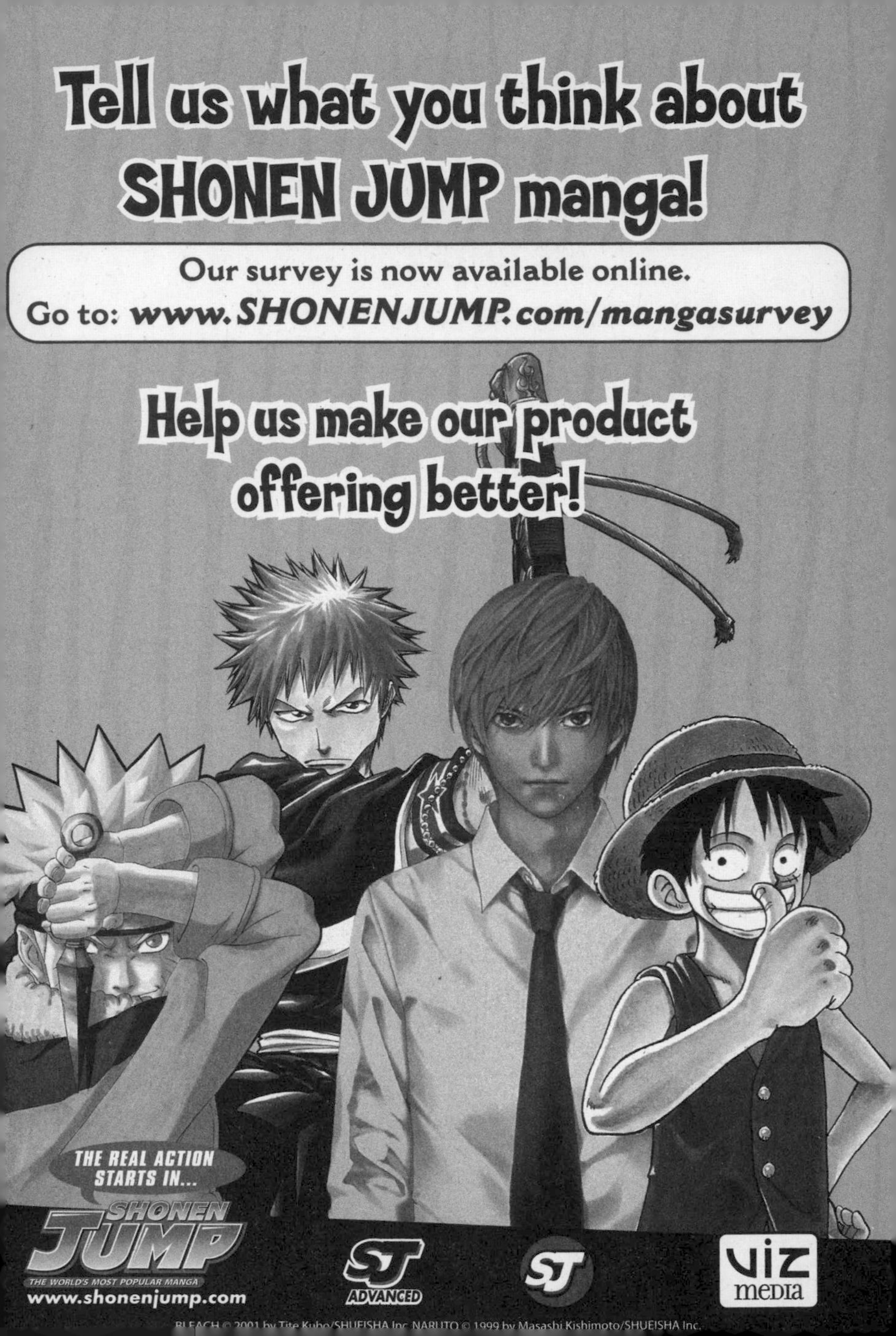
Tell us what you think about SHONEN JUMP manga!
Our survey is now available online.
Go to: www.SHONENJUMP.com/mangasurvey
Help us make our product offering better!
THE REAL ACTION STARTS IN...
SHONEN JUMP
THE WORLD'S MOST POPULAR MANGA
www.shonenjump.com
SJ ADVANCED
SJ
VIZ media
BLEACH © 2001 by Tite Kubo/SHUEISHA Inc. NARUTO © 1999 by Masashi Kishimoto/SHUEISHA Inc.